I0099576

The Benefits of Friends

The Benefits of Friends

INSIDE THE COMPLICATED WORLD OF
TODAY'S SORORITIES AND FRATERNITIES

Jana Mathews

The University of North Carolina Press

Chapel Hill

© 2022 Jana Mathews

All rights reserved

Manufactured in the United States of America

Designed by Jamison Cockerham
Set in Scala, Scala Sans, Klavika, and Calt
by codeMantra

The University of North Carolina Press has been a member
of the Green Press Initiative since 2003.

Complete Library of Congress Cataloging-in-Publication
Data is available at https://lccn.loc.gov/2022015052.
ISBN: 978-1-4696-6964-9 (cloth: alk. paper)
ISBN: 978-1-4696-7210-6 (pbk.: alk. paper)
ISBN: 978-1-4696-6965-6 (ebook)

Material in the preface originally appeared in somewhat different form in
Jana Mathews, "The Oldest Sister: Lessons Abound When a Professor
Becomes a Student of Sorority Life," *Rollins* magazine, Fall 2014,
https://www.rollins.edu/magazine/fall-2013/the-oldest-sister.html.

CONTENTS

. . . .

Preface vii

Introduction: More Than Friends *1*

1 Fraternity Party Population Control *23*

2 Group Sex *41*

3 Hooking Up Hammered and High *77*

4 Going After Girls *101*

5 The Sorority Superchapter and the End of the Best Friend *129*

6 Playing War and the Case for Fraternity Hazing *151*

7 Friends Who Fit *176*

8 Friends in High Places: The Fraternity Power Pipeline and Opportunity Hoarding *205*

Conclusion: Preference *233*

Acknowledgments 247

Notes 249

Bibliography 271

Index 317

PREFACE

Like many women at Rollins College, I joined a National Panhellenic Conference (NPC) sorority during my first year on campus.[1] In lots of ways my experience in the white Greek system was typical: I went through new member education training and sorority initiation, participated in service projects and chapter events, and attended mixers and formals. The only difference between me and the rest of the members of my pledge class is that when I joined the organization in the spring of 2011, I wasn't an eighteen-year-old first-year student but a thirty-something-year-old college professor.

My age and profession aren't the only reasons why I am not the first person you would expect to join a sorority. I grew up in a devout Mormon household in an insular and extremely conservative social community. When it was time to go to college, I enrolled at Brigham Young University (BYU), the institution of higher learning best known outside of Utah for being named Princeton Review's "most stone-cold sober school" for twenty-two years running.[2] Needless to say, there aren't any sororities and fraternities there.

My postgraduate résumé mirrors that of other upper-class white and straight women who attended BYU in the 1990s: I got married at twenty and spawned half a basketball team by the time I turned thirty. During the same period, however, I also did something that was very atypical for Mormon women of my generation: I enrolled in graduate school and earned a PhD.[3] My field of study was medieval British literature (think *Beowulf* and Chaucer's *Canterbury Tales*). Shortly afterward, I won the professional lottery when I was offered a teaching and research position at Rollins College, a small four-year liberal arts institution comprised of roughly 2,000 undergraduates in Winter Park, Florida. Like other colleges with small class sizes and low faculty-to-student ratios, Rollins expects its professors to cultivate tight-knit mentoring relationships with their students.

The problem was that I didn't have very many students.

I started my tenure-track professorship at Rollins the same year that the college made *Playboy Magazine*'s list of the top-ten party schools in America.[4] I learned two things right off the bat: first, I was woefully unprepared for the culture gap between my sheltered religious upbringing and the secular college experience; and, second, that I had grossly overestimated how much my new students would enjoy reading fourteenth-century Middle English poetry.

As the semester progressed, I invested an enormous amount of time trying to find ways to engage my students, all of whom showed visible signs of distress when they came into my classroom. After one particularly disheartening class session, my wise husband staged an intervention. "How can you expect your students to be interested in something that is important to you," he asked, "if you don't show any interest in what matters to them?"

He made a valid point.

I didn't have to look far to find my students' shared interest. Nationally, only about 10 percent of the student population is part of the sorority and fraternity system on campuses where Greek letter organizations exist. By comparison, 35 percent of the Rollins undergraduate population at the time was involved in one of these organizations, making it one of the highest per capita sorority and fraternity populations in the country.

A few days later, I happened across a group of women students wearing matching sorority T-shirts huddled around a study table in the library. One of the women would later tell me that she found it slightly unnerving when I slid into the chair across the table from her and began asking her the same set of questions that one would pose to a spaceship full of aliens: Where did you come from? How many of you are there? What do you want?

The two-hour conversation that followed culminated with an invitation to attend one of the sorority's upcoming chapter meetings. My attendance at that meeting—and several other chapter events in subsequent weeks—led to an invitation that took me by surprise. The chapter had solicited and received formal approval from their international headquarters to initiate me as an alumna member of their organization. Usually, these kinds of membership requests are processed by a local alumnae chapter of the sorority, but since I was affiliated with Rollins and knew so many of its active collegiate members, I had been given special permission to join the chapter's current pledge class. "Are you in?" one of the sorority women asked me.

Once I stopped laughing, I realized that she was serious. As I weighed the choice before me, I found myself hovering between thinking, "Why in the world would I do this?" and "Why not?" Ultimately, I was swayed to acceptance by a combination of curiosity and the hope that some of Rollins's undergraduate students would be inspired to step out of their academic comfort zones and take my classes if they noticed me orbiting so far outside of my own social universe.

Shortly after being initiated into the sorority, I took on the role of faculty advisor for the chapter. Almost immediately after rotating out of that role, I rotated into the same one for another NPC sorority chapter. Then, right after that, I served as the executive chairwoman (i.e., head chapter advisor) for a white North American Interfraternity Conference (NIC) fraternity.[5]

During the roughly seven combined years (2011–18) that I served as a sorority and fraternity advisor, I attended chapter meetings, philanthropic fundraisers, Greek Week competitions, new member education seminars, leadership training retreats, and sisterhood and brotherhood events. I also chaperoned mixers, crush parties, and formals. I have dealt with serious questions about where to rehome a live chicken and what to do with a live alligator after it successfully fulfilled its role as the guest of honor at a party.

I also have spent countless hours engaged in emergency problem-solving and one-on-one mentoring. I got calls from spring breakers in Mexico who wanted to know how to help a brother who was threatening suicide. I was summoned to the hospital emergency room following an interfraternity bar fight and helped talk my chapter's members out of a plan to enact vigilante justice. I have had fraternity men ask for help addressing their brothers' mental health struggles and alcohol and drug use.

I have received texts sent by sorority women from restroom stalls in bars and nightclubs that said things like "I'm scared" and "I think I've been slipped something." I have held way too many before-dawn emergency meetings in my office with sorority women who weren't sure how to define what happened to them the night before. I have had sorority and fraternity members make appointments with me on the pretense of wanting to talk about law or graduate school but really wanted to talk about sexism, homophobia, and classism within their ranks.

When my doorbell rang at odd hours, my family was conditioned to expect a sorority woman or fraternity man standing on the doorstep, just barely holding back tears, or already sobbing. We remodeled our upstairs bonus room and outfitted it with an air mattress and blankets for unexpected guests. The mattress stayed inflated throughout the academic year.

I continued working with the sorority and fraternity community at Rollins long after I needed to because of the relationships I formed with individual students and the personal rewards that came from helping them navigate the treacherous waters of early adulthood. While I can genuinely say that I liked all the fraternity and sorority members with whom I worked, I didn't always like the way they thought or things they did. I didn't pull back despite this ideological tension because of my strong commitment to the liberal arts educational ethos, which holds that transformative growth happens when we are uncomfortable. Of course, my motivations were not exclusively altruistic. I also will confess that I leveraged these relationships for my professional gain. My mentoring of fraternity men and sorority women certainly aided the individuals and organizations with which I worked, but it also benefited me in clear and measurable ways: my classes were packed, I was nominated for teaching awards, and, because of both these things, I sailed through the early stages of the tenure process.

Like the first-year women in my pledge class, my journey from unaffiliated woman to sorority member was short, exciting, and chaotic. As someone who is a researcher by trade, however, I quickly was forced to admit that I had joined an organization that I knew very little about. My failure to subject the white Greek letter system to the same type of rigorous intellectual scrutiny that I did with every other facet of my professional life morphed from a regretful oversight into an urgent inquiry when my children entered middle and high school and started talking openly and excitedly about joining Greek life when they went to college. Was that a pursuit that I wanted to encourage? I wasn't sure.

I set out to read everything about fraternity and sorority life I could get my hands on. Diana Turk's pioneering study *Bound by a Mighty Vow: Sisterhood and Women's Fraternities, 1870–1920* tells the origin story of white sororities and, in doing so, illuminates the role that these organizations played in the construction of femininity and womanhood. In her 2020 book, *Women of Discriminating Taste: White Sororities and the Making of American Ladyhood*, Margaret L. Freeman elegantly pulls the history of sororities forward by showing how from the 1920s to the 1970s white Greek letter organizations reinforced gender binaries and became emblems of heteronormativity.[6] The foundational history of white fraternities is Nicholas Syrett's *The Company He Keeps: A History of White College Fraternities*.[7] In this study, fraternities emerge as a powerful agent in the construction of American masculinity. How fraternity men see themselves, Syrett argues, bears crucially on how they perceive and understand issues of race, class, gender, sexuality, and religion.

One can't work so intimately with sororities and fraternities for so long and not witness in current fraternity and sorority chapters the complicated legacy of the beliefs, values, ideologies, and traditions that Turk, Freeman, and Syrett describe. While I knew that my position as a professor and fraternity and sorority advisor afforded me a unique lens through which to analyze the contemporary white Greek letter community, I didn't have a concrete plan for what to do with the narrative that was starting to form in my head until I attended a conference for sorority and fraternity advisors in Nashville, Tennessee, in December 2014. One of the guest speakers at the event was Caitlin Flanagan, an investigative journalist who, a few months earlier, had penned an inflammatory cover story for the *Atlantic* on fraternity violence.[8] In her talk, Flanagan said something along the lines that what the national fraternity and sorority scene needed was an ethnographic study of its current community, one conducted by someone from the outside who would, she imagined, study fraternities and sororities with a critical eye toward determining the root cause of their consistent and puzzling allure. After the talk, I went back to my hotel room and called my husband to break the news. "I'm pretty sure Caitlin Flanagan was talking directly to me," I told him.

I came into this project well aware of how my kind is perceived by this community, and I am equally aware that rolling up to strange chapter houses and interviews with fraternity and sorority life (FSL) executives dressed in mom jeans and Target sweaters instead of academic regalia curbed the instinct of many to shut the door in my face. My Mormon background (signaled by the BYU degree on my résumé) was surprisingly cited more than once by sorority leaders as the reason why they were swayed to take my meeting. Some noted that they felt inclined to trust me because of what they perceived and openly referred to as "our shared history of institutional persecution," a view that I don't share but also with which I didn't publicly disagree. For others, the fact that I attended a religious university that didn't have Greek letter organizations enabled them to imagine me as someone who didn't reject them on principle when I had the chance, but instead might have joined their ranks if I had the opportunity. Another key but unstated part of my golden ticket: I'm a blonde-haired, blue-eyed white woman and, thus, aesthetically read like an older model of the stereotypical collegiate sorority member. I'm not under any delusion that this didn't play a part in the reason why I was invited to join the sorority in the first place. While my age and religion may make me the last person you would expect to join a sorority, everything else about me signals that I am exactly the kind of person you would expect to find hanging out at a sorority house. I like to tell people in the FSL community that I am a magic unicorn who happened to be the right kind of scholar at the right place and at the right time to do this work. That is a gentler way of stating the bald truth that I used my white privilege to tap into theirs.

Currently, there are about 750,000 undergraduate members of white fraternities and sororities, spread across 800 campuses in the United States and Canada, with dozens of new chapters opening every year.[9] While Greek letter membership is not at its highest level in history (that honor belongs to the 1920s), white sororities and fraternities are hugely popular and are growing at unprecedented rates. In an era where heteronormativity is, to borrow the words of a writer for *Teen Vogue*, "a bad thing," and promoting inclusivity of all kinds is a strategic priority of higher education writ large, the flourishing of these single-sex social groups that uphold traditional gender identities and roles is an enigma that defies common sense.[10] Even from a perspective that heterosexuality is the norm, sororities and fraternities challenge the foundational notion of human relations that privilege romantic relationships over same-sex platonic friendships. If straight men and women are programmed to prefer the company of one another over their same-sex friends, then why are so many straight college students clamoring to join these groups?

At a moment when the call to abolish white sororities and fraternities grows louder and more persistent by the day, *The Benefits of Friends* foregrounds the questions that undergird their continued existence—namely, what do these organizations do and what are they good for? I am not talking about the mechanics of how fraternities and sororities operate but, rather, the social, economic, and cultural benefits conferred by membership in them. As higher education's most enduring and pervasive single-sex organizations, white fraternities and sororities collectively emerge in this book as a powerful social influencer that extends the definition of heteronormativity to include platonic relationships between same-sex friends. Taking seriously the popular fraternity and sorority life mantra that "friends are the family you choose," this book takes up questions that nag at higher education and society. How specifically do fraternities promote straight hookup culture, and what are its effects? What happens to relationship culture when sex and intimacy are decoupled and reassigned to different actors? How does the concept of family change when all its members are the same age, sex, and race? What is at stake socially, politically, and culturally when one romanticizes the figure of the friend?

In order to get at these questions, you'll have to venture with me into the sorority house on a typical Friday night.

The Benefits of Friends

More Than Friends

It was close to midnight by the time that I flipped off my office light and called it a night. I had spent the past several hours attending a guest lecture, and while my mind was buzzing with new ideas, my middle-aged body was telling me in no uncertain terms that it was time to pack it in. As I made my way to the faculty parking lot, a plate of leftover brownies in hand, I passed by the sorority house of the chapter for which I was serving as faculty advisor. There were several women hanging out on the benches outside of the building. After exchanging pleasantries, the women invited my desserts inside and said that I could come too if I wanted.

Although it was well past my bedtime, the night was still young for the eighteen-to-twenty-two set, which is why I was surprised to find more than a dozen women sprawled out over the common area, binge watching a previous season of *The Bachelor*. "What have you all been up to?" I asked the group. One woman, whose body parts comprised one-fifth of a corporeal mass covered by a furry blanket on an upholstered sofa, recounted in detail the activities of the evening so far, which included drinks at a bar, dinner at a trendy downtown Orlando restaurant, and film viewing at a local movie theater. As this woman spoke, I couldn't help but notice that the women curled up around her were engaged in various forms of peer grooming: one twirled her neighbor's hair around her fingertips, another massaged the back of her friend's neck, and two others cradled their heads in the crooks of the shoulders of the women sitting next to them.

At different times in the past, the so-called dinner-and-a-movie outing, followed by a late-night couch cuddle session, served as shorthand for what a straight woman did with her date, boyfriend, "steady," or the man who was on the fast track to becoming one.[1] One need only to glance around the sorority chapter house or the bar and restaurant where these women were hanging out a few hours earlier to see how things have changed.

Choosing to spend a day and time of the week known colloquially as "date night" with one's same-sex platonic friends over a romantic partner of the opposite sex marks a shift not only in romance culture but also in identity politics. While sororities and fraternities are inherently heteronormative organizations in structure, they are comprised of individuals belonging to a generation that both acknowledges and embraces sexual fluidity. While all of the women in the sorority house that night self-identified as cisgender and straight, their behavior falls into what Eve Kosofsky Sedgwick describes as the "open mesh of possibilities, gaps, overlaps, dissonances and resonances, lapses and excesses of meaning when the constituent elements of anyone's gender, of anyone's sexuality aren't made (or *can't be* made) to signify monolithically."[2] I follow Sedgwick and Adrienne Rich in holding that a continuum exists between heterosexuality and homosexuality. Participating in homosocial activities that border on the homoerotic (or cross over to homosexual) does not necessarily constitute the basis for exclusion from straight male and female identity but rather is often a qualifying requisite of it.[3] Sociologist Jane Ward of the University of California, Riverside, has recently shown how straight-identifying men in hypersexualized environments like fraternities go out of their way to manufacture opportunities for sexualized contact with other men.[4] This brand of homosociality, which Henning Bach calls "absent homosexuality," structures the way that men view society and their place within it.[5]

Straight sorority women (and men), I argue, do the same thing. As some of society's most powerful current and future social influencers, sororities and fraternities endorse a social model where the reproduction of heterosexuality is fueled by homosocial and homoerotic relations. This is manifest in lots of ways, including and especially in the expanding job description of the "sorority sister" and "fraternity brother." The structure of traditional straight romance culture, which promoted pairing off and formalized coupling via the appropriation of the titles of "girlfriend" and "boyfriend," fostered the perception that the romantic partner is a kind of human one-stop shop for all their partner's emotional and physical needs. The nature of today's chaotic and noncommittal hookup culture, however, privileges job sharing and outsourcing over consolidation.[6] What exactly is a hookup? Journalist Laura Sessions Stepp perhaps put it best when she said that "it isn't exactly anything."[7] What individuals call a "hookup," a term whose power is derived from the ambiguity of its reference, can run the gamut from kissing to penetrative sexual intercourse, and everything in between. As a result of its flexible signification, hookup culture fosters the belief that everyone is having sex, and all the time.[8] No longer is the expectation or even necessarily the desire that sexual and emotional intimacy will be provided by the same person. In this new relationship model, sex is an act that you do with the opposite sex, while intimacy is something that you have with the same sex.

Despite veering away from tradition in some ways, straight hookup culture doesn't completely kill off the traditional dating script; rather, it reassigns its roles to same-sex actors. What happened next in the sorority house serves as an illustrative case in point. Starting at about midnight, the women's phones began to wake up by texts from men. Some of the correspondence was unsolicited, while other conversations had been initiated earlier in the evening by the women themselves. The group curled up under the blanket were the fortunate recipients of an array of tantalizing offers. One was invited to the apartment of a man she had been "talking to" for several weeks. Another received a text from a drunk fraternity man asking her to meet him at a local bar. A third held up her phone to show everyone the text she had just received from her self-described "fuck buddy." It was just a string of question marks.

None of the text recipients jumped for joy when the invites started rolling in, but they didn't seem to be particularly offended by their clinical directness, either. Indeed, the collective attitude toward the invitations might best be described as a kind of amused ambivalence. Eventually, the chuckling gave way to hemming and hawing over the options at hand. A factor bearing heavily on the decision-making for everyone on the sofa was the inconvenience of having to extricate themselves from the web of bodies and change out of their pajamas and put on "real clothes." Eventually, one of the women disentangled herself and stood up, making a loud, exasperated sigh in the process. "I'll be back in an hour," she promised. Turning to the woman controlling the TV remote she asked, "Pause it until I get back?"

Scholars have shown how hookup culture fosters an environment where women sometimes have sex with men in order to keep their attention.[9] The sorority women's lukewarm response to males' text invitations seem to suggest that a sense of obligation and duty might have played a role in at least some of the decisions that were made.[10] If the choreographed exit was a veiled complaint against a relationship culture that privileges male over female desire, it was also a powerful statement about loyalty and allegiance.

While sorority women were willing to give men an hour of their time and bodies, they gave other women the rest of the night.

Romanticizing Friendship and Friendifying the Lover

What took place in the sorority house that night is one manifestation of the new model of campus relationships in which sexual intercourse is outsourced to members of the opposite sex and intimacy in all its forms, save sexual, is kept proverbially (or, in the case of sororities, literally) in house and provided by members of the same. Sorority women's decision to pour more time, money, and energy into platonic same-sex friendships than into relationships with their male sexual partners, however, doesn't make sense from an economic point of view. The sex ratio on many campuses nationwide is forty men to sixty women.[11] In recent years, we have come a long way in recognizing that a two-gender demographic model is too restrictive and doesn't account for the full range of ways that individuals self-identify. While I recognize that using terms like "sex ratio," "gender ratio," and "same-sex friends" to talk about human relations is noninclusive, the terms' stubborn persistence in official head counting and popular discourse makes their usage within this study a necessary evil. Specifically, it's difficult to quantify and properly recognize nonbinary and gender-nonconforming individuals when colleges and universities present their demographic statistics in terms of male and female or women and men. The same critique can be made on a broader societal level, especially after it was revealed that the 2020 national census gave respondents only two sexes from which to choose: male and female.[12]

The law of supply and demand suggests that the excess number of cisgender straight women on college campuses should make same-sex friends expendable—but they aren't. Sorority women are not discarding friends with the careless abandon derived from the knowledge that there are more where they came from, but instead are cultivating these relationships and going to unprecedented lengths to preserve them. Cisgender straight fraternity men are doing the same thing.[13]

Privileging same-sex friends over romantic partners is not just a prudent strategy to help individuals navigate through the situational benefits and challenges of collegiate lopsided sex ratios; it also functions as a kind of insurance policy for later in life. The number of people who are marrying later or not at all is on the rise.[14] Unlike seventy-five years ago, when the average cisgender person might have spent their twenties living with their opposite cisgender spouse, today's young adults spend the bulk of the same decade in the company of friends. A 2017 study conducted by Michigan State University assistant professor of psychology William Chopik looked at data collected from 270,000 individuals in 100 countries.[15] The first thing that the study revealed wasn't really a surprise: friends and family members both contributed to individuals' well-being and personal happiness. What took Chopik off guard, however, was which group had a greater positive influence. "I went into the research sort of agnostic to the role of friendship," he told *Time* in 2017. "But the really surprising thing was that, in a lot of ways, relationships with friends had a similar effect as those with family—and in others, they surpassed them."[16]

The elevated status and role of the same-sex friend in contemporary relationship culture goes a long way in explaining why the process of acquiring one has begun to mirror and mimic the conventional dating script. The term that we use to describe the first peer interactions that children have today—"play date"—serves as a compelling case in point. It's unclear exactly when this term first entered the English lexicon, but based on two dictionaries' combined etymological research and the discussion about the term on several online parenting forums—in which no one remembers it being used when they were kids—it appears to be an invention of the late 1980s.[17]

Play dates don't just borrow from the vocabulary of traditional courtship culture; they also appropriate the structure and expectations of it as well. As *Huffington Post* blogger Chris Bernholdt humorously put it, adding the word "date" to the phenomenon of play "gives off this connotation that I should be opening doors for you as you drop off your kid."[18] In theory, friend-making follows traditional courtship culture along a parallel pathway through time and space. Both types of relationships are formed through progressively longer intervals of less-supervised time together and located in increasingly private spaces. The dating analogues to school playgrounds, mall food courts, backyards, and dark basements are bars and restaurants, movie theaters, and the dimly lit living room. Both relationships migrate by stages toward the most intimate and private space: the closed-door bedroom.

The contours of same-sex friendships and romantic relationships become increasingly muddy as one passes through adolescence and into adulthood. Like their romantic counterparts, friends move in together and go away together on girls' weekends and men-only camping trips. It is not uncommon for straight couples to find themselves lying on cruise ship lounge chairs next to a pair of women who are similarly sharing piña coladas and finishing each other's sentences. In recent years, *Bustle*, *Cosmopolitan*, and a slew of other women's pop culture magazines have extended the metaphor of friend-as-sexless-lover by cataloging the ways in which a woman's female best friend does a better job of fulfilling boyfriend duties than the boyfriend himself.[19] Brittney Cooper, a Rutgers professor and author of *Eloquent Rage*, writes about #ThottieThursdays, a custom where women in her friend group "sext one another slyly seductive pics of our asses, or thighs, or cleavages, sometimes bare, or sometimes clothed in the perfect way that all our curves are accentuated."[20] Gender studies scholar Michael Kimmel says the same things about platonic relationships between men. Men subscribe to the traditional ideals of masculinity not because they want to impress women, he says, but because "they want to be positively evaluated by other men."[21]

While popular culture has been romanticizing the friend, it also has been engaged in the reverse project of friendifying the lover. Many have pointed out that ambiguity governs the domain of hookup culture vocabulary, so much so that even the meaning of "hook up" itself is fluid and uncertain.[22] Throughout most of the twentieth century, the term primarily referred to the act of meeting up with friends.[23] Hookup culture's other favorite words and phrases—"hanging out," "talking to," "seeing," "hitting it off," "sleepover," "fuck buddy"—all are sexualized versions of activities you do with friends or synonyms for the people you do them with. Either despite or because of their symbolic and functional proximity, the interface of friend-finding websites like MeetUp, Friender, and Next Door look a lot like matchmaking websites. Dating websites and apps also have gotten into the friendship-making business. In 2016, Bumble launched a new platform called Bumble BFF that lets users use the same swiping and matching algorithms for friendships that they do for dating. After switching into BFF mode, users see their potential dates replaced by people of the same gender whom Bumble thinks they would want to be friends with based on shared interests and hobbies reflected on the users' social media profiles.[24] Although still less popular than its romantic other half, Bumble BFF and its copycat platforms saw a dramatic uptick in usage when the COVID-19 pandemic thrust the world into a prolonged period of quarantine and social distancing.[25]

Regardless of where or how they originate, not all the individuals who start down the parallel pathways of friendship and dating will reach their respective final stages. The related processes of sifting and weeding out confer upon the lucky a series of more impressive and intimate titles: a "friend" progresses to "close friend" and then "best friend." Articles on popular sites like Elite Daily and *Cosmopolitan* routinely blur the distinction between friend and lover even further by listing reasons why the former is better than the latter and arguing that the closest best friends deserve an even more privileged and rare title: that of soulmate.[26] In his 1976 ethnographic study of the relationship between love and friendship, anthropologist Robert Brain conceded an inherent slipperiness between the two terms, but he also pointed to a specific distinction between them: "We don't 'marry' our best friends."[27] Almost fifty years later, this long-standing cultural truth has bent so far that red flags are raised about any betrothed individual who does not use this moniker to describe their significant other.[28] What is the reward for making the final cut in both the friendship and the dating arenas? A piece of sparkly jewelry. Given the ideological and linguistic overlaps between friends and lovers in America, it is not surprising that the platonic counterpart to the diamond engagement ring is a heart-shaped "best friends" charm necklace if you are a ten-year-old girl, a Pandora or Alex and Ani bracelet charm if you are a forty-year-old woman, and a sorority pledge pin if you are an eighteen-year-old female college student.

By foregrounding the impact of homosocial bonding on campus social relations, *The Benefits of Friends* extends histories of sororities and fraternities and examines their practical and ideological legacies. Much of the scholarly research on Greek letter organizations falls into two camps: well-researched histories of systems or individual organizations and article- and book chapter–length case studies that illuminate a broader phenomenon or problem endemic to higher education such as hookup culture, racism, hazing, and binge drinking.[29] Sororities and fraternities are a favorite topic of investigative journalists, and while these writers have ample reason to be critical of these organizations, the stories they tell often closely follow the prescriptive plotline of the sensationalistic exposé.[30] This study combines academic theory—culled from sociology, cognitive psychology, evolutionary biology, anthropology, and economics and translated for a general audience—with ethnographic fieldwork and journalistic storytelling to create an innovative conceptual framework for understanding what sororities and fraternities do and why. In the context of sororities and fraternities, it no longer makes sense to rely on a secure split between friendship and romance. These same-sex friendships are now more intimate than dating, take on the structure and expectations of courtship, and unmake traditional dating scripts to create new patterns controlled by the same-sex group. At their best, these new social molds can offer dynamic new relationship possibilities and social and economic security for their members. This book will also reveal, however, how elevating the ingroup demands of these fictive brothers and sisters can reinforce insularity, entrench privilege, and (at times) threaten physical safety. Speaking more broadly about individuals who make friends instead of romantic partners the center of their lives, Rhaina Cohen writes in the *Atlantic* that "these friendships can be models for how we as a society might expand our conceptions of intimacy and care."[31] *The Benefits of Friends* reveals collegiate fraternities and sororities to be powerful social influencers that actively shape the contours of social relations on American college campuses in ways that affect how everyone sees and understands what it means to be a friend.

Methodology

I started working on this book roughly three years into a seven-year stint as a campus sorority faculty advisor and fraternity chapter advisor. Within this time frame, I worked directly with hundreds of members of three white Greek letter organizations. This experience provided me with a set of observations and questions that guided the early stages of my research. In my capacity as a formal invited researcher, I visited the national and international headquarters of multiple National Panhellenic Conference (NPC) sororities, attended three national sorority conventions, a national fraternity leadership conference, and several hazing prevention workshops. I also shadowed sorority recruitments at three institutions other than my own and interviewed members of multiple organizations' leadership teams (including three international presidents), industry consultants, campus fraternity and sorority life (FSL) professionals, and representatives from the industry's two largest and prominent trade organizations—the NPC and the North American Interfraternity Conference (NIC).

My in-group status as an alumna initiate and chapter advisor opened doors that would have been closed to other academics, and I am enormously grateful for the generosity of the individuals and organizations who welcomed me into their spaces, gave me access to their archives, and took time out of their busy schedules to patiently and thoughtfully answer my questions. For every request that was granted, however, there were a dozen unanswered emails, polite rejections, or last-minute cancellations. While the white fraternity and sorority community has made progress in opening itself up to the outside world, the fact remains that almost all the decision-making power is consolidated in the hands of a small group of people in the organizations' office headquarters—and has been that way for decades. In 1965, John Finlay Scott observed that collegians may hold leadership positions within their chapters, but it's the parent-age alumnae and chapter advisors who really are calling the shots. "The prototypical sorority," he said, "is not so much a servant of youthful interests as it is an organized agency for controlling them."[32] In my humble opinion, not much has changed. Very few of the organizations' on-the-ground representatives—and by this I mean alumni volunteers, leadership consultants, and campus FSL professionals—felt authorized to speak with me or grant me access to the events they were organizing without first consulting the higher-ups. If I had a dollar for every time someone responded to an interview request with the phrase "I need to check with nationals," I would be a rich woman. More often than not, the answer that came back was "No."

If my quest to land interviews with FSL professionals wasn't so frustrating, it would make a hilarious extended joke. In one instance, I drove two hours to meet with the president of one of the nation's largest sororities at a coffee shop near her home. A few minutes before the scheduled meeting, the woman canceled and never responded to my repeated attempts to set another date. Another sorority asked me to submit a cover letter, CV, and book proposal before granting me a screening call. Fair enough. After passing the baseline litmus test for credibility, I was granted an in-person meeting with the organization's executive leadership team. When I arrived at the national headquarters three weeks and a long plane ride later, a small group of women ushered me into a boardroom and announced that they would be happy to show me their sorority's trophy case but that access to any of their chapters' events were off-limits. Another organization granted me use of its historical archives but insisted on making photocopies of my handwritten notes before I left the building. I engaged in a protracted negotiation with another organization to profile its innovative diversity and inclusion workshop series. Everything was going great, until it inexplicitly terminated all communication.

I don't tell these stories out of spite; in fact, I've changed the identifying details of all parties to prevent detection. I understand their concern about speaking with outsiders: journalists and academics have not been historically kind to the white Greek letter system, and for organizations that place an extraordinarily high value on public perception, the risk of letting anyone muck around in your archives is not worth the reward. I also respect these organizations' right to privacy: just because I want access to something doesn't mean that I'm entitled to it. At the same time, I will say to you what I said to them: if they don't tell their story, someone else will. By opting out of conversations about their community or offering up heavily mediated, overtly biased, and fragmentary access, fraternities and sororities believe that they are controlling the narrative about who they are and what they do. In reality, they are doing exactly the opposite.

While many people occupying the top rungs of the sorority and fraternity ladder remained elusive and frustratingly out of reach, those clinging to the lowest rung were everywhere and easily accessible. I approached young adults sporting sorority and fraternity paraphernalia at airports, dog parks, grocery stores, and community swimming pools, as well as at a trailhead at the bottom of the Grand Canyon and a scuba shop in the Florida Keys. While some of my interviews were culled from sorority and fraternity members whom I met by chance, most were secured by referral. Using a strategy commonly referred to as "snowball sampling," I started out by interviewing current and recently graduated (within three years of the interview date) Rollins students who were members of white sororities and fraternities. At the end of each interview, I asked the individual if they would be willing to reach out to their high school friends who were currently members of white Greek letter organizations at other colleges and universities to see if they also would be willing to speak with me. The interview pool would continue to grow or "snowball" when the second set of students referred me to their friends, roommates, relatives, and so on.

Each interview typically began with me explaining my project and asking the open-ended question "Why did you join a sorority/fraternity?" The conversation that followed was loosely structured around the themes of this book but left broad enough, I hoped, to avoid leading questions. Oftentimes it was enough to simply say, "Tell me about the defining moments that shaped your fraternity/sorority experience." From there, students took me to the places where they wanted to go. I recognize that there is a difference between describing events that I personally witnessed and telling stories that were reported to me secondhand. In considering the latter, I followed the rule of recurrence. Specifically, I had to hear similar stories multiple times from individuals at different institutions for the narrative to make it into the book. In this way, I hoped to avoid representations of Greek culture that were localized and unique to specific campus environments.

Thanks to my students' generosity and the kindness of collegiate strangers, I was able to speak with current or recent sorority alumnae from twenty-three out of the twenty-six NPC member sororities. I was similarly able to interview current or recent fraternity member representatives from twelve NIC member organizations and three former NIC organizations. In total, I interviewed sorority and fraternity members from fifty-five colleges and universities. These institutions range from massive flagship state universities to small private liberal arts schools and everything in between. Thirty-six of these institutions are in states located in the east quadrant of the country whose imaginary borders draw a line from Florida to Texas, up to Missouri, east to Virginia, and back south again.

Because this book draws disproportionately on the experiences of fraternity and sorority members attending colleges and universities in the South, one could reasonably argue that this is a regional study. In some respects, this is true. Early editions of *Baird's Manual of American Colleges and Fraternities* (first published in 1879) classified fraternities as northern or southern based upon the location of their origin.[33] On the whole, institutions in the South are more racially homogenous and located in more politically conservative states than in other parts of the country. Without a doubt, sociopolitical forces fundamentally inform conceptions of race, gender, and sexuality. While examples of racism, misogyny, and homophobia abound in southern fraternity and sorority chapters, the South doesn't lay exclusive claim to all that is bad or good in white Greek letter culture. Margaret L. Freeman's recent study of white sororities' role in fashioning the national ideal of womanhood in the twentieth century reveals that southern sorority chapters exported the idea of the "southern belle" and culture of the imagined South to sorority chapters outside of the region.[34] This "southern aesthetic," as Freeman calls it, took the form of southern-themed parties that drew on Old South imagery and motifs, plantation-style chapter houses, and affected southern hospitality. The ideal sorority woman as emblematized by the imagined figure of the southern belle is characterized by her conventional physical beauty, polished dress, impeccable manners, and social and political conservatism.[35]

In her early 2000s ethnographic study of white sororities at universities in Texas, Diana Kendall similarly observed that sororities reproduce social class and "sisterhood" by communicating their expectations for appearance and behavior to their members not only directly, through dress codes and codes of conduct, but also indirectly, through peer modeling and carefully crafted histories.[36] Central to the new member education process is learning about the organizations' founding members and their families. New fraternity members are similarly taught to revere their founders with a respect and devotion that borders on the religious. In the course of my research, I attended a fraternity leadership conference held at the university where that fraternity was founded 150 years ago. Part of the conference agenda included participating in a small group tour of the dorm room where the organization's first collegiate members drafted the founding charter. The short walk from the conference venue to the residence hall was viewed by the fraternity members in my tour group as a kind of pilgrimage. "This is one of the coolest experiences of my life," one of them told me. The room where it all began had been remodeled so many times over the past century that it was hard to see the space, which was occupied by a bunk bed, two nightstands, and matching desks, as unique or special—that is, until the tour guide gestured to a small commemorative plaque on the wall. The fraternity men glanced at each other nervously, belying the fact that they all had been taught how to respond to the story of their founding members but hadn't been coached on what to say or do in this space. Before the awkwardness became unbearable, the tour guide volunteered a suggestion of how to engage with the plaque: "Take a photo of it!" With a sigh of relief, every man in the room whipped out his phone and began snapping away.

The fraternity whose leadership conference I attended treated their founding members' residence hall as a kind of consecrated holy space. This was evidenced not only in the language they used to describe the dorm room but also by the fact that the men asked me to step outside so they could perform a fraternity ritual in it. While this fraternity sacralizes the site of its founding to make a case for the value, prestige, and power of the organization, others employed different strategies to create what Nicholas Syrett describes as an imagined nation "composed solely of white, moneyed men."[37] Freeman shows how southern sororities did the same thing by constructing origin stories that glorified the antebellum South and cast the first sorority women as heirs to an aristocratic white gentility, an inheritance that they figuratively bequeathed to all women who are grafted into the family tree through initiation into the organization.[38] When these sororities spread outside the region, they took their romanticized histories and white supremacist ideas with them. At the same time as southern sororities were spreading southern identity up and out, nonsouthern sororities, enamored with the "belle character," refashioned their organizations' histories and culture to align with the southern aesthetic.[39]

Many attributes of the southern aesthetic, far from being a relic of the past, and its accompanying rhetoric feature prominently in contemporary white FSL culture. Charlotte Hogg's and Leigh Ann Jones's examinations of sorority and fraternity rhetoric collectively demonstrate "a propensity for behaviors that sustain traditional gender norms, particularly by modeling a kind of sisterhood that does not transgress the cultural values the founders came from and forwarded."[40]

Southern Living magazine regularly publishes photo albums and rankings of the nation's "most beautiful sorority houses," which unsurprisingly feature a disproportionate number of massive white mansions at universities in the South. Recently, periodicals with a broader and more diverse readership like *Cosmopolitan*, *Teen Vogue*, *Architectural Digest*, and *Town & Country* have gotten in on the act, publishing their own lists and accompanying photo spreads that feature gleaming white sororal mansions in Louisiana and Mississippi next to lookalike white mansions in California and Nebraska.[41]

Popular magazines aren't the only form of media that work to nationalize the southern sorority aesthetic. Social media has popularized iconic southern fashion styles including preppy button-ups and shift dresses, whipstitched sandals and boat shoes, and simple pendant jewelry. The southern sorority women's devotion to specific designers and brands (Kendra Scott, Tory Burch, Longchamp Le Pilage, Golden Goose, Steve Madden) has exported both these styles and brands to the rest of the sorority and fraternity world.[42] Southern Tide's classic skipjack polo shirt (designed by a University of South Carolina fraternity member in 2006) is a staple of fraternity men's wardrobes nationwide; so are bright pastel-print Lilly Pulitzer dresses. The latter's Miami-based headquarters famously ran a social media contest in 2011 that promised the NPC sorority with the most votes a custom floral print in the sorority's colors that could be turned into clothing, bags, phone cases, and other accessories. The winner of the 2012 nationwide contest was announced with fanfare at my college and with the assistance of the Rollins sorority chapter with which I worked at the time.[43] A few years later, Jack Rogers, a sandal company with a cult-like sorority following, unveiled a specialty line of sorority letter sandals.[44]

If southern fashion trends and brands were introduced to other parts of the country through social media, the region's Greek life culture took on a life of its own with the 2010 creation of Total Frat Move (TFM) and its sister website, Total Sorority Move (TSM). Geared toward eighteen-to-twenty-four-year-old college students, these microblog sites epitomized the "fratire" genre of comedy by posting clever memes and one-liners, crazy party stories, photos of attractive sorority women and "fratty men," and weird and shocking campus news. In a 2014 interview with Business Insider, the website's founders—two former fraternity brothers from Texas State University named Madison Wickham and Ryan Young—said that they focused their early marketing efforts on Twitter. "We started following people who fit the part," Wickham said, "not just any fraternity guy, but that Southern, stereotypical fraternity guy who we thought had a high probability of sharing it with friends."[45] Before long, it wasn't just southern fraternity men who were viewing southern fratire. In 2014, the sites generated 18 million monthly unique visitors. The book *TFM* debuted on the *New York*

Times best-seller list.[46] The websites came under fire for being distasteful and sexist, but the criticism did nothing to diminish their popularity—for awhile.[47] By 2019, the content that made TFM and TSM all the rage in the early 2010s had shifted to other platforms (specifically the photo- and video-sharing apps Snapchat and Instagram); eventually the websites were absorbed within a competing media conglomerate called Barstool Sports, and its content disappeared from the Internet. If TFM's and TSM's unceremonious departures from the web signal these sites' cultural expiration date, their collective nine-year tenure serves as a poignant reminder that the websites served as a primer for Greek life—or at least an exaggerated and imagined version of it—for almost a decade's worth of college students.

Photo- and video-sharing platforms quickly picked up where TFM and TSM left off. Sorority recruitment videos (short promotional videos of individual chapters set to music) began popping up on YouTube in the early 2010s but exploded in popularity after the University of Alabama's 2015 Alpha Phi video went viral.[48] A recent research study of the 100 most viewed sorority recruitment videos in 2017 revealed that over half featured sorority chapters at colleges and universities in the South.[49] In August 2021, TikTok solidified its status as the runaway favorite for sorority- and fraternity-themed content of the moment when sorority recruitment at the University of Alabama (the nation's largest Greek letter community) went viral. During the week-long event, more than 20 million people viewed TikTok videos with the hashtag #AlabamaRush and over 55 million viewed those with the hashtag #BamaRush.[50] Less than a week later, the number of views of videos with the latter hashtag had climbed to 327 million.[51] Many of these videos featured potential new members (PNMs) of sororities modeling their daily outfits and identifying each clothing item's brand or where they purchased it.

Thanks to these platforms, when rising college students think of sororities and fraternities, they don't think about small chapters who hold their meetings in university classrooms and have modest social calendars; they think of supersized campus Greek Villages filled with megamansions that exist in many parts of the country but are emblematic of those in the South. While it is true that Greek culture in the South does not accurately represent what fraternity and sorority life is like in other parts of the country, it is also true that the southern Greek aesthetic represents how sororities and fraternities are perceived in the nation's cultural imagination—and this is arguably more important. This study doesn't try to dismantle this perception or glorify it; rather, it seeks to examine the power of it.

There is another way that this book is grounded in perceptions that are more culturally than factually accurate. Every Greek letter chapter has its own personality, or, as my students put it, "vibe," and the one that I joined as an alumnae initiate was and still is filled with academically high-achieving women. Because the chapter privileges GPA over physical appearance and body type in recruitment, it proudly occupies the so-called bottom tier in the school's unofficial chapter ranking system. The other sorority chapter and fraternity chapter with which I worked were, by all accounts, top tier. The criteria with which sorority and fraternity chapters across the board use to evaluate themselves and others is vague and subjective but is generally based on the chapter's perceived desirability by PNMs and popularity among other chapters. Because of this, top-tier chapters usually are those whose members are conventionally attractive, wealthy, cisgender, and straight.[52] Lower-tier chapters tend to be those whose membership is more diverse in every way. Mid-tier chapters fall somewhere in between. Because people tend to surround themselves with individuals from similar backgrounds, many of the sorority and fraternity members whom I interviewed from other institutions were self-professed members of top-tier chapters. By giving this demographic a prominent voice in this study I am not suggesting that its members speak for everyone within the national sorority and fraternity community. I am arguing, however, that by embodying the stereotypes of their kind they represent the cultural construct of what contemporary American society has imagined the current sorority woman and fraternity man to be.

Because I started working on this book while I was actively working with a campus fraternity chapter, questions about ethics and conflicts of interest played a big role in guiding my research process. While my omnipresent name badge clearly marked me as a researcher when I visited other institutions, I was acutely aware that the same tag didn't convey the same meaning at my own institution. After constantly struggling to determine which of my roles was most dominant in the moment—teacher, faculty advisor, chapter advisor, researcher—I gave up on the grounds that they were all too interconnected to be meaningfully and effectively separated. Did the fraternity chapter with which I worked at Rollins know that I was writing a book about sororities and fraternities, and that their chapter might show up in it? Yes. Were these key facts on the top of their members' minds as they went about their day-to-day operations? No. I took my concerns about informed consent to my institution's Institutional Review Board (IRB) and got the go-ahead. Still, the uneasiness that comes from not being able to draw a clear line between my roles prompted me to implement several measures to protect individuals' privacy.

Industry professionals and experts whom I formally interviewed appear under their real names and titles, as do the names of the universities and colleges that I visited. No sorority or fraternity member, however, appears under their own name, and all identifying features have been obscured, even when individuals professed that neither was necessary. I insisted on anonymization for one simple reason: sorority and fraternity members (my own and those affiliated with other institutions) have trusted me with their stories, some of which are extremely personal. With this trust comes the responsibility to protect them from themselves. What eighteen-to-twenty-two-year-olds may be proud to share with the world in the moment may not be something that they particularly want their names attached to when they are, let's say, applying for full-time jobs, meeting future in-laws, or running for public office. All individuals who were interviewed for this book signed IRB interview consent forms. One individual is featured briefly in two chapters of this book and, for an added layer of privacy, asked to be represented under two different names. In the interest of transparency and to make sure that I represented events fairly and accurately, I invited individuals who are featured prominently in this book to review and offer feedback on the sections or chapters in which they appear.

What You Won't Find in This Book

This is not a book that will weigh in directly on whether sororities and fraternities should stay or go. Each side has passionately made its case, and joining one chorus may help drown out the other, but it won't move us any closer to understanding what essential things these organizations provide individuals that college students can't get anywhere else. If we are going to talk seriously about abolishing sororities and fraternities, then we need to know what holes we are going to have to fill when they are gone. Conversely, if white sororities and fraternities are here to stay, then we need to start talking seriously about how their model of friendship operates. This starts with recognizing that the scope of these organizations' social and cultural influence extends far beyond the college campus.

This is also not a book explicitly about African American or multicultural Greek letter social organizations. All single-sex organizations place a high value on same-sex friendship, and, thus, much of the discussion that follows will be both relevant and revealing. The point of departure comes in the argument's framing. At its core this book is about whiteness and power, and particularly how a dominant racial group consciously and unconsciously mobilizes race and class to its advantage. My discussion is premised on the fact that social, economic, and political capital is consolidated in this country in the hands of white elites, and that, as organizations overwhelmingly populated by this demographic, white sororities and fraternities are inexorably bound up in the protection and promotion of this model of race and class relations. My understanding of "white privilege" aligns with Cheryl Harris's notion of whiteness as property and Peggy McIntosh's classic metaphor of it as an "invisible weightless knapsack of special provisions, assurances, tools, maps, guides, codebooks, passports, visas, clothes, compass, emergency gear, and blank checks."[53]

I use the terms "white sorority" and "white fraternity" throughout this book instead of the traditional way of referencing these organizations—"historically white"—as a way to put pressure on industry terminology and the beliefs governing it. As critical race theorist Crystal M. Fleming reminds us, referring to any form of systemic racial discrimination as something "historic" gives the false impression that racism is a problem confined to the past.[54] This is certainly not the case when it comes to the organizations featured in this book. With one noted exception, case studies are drawn from the twenty-six white sororities comprising the NPC and the white NIC fraternities. At their founding and up through the middle of the twentieth century, most of these organizations only admitted individuals who were not only racially white but also from Anglo-Saxon Protestant heritage. Julie Park's analysis of data compiled from the National Longitudinal Study of Freshman revealed that 97 percent of members of white sorority and fraternity members enrolled in college between 1999 and 2003 reported that their organizations were primarily white.[55] The NPC and the NIC don't keep demographic records of their members, so it's hard to tell how much the needle has moved since then, but if the group photos that are posted on chapters' websites are any indication, it doesn't appear to be much in most places.

Another gap in this book is a nuanced portrayal of LGBTQ+ sorority and fraternity members. This book focuses primarily on the role that wealthy, straight-passing white gay fraternity brothers play in facilitating and orchestrating sexual encounters between their straight friends. I recognize that this snapshot captures only a fraction of the range of gender identities, roles, and experiences of LGBTQ+ Greek members, and I ask that readers don't take my short-shrift treatment as a sign of disinterest or attempt at dismissiveness, but rather as an invitation to continue the conversation about a critically important and underresearched population.

Religion is another topic that hovers around the margins of this book but does not get direct treatment within it. Many but not all NPC and white NIC organizations were founded by Protestant Christians. Over time, sororities and fraternities have amended their charters and revised their rituals in ways that preserve tradition but also signal that they are no longer religiously homogenous organizations. Despite having been subjected to editorial red pens, many sorority and fraternity rituals still ideologically position themselves as distinctly Christian. During my own sorority initiation ceremony in 2011, I was so startled by the ritual's heavy deployment of biblical language and Christian symbolism and imagery that I made a point to later ask several non-Christian and nonreligious women in the room about it. Without exception, the women told me that they found the religious content both strange and seemingly unnecessary, but that its inclusion in the sorority ritual didn't really bother them.

These women's views were consistent with what I heard from non-Christian and nonreligious sorority and fraternity members at other institutions—even those located in the most conservative Christian pockets of the Deep South. Many of the women and men that I interviewed view Christian rhetoric as an accepted part of their lived existence: the "Jesus talk" that they hear in the sorority and fraternity houses isn't any different than what they encounter at the grocery store or have heard in their hometown high schools. If part of their response to their chapters' rituals are to treat them like the Pledge of Allegiance—the reference to God in both isn't something they've ever thought to be troubled by—another is to redefine their meaning and significance. The most common strategy that I encountered was to contextualize ritual religious terminology and practice within the broader context of the organization's revered history. By viewing rituals through the lens of tradition, non-Christian sorority and fraternity members find a way not only to defend their existence but also to advocate for their continued use. Unpacking the layers that undergird this stance could fill a book itself, which is why I have left it largely alone. With this being said, much of what I will say about sororities' and fraternities' attitudes toward racialized and nonstraight "others" applies to non-Christian members as well. To the list of individuals and agencies that Y. Joshi Khyati identifies as being subjects of "white Christian privilege," I add non-Christian and nonreligious members of white sororities and fraternities.[56]

What You Will Find in This Book

Women outnumber men on college campuses nationwide, and studies show that campuses with higher women-to-men ratios have more pronounced hookup cultures. In chapter 1 I show how fraternities have a long tradition of controlling the campus dating script by artificially manipulating sex ratios to create an even more pronounced hookup culture. In the early twentieth century, when men were the numeric majorities on college campuses, fraternity chapters created artificial male scarcity by prohibiting some of their members from attending their own parties. Today's campus demographics combine with current NIC policy—which does not establish a minimum membership size of fraternity chapters—to do the same thing. The uneven size of many fraternity and sorority chapters means that every time a sorority mixes with a fraternity, there are upward of three times the number of women at the event than men.

Chapter 2 illuminates how sorority women have uniquely adapted to the dynamics of modern hookup culture and work to subvert it, not by pursuing a romantic interest on their own, but by forming sororal teams that mobilize their collective resources in sequence to secure romantic partners from a targeted fraternity for all members of the group. If one of the strengths of a team-based dating culture is increased access to a scarce commodity (men), a weakness is romantic mobility. Because sororal teams form romantic alliances with specific fraternities, to pursue someone in an alliance other than your own often means taking on an entire sorority. This chapter also considers the role that LGBTQ+ fraternity and sorority members play in straight hookup culture. Despite championing gender binaries and privileging straight identities, some chapters actively recruit queer members to serve as matchmakers, diplomats, and mediators. Torn between competing loyalties, LGBTQ+ members find themselves occupying the nebulous space between empowerment and exploitation.

Chapter 3 examines the role that alcohol and prescription drugs play in sorority and fraternity matchmaking to illuminate why being under the influence is a requisite for engaging with the opposite sex. It also looks at how the rhetoric of fictive families both muddies the narrative of sexual assault and raises the social stakes of its reportage beyond what is reasonable to handle. If reporting isn't an option, then the best alternative available to sorority women is to prevent sexual assaults from happening in the first place. The chapter concludes by arguing that the so-called buddy system still works even when it fails by displacing the blame of sexual assault from the male assailant (who won't make amends for the harm inflicted) to the victim's sorority sisters (who will).

Blurring the boundaries between friend and lover works to diminish the importance of the latter while elevating and essentializing the existence of the former. In chapter 4, I revisit the sorority community made infamous in Alexandra Robbins's 2004 best-selling sorority exposé *Pledged*. In the eighteen years since the book's publication, there has been a marked turn in the recruitment practices at Southern Methodist University (SMU) from one that picks women apart to one that marks them as objects of desire. From unabashedly erotic recruitment videos in which women signal their desire to enter into platonic relationships with other women through sexual innuendo to recruitment activities that are thinly veiled imitations of *Bachelor*-style marriage proposals, wedding ceremonies, and honeymoons, SMU's sorority recruitment reimagines the friend-making process as a series of rituals that culminate not in sexual intercourse but in the creation of a sexless sanctuary.

The physical embodiment of this sanctuary is, of course, the sorority house. Since their first inception in the 1870s, sorority houses have served as material manifestations of the aspirational family home. Chapter 4 uses readings of digital and in-person house tours, magazine spreads, and interviews with current and former sorority house residents to show how the long-standing trope of the "dream home" has shifted from being a residence designed for the traditional nuclear family to a palatial mansion where men are not welcome. As a training ground for adulthood, living in a sorority house is a ritual that both prepares female college students for a life with a husband but also a future spent in the company of women.

The glittering megamansions that line many college towns' proverbial sorority rows aren't struggling with the same empty bed syndrome that plague other forms of student housing. Rather, many are bursting at the seams. Chapter 5 examines the rise of the so-called sorority superchapter (chapters with upward of 300 members) to explore what happens when the number of your friends exceeds that which scientists claim your brain can maintain. Applying the pioneering theories of evolutionary anthropologist Robin Dunbar to the fraternity and sorority communities of the University of Arkansas and University of Alabama, we see how members of these and other sorority superchapters adapt to the problem of having too many friends by forming microcommunities, often consisting exclusively of members of their same-aged pledge classes. The substituting of horizontal friendships for vertical ones reflects broader societal trends (individuals between eighteen and twenty-four spend more time with each other than any other demographic). As we will see, this dynamic within the sorority house promotes the formation of deep peer bonds but also makes these relationships susceptible to bullying, slut-shaming, and hazing.

Chapter 6 extends the previous chapter's exploration of the negative ramifications caused by horizontal friendships by examining the function of fraternity hazing. This chapter puts the origin story of fraternal organizations in America in dialogue with contemporary military theory and the media coverage of recent alcohol-related hazing deaths to argue that hazing fails not when it goes too far but when its success is contingent upon it going too far. Today's hazing rituals, I show, function as crude proxies for the types of salvific acts performed on battlefields. In particular, binge drinking is designed to mimic the condition of submission that soldiers inherently place in their comrades during active combat in that both soldier and drinker relinquish their bodies to their friends for safekeeping. Through alternately assuming the roles of protector and the person needing rescuing, fraternity members embody the defining principles of fraternal brotherhood—namely, solidarity and mutual assistance. Following the logic that practice makes perfect, the best soldiers and fraternity brothers are those who are consistently successful in playing each role. By extension, bad soldiers/fraternity brothers are those who either don't perform their assigned jobs well or don't do them at all. In this backhanded way, the fact that fraternity members of other chapters are dying by hazing affirms the value and exceptionalism of the chapters whose members survive.

At the same time as hazing manufactures the conditions of battle to make the case that the white fraternity man is entitled to special powers and privileges, the growing influx of women, LGBTQ+ students, and men and women of color onto the contemporary college campus simultaneously positions this figure as a combatant in a turf war that he is destined to lose. Chapter 7 explains how fraternities (and the sororities who emulate them) became bastions of racism, and why unmooring them from traditional ways of thinking and viewing individuals outside of their racial in-group is so difficult. In particular, I examine the recent push by white organizations to diversify their ranks by taking a close look at the specific offer that is being extended. While adding a few brown and Black faces to a chapter composite technically may justify calling oneself a "historically white" organization, I argue that the industry's historicization of racial oppression is a rhetorical move that does exactly the opposite of its intended effect; instead of demonstrating the community's commitment to moving beyond single-race friend groups, it reveals it to be structurally incapable of supporting a different relationship model.

Chapter 8 continues the conversation about white privilege by examining how the social bonds forged through fraternity membership extend beyond current collegians to include the alumni members of these organizations. The pervasiveness of so-called fraternity pipelines into Fortune

500 companies and high-ranking government positions goes a long way in explaining why former fraternity members occupy the highest rungs of our nation's socioeconomic ladder in disproportionate number. This chapter starts out by illuminating how and why the vitality of this fraternity pipeline depends on maintaining a clear distinction between whites and "white trash." It also considers why sorority women, who, by virtue of their sheer number on campus, socioeconomic background, and representation in the current workforce, have enough force to create a parallel professional pipeline that rivals the depth and breadth of that run by their fictive brothers. The chapter concludes by considering what's stopping them from doing so.

The book ends with an examination of what happened when sorority and fraternity houses were shuttered, and their organizations' programming moved online. The COVID pandemic upended society by essentially shutting it down for a season. Running alongside the ongoing concerns about public health was a parallel concern about the mental health of young adults. As experts in the relationship business, sororities and fraternities were uniquely poised to provide college students with what they most craved: peer friendship. Taking a close look at sorority and fraternity life in the time of COVID reveals fascinating insights about the allure of these organizations at the same time as it allows society to imagine a world without them. The global pandemic, I argue, doesn't make a case for whether these organizations should stay or go but rather fundamentally changes the question to something that might have an easier answer.

ONE

Fraternity Party Population Control

The Manor, as it is affectionately known around town, has seen better days. The 1960s-era rambler's notable architectural features include a sagging roof, a splintered front door, and a chipped and faded stucco façade. A single scraggly miniature palm tree poking out of the sand pit that is the front yard is the only surviving evidence of the futile attempts to stave off the property's descent into the neighborhood eyesore.

What the house lacks in curbside appeal, it more than makes up for in interior charm, if by charm one means smelly, roach-infested squalor. When I entered the house one afternoon, I was greeted by a fraternity man frying up breakfast on the stove. "Wussup?" he asked, nodding in recognition of my presence. On the kitchen counter, casually sitting next to the carton of eggs and package of uncooked bacon, was an industrial-size box of condoms. Just a few feet away from the stove and the man cooking on it was the abode's piece de resistance: a large jetted hot tub. The fact that the tub was built into the floor and boasted an elaborate tile surround revealed that the object didn't wander into the kitchen by chance but was placed there deliberately by a creative homeowner who wanted a fancy bathtub and didn't want to tamper with the home's existing plumbing. The location of the hot tub explains why the Manor might struggle on the conventional residential resale market. It also explains why my fraternity members would find the prospect of living there immensely appealing. Indeed, the gift that was this multipurpose workhorse endowed the house with almost reverential qualities. It wasn't quite a temple, but definitely worthy of its stately name. Where else other than a manor could you cook dinner from your bathtub? What other object, through its ability to hold 200 pounds of crushed ice, could serve so perfectly as a surrogate cooler for an equal number of cans of beer?

The half a dozen aluminum corpses that were floating in the tub revealed the capacity in which the object had most recently been pressed into service. It was approximately eighteen hours after the Manor had played host to one of the biggest fraternity parties of the year. The material residues of the previous night combine to construct a narrative where alcohol and sex are consistent and defining components of fraternity culture.

There are lots of reasons for the fraternity house's long-standing claim to this honorific title, including the proximity of party space to bedrooms, accessibility of free alcohol, and the demographic of the partygoers. Fraternity houses also have a competitive edge over other party venues in that they typically are located on, directly adjacent to, or within walking distance of school property, but often are privately owned residences. While technically subject to the school's code of conduct (which prohibits underage drinking), its status as private property means that school officials can't just barge in at will, making enforcement of these codes notoriously tricky.

Because of its proximity to and away from campus, the fraternity house and its surrogates—local restaurants, bars, pool halls, and hotel ballrooms rented out by fraternities for social events—long have served as combined speakeasies and collegiate ancestral mating grounds. One of the first events I attended as a fraternity and sorority advisor was held at an Orlando nightclub. While circling the premises, I stumbled on what would become a familiar sight: a fraternity man and sorority woman making out in the bushes. A few days later, the woman, named Tatum, stopped by my office. She reported that her friends were teasing her for hooking up with the man, whom she described as someone who "is afflicted with the double curse of being unattractive and socially awkward." If you aren't interested in him, I asked, why kiss him? The woman sighed and chalked her decision up to desperation: "I wanted to hook up with *someone*, and he was all that was left." Tatum's insistence that her hookup partner literally constituted her only option for straight romance made me laugh, until I reviewed the guest list and saw that approximately two-thirds of the party guests were straight women. As we shall see, on one level, the party's gender imbalance made sense, but on another, the math simply didn't add up.

Imbalanced Sex Ratios and Campus Hookup Culture

Wander around the grounds of many colleges and universities in America and you will encounter no shortage of women. Cisgender female students outnumber their cisgender male counterparts in nearly all sectors of undergraduate higher education today.[1] Of course, that wasn't always the case.[2] Colleges and universities opened their doors to women in stages, and some of the biggest dominoes to fall—Princeton, Yale, and the University of Virginia—were among the most recent. Jane Leifer, a member of the first cohort of women students to study at Princeton, famously described her matriculation in the fall of 1969 as a "blind date with history."[3] When Leifer and her 170 female classmates stepped foot on campus, they joined 820 men, making the sex ratio of men to women a staggering eight to one.

While Princeton's lopsided sex ratio quickly righted itself, many of the institutions that went coed during the first wave of integration had significantly higher male enrollments throughout most of the first half of the century. During the 1930s at Cornell, for example, the ratio was three men to one woman. During the same period, the sex ratio at the University of Michigan was two to one.[4]

While the sex ratio imbalance was visible on all coed campuses, it was even more pronounced at then-rural institutions like Pennsylvania State University University Park (Penn State), where male students outnumbered their female cohorts in the 1930s by a ratio of six to one. The students attending these institutions weren't the only ones to take note of the lopsided ratio on campus; coeducation was *the* hot topic of conversation in academia. While his colleagues debated the merits of coed classrooms (the consensus in the early years of the initiative was that having women around was distracting to male students and threatened to dilute the value of the curriculum), Penn State sociologist Willard Waller observed that the skewed sex ratio meant that men had to work hard for love at his university, regardless of how ideal the specimen.[5]

Waller's research methodology has since been called into question, but his observation that gender imbalance impacts romance customs found solid theoretical grounding forty years later in the Guttentag-Secord theory, so-named after the Harvard psychology professors who developed it.[6] This theory holds that the gender that comprises the numeric minority inherently has more partner options and thus controls the script of romantic and sexual relationships. Historically speaking, when women have held this position of power in dating culture, they have leveraged it to promote the formation of monogamous bonds.[7]

Since sex ratio theory privileges the less populous gender, the first generation of female college students should have been overrun with male suitors. Proving that every rule has an exception, this largely wasn't the case, as women were seen as intruders in male space and whose presence in the classroom had a feminizing effect.[8] Cultural change and increased educational and professional access for women spurred by the suffrage, women's liberation, and civil rights movements helped push the campus sex ratio closer to equilibrium. The number of women attending college increased in the 1960s and accelerated in the 1970s and 1980s. In 1994, the sex ratio was balanced at 50:50.[9] In the almost thirty years since, the gap has widened in the opposite direction. Today there are about forty men for every sixty women on many college campuses. This may not sound like a significant disparity until you frame the numbers in the way that economics and business journalist Jon Birger does. Specifically, when we convert ratio to a more familiar mathematical form (percent), we see that a 40:60 sex ratio means that there are 50 percent more women than men on today's average campus.[10] As we shall see, this number has an underrecognized but monumental effect on all facets of the college experience, including and especially students' social lives.

The F*%k Boy Next Door

Although only about an hour's drive apart, Georgia Institute of Technology (Georgia Tech) and the University of Georgia (UGA) might as well be housed on different planets when it comes to their campus relationship culture. Located in midtown Atlanta, Georgia Tech prides itself on being on the cutting edge in technological innovation, but, by multiple accounts, it is a virtual dinosaur in the straight romance department. According to current and former students, some hookup culture exists on this campus, but individuals are more likely to pair up in long-term monogamous romantic relationships. Contrast this with UGA, which, in 2016, earned the dubious honor of being named the "kinkiest college" by the dating app Clover.[11] While the app didn't expound on its terminological choices, in any college thesaurus "kinky" appears closer to "hookup" than it does to "long-term boyfriend."

Despite the popular perception that colleges and universities are sexual playgrounds, the reality is that college students today aren't having more sex than their predecessors.[12] While hookup culture may trade in illusion, sociologist Lisa Wade's research shows that it is still very much real.[13] If the dynamics of contemporary campus relationship culture portray Georgia Tech as a place where it is still possible for a straight woman to fantasize about being asked out on a traditional date—and have reasonably good odds that her dream might actually come true—UGA falls into the category of schools where the word "date" itself might as well be stricken from the campus lexicon. Applying the logic of sex ratio theory, part of this might have to do with the fact that Georgia Tech's sex ratio is 61:39 and UGA's is 43:57.[14]

My institution is on the same 40:60 sex ratio list as UGA; the University of California, Los Angeles; James Madison University; New York University; Boston University; the University of North Carolina at Chapel Hill; and multitudes of other campuses. The sex ratio imbalance across institutions of higher education in America is fundamentally changing the contours of the campus relationship dynamics for both women and men. If college men are not asking their female classmates to go out to dinner and a movie, what, might you ask, does a straight male student's love life look like on today's campus? That varies according to campus, social group, and individual, of course, but when asked to recount the details of their previous weekend's social calendar, here is what three white Rollins fraternity members from different chapters professed to have been up to.

Tom, a tall and gregarious senior from New York City, accepted an invitation to attend a sorority semiformal with his close friend Molly, whom he's known since his first year and with whom he engages in frequent noncommittal hookups. Once Tom arrived at the party, he was delighted to discover that instead of bringing men to the event as dates, many of Molly's sorority sisters either went to the event solo or brought a woman friend, making the sex ratio of the room approximately one man to two women. Once the alcohol started flowing and everyone had downed a few, Tom admitted that "things got pretty wild." Reports differ on what exactly transpired. According to Molly, Tom "stuck his tongue down the throats of five or six of her friends." Tom insists he only hooked up with three.

Ryan's fraternity threw a small invite-only house party at the apartment of one of its members. Although the third-year business major from Miami wasn't personally in the market for a random hookup, Ryan was committed to helping his roommate and fellow fraternity brother find love—or at least have sex. As the party got going, Ryan did a quick headcount of attendees. What he discovered—that there were twenty fraternity men and over thirty women in the house—boded well for his roommate. The next morning,

Ryan checked in on his friend via text. In response to his query about how things went, Ryan received a single-word text response: "Sexcess."

Parker, a second-year student from Kansas City, had to get up early on Monday morning for his internship at a local insurance firm, so he made plans to spend Sunday afternoon hanging out with some of his buddies at a local sports bar with the intent of calling it an early night. At the bar, he ran into Madison, a communications major from Atlanta, who was part of his extended fraternity and sorority friend group. After chatting for a few minutes, the two made vague plans to "maybe hang out at some point in the future." An hour after arriving home, Parker texted Madison and invited her over to his house to "Netflix and chill." Madison promptly declined the coded offer for casual sex. Parker shrugged his shoulders and texted back "np [no problem]; mb [maybe] next time." He then scrolled through his phone's contact list until he landed on another prospect. "Netflix and chill?" he typed.

If research tells us that most college students aren't hooking up all that often, the self-reported nature of these stories draws their factual accuracy further into question. But whether or not the alleged romantic escapades played out exactly as the men described them doesn't really matter; it's precisely because any hookup story could be partially true that allows all hookup stories to be taken seriously.

While the landscape of college hookup culture has been fashioned into something of a straight male fantasy, according to a group of female students who run in the same crowd as Tom, Ryan, and Parker, this romantic terrain turns college men into so-called fuck boys. Sociologists offer a less crude explanation of the situation. Using data from a survey of 1,000 straight female American college students, professors Jeremy Uecker and Mark Regnerus have showed that on campuses like Rollins, where women comprise a higher proportion of the student body, women reported going on fewer traditional dates, were less likely to have boyfriends, and engaged in more hookups with more men.[15]

My anecdotal account of the form that hookup culture takes at Rollins is buttressed by qualitative data compiled by researchers at Indiana University Bloomington. Between 2004 and 2008, professors Elizabeth A. Armstrong and Laura T. Hamilton tracked a cohort of fifty-three female students throughout the entirety of their undergraduate tenure. All the women in their study lived on the same floor of a campus residence hall during their first year and, to get a comprehensive and nuanced view of how their personal and academic lives unfolded, Hamilton moved in alongside them. One of the things that Armstrong and Hamilton discovered and wrote about in

Paying for the Party was that many college women see men the same way that men see them—namely, as sexual objects, ephemeral playthings, and forms of entertainment and amusement.[16]

Since the publication of Armstrong and Hamilton's research in 2013, the buzz about women's engagement in hookup culture has grown into a chorus of voices that catalog the ways that women are mobilizing hookup culture to serve their own ends. Indeed, one of the upsides of living in a society where women have autonomy over their sexual lives is that it opens up opportunities for women to pursue their own sexual desires. Specifically, when women and men are free to follow the same romantic script (i.e., hookup culture), researchers notice that they pursue similar lifestyle pathways after graduation in that they choose to privilege their careers over romantic relationships.[17]

Although hookup culture has benefits and drawbacks for both genders, sociologists don't see the embracing of hookup culture by today's college women as a sign that sex ratio theory has been either rendered irrelevant or has gone off the rails. Rather, many see it as an adaptation to a social environment that women don't have the power to control or change.[18] While straight college women may not be looking to pair up with the intent of settling down at the rate they used to, sex ratio theory posits the uncomfortable hypothesis that some women are choosing this course, in part, because there aren't other options. To put it bluntly: even if a straight college woman on a 40:60 campus wants a serious boyfriend, there might not be a whole lot of men raising their hands to volunteer for the job. Women who attend universities with more equal sex ratios often don't have it any easier because the population who controls the campus social scene systematically manipulates party demographics to create a hookup culture where numerically there shouldn't be one.

"The Sex Ratio Is Way Off. We Have to Get More Girls."

The gender imbalance at Rollins explains why there will be more women than men in attendance at all-campus functions. But the skewed ratio at the fraternity and sorority party where Tatum and I were both in attendance didn't make sense when situated within the demographic context of the national Greek letter community. According to the trade associations of which white fraternities and sororities are members—the North American Interfraternity Conference (NIC) and the National Panhellenic Conference (NPC)—there were a combined 750,000 active fraternity and sorority members on North American college campuses during the 2017–18 academic year. Out of this number, the number of men and women was roughly split right down the middle.[19] While the gender breakdown was basically even, how white fraternities and sororities structure themselves on college campuses differ in a small but an enormously important way.

Before 2003, white sororities didn't have enrollment caps and quotas.[20] Each chapter could admit as many or few members from an applicant pool as its current members wanted, resulting in a campus Greek letter community with chapter sizes all over the board. While there were certain benefits to this model—total control over one's membership population being chief among them—the lack of an umbrella admissions policy threatened to breed divisiveness among the organizations by allowing the growth of a few supersize chapters that would consume competition while permitting the exclusion of individuals from the broader Greek letter community who wanted to join a fraternity or sorority but weren't invited to join these specific groups. In a move designed to promote greater inclusivity, the twenty-six sororities belonging to the NPC switched to a supply and demand admissions model. In its most basic sense, what each campus sorority community does is take the number of women who sign up to participate in sorority recruitment that year and divide that number by the number of campus organizations. While a woman may not gain admission to her first-choice house, exceptional circumstances aside, this system greatly improves the odds that she will be placed in a house. This also means, by extension, that all the sorority chapters on any given campus have roughly the same number of members. In a phone conversation, NIC spokesperson Todd Shelton told me that NIC member fraternities didn't actively reject the idea of adopting a similar membership quota system as much as they didn't see a need to seriously consider it. As a result, it's possible to have a fraternity chapter with as few as a dozen members on the same campus with one that has several hundred. The commitment to autonomy by white sororities and fraternities on this issue is strange given the extent to which these groups intermingle and interact.

The unwillingness of the NPC and the NIC to consider the implications of having different membership models means that no one is paying attention to how uneven fraternity chapter sizes affect the nature of the fraternity and sorority social scene. Even while acknowledging that they are part of a larger Greek letter community, the complete body of fraternity and sorority chapters rarely come together to do things as a group, unless they are forced to. The primary form that interaction between groups takes is through mixers, a vague and amorphous term that refers to everything from pumpkin-carving contests and cupcake baking to pool parties and paddleboard outings. In the spirit of avoiding cliquishness and promoting inter-group relations, many schools' student-run NPC and Interfraternity Council (IFC) governing boards require each sorority and fraternity chapter to socialize formally with each other at least once per school year. What this means for a community with uneven demographics is that every time a fraternity "mixes" or pairs up with a sorority for an event, there usually will be more women than men at the event. At a growing number of schools, the numeric difference between the genders is measured not in tens, but hundreds. The average IFC fraternity chapter size at Washington State University Pullman, in 2018 for example, was 60, while the average NPC sorority had a whopping 157 members.[21] In 2019, there were 5,194 women spread across twenty-eight Panhellenic and multicultural sororities and 2,562 men spread across thirty-five fraternities at UGA, making the average number of women in each sorority 187, compared to 73 for each fraternity.[22] While a mismatch of male and female partygoers doesn't necessarily guarantee that hookups will occur, the sex ratio theory has taught us that it increases the odds that they will.

While white sororities' well-meaning attempt to be fair to women creates a dating milieu that is markedly unfair to them, fraternities have a long history of engineering circumstances that tip the scale even further in men's favor. In the 1930s, Waller observed a pervasive culture of "petting" (a mid-twentieth-century term that refers to sexualized kissing and touching that includes in its most expansive form, nonpenetrative forms of sex) within the fraternity and sorority community at Penn State. This was strange because the college's sex ratio at the time was 6:1, and, because of this, it should have created a dating script that privileged monogamy over casual sex. After digging around a little bit, Waller discovered what was going on: fraternity members were artificially manipulating the sex ratio to give men a numeric advantage. They did this by prohibiting first-year members from dating coeds, limiting nonmember male access to fraternity parties and cultivating a culture of social ranking and prestige that made dating anyone other than a fraternity member a form of social suicide. Through blackballing their competition and making the social status of women contingent upon their association with a small group of men, fraternities successfully engineered a dating culture that rendered the sex ratio theory impotent.[23]

The genius of this maneuver did not go unnoticed by subsequent generations of fraternity men, and long after the campus sex ratio tide turned in their favor, they continued the practice. Not surprisingly, the current heirs of these strategies are more than a little reluctant to give them up. After all, evening out the playing field does nothing to benefit them, but, conversely, creates an environment where they must exert more effort to generate a romantic encounter. This is opposed to now, where, in the words of Tatum, "the only thing a guy needs in order to get in a girl's pants is a pulse."

This is obviously an overstatement, but, in some cases, not by much. The fraternity chapter with which I worked at Rollins kicked off the spring semester every year by hosting a "darty" (day party) on the shores of an alligator-infested lake. Urban legend has it that when the developers of Disney World were building the theme park in the 1970s, they collected the reptilian residents living in the area's boggy marshland and relocated them to said lake, which is just twenty miles up the road from the college. Even the biggest skeptic of the tale doesn't have to venture far along Lake Jessup's shoreline to transform into a believer. Alligators are everywhere: sunbathing on the beach, watching motionless with eyes just above the surface, and clustered in groups at the base of large trees, with their heads tilted back and massive jaws gaping wide open toward the sky. This is an especially popular activity in the springtime, when the eggs of the various bird species that live in the trees begin to hatch, and the newborn chicks embark upon their first flights. For the alligators, it's almost too easy; the baby birds literally just drop into their mouths.

During the 2018 darty, a different form of opportunism took place. The event began when two buses arrived and expelled their contents—about thirty men from one fraternity and roughly eighty women from multiple sororities. The group spent the next few hours drinking, dancing, and being warned by bartenders to keep a safe distance from the gators. For Corbin, a portly and affable senior from New Hampshire, this event marked his fourth trip to the lake. The luster of the experience had started to wear off, but not so much that it dampened the memory of his first time around: "Coming here for the first time, it's just you, your fraternity brothers, and all of these women," he told me. "So many that it's almost overwhelming. And then you realize: they are all here for you." Perhaps sensing that his last statement came across as bad as it sounded, he quickly corrected himself. "That they are all here *because* of you."

Corbin's tenure in his fraternity evolved from party attendee in year one to party organizer by years three and four. An avid golfer, Corbin found in the sport an apt metaphor for the overarching goal of the event: "You always aim to tee it up for yourself, you know? You want at least a 1:1, but obviously we prefer it to be higher." For Corbin, having more women than men at the

Fraternity Party Population Control

annual party is a win-win situation. Women, he claims, feel comfortable and thus safe when there are more of their kind around. Of course, perception does not always align with reality. Regardless of how things pan out for the women in attendance, the upside of their sheer number for the fraternity men is that the scenario significantly increases the chance that they will have sex. At the lake party, a guy's odds of getting laid were, in Corbin's words, "astronomical," and not just because of the sex ratio disparity and implied sense of obligation, but also because of the bus ride home.

The sheer number of passengers crammed onto the buses made it necessary for women to sit on fraternity men's laps during the thirty-minute ride back to campus. The story that Corbin told me about his bus ride home—and the events that transpired afterward—follows the same rote plotline as the sexual tales told by other members of his fraternity community: college boy has his pick of romantic partners and when given the opportunity, chooses them all. In this case too, all the red flags (the fact that drunk fraternity members aren't the most reliable of narrators being chief among them) that signal that his story might not be wholly true are overshadowed by the possibility that parts of it might be. According to Corbin, he kissed and fondled the breasts of the woman who was seated on his lap ("woman number one," as he called her) on the bus ride back to campus. Unfortunately, the two were separated in the push-and-shove chaos that ensued upon arrival. Corbin made a half-hearted attempt to locate woman number one in the crowd, but, in the process, he fell into step with and started talking to "woman number two." He ended up walking this woman back to her apartment, "where one thing led to another." In the awkward aftermath of the encounter, Corbin excused himself on the pretense that he had to attend to a prior commitment. That commitment was stopping by woman number one's place, where the couple "finished what they started."

Schools with 40:60 sex ratios aren't the only places where you will find fraternity members manipulating the law of supply and demand to serve their own interests. The same thing is happening at universities where male students far outnumber female students. Nicole and Elizabeth are second-year sorority members at 57:43 Purdue.[24] They report that fraternity chapters will routinely invite five to six sorority chapters to a function and then "want us to compete for them [the fraternity members]." They attended the parties as first-year students because the social scene was new and exciting but have since stopped attending because after awhile "it gets annoying." Amanda is a third-year student at 67:33 Rochester Institute of Technology (RIT), who told me that she arrived on campus feeling empowered by the knowledge that she had the upper hand in the romance department.[25] "The boys all know that women have the ability to be more selective," she told me. Although she attended fraternity parties with the confidence of knowing that she could have her pick of men, Amanda was all too aware of the ways that fraternity men tried to manipulate the sex ratio in their favor. In addition to barring entry to outside men, older fraternity members excluded younger members from socializing with female guests by making them serve as doormen, bartenders, bouncers, DJs, and designated drivers. Amanda's view of the last group was mixed. While she appreciated the fraternity's assistance in getting to and from their parties safely, she learned the hard way that giving her contact information to one fraternity member (by requesting a pickup/drop off by text) was tantamount to giving it to all of them.

Rose was a rising senior at Duke (52:48) when I spoke to her about her experience in her university's Greek system.[26] When she was in her second year, she and a group of her sorority sisters attended a fraternity mixer. When they arrived, they were surprised to find a lot more men than women in the room. After a few minutes, Rose asked her friend, who was playing the part of DJ, if she could change the music. The man told her "sure" and pointed her in the direction of his cell phone (which was linked via Blue-tooth to the room's speaker system). When she got on the phone, she discovered a bunch of messages in the fraternity's group chat. One of the messages said, "The sex ratio is way off. We have to get more girls." Rose confronted her friend about the comment and his dismissive response—"You just saw something that you shouldn't have seen"—infuriated her. Reenacting for me what happened next, Rose said she told her sorority sisters, "I'm going because he acts like his fraternity is a sanctified space. I have no interest in being anyone's ratio." Rose reported that the fraternity men got upset when she and her friends left the party, but later "we got all these apology messages in an attempt to fix relations between the organizations."

A few years ago, an undergraduate at the University of Southern California (USC) named Sean Fernandez was people watching from his fraternity house's balcony and noticed something that struck him as strange: despite being in the heart of fraternity row, all the individuals coming into and out of the fraternity houses were female. One explanation for this has to do with a controversial policy held by all Panhellenic sororities that prohibit alcohol consumption inside sorority houses. This rule—which chalks its necessity up to liability concerns and insurance regulations—means that any social get-together involving alcohol (which is pretty much all of them) is displaced to fraternity houses or third-party venues.[27] The cost of renting

Fraternity Party Population Control

an off-campus space to host parties (and shouldering the liability on their own) is what keeps sorority women from reversing the tables and inviting five fraternities to their next mixer.

NIC fraternities have the same liability concerns, and until recently were content to accept the additional risk and added insurance costs to keep throwing parties. According to Caitlin Flanagan, the second most common type of insurance claim against the fraternity industry is for rape.[28] She continues: "The more you supervise the fraternities, the more you establish a legal duty of care. The national administrations of the fraternities don't closely supervise the individual chapters for the same reason."[29] In 2018, in response to an ongoing pattern of alcohol-related deaths and skyrocketing insurance premiums, the NIC banned consumption of alcohol above ABV 15 percent, or just about everything except beer, wine, and malt beverages in fraternity houses.[30] While the NIC's hard-liquor ban moves fraternity and sorority alcohol policies closer together, the NPC's "no tolerance, no alcohol" rule keeps fraternity row as the de facto campus party headquarters. A 2021 research study revealed what we already knew: underage college women who want to drink but don't have fake IDs have very few options other than fraternity parties for where to get and consume alcohol without risking arrest or disciplinary action from their college or university.[31]

At USC, the differences between the sorority and fraternity alcohol policies alone didn't sufficiently explain to Fernandez why women were doing so much work to attract male attention when the script crafted by the university's 52:48 sex ratio suggested that they shouldn't have to. This prompted Sanchez to take up the question in his master's thesis. The results from his survey of USC's Greek letter community substantiate what students have told me: that fraternities engineer sex ratio imbalances by instituting creative mechanisms of male population control.[32] Like their peers at Purdue and RIT, fraternity men at USC restrict access to their social events by unaffiliated men. At the same time as they exclude potential competitors from their parties, fraternities also further manipulate the sex ratio in their favor by opening their party doors to unaffiliated women students and multiple groups of sorority women.

Even with the numbers stacked against them, women are not in such oversupply at USC that their individual stock should be devalued. This especially goes for the campus's most desirable women—those who, by virtue of their membership in top-tier organizations, have accrued the most social capital and greatest number of partner options. While it would make sense that women from less prestigious sororities or those occupying lower rungs of the social ladder would hook up more often and with more partners to preserve their status and relationship with men, Sanchez didn't find this to be true. A 2017 research study of hookup culture at an elite liberal arts university yielded the same results.[33] Specifically, what Sanchez and the researchers discovered was that the most coveted women hook up at roughly the same rate as women lower down on the popularity totem pole. While many factors play into this, the numbers suggest that they have no other choice. The oversupply of women means that hooking up has become a requirement for preserving their relationship status with fraternity men. Put another way, the informal romantic code within USC's fraternity and sorority social life is "hook up or get out." By manipulating their guest lists so that women always outnumber men at their house parties, fraternity members make women essentially disposable. Like all great ideas, another enterprising USC fraternity member devised a way to capitalize on the phenomenon described by Fernandez by bequeathing it to the masses. The material form that this tool takes is an app launched in 2012 called Tinder.

Tinder and the Franchising of Fraternity House Romance

The origin story of Tinder is mired in controversy. Depending on who you ask, the hugely popular cell phone dating app—whose famed double opt-in "swipe" system facilitates meeting strangers—was founded either by former USC Alpha Epsilon Pi fraternity member Justin Mateen and his friends Sean Rad and Jonathan Badeen, or by this group along with another trio of colleagues that include Joe Munoz, Dinesh Moorjani, and Whitney Wolfe. What isn't in dispute is where the app was seeded and first went viral. In a 2017 podcast interview, Rad told *Business Insider* journalist Alyson Shontell that the app launched in September 2012 at a huge USC house party and then was systematically introduced to Southern California's fraternity and sorority community:

> Every afternoon, the whole team would leave the office, get in a car, and we would drive by every fraternity and sorority in Los Angeles, then San Diego, then Orange County, and every school we could cover. Every time we would go to sororities and fraternities and talk about Tinder, we would that night see 100 sign-ups. Every single sign-up in the beginning mattered. We were stopping people on the street, and we'd go into coffee shops and talk to each other like, "Oh, have you heard of that app Tinder? It's such a cool app!" Anything

we could do to get the word out we were doing. I'd take out the app and say "Oh, this is interesting! Who told you about this great app called Tinder?" and yell it in the coffee shop, so people keep hearing "Tinder" in LA. And then what happened—and this was nuts—we sort of cornered the West Coast, which is where we lived. Then in January, everyone went home for break and I guess told their friends. So in the beginning of January, we had about 20,000 users, and at the end of January, we had 500,000 users—all organic. The growth curve was unimaginable. It was pretty amazing.[34]

Since 2012, Tinder's popularity has continued to rise. In 2020, it was the most used dating app, with an estimated 50 million users worldwide.[35] Just because a lot of people have Tinder accounts, however, doesn't mean that everyone makes equal use of them. Studies show that the number of men on Tinder outnumber women by up to a ratio of 3:1.[36] Assuming this is true, then Tinder should be fostering a dating culture where women control the romantic script. But it doesn't. The genius of the app is that it manipulates user demographics to create a virtual dating scene that mimics a fraternity party. Specifically, technology solves the problem of having too many straight male fishermen in the sea by allowing them to cast wider nets. We see this on college campuses like Georgia Tech, where the app allows male students to broaden their romantic prospects beyond the campus to the greater Atlanta region, and particularly schools with high female to male student ratios. "Pretty much every single male at Georgia Tech that I know uses Tinder, Bumble, and Hinge to connect with women," a senior business administration major named Natalie told me. "I find that guys at Georgia Tech frequently use these apps to date or hook up with girls at other state schools such as Georgia State, Kennesaw State, and even UGA."

There is something to suggest that this massive influx of outside women into the dating pool is working to change the contours of campus romance. While monogamous relationships may still be the norm, hookup culture is on the rise, in part because of the inflated egos acquired by men who have more options. "I've met many decently attractive guys at Georgia Tech who genuinely think they are the hottest thing to walk this earth," quipped Natalie. "If this guy were to visit the campuses of other state schools, however, he would find that he is on the lower end of the spectrum attractiveness wise." Kayla and Nikki also referenced the shift in self-perception of the men on campus during their tenure at Georgia Tech. The sisters graduated in 2016 and 2017, and both were members of sororities during their time there. It had long been standard operating procedure, they told me, for fraternities to manipulate sex ratios at their house parties so that there were an equal if not higher number of women in attendance than men. However, both felt a notable uptick during their tenure in the number of fraternity men—particularly those who were members of the "best" chapters (i.e., those with the most attractive members)—who not only wanted to hook up with female party guests but also felt entitled to do so. The sense that fraternity parties were getting increasingly "rapey" was buttressed during Kayla and Nikki's second and third years when an email authored by the 2013 Phi Kappa Tau social chair went viral. The letter, which was addressed to the man's fraternity brothers, reads in part:

> If the party is going good (a.k.a. there are a lot of open girls) try to escalate cause it's awesome. . . . A short guide consist of the 7 E's of HOOKING UP! 1. Encounter (spot a girl or group of girls) 2. Engage (go up and talk to them) 3. Escalate (ask them to dance, or ask them to go up to your room or find a couch, depending on what kind of party) 4. Erection (GET HARD) 5. Excavate (should be self-explanatory) 6. Ejaculate (should also be self explanatory) 7. Expunge (send them out of your room and on their way out when you are finished. IF ANYTHING EVER FAILS, GO GET MORE ALCOHOL. I want to see everyone succeed at the next couple parties.[37]

Currently, there are over thirty fraternity chapters at Georgia Tech, and it would be unfair to make sweeping claims about the whole community based on the actions of one chapter. However, if the student contributors to a popular online forum about Tech are right in saying that fraternity and sorority life dominates the social scene at the university, then the principle also holds that one's community is only as good as its worst member.[38] That it's been several years and the Phi Kappa Tau "rape bait" email not only is still coming up in casual conversation about the school but is also the first thing that Kayla mentions to me suggests that at least some men on campus perceive that the dating script has not only flipped in their favor but, by self-authored decree, authorized them to rewrite it in the most misogynistic and predatory terms.

Pan outside the walls of academia and we see how Tinder is similarly creating fraternity party hookup culture in places where demographics dictate that there shouldn't be. Richard Florida, a professor at the University of Toronto, used data compiled by the Martin Prosperity Institute to create a population map of the United States that shows where individuals between the ages of eighteen and twenty-four live. In all major metropolitan areas, the number of men in this age range exceeds the number of similarly aged women—sometimes by a lot. In cities like Houston, Chicago, San Diego, and New York City, for example, there are upward of 50,000 more young men than women.[39] Tinder's success at subverting the laws of supply and demand are registered everywhere in writing about the dating landscape in the Big Apple, the gist of which is summed up in the title of Jo Piazza's 2015 *Vanity Fair* piece, "Tinder and the Dawn of the Dating Apocalypse."[40]

If we've blinked and Tinder has turned America's dating scene into a pseudo–fraternity party, then a competitor dating app positions itself to be a partial corrective. In 2014, when Tinder was still a toddler, cofounder Whitney Wolfe abruptly parted ways with the company. She used her reported $1 million out-of-court settlement from the gender discrimination suit she filed against Mateen and the company's other male cofounders to launch a filtered double-opt-in version of the dating app called Bumble. The key difference between Tinder and Bumble—and what makes the latter women-friendly—is that women must make the first move by accepting potential suitors before they are formally matched with them. Borrowing the successful marketing strategy from her days at Tinder, Wolfe returned to her undergraduate stomping grounds—the Kappa Kappa Gamma house at Southern Methodist University—to unveil her product.[41] Five years later, Bumble's valuation hovered at around $1.2 billion, a staggering figure that is due in no small part to the grassroots marketing efforts of the company's paid brand ambassadors called Bumble Honeys, many of whom are sorority members.[42] For a semester, Natalie was one of them. Since she matriculated at Georgia Tech three years after Tinder launched, the only adult social universe the sorority woman ever inhabited is one that includes dating apps. At Georgia Tech, Natalie not only had a front row seat to the benefits reaped by her male classmates who used the technology to connect with women outside the campus community, but she also witnessed the consequence for Georgia Tech women:

> It's very interesting to observe because these guys are often extremely intelligent and hard-working, yet I often see them dating or sleeping with these really ditsy or less focused girls from other schools (not saying all girls at other schools are this way of course). Women at Georgia Tech are incredibly smart, talented, hard-working, and intense. For generations, men have been intimidated by or disapproving of extremely career-driven women. I think the way GT guys go

for girls from less challenging schools is an extension of this age-old gender dynamic. Men want to be the ones making the most money and they want to be the smartest. A GT woman will tend to challenge these expectations because she very well could make more money or be smarter.

Vivacious and conventionally beautiful, Natalie is also smart and driven. Throughout her undergrad years, what she saw again and again was how Georgia Tech's fraternity men were using Tinder to expand their dating pool beyond the campus.

Bumble is helping women like Natalie to fight back, not by reclaiming Georgia Tech men who have passed her friends over, but by forcing men who use the app to come to where the women are . . . and, in doing so, play by their rules. What this looks like at Georgia Tech is mobilizing women to either cast Tinder aside, or, if not, declare a primary loyalty to Bumble. Following the metaphor of the beehive with which the company's name and branding strategically plays, all women's romantic prospects are better served if they gather in a social space that is governed by and operated for women. This is a message that resonates well with sorority women, not just at Georgia Tech, but all over the country. The success of this mass gathering of women on the site is registered in numbers. In 2017, Wolfe reportedly rejected a $450 million acquisition offer by Tinder's parent company.[43] If the decision to hang tight was bold, it was also fortuitous, as Wolfe Herd (as she is now known) became the world's youngest self-made female billionaire when she took Bumble public in February 2021.[44]

As Bumble digs in and not only holds but continues to gain ground among users of dating apps, the women who use these apps are doing what many of the sorority women with whom I have worked aren't doing in-person on their college campuses—restructuring the social scene so that the sex-ratio works in their favor. Instead, they are banding together to mobilize a different strategy to promote and fulfill their romantic interests and desires.

TWO

Group Sex

"Omigod, look at this!" Ali flipped her cell phone around to reveal the pair of text messages that she had just received. The first consisted of a simple introduction: "This is Brady." The second—"come over?"—was a thinly veiled invitation to engage in a hookup. The second-year student from Cleveland explained that she had just met Brady the previous weekend at a "CEOs and office hoes"–themed party hosted by his fraternity. She hadn't given him her cell phone number but figured that he had acquired it from one of her friends.

What Brady knew at that moment was that he was texting a woman in whom he had a romantic interest. What he didn't know was that he was simultaneously conversing with five of the woman's female classmates and her two female college professors.

The eight of us were huddled around a restaurant table in Munich, Germany, during a spring break field study trip, when Brady pulled up a digital chair. Ali puckered her lips and smiled. "You guys have gotta help me," she begged. "What should I say?" My colleague and I shot each other amused sideways glances and graciously declined the offer to ghostwrite our student's texts. Fortunately for Ali, the other women at the table were more than happy to provide their literary services. Everyone agreed that Ali should leave out the fact that she was currently in a different country and not alone. They also agreed that Brady should suffer some form of public humiliation for his unapologetic forwardness. "What the fuck?" Ali scoffed as she reread Brady's text. "How do I even respond to this?" The women were full of thoughts and good ideas.

The options were discussed and voted upon before Ali typed out the winning reply. The collaborative writing activity continued until the meal arrived and Ali became more interested in the food that was in front of her. When Ali exchanged her phone for a fork, one of her classmates snatched the device and, without missing a beat, took over the role of scribe.

Even if this scene makes you feel a little bit sorry for Brady, it's a scenario that shouldn't strike anyone as new: communicating with the opposite sex has long been a collaborative effort involving behind-the-scenes players. In nineteenth-century Jane Austen novels, the female protagonists' coterie of sisters, girlfriends, aunts, and mothers orchestrated and performed dress rehearsals of courtship rituals and listened through parlor doors as they were enacted. In the 1940s and 1950s, this role was taken up by sorority sisters who spied on their friends' dates from balconies and secret alcoves like the "Goon Room" in the University of Arizona's Alpha Pi's chapter house.[1] In the 1990s, romantic assistance was rendered via creative use of the landline telephone mute button.

The arrival of more advanced forms of communication technology on the dating scene makes it unnecessary for middle schoolers to listen in on their friends' phone conversations and to shuttle them handwritten notes with instructions on what to say next. Now, the rise of social media and texting make third-party interventions easier than ever. A 2020 study found that Stanford University students spent over twelve hours a day on their laptop, tablet, or phone.[2] The sheer amount of time that teenagers and young adults spend texting, talking, and interacting with their friends on social media on their phones means that, for better or for worse, most college students' social life now takes place online.

One of the reasons why college students like to mediate communication through technology is that it gives them a greater level of personal control. Face-to-face conversations are intimidating, and, in the opinion of Sophie, a Rollins senior from New Jersey, "weird" because they incur a level of risk. The human tongue is a notoriously unpredictable organ, and one never knows what may fly out without warning. A text, by contrast, can be edited and wordsmithed to perfection. "You can spend twenty minutes writing a text if you need to," Sophie explained. "When you talk, there is more of a chance that you will say the first thing that comes to your mind." When I asked why that was such a bad thing, she looked at me like I was a single-celled organism incapable of rational thought.

Besides lost time, there are other hidden costs to texting. Voice inflections, gestures, and body language aid in interpretating the meaning of spoken, in-person conversations. When communication is restricted to an abbreviated form of the written word—as is the case with texting—meaning is freighted by things that we normally ignore or take for granted. Included among the minutiae-turned-monumental are punctuation and spelling. As anyone under the age of thirty will tell you, responding to a text with "OK" instead of "k" or "kk" signals anger and irritation equivalent to stomping out of the room or at least a good door slam. Putting a period at the end of any sentence in a text message is another middle finger. Emoji happy faces and gifs of dancing animals generally convey excitement and happiness, but also have the potential to be satirical and mocking, and thus should not be completely trusted. Even the humble exclamation point—punctuation's most long-standing one-trick pony—should, from the viewpoint of many millennials and Gen-Zers, be viewed with suspicion.

In short, decoding texts requires an advanced skill set and is a feat not easily accomplished single-handedly. In an Elite Daily article, Ashley Fern lays bare the hard truth to men: "If you think the only person reading your texting conversation is the person you sent it to . . . you are very sadly mistaken. Gentlemen, there's actually little to no chance that whatever message you just sent will go unread by at least three of a girl's best friends."[3] I pitched this figure to a group of Rollins third-year students, who were also close friends and sorority sisters. These women had come to Florida from places like New York City (Stella), Atlanta (Stacy), and Boston (Monica). Kylie, the only international student in the group, was from Brazil. Based on their own experiences, they collectively estimated this number to be a little low. "There are five girls behind every conversation," asserted Monica matter-of-factly. The others gestured in agreement.

Third-party involvement in romantic relationships extends beyond the jobs of consultant, editor, and support group. A 2016 Pew Research Report revealed that friends also help construct each other's personal brands and online personas. About a third of female online dating users, for instance, enlisted a friend to help them craft the so-called perfect profile.[4] For social media accounts, the number is even higher. Among my female students, soliciting advice from friends on which photos to post to Instagram and other social media sites is standard operating procedure and takes place at least daily, and often more. "I'll text a photo I like to my friends in a group chat," Stella explained, "and then ask them, 'Is this a good one of me?'" When I asked the group if they ever grow tired of offering feedback on their friends' photos, they blinked at me and answered the question by responding with one of their own: "What do you mean?"

While friends' solicited advice and opinions on photos, posts, and texts work in direct ways to shape an individual's online persona, journalist Nancy Jo Sales points to a subtle but arguably more powerful way in which friends wield influence over each other's identities on social media. In her 2016 best seller *American Girls: Social Media and the Secret Lives of Teenagers*, Sales tells the story of a sixteen-year-old girl from Los Angeles named Padma who she interviewed—and then followed on social media—over the course of several months. Since middle school, Padma had self-consciously curated a profile that portrayed herself as a wholesome, all-American girl. Sales isolated the sudden and marked pivot in Padma's personal brand to the moment that the girl posted a sexy selfie in which she was wearing lots of makeup and revealing exposed cleavage. Whereas previous photos of Padma got just a few or no "likes," the sexy photo garnered almost a hundred.[5] In what may be a vestige of the hunter-gatherer in all of us, collecting "likes" on social media is instinctive and addictive. Young girls learn very early what aesthetic version of themselves gets attention, and, importantly, comments from both male and female friends reveal that both genders prefer the representation of the self that is glamorous and hypersexualized.

Like scores of other college professors, I am "friends" with many of my current and former students on social media. Scrolling through their feeds, I struggle to recognize the women in the photos—who are sunbathing at the beach in thongs and wearing bandage dresses and fake eyelashes in fancy restaurants—with the women who are enrolled in my classes, and whom I have only ever seen dressed in yoga pants, trainers, and oversized sorority T-shirts. "It's like a work of art," Kylie told me, describing her Instagram feed. "I'm really picky about what goes on there and how everything looks." Nothing makes the cut until it's been vetted by her sorority sisters. She paused on a tinted photograph of her bikini-clad body stretched out on the beach at sunset and sighed in self-appreciation. "It's really pretty, isn't it?"

While helping one's same-sex friends gain a competitive edge in the contemporary dating market by literally putting their best faces forward demonstrates kindness and generosity, it isn't a particularly smart move, at least according to the principles of economics and laws of science. This is especially true on college campuses with a sex ratio imbalance that favors men. The surplus of women in these milieus creates a supply and demand problem. In these situations, women should be trying to minimize competition for male attention, not intensifying it—especially when the cost is so low. In a 2011 survey of over 500 men and women, a behavioral research team found that entering a romantic relationship comes at the cost of losing two close platonic friends.[6] The logic follows that in an environment where there is a surplus of women, women have friends to spare. The fact that female friend groups on contemporary college campuses are circling the wagons and shoring up homosocial bonds with their friends instead of cutting ties with them illustrates the way that women have uniquely adapted to the dynamics of modern courtship culture and simultaneously work to subvert it. On college campuses, women collectively compete for scarce resources (men), but they don't usually face off one-on-one in gladiator style. Rather, they form teams that compete against other teams in ways that benefit both the individual and the group.

The way that it works is not unlike professional road cycling. In the major races (the Tour de France being the granddaddy of them all), a designated team leader pairs up with eight other riders, called "domestiques." The job of these cyclists isn't to try to win the race themselves, but, rather, to do everything they can to help the team leader increase his odds of winning. The most common and important thing that domestiques do is to ride in front of the team leader and, by cutting the wind, make it easier for him to pedal. Cycling experts say that drafting like this can save leaders between 20 and 40 percent of their energy in a long event. What's in it for domestiques? Money, for one thing. It's customary for the race winner to split the cash prize with members of his team. Another shadow benefit is that, when called upon, teammates often return the favor in other races.

While this metaphor isn't exact, female friend groups often operate in strikingly similar ways. By working together to secure a romantic partner for one member of the group, the interests of the whole group are served. As roles rotate, each team member (at least in theory) gets a guy, and, with each match made, the reputation of the group increases. This strategy is employed informally across the board with friend groups ranging from prepubescent middle schoolers to divorced moms to women in retirement communities, but, as the next section argues, may find its fullest and most effective expression in the college sorority.

Matchmaking via Sorority Squad

Ask any sorority woman to enumerate the benefits of membership in her organization, and she will talk a lot about how being in a sorority means that other women "have your back" and "are always there for you." These phrases refer to different things in different contexts, but within the dating milieu, they refer to the notion that the sorority functions, in sociologist Lisa

Handler's words, as a "haven from the chaos of the unregulated romantic marketplace."[7] Put simply, sororities confer upon their members the promise that all sorority sisters are your friends and that friends don't compete with each other for men. The formal designation of friendship is important because, as it turns out, we aren't great at identifying our friends. This is, at least, according to a 2016 study conducted by Massachusetts Institute of Technology researchers, which showed that only about one-half of perceived friendships are mutual.[8] Evidently, many of the people that we think of as our friends don't think of us in the same way.

Joining a sorority claims to relieve individuals of the need to be supernaturally gifted in perception and eliminates doubt over who is and who is not really one's friend. In addition to delineating teammates and establishing a bond of trust between them, this sororal pact also sets the rules of engagement for the college dating and mating game and establishes each team member's roles and responsibilities within it. As a discrete dating team, each sorority chapter's overarching goal is to create as many romantic matches for as many of its members as possible. Its members do this by working behind the scenes to promote candidates from within its own ranks while blocking competitors who are members of other sorority chapters/teams. This matchmaking strategy doesn't render friends irrelevant but makes them necessary and integral to the entire process. Based upon my years on the ground working with the white Greek letter community, here's what a sorority matchmaking squad looks like in action:

1. Someone stakes a claim. A sorority woman articulates to her sororal sisters a romantic interest in a particular fraternity member. This vocalization—via text, group chat, or in person—marks a provisional claim to him. Of course, a woman can't call dibs on every man she finds attractive; for this claim to hold and earn the support of her sisters, she has to make a compelling claim, ideally backed by evidence, that the woman's romantic gestures have the potential to be reciprocated. Acceptable forms of evidence include a previous hookup or proof that the fraternity member has commented on or liked the woman's posts on social media.

2. Her teammates lock their hearts. While sorority membership guarantees that you will have a turn, in professional cycling terms, to be the lead rider and have other women work on your behalf, the sheer number of team members means that you will be spending most of your time inhabiting the role of the hookup culture's version of the

domestique: the wingwoman. This figure, a frumpy sidekick and third wheeler who plays the part because there are no other roles available to her, has been rehabilitated by sorority culture into a devoted friend who can attract the object of desire for herself but opts out of the competition to benefit someone else. Sorority-themed websites put the wingwoman on a pedestal tantamount to that of Jesus in large part because of her similar act of self-sacrifice. An article in Total Sorority Move explains: "You two are probably friends because you have similar tastes, but when you're her wingwoman, it's important that you aren't going after the same guys she is into. Nothing can crush a girl's confidence more than when a dude she's interested in is more into her friend. So even if he normally would be your type, when you are her wingwoman, he's not."[9]

3. The wingwomen spring into action. Digital communication with the fraternity member is mediated and facilitated by sorority sisters. In addition to offering advice and feedback on texts and social media posts, the woman's friends also may initiate conversations with the subject's friends in which they stealthily praise the virtues of their sorority sister or otherwise nudge the guy's fraternity brothers to push the relationship along.

4. The wingwoman's job continues at the bar. Once digital interactions graduate to flesh-and-blood encounters, the wingwoman serves as a social buffer and conversational lubricant. Perhaps more important than clearing the space is to block potential competitors from other teams from horning in. This may take the form of simply talking up the friend to the subject (or subtly criticizing the opponent), or lurking nearby and intercepting any other female interlopers by engaging them in conversation or diverting them strategically to other men.

5. The wingwoman takes one for the team. This includes a broad range of actions, including sacrificing opportunities to pursue a romantic interaction with a man in whom she is interested to support her teammate by socializing (or going to fraternity formals) with the subject's fraternity brothers instead. It also may mean proactively hooking up with the subject's friends to put pressure on the subject to accelerate the pace of his romance with her sorority sister.

Wingwomen do a lot of the heavy lifting for their friends and, like the domestiques of the cycling world, feel entitled to part of the victor's spoils. While supporting one's friend behind the scenes is a demonstrable act of loyalty, compassion, and kindness, the generosity is also self-serving. Matching one of its members with a member of a specific fraternity gives a sororal team privileged access to that fraternity members' friends, thus increasing the likelihood of other hookup matches. By laying proverbial claim to enough members of a specific fraternal group, a sorority blocks out competing teams of sororal women and lays claim to the entire chapter.

The sororal contract means that sororities compete against other sorority teams/chapters for access to men, but not with members of their own. The bonds of trust that privilege group interest over individual desire is why hooking up with a man that your team has secured for one of your sisters—regardless of how long ago—is considered taboo. The same girl code that holds the team together and makes hookups possible, however, also restricts its members' social and romantic mobility. Because of the strength of the team-based romance culture within sorority life, it can be difficult for women to gain access to male friend groups outside of which they have established alliances. This is because pursuing someone in a different fraternity would mean taking on the entire sorority with which that group or organization is paired.

While the sororal team member who is sexually linked to a fraternity man has long served as her friends' primary gateway agent to the fraternity, on many campuses this figure has a new partner in crime who works from the inside to grease the wheels for sorority women. That figure is the gay fraternity brother.

The Gay and Queer Fraternity Men and Sorority Women behind Straight Hookup Culture

Chase is tall and sinewy and speaks with an unmistakable Boston lilt that drives the ladies wild. While Chase's entrance into a room makes all the straight women in attendance swoon, the fairer sex knows their chances of hooking up with him are negligible, because ever since his high school years at a prestigious northeastern boarding school, Chase has been very open about the fact that he's only romantically interested in men.

As a society, we still have a long way to go in the areas of gender and sexual equality, but there's been a markedly positive shift in the public's attitude toward and acceptance of the LGBTQ+ community over the past few decades. The little research conducted on LGBTQ+ fraternity and sorority members in 1990s and early 2000s revealed feelings of marginalization and intense social pressure to stay closeted.[10] Today's college students grew up in the wake of the legalization of gay marriage, and many spent their formative years surrounded by gay role models, family members, and friends and watching LGBTQ+ characters on television. Given Generation Z's increased exposure to diverse sexual and gender identities, it makes sense that studies reveal this generation to be the most tolerant and open of the bunch.[11]

With a few exceptions, it isn't socially acceptable to be openly antigay on any college campus, including those in conservative-leaning southern states. Still, this doesn't mean that homophobia doesn't exist. And when such language does rear its ugly head, one of the places where it frequently shows up is in the mouths of fraternity members. "Faggot," "homo," "butt rammer," and "dick licker" were terms of endearment within the fraternity that I advised, used in sentences like "Stop being such a homo and come out with us," and "Get off your ass, faggot, and help me clean this shit up." These same terms also could be mobilized to alienate a member of the group and signal his disenfranchisement. This is what happened to a Pi Kappa Phi fraternity member at the College of Charleston after he punched a fraternity brother for talking to his ex-girlfriend at a party. "We will get 80 bros behind us to bury you, you (expletive) queer," read a Facebook message sent to the man after he was sent home.[12] In addition to using homophobic slurs to communicate with each other, fraternities also have been known to hurl them at others. In 2018, a gay student was assaulted at a University of Delaware fraternity party.[13] A year later, two University of Memphis students were kicked out of a fraternity party for being gay.[14]

All of this serves to illustrate the point that while higher education may be more socially progressive than many other corners of America, the fraternity house's reputation for being both an incubator of and safe space for toxic masculinity arguably makes this locale one of the last places on campus where an openly gay male should feel welcome. This is doubly true of a Rollins chapter whose ranks are, according to Chase, filled "with athletes, gym rats, and guys with concealed weapon permits and multiple deer hunting jackets." From the outside looking in, it makes no sense why Chase would want to join this organization, or why, as he put it, "the most broey fraternity on campus" would aggressively pursue him.

I talked with Chase six months after he had graduated from Rollins. Now living back in the Northeast and working for a marketing firm in Boston, he has had some time and space to reflect on his fraternity experience. Chase came to college not hiding the fact that he was gay, but not shouting it from the rooftops either: "I went through so much internal shit in high school grappling with my identity and figuring out who I was, that by the time I came

[here], I didn't give a shit." The fraternity community took note of Chase's self-confidence—in a sea of first-year students who were clamoring for older students' approval, Chase's self-professed "fuck you" attitude stood out—and was admired.

Chase's ability to hold his liquor also earned him additional credibility within this community. Chase grew up with three older brothers and had what he described as a hypermasculine friend group in high school. It was because he was surrounded by so many heteronormative straight men for so long that he inherently developed an uncanny knack for making straight guys feel like he "wasn't trying to get into their pants." Part of this strategy involved cultivating an interest in sports and opting out of conversations about sex; another was learning how to drink everyone else under the table.

Like many schools, Rollins practices deferred recruitment, meaning that instead of joining a fraternity before the start of their collegiate experience, first-year students join at the beginning of their second semester. During that first semester of his freshman year, Chase brought his drinking skills to fraternity parties. He also brought along something else: women, and lots of them. In his dorm, Chase held the self-described role of "the gay best friend of all of the hot girls." Because he roved around campus in a pack with them, it didn't occur to him not to accompany them to fraternity parties. Even if fraternity members weren't thrilled to see him standing on the front porch of their chapter houses, they couldn't do anything about it. "When I came to a fraternity door with a dozen beautiful women, they weren't going to turn me away," Chase said. "Over time, fraternities understood that we were a package deal."

When Chase decided to go through fraternity recruitment, his application presented a conundrum to his campus's fraternity community. Since organizations had reputations to preserve that had everything to do with heteronormative masculinity and nothing to do with inclusivity, no one was particularly clamoring to be known as the chapter with the gay guy. If Chase was high risk in this regard, he was high reward in another. For a community deeply invested in keeping the sex ratio of their parties slanted in their gender's favor, a gay brother is a win-win: not only does he not compete with his fraternity brothers for women, but he also hand delivers women to them.

Throughout our conversations, Chase mentioned several times that fraternity experiences are individualized, and if he was less gender conforming, had attended a college in a more politically conservative city, or joined a chapter with less open-minded and tolerant men, his experience likely would have been dramatically less positive than it was.[15] A 2013 study found that the sorority community at an unnamed midwestern university was generally accepting of lesbian and bisexual members but expected all sorority women regardless of sexual orientation to present themselves in conventionally feminine ways.[16] Studies conducted in 2009 and 2015 revealed that traditionally masculine men fared better during fraternity recruitment and were more readily accepted into the fraternal community.[17]

Sadly, this sentiment is one that was echoed by many of the LGBTQ+ and straight sorority and fraternity members at Rollins with whom I spoke. Davis, a straight member of another top-tier fraternity at Rollins known for its sizable population of wealthy southerners and lacrosse players, imagined what it would be like to encounter a "nonmasculine" gay potential new member (PNM) during recruitment. "I'd tell him honestly that my fraternity was not a good fit for him," he said. "I'd want him to have a positive experience, you know, and wouldn't want to put him in a situation where he was set up for disappointment." Davis's biological brother is gay, so his advice, he said, came from a place of empathy and support. While his chapter's culture doesn't reflect his personal beliefs, Davis is a realist: queer individuals have a place within the fraternity and sorority community in the South, but it's one that is largely assigned to them based on their gender expression. Less competitive chapters typically are more inclusive, in part because they have to be. While there are always exceptions to the rule, the LGBTQ+ individuals who gain admission to the most competitive "top-tier" chapters are usually those who can and are willing to pass as straight. George, a recent graduate of a top-tier fraternity at the University of Mississippi (Ole Miss) quickly told me "No" when I asked him if there were any openly gay men in his chapter, and despite not being able to think of any gay men in any chapters on Old Row (the nickname for the seven "top" chapters), assured me that he has no doubt that they are around. Mackenna, a bisexual sorority woman who graduated from Rollins in 2018, serves as a representative case in point. Now attending graduate school in California, the self-described "femme-presenting" woman reminisces: "I'm a nice introduction to the queer community. I would get all dolled up and put on a push up bra and giggle during the sorority serenade, and then [go back and] have a girl in my room." Suzanne, an openly lesbian member of an upper mid-tier Rollins sorority said the same thing: "I don't think [my organization] would want a clearly butch lesbian. The reason why I got into [my organization] is because during recruitment I wore earrings and lipstick and my hair down."

Bailey is the only out member of her top-tier sorority at Wake Forest. Incredibly self-aware, Bailey matter-of-factly explained that the number of attributes she shares with her sorority sisters—conventional beauty; boarding school education; a well-heeled southern pedigree—was enough to trump the fact that she also had a girlfriend. Still, Bailey felt that her sexual orientation was enough of an elephant in the room that she brought it up with the sorority woman who talked with her on the final night of recruitment. "Oh, yeah, I know," Bailey recalls the woman saying. "I think everyone knows that." Two years later, the woman's casual shrugging off of the announcement still makes Bailey smile. She didn't see her sexual orientation as a big deal and knew she had found the right sorority when she met women who didn't see her primarily through that lens either. During our conversation, however, I unintentionally swapped out the soft pillow for a hard rock when Bailey asked me how I learned about her sexual orientation, and I said the name of one of her sorority sisters. "Huh," she replied. "I don't really know [her]." For someone whose connection to her organization derived in part from the perception that its members didn't find her sexual orientation relevant or noteworthy, being identified to an outsider as the "token lesbian" was both jarring and disappointing. Bailey admits to struggling with internalized homophobia and doesn't engage with the broader LGBTQ+ community on campus because "gay people are weird." "I am straight passing, and I get away with that," she told me. "My socialization into what is normal and perceived as normal is within heterosexual ideals. I feel comfortable in that space."

The same goes for Preston, who enrolled at Rollins two years after Chase. While the latter had to make a case for his value within the straight campus romance milieu, Preston entered into fraternity recruitment as a clear beneficiary of Chase's legacy. While Preston chose to join Chase's fraternity because of the chapter's positive track record of treating Chase with respect, he learned after his initiation that the chapter had reservations about taking a second gay member, lest they garner a reputation as the "fag fraternity." According to Preston, what ultimately turned the tide in his favor was that he "knew every single girl at Rollins but was even less gay than Chase."

At the same time as Chase and Preston helped their fraternity brothers by bringing the most coveted and beautiful women on campus to their parties, the men also helped their female friends (all of whom joined sororities) attract the attention of fraternity men. Throughout the duration of their undergraduate experience, both Chase and Preston served as the unofficial puppet masters of straight fraternity and sorority romance on campus. Working both sides to orchestrate matches, they scripted texts and responses to texts, prodded brothers into inviting specific women to events, encouraged women to accept the invitations, and reprimanded brothers for disrespectful behavior.

Like Chase and Preston, Bailey serves as a wingwoman for both sides. Because she isn't competing with other women for men's romantic attention, she has carte blanche freedom to befriend any man she wants, even if that man and his fraternity are currently "claimed" by a rival sorority. Relishing her role as an unpaid therapist and relationship coach, Bailey says that she is the recipient of a significant amount of straight male gossip and frequently solicited for sex tips by fraternity members. "It's such a fun conversation," she said, "because we both have similar experiences."

There is no "normal" when it comes to gender identity and gender expression. Because of this, the aforementioned roles don't comprise a universal script to which all LGBTQ+ fraternity and sorority members adhere or are expected to follow. The dearth of formal qualitative studies on this topic leaves me with only anecdotal evidence on which to base my analysis, but the common threads that ran through my conversations with LGBTQ+ fraternity and sorority members at several colleges and universities in the South suggest that their experiences are not unique. An anonymous 2018 Reddit post titled "Any Gay Frat Guys? What Has Your Experience Been Like?" yielded fifty-two responses, including a thread seemingly authored by straight fraternity members who didn't have answers to the guiding question but wanted to sing the praises of having gay fraternity men in their ranks.[18] Johnny_Fratkins wrote: We had a very handsome, jacked gay guy in our chapter—he was straight (no pun intended) up with us from the get-go. In fact, he was my pledge brother too. Everyone treated him the same; he was a good brother, period. That's all we cared about. That's the way it should be. In fact, he brought so many girls to our party. Total chick magnet and a great guy."[19] PingPongx then chimed in, "Have a guy that's bi in our house and he's so good with the ladies it's ridiculous. Brings so many girls around, such a cool dude."[20] Another respondent similarly reported, "In our chapter of 86 people I believe at least 4 people are gay. Awesome dudes and they invite a lot of cool chicks. Sorority girls love them."[21]

The anonymity of the platform means that the identities, organizational affiliations, and schools of these posts' authors are all unknown. What is striking about these comments is that in the same breath that their authors insist that their chapter's fraternity men treat their gay and queer members the same as straight members, they also demand something from the former that they don't of the latter. Straight men aren't expected to cultivate the adoration and trust of women, nor are they called upon to bring them to their parties. What makes a gay or queer fraternity man a "great guy," "a cool dude," and a "good brother" is his willingness to be an exceptional embodiment of the fraternal principle of selfless brotherhood by relinquishing his claim to mutual assistance in the area of romance.

While Chase and Preston enjoy a wide social circle comprised of people of all sorts of sexual orientations, their fraternity brothers orbit in a narrower social universe. Taylor Phillips, a model and former fraternity member at Ole Miss told his coming out story in a 2019 YouTube video. "I was at a school, in the South, in a fraternity where being gay was not OK, period. Like it just wasn't welcome, it wasn't even really tolerated, it was frowned upon."[22] With the encouragement of his close friend and pledge brother, Taylor came out to the rest of his pledge class during his third year in the organization. While the reaction to his announcement was mixed, Taylor recalls more than one of his friends commenting on the novelty of the relationship by telling him, "I've never even, I don't even know a gay person. I've never met a gay person. I don't know anything about the gay community or gay people."[23] While Taylor never articulated any expectation that his fraternity brothers would help him find love (in fact, he says that he spent much of his remaining time at Ole Miss apologizing to his friends for being gay), it goes without saying that even if they wanted to, they wouldn't have been able to offer Taylor much in the way of reciprocal matchmaking services.

Suzanne's sorority sisters professed not to care that she was gay but didn't exactly go out of their way to be accommodating to her needs. Suzanne recalled a time during her second year when her chapter's student leadership team (executive board) mandated that its members bring a date to an upcoming semiformal, and that to avoid the appearance of dirty rushing and to keep the sex ratio equal, the date had to be a man. When Suzanne asked in the middle of a chapter meeting if that rule applied to her, she said that her chapter's executive board looked around and said, "We never thought about you."

Preston's social media accounts include photos of the fraternity man embracing, kissing, and holding hands with other men, so it's not like he's hiding his romantic life from his fraternity brothers. But when I asked him why he never brings male dates to his chapter's mixers and formals, he looked at me aghast: "I would never." There is a difference, Preston explained, between knowing someone is gay and witnessing a same-sex romantic relationship in person. When I pointed out that Rollins is an allegedly LGBTQ+ friendly campus, and his fraternity brothers all have had exposure to gay and queer couples, Preston clarified that his decision to bring women as dates to his group's social events was a matter of respect and social courtesy, since he would never want to make any of his brothers feel uncomfortable.

Privileging others' possible discomfort over their own desires is one way that LGBTQ+ members of high-status Greek letter organizations perform their second-class status; another is managing their fictive brothers' and sisters' homoerotic anxieties. Assuring their same-sex, straight friends that they love them but aren't sexually attracted to them isn't a one-and-done event but an ongoing process. Even then, Mackenna said that she always hovered in the margins of suspicion. "There was one girl who was convinced I had a crush on her, and I think she was going through a lot and needed someone to feel special, and so she glommed on to me," Mackenna recalled. Instead of seeking out support in a healthy way, the woman went around the chapter saying, "I think Mackenna has a crush on me, but I don't know for sure." Mackenna spoke of the incident with nothing but compassion and generosity for her sorority sister, but also noted that, regardless, the gossip required immediate intervention. Assuring one's sorority sisters that you aren't going to try to hit on any of them without casting doubt on their sexual desirability is no easy task, but one that Mackenna accomplished through making a self-deprecating declaration that femme-presenting women aren't her type, "at least not until she's had a couple of glasses of rosé."

Mackenna's strategy of building trust and finding acceptance with her sorority sisters involved borrowing a play from the proverbial gay male best friend's playbook by positioning herself squarely outside the women's possible dating pool. If the power of the gay best friend derives from its perception of safety grounded in the lack of ulterior motives, then the openly gay fraternity man who serves as the bridge between his fraternity chapter and the campus sororities is put in a tug-of-war battle of loyalty. "My job is to keep my fraternity brothers in good graces with the girls," Preston stated matter-of-factly. He and many of the other gay fraternity men with whom I spoke rattled off times when they were called upon to apologize on behalf of their chapter or smooth things over with sororities after members of their chapter were rude, disrespectful, or otherwise acted inappropriately. Preston's close relationships with sorority women—and the fact that they see him as a male ally in a sexist and patriarchal community—makes him a reliably successful peacemaker. He told me that most women don't trust fraternity men, but they trust him.

Maybe they shouldn't.

Loyalty is always conditional, and the line in the sand of every relationship is different for everyone. For fraternity men like Chase and Preston whose acceptance by their straight fraternity brothers is often predicated on the number of women that they can recruit to attend fraternity parties, the question "To whom are you more loyal?" is not an easy one to answer, partly because the stakes are so high on both sides. Fraternities employ a wide range of strategies to skew the demographics of their parties in their favor. One of their newest tools (and I use this term intentionally to signal a lack of agency) is gay fraternity men. While all the gay fraternity men with whom I spoke were strong and vocal advocates of the #MeToo movement and said that they would never put their female friends in harm's way, they simultaneously admitted that their fraternity houses were dangerous places for women. Facing pressure from their fraternity brothers to provide access to sorority women and from sorority women to keep them safe from fraternity men, gay fraternity brothers are, in Chase's words, by virtue of the role to which they've been assigned, "screwed either way." Let me clear: none of the fraternity men with which I spoke intentionally facilitate sexual harassment and assault, but for some individuals in some chapters, that is exactly what they are set up to do. In a 2015 *Salon* article, Skylar Baker-Jordan wrote about his experiences as a gay fraternity man. Ostracized and excluded by straight men in high school, his relationship with beautiful women and life-of-the-party demeanor gave him a kind of "patriarchal currency" in college that he'd never had before. For Skylar, "fraternity life is about gross displays of masculinity, and when boiled down, that means oppressing and objectifying women." The pressure to prove his superiority to women took the form of demonstrating that he had "sexual control over them." Skylar continued:

> It's why, one night, I made out with four different women. I still remember carrying a petite young blonde around, her legs wrapped around my torso, as I made out with her. There was nothing sexual about it to me, yet it was overtly sexist. I was using her to prove a point to the other men; I could get more women than they could. Such a display raised me in their esteem, even as I posed no threat. I could bring the hot women, and I had the ability to score the hot women, but I "chose" not to. Even as a gay man, my sexual currency was defined through heterosexuality.[24]

A gay TikToker named Jake articulated a similar awareness of his social power when in 2021 he posted a video of himself dancing with the caption:

"Pike might be able to blacklist me from their frats, but i'm the gay best [*sic*] friend I can blacklist yall from pussy, your move tho!"[25] Six months after conducting my initial round of interviews with Preston, I went to his apartment and showed him the draft of this chapter. When he got to Skylar's quote (above), he stopped reading and looked up at me. "This dude is gross," he declared. "I don't use women like this." One of the other people in the room—a sorority woman named Morgan and one of Preston's best friends—begged to differ. She reminded Preston of when his fraternity asked him to find the "hottest woman on the planet" to bartend one of their parties and he cajoled a buxom sorority friend into doing the honors in a crop top and cut-off shorts. And then there was the time, she continued, before Preston joined a fraternity, when he piled eleven conventionally gorgeous women into his car and drove them to a party held at his future fraternity house. Preston was stopped at the door and told that he wasn't allowed in unless he brought a handle of vodka with him. Preston told him that he brought something better and then stepped aside to allow the women passage. The uncomfortable realization that he unconsciously used his girlfriends to curry favor with fraternity men didn't sit well with Preston, and he texted me a few days later to say that he brought the subject up with his therapist and was working through what it means "to be a Jeffrey Epstein." Preston, in my opinion, is more victim than perpetrator in this situation. While Preston is being too hard on himself, the fraternity chapters that recruit gay men as party promoters need to be harder on themselves. Once stripped of its thin patina of brotherhood, the manipulation and abuse that lies at the heart of the relationship between straight and gay fraternity brothers is laid bare: the former is using the latter to fulfill their sexual desires. Look a little closer and you'll find that gay fraternity men (and, by extension, LGBTQ+ sorority women) serve an additional role beyond facilitating heterosexual sex; in some cases, they also are the recipients of romantic advances by their straight-identifying brothers and sisters.

I Love You, but I'm Not Gay

Tall and blond with a quick wit and easy charisma that makes him popular with Rollins's sorority women, Aidan is, in Preston's words, "the poster child for man whores." Because Aidan spends so much time conversing with women on social media, Preston was taken aback when Aidan initiated a friendly Snapchat exchange with him. He was doubly surprised when, after two weeks, the duo reached yellow heart status (signifying that both individuals had sent the most snaps to each other). While the conversation started out innocently enough, Preston reported that it wasn't long before Aidan was sending him shirtless selfies and videos of himself lying seductively in bed. A few days after Preston and Aidan's Snapchat streak reached pink heart status (two months of most exchanged snaps), Aidan texted Preston: "What are you doing tomorrow night?" Preston showed me the exchange that followed on his phone. "Hopefully you," he replied. Later that night, Aidan texted Preston: "I'm coming over." Preston said that a few minutes later Aidan knocked on his door and, in drunken, slurred speech, begged Preston to let him in. Preston said that he wanted to open the door but didn't because he was nervous that other fraternity members might be around and that, because Aidan was drunk, he couldn't be sure that a same-sex romantic encounter was really what his friend wanted. The next morning, Preston asked Aidan via text about his intentions the previous night. Aidan accused Preston of misreading him and firmly denied any past flirting. "I love you but I'm not gay," he texted. Aidan never sent Preston another text, and the Snapchat streak ended that day.

The episode left Preston with a swirl of emotions: shame, embarrassment, anger, and confusion. As he sorted through his feelings over subsequent weeks, he couldn't decide if he was a victim of gaslighting or had read too much into the relationship. His confusion is well founded, as there isn't a straight line between behavior and identity. Scholars argue that sexuality emerged as a form of selfhood and an identity category in America in the late nineteenth century; before that, gay sex and straight sex were more commonly seen as behaviors.[26] While displays of same-sex physical affection such as hand-holding, kissing, hugging, passionate letter-writing, and bed-sharing were accepted parts of the masculine and feminine culture in the early nineteenth century, many of the same behaviors were viewed with growing suspicion at the end of the century. In his comprehensive history of fraternities, Nicholas Syrett tells the story of what happened when Dartmouth administrators were confronted with a campus fraternity chapter comprised of proudly effeminate men. According to Syrett, several members of Epsilon Kappa Phi and at least two of the chapter's alumni rented a nearby farmhouse and converted it into a kind of clubhouse. When rumors began swirling that the fraternity was throwing parties there that involved drug use and "moral degeneracy" (the latter being code for homosexual behavior), Dartmouth's president took action to shut the party house down for the safety of other fraternity men. This decision was consistent with the prevailing notion that homosexuality was contagious and that partygoers risked being tricked into becoming "inverts."[27]

Dartmouth's fretting over rumors of gay sex illustrates the popular perception that same-sex interactions are unnatural and morally degenerate while at the same time obscures how central they are to straight self-fashioning. In 2015, sociologist Jane Ward laid bare what a *Gawker* reporter said: "people maybe were thinking but just weren't saying"—namely, that same-sex sexual encounters are still a ubiquitous feature of the culture of straight white men in America.[28] Specifically, Ward shows how "white straight-identified men manufacture opportunities for sexual contact with other men in a remarkably wide range of settings, and that these activities appear to thrive in hyper-heterosexual environments, such as universities, where access to sex with women is anything but constrained."[29] One of the places where sexualized rituals and behavior is most pronounced is the fraternity house. Some of this behavior is visible, like at the fraternity chapter meetings I supervised where men greeted each other with half-hugs and slaps to their friends' shoulders, chests, and butts. Other forms of it are hidden and only come to light when fraternity members show or tell outsiders or document their actions in photographs or video. Andrew Moisey's critically acclaimed and highly controversial 2018 book, *The American Fraternity: An Illustrated Ritual Manual*, includes photographs the author-artist took of members of an unnamed University of California, Berkeley, fraternity between 2000 and 2008.[30] One of them shows a man wearing cutoff jean shorts with his testicles exposed crawling on the ground, while others show, respectively, a naked man tackling a clothed man on the ground, and a man, naked from the waist down, being hand-fed a drink by two other men.[31]

The scenes that Moisey documented are variations of similar behaviors on other campuses. In 2013, Cornell disbanded one of its fraternity chapters after it was revealed that part of the organization's initiation ritual involved fraternity men stripping their new pledges nude.[32] An economics class at Princeton was disrupted in 2014 when a group of twenty suspected fraternity pledges wearing nothing but ski masks, scarves, and sneakers ran through the classroom.[33] In 2017, twenty-one members of a fraternity at the State University of New York at Plattsburgh were charged with hazing violations that including paddling new members and urinating on them.[34] In 2018, a leaked video allegedly showed members of a University of Idaho fraternity chapter dancing naked in front of party guests.[35] A year later, a photo taken in 2016 surfaced that seems to show fully clothed fraternity members at Sacramento State University simulating the elephant walk (a ritual that involves men forming a line and walking as a group while grasping the penis of the man in front of them).[36]

Such forms of sexual hazing are commonly thought of as degrading and a form of bullying, and sometimes they are. According to Ward, it doesn't mean that these acts are nonsexual or devoid of erotic pleasure. Male sexuality, she contends, is just as fluid as female sexuality, and sexual hazing can also be read as an acceptable fetish within white heteromasculinity.[37] As other scholars have shown, sexualized encounters that occur outside of the sphere of fraternity initiation simultaneously normalize homosexual acts and work to inscribe them within the definition of heterosexuality.[38] The elasticity of heterosexuality within fraternity (and sorority) culture is what makes the interaction between Preston and Aidan so tricky to understand. Aidan's erotic selfies and flirty DMs and texts could be read as forms of sexual experimentation; they could just as easily be viewed within the sphere of the fraternity house as expressions of straightness. As Tony J. Silva and Rachel Bridges Whaley succinctly put it, the practice of straight-identifying men having sex with men can be compatible with straightness because "heterosexual identification is neither uniform nor monolithic."[39]

While contemporary Greek life culture may work to expand the definition of heterosexuality, in some chapters the line between homoerotic desire and revulsion is murky and shapeshifting. Dan, a member of a University of South Carolina fraternity chapter, laughed as he told me stories about fraternity brothers who "act gay" through flamboyant behavior and homoerotic banter as a way of being funny, but also reported that there are a few guys who take things too far. It's OK to hump each other in the fraternity house, Dan reported, "but when you do it in public, we're like, 'OK, man, what's going on?'" The moving target that is social acceptance, coupled with the reality that not all sexual identities have equal status (there are powerful cultural incentives to identify as straight), offers up little incentive to openly embrace sexual diversity.

A same-sex sexual encounter between a gay fraternity man and his brother who identifies as straight has the potential to generate mixed feelings, but the power differential between the two leaves the gay brother more isolated and vulnerable. This was at least the experience of Gabe, who was a member of a top-tier fraternity at a private university in Texas between 2014 and 2017. When Gabe was a second-year student and in the early stages of coming out, he was befriended by two older fraternity brothers who shared a common interest in cars, snowboarding, and Texas professional sports teams. At a time when he was questioning his own masculinity, Gabe found much-needed reassurance by hanging out with two of his chapter's most "southern gentlemen" and notorious womanizers. One night, Gabe had too much to drink at a fraternity party and was helped back to his apartment by his new friends. As he flitted in and out of consciousness, he was aware that his fraternity brothers undressed and performed sexual acts on him, but he was powerless to stop it. That was Gabe's first same-sex sexual encounter. The incident served as a starting point for a secret on-again, off-again relationship with one of the men. Gabe reported that the man "would make fun of me and call me faggot in public at the same time as he was fucking me in private." Per the man's wishes, Gabe agreed to hide their relationship, even going as far as to sneaking into the man's apartment through back doors and windows to avoid detection from the man's roommates (who were also fraternity brothers of both men). Gabe didn't see it then, but with the wisdom afforded by time and therapeutic intervention, he now sees that the physical abuse that kickstarted the relationship pervaded it all the way through. One evening about a year into it, Gabe and the man got into a silly argument that escalated to the point where the man yanked his fraternity paddle off his bedroom wall and held it up to Gabe. "What are you going to do?" Gabe asked. "Hit me with it?" According to Gabe, the man answered the question by striking him with the object . . . and didn't stop until the sound of Gabe's bones snapping prompted the man's roommates to break down the door.

The story is horrifying to listen to, but, as I sat across a restaurant table from Gabe almost four years after the incident watching his hands shake and his voice waver, it was clear that his telling of it is the greater trauma. If the details of the event weren't so hideous, the irony of the situation would make me laugh. Wooden paddles used to play a starring role in fraternity and sorority hazing rituals, but after the North American Interfraternity Conference (NIC) and the National Panhellenic Conference (NPC) formally banned hazing, the objects were repurposed into symbolic tokens of Greek letter membership. The tradition varies per organization and chapter, but it's commonly the role of "Big" brothers and sisters to decorate premade blank paddles (sold at many national chain craft stores expressly for this purpose) for their "Little" brothers and sisters. Even if the gifts aren't crafted with any malintent, no amount of puffy paint, ribbon, or three-dimensional stickers can disguise the fact that the object is a weapon. While fraternity and sorority members aren't supposed to be paddling each other anymore, there's evidence that some still do. And for those who are staunchly against violent hazing but have decorative paddles hanging on their walls, I would ask: What is the difference? The first establishes and maintains social hierarchy through physical violence. The latter accomplishes the same goal through the threat of imagined violence that is conjured by gazing at the object every day. In response to the bad optics, several fraternities and sororities have banned the sale of premade paddles decorated with their letters or logos, but a licensing adjustment can't erase the reality that Gabe's story lays bare: Greek letter culture authorizes members of the community to hurt each other and provides them with the (in Gabe's case, literal) tools to do it.[40] Thanks to technology, it's no longer necessary to make physical contact with a person in order to affirm or injure them. Both can be accomplished with a couple of swipes and a push of a button that says "post" or "share."

Frexting Your Sisters

The centrality of sorority wingwomen and gay wingmen in the creation and perseverance of romantic relationships within campus Greek life makes such relationships inherently collective and communal. Despite the number of porn flicks that feature sorority threesomes, none of the sorority women with whom I spoke made a practice of sharing their boyfriend or hookup partners' bodies with their friends. But that doesn't mean that they don't bring their sorority sisters into the bedroom with them. According to Indiana University–Purdue University Fort Wayne researchers, sexting—described as sending sexually suggestive messages, photos, or videos via cell phone—is common on college campuses (i.e., 62 percent of college students surveyed either sent or received such picture messages).[41] A similar study published in *Sexual Health* revealed that one in four sexually explicit texts are shared with at least three different people.[42]

These numbers certainly matched up with those reported by Stella, Stacy, Monica, and Kylie when I met up with them again a year later. Now seniors, the women hadn't even sat down at the restaurant where I met them before Stella launched into the story of her most recent sexting escapade. Her new hookup partner had sent her an explicit and lengthy step-by-step description of what he wanted to do with and to her. Immediately after receiving the erotic text, which the women described as being so long that it could have been a novel, Stella instinctively screenshotted the message and forwarded it to all her friends. "It was intense," Kylie sighed. "I'll admit that I felt something," Monica said with a smile. Stella didn't forward her sext with the intent of arousing her friends per se, but both the sender and the recipients viewed it as an acceptable byproduct of information sharing. Like the paperback romance novels that their mothers and grandmothers used to pass around among their female friends, good sex stories are circulated and shared.

The pictorial analogue of the sext message is, of course, the nude. According to the 2019 SKYN Condoms Sex & Intimacy Survey, 50 percent of its millennial and Gen Z respondents have sexted, and 37 percent have filmed themselves having sex.[43] According to Sean Young, the director of the Center for Digital Behavior at the University of California, Los Angeles, one reason why sending nudes is so common among college students has to do with the fact that individual actions are heavily influenced by one's perception of what one thinks is normal and ubiquitous. Seeing or hearing about someone else receiving or sending a nude selfie (regardless of how widespread this behavior really is) accelerates the normalization of this behavior.[44]

The corner of the mainstream media that targets the collegiate audience plays a big part in minimizing the professional and personal consequences of circulating nude selfies by focusing one's attention on how to take a good one. Recent articles in popular online magazines boast titles like "How to Take the Perfect Nude Selfie," "7 Tips to Elevate Your Nude Selfie Game," and "7 Things to Know Before Taking the Perfect Vagina Picture."[45] The banal, matter-of-fact way that another article talks about staging one's genitals for a photo shoot—"No flashes. Ever. *Ever.* A camera flash will turn the most regal peepee or veevee into a blinding physiological hell demon, exploding forth from the screen. You should never look terrifying naked. A flash will clinch this"— further promotes the specter of ubiquity and the sense that everyone is taking nude selfies and launching them casually and randomly into cyberspace.[46]

During my research, I asked a group of my chapter's fraternity men about the particulars of the nudes that they had stored on their cell phones. "Are all of them selfies?" I wanted to know. They started to answer in the affirmative, but then stopped short. Now that they thought about it, they realized that many of the nude photos they received weren't taken by women posing in front of a bathroom mirror. A surprising number, in fact, seemed to be curiously taken by an external agent.

"How do you think these photos were generated?" I asked.

They mulled over the possibilities. "It could have been a tripod," one proposed.

"Sure."

"Or maybe the camera was propped up on something and taken with a timer."

"That also could be the case."

There was one other possibility that dangled right in front of them, but all were unwilling to acknowledge it. When the awkward silence became unbearable, one finally articulated the truth that had just dawned on them. "Maybe one of her friends took it?"

The reluctance to consider the existence of another person behind the camera doesn't signal that these men are missing a few brain cells as much as it represents a natural and expected attempt to preserve the fantasy that they are the photographs' exclusive audience. If what was making my fraternity members uneasy was the suspicion that the nudes weren't just for them, odds are that they were right.

According to the media, "frexting," or the practice of sending erotic images to one's platonic friends, is all the rage.[47] *Sports Illustrated* swimsuit model Chrissy Teigen did it when she made a digital birthday card for her friend that featured a naked photo of herself.[48] Bypassing the clichéd body lotion or scented candle birthday gift that women friends often give one another, comedian Chelsea Handler opted instead to celebrate her celebrity gal pal Reese Witherspoon's fortieth birthday by posting an almost nude of herself to Instagram.[49]

Exchanging sexy selfies with your girlfriends or having them take steamy pics of you isn't an activity exclusive to the rich and famous; some sorority members admit to sexting with their friends almost as much as they do with men. Just a week before I met with Monica, Stella, Stacy, and Kylie, the women had staged an impromptu sexy photo shoot in their apartment, with each woman taking turns as photographer and subject. "We don't spread our legs for each other or anything like that," Monica clarified, "but we do take lots of sexy, fun shots that fall into the category of cleavage and peekaboo breast pics, just-out-of-the-shower towel shots, and various nude and topless poses." Motivations or occasions inspiring these photo shoots include the acquisition of new underwear, the desire to have some sexy pics "in the bank, 'cause you never know when you'll need them," and, in this case, boredom and a few free hours.

While many of the photos taken during these sessions ultimately would be sent to men and, through their self-consciously erotic staging, were intended to arouse them, the women talked about their hookup partners' cell phones as if they were the last stage of an assembly line: they might be the final destination, but the images are filtered through hands and minds and eyes of countless other women before reaching that point. As the creator of the online matter project Everyone Sexts, writer/artist Jenna Wortham told Medium that frexting is about reclaiming the nude and rewriting its meaning. Specifically, they are "coopting a device that was built for one specific intention and turning it into something that's used for female bonding."[50] A 2021 study conducted by a researcher at the University of Surrey in England found the same thing.[51]

For today's college women who inhabit the largely male-centric hookup terrain, frexting represents a safe zone where they can explore and express one's sexuality without extending an invitation for anything more.[52] Writing for *Bustle*, author Beca Grimm concurs: "Sexts can be like a weird, unspoken language between two people. Who knows what you're actually communicating or agreeing to when partaking in such a confusing channel? But frexts are always transparent and clear—and have no strings attached."[53]

The safety and security that frexting offers derives from the contract between its participants.[54] While nudes sent to the opposite sex run the risk of being ignored, mocked, picked apart, or otherwise rejected, the only appropriate response to a frext is affirmation. Frexting etiquette includes replying with heart emojis, the words "gorgeous" or "stunning," and animated gifs of animals clapping or doing backflips. The rigidity of the script and predictability of the response is what empowers women to take risks. Take, for example, the case of New Yorker Sebastian Lavender. Her first frext was an RSVP to a "send nudes" party hosted by her female friends. The premise of the gathering was to celebrate the female body. Lavender's contribution to the party decor—nude photos of the all-female party attendees—was a stylized topless selfie with her pet rat perched on her shoulder.[55]

In one of life's little ironies, I have found myself in a G-rated frexting relationship with two now former students (both of whom were members of the Rollins Greek system). It started in 2017 when Elizabeth, then a rising second-year student, reached out to me via text. She explained that she was stuck in a depressive slump and needed help digging herself out. In addition to connecting her with professional counseling services, I also looped her into a group chat with Charlotte, a recent graduate and upperclassman peer mentor who a year earlier was assigned to help Elizabeth and a cohort of seventeen other first-year students navigate their first year at Rollins. The first weeks of the chat's existence were dedicated to wellness checks (e.g., Have you gotten out of bed yet? When is your next therapy appointment?). In the past, similar group chats between me, a peer mentor, and a student have tapered off into nonexistence once the crisis at hand is resolved, but quite unintentionally this multigenerational mentorship text chain persists five years later. Over time, the chat's initial focus—to remind Elizabeth of her inherent value and intrinsic worth as a woman—has evolved into a daily text chain comprised almost exclusively of "This is what I am wearing today" selfie shots taken by Elizabeth and Charlotte in front of their bathroom mirrors. Throughout all of this, my role has remained consistent: to praise any wardrobe selection with which I'm presented, whether it be a first-day-of-work business suit or floor-length gown.

While many of the selfies that Elizabeth and Charlotte send me eventually make their way to Instagram and other public-facing venues, they report routinely sending more racy photos of themselves to girlfriends and former sorority sisters via private text or Finstagram (a private Instagram account meant to be viewed only by the users' best friends) when they are feeling lonely or rejected by men, when they feel fat or ugly, or when they need an overall confidence boost. Charlotte recently confessed that she and Elizabeth have a separate text chain reserved for more racy selfies that they don't want me to see. "FYI just sent Elizabeth a nude," she recently texted me. "Don't be mad." That the women apologized for leaving me off the text chain instead of presenting the exclusion as a gift speaks to the status of the nude as one marker of a kind of social bond between girlfriends that friendship guru Shasta Nelson calls "frientimacy."[56]

In addition to sending out nudes when they need a pick-me-up, some sorority women also distribute them when they are feeling at the top of their game, not to rub their good fortune in their friends' faces, but to inspire and uplift them—and share their creativity. "I always send sexy pics of myself to my friends so they can see what I do," Stacy told me. "Especially the good ones." Motivating this action is a kind of generosity that models itself on friendship culture from earlier eras but takes a different form. The racy lingerie shot or sexy nude can be seen as the new Jell-O mold recipe. If you find a good one, it is selfish and uncharitable not to share it with your friends, neighbors, or, if you are feeling especially generous, the entire Internet.[57]

While men get a bad reputation for having iCloud libraries filled with photos of nude women, women likewise keep their own stashes of naked and seminaked women. Peruse your average Pinterest board, and you'll find scores of photos of women—pulled from fashion, fitness, and weight loss blogs, Facebook posts, and Instagram accounts—in varying states of undress and exposure. The most popular of these specimens (like the Instagram account of fitness model Michelle Lewin, which boasts over 13 million followers) exceeds many porn sites in the number of daily clicks and views.[58] The gravitational pull of women to these PG-13-rated photo albums of seminude women marks the female body as an object of universal infatuation and desire. When curated by their subjects, image collections of women's nude and seminude bodies serve as powerful expressions of agency and power, albeit ones that largely reinforce conventional standards of beauty.[59] When nudes are taken or circulated without the consent of their subjects, however, these images can and do have the exact opposite effect.

Fraternity Group Chats and "Tits of the Hour"

On a bright and cheery morning in October 2017, members of Florida International University's student-run fraternity and sorority governing boards (i.e., the NPC and IFC councils) woke up to find photos of naked women in their inboxes. The nudes were embedded within screenshots of a campus fraternity's 108-member GroupMe chat and sent anonymously by a whistleblower.[60] Two years earlier, a Penn State fraternity was penalized for posting nude photos of women on a secret Facebook page.[61] Leaked "meeting minutes" (basically a weekly roast of fellow fraternity men by other fraternity men) from the Phi Psi chapter at Swarthmore College in 2013 describe a witnessed sexual interaction between a fraternity member and a woman where the latter allegedly "tickled his tits, groped his cock, and rubbed her wet vag all over his neatly pressed khakis." In addition to describing the act, the author of the document inserted a now-deleted twenty-six-second video of the "molestation," as well as three screenshots.[62]

Three-fourths of the sorority women with whom I spoke at the restaurant had nudes of themselves on the loose—that they knew about. When Stacy learned that one of her photos was circulating through several fraternity group chats on campus, she was both upset and embarrassed. Her views of the situation changed, however, when she saw that the photo in question was, as she described it, "an old one." As she went on to minimize the event by talking about the image as if its age made it analogous to a naked baby photo pulled from her childhood scrapbook, I pressed her for clarification. How old exactly was the nude? "Super old," she replied. "Like from my freshman year [of college]."

Like Stacy, the other two women in the group whose nudes were made public weren't particularly surprised about the leaks. While they were none too pleased in the moment of their release, they had long made their peace with their existence on the grounds that naked bodies are no big deal. "We all grew up on porn," Kylie explains. "There are naked people on Instagram."

The idea that no one's private parts—including their own—are particularly precious or noteworthy is reflected in a story Monica recounted about the summer after her second year at Rollins, during which she had a brief fling with a campus fraternity member named Jack. She didn't think about Jack again until three months later, when his penis showed up uninvited at her Thanksgiving dinner table. As the turkey was being sliced, a text came in that contained a video that Jack took without her knowledge of Monica performing oral sex on him. "I was totally freaked out when I got that video, and even more devastated to learn that Jack had sent the video to all of his fraternity brothers in a group chat, as you can imagine." I could imagine. And, based on the suddenly somber mood at the table, her friends could too. "What was Jack's fraternity brothers' response to the video?" I wanted to know.

To their credit, the fraternity kicked Jack out of their organization. However, if the rumor mill can be trusted, Jack didn't lose his membership because he videotaped a sex act and circulated it without Monica's consent. Rather, the alleged reason he was expelled from the group was because he revealed the existence of the chapter's group chat to someone outside of the fraternity. In the weeks following "the incident," as she called it, Monica received several texts and calls from Jack's former fraternity brothers, apologizing for the leaked video and assuring her that what they had seen "wasn't a big deal."

"But you thought it was a big deal," I said softly, echoing what she had said moments earlier. "How did you respond?" Monica talked about feeling betrayed and violated by what happened but said that she felt a lot better after learning how many pornographic images of women passed through the fraternity group chat. The point that the fraternity men kept making to her over and over was one about perspective. Instead of being the star attraction of the daily group chat, the men downplayed her appearance. "My breasts were basically the tits of the hour," she explained.

For women who have had sexual videos or photos taken of them and distributed without their consent, there are not many ways to spin the story other than the one chosen by Monica. The trivialization of nude photo sharing speaks to the larger problem with technology-based sexual misconduct on college campuses and its normalization within the fraternity and sorority community.[63] A 2021 study of 1,867 college students at a large Midwestern university found that fraternity members were more likely than nonmembers to post and share nude images and videos online without consent.[64]

But just because individuals see lots of breasts and vaginas throughout the day doesn't make the unauthorized exposure of yours any less of a violation. At Rollins and lots of other places, viewing nudes of friends' hookup partners is a way men participate in each other's sex lives. "Fraternity guys would fuck each other if they could," Monica said matter-of-factly. And even though that option is on the table, they sometimes opt to share the next best thing: nude photos and illicit sex tapes of the girls they fuck.

That's what Kathryn Novak said happened to her. According to a lawsuit filed in 2018, Novak was spending spring break with her boyfriend, University of Central Florida (UCF) fraternity member Brandon Simpson, when she discovered a disturbing text on Simpson's phone that referenced a nude video of Novak.[65] Simpson admitted to directly distributing the video to at least five of his fraternity brothers without her consent. Novak also learned that Simpson and other fraternity members also sent the video to more chapter members to view during a chapter meeting.[66] At the time of the lawsuit's filing, Novak claims that over 200 fraternity members and UCF students received the video.[67] In addition, Simpson allegedly revealed the existence of a private Facebook page called the "Dog Pound," where fraternity members posted nude photos and videos of their girlfriends and other women engaged in sexual activities—all without their consent.[68]

Nudes are shared through a variety of platforms (GroupMe, DM, text), but the runaway winner in the sexy-photo-sharing contest is Snapchat. It's an open secret that porn has been the driving force behind some of society's most exciting technological innovations. Video streaming, online credit card transactions, and tracking devices all started out as inventions created for the porn industry.[69] Snapchat is part of this legacy, though one not born in the seedy porn hub of Los Angeles's San Fernando Valley but several hundred miles north, on the campus of one of our nation's most elite universities. Evan Spiegel was a Sigma Kappa fraternity member at Stanford when, in 2011, one of his fraternity brothers sparked the idea for Snapchat with an offhand musing about how great it would be if raunchy texts and racy photos could magically disappear after being viewed. Billy Gallagher, a Silicon Valley tech writer and former fraternity brother of Spiegel and the company's other cofounders, writes how the fraternity brothers immediately envisioned all the problems that such an app would solve: one could send "dick pics" without the fear of recrimination; disappearing photos would encourage women to send nudes of themselves.[70] One of the app's most popular features, My Story, allows users to compile a sequence of captioned photo snaps into a pictorial chronological narrative. Emails authored by Spiegel during his fraternity days and leaked to the public in 2014 reveal that the feature bears an uncanny resemblance to one of Spiegel's favorite college storytelling strategies—the narrative timeline. Consider this leaked email Spiegel sent to his pledge class in 2009:

Last Night and This Morning
(as depicted by a series of colorful vignettes)
by Evan Spiegel
9:30pm
Fuck, I hope we finish this keg before the Pi Phis get here.
10:00pm
Pi Phis are more frigid than previously anticipated. Maybe if I get
    more fucked up they will stop huddling in corners.
10:30pm
Each team completed one station. Progressive= success. Let's throw
    a rager.
10:35pm
Wait, Pi Phis don't rage. Bummer. At least we have another tray
    of rubbing alcohol/jello-flavored shots. Note to self: Thank
    Coggeshall and Cam.
11:00pm
Drunk sex would be a ton of fun right now.
11:30pm I'm definitely too drunk to have sex.
Probably too drunk to not have sex. Let's give this a shot.
4:00am
Did I just pee on Lily while assuming the big spoon position?
4:30am
Uhoh.
4:01am
Maybe I can blame this on her.
4:02am
The back of her shirt is soaked. She's gonna be super irritated. This
    is pretty gross.
4:06am
Walking to Pi Phi sucks. Note to self: don't pee on Lily again.
4:20am
At least this bed doesn't have pee on it. Why do girls always have
    their shit together?
8:10am
Late to my first chem section. I need a bike. I wonder if my TA has
    ever been
peed on. She's pretty hot for a TriDelt.
8:11am
Let's throw a TriDelt progressive.

8:11.15am

Did I really just think that?

8:12am

I need to go to sleep.[71]

The goal of this narrative mode is to transport the audience to the scene of the action and enable them to vicariously experience what's going on both in the room and in the mind of the first-person narrator. Snapchat's My Story feature is an amplified form of this narrative technique that allows the narrator to tell the same story with visuals.

If the problem that Snapchat was trying to solve is the inadequacy of words to capture the full range of degradation of women, the app and its features have been wildly successful in accomplishing its goal. The above email tries to be a snap by constructing a clear mental image of the main event. Why else would Spiegel name the woman on which he urinated if not to conjure a detailed image of her degradation? Had the scene played out a few years later, after Snapchat was operational, it's easy to imagine the kinds of photos that would have replaced or accompanied the narrative: an image of a group of "frigid" sorority women ignoring the advances of fraternity men, one of a sleeping woman that is drenched in the author's urine, and a photo of another sorority woman taken from the back of a college classroom while she's listening to a lecture.

Snapchat's creators insist that the app wasn't devised exclusively as a way for fraternity brothers to share damning and risqué photos with one another and hide the evidence, but the ease with which the app makes this practice possible is undoubtedly part of its appeal.[72] If Snapchat's design makes it easy to share nonconsensual photos and videos, the way that the app is operated and maintained makes it incredibly difficult to police the sending and receiving of unlawful content. This is because Snapchat doesn't save copies of snaps after they are opened by a recipient and deletes unopened snaps from its main server after thirty days. Because Snapchat content has such a short life (evidence disappears from the company's main servers often before it can be authenticated by law enforcement), users can send and receive content with relative impunity. As the fraternity community's gift to the world, Snapchat democratizes risqué photo sharing and, in doing so, provides the public with the ability to act like fraternity members or to be on the receiving end of those who do.

Snapchat and related platforms make it easy to perpetuate the misogyny that seems to lie at the core of Snapchat's founding. Spiegel's leaked emails reveal a pattern of disgusting comments about women, from expressing a desire to shoot lasers (referring to laser tag) at "fat girls" and encouraging his fraternity brothers to "give yourself a pat on the back or have some girl put your large kappa sigma dick down her throat" to thanking his brothers for throwing a Hawaiian-themed party by expressing hope that "at least six girl [sic] sucked your dicks last night" and signing off with his name and the phrase "Fuckbitchesgetleid."[73]

Predictably, Spiegel was horrified when he learned about the leaked emails. His written response to CNN says: "I'm obviously mortified and embarrassed that my idiotic e-mails during my fraternity days were made public. I have no excuse. I'm sorry I wrote them at the time and I was a jerk to have written them. They in no way reflect who I am today or my views towards women."[74] Spiegel's response downplays the significance of the emails while simultaneously normalizing them by situating the missives within the context of fraternity membership. The thinly veiled subtext of his response goes like this: fraternity men are all jerks, and when he was a fraternity member, he did what fraternity men inherently do and sent "idiotic" emails. Even if we believe that Spiegel's emails didn't reflect his views toward women (and I'm not sure that we should), Snapchat has been dogged in recent years by persistent complaints of having a sexist company culture.[75] By suggesting that fraternity culture shouldn't be taken seriously, Spiegel is asking us not to take seriously what he said when he was a fraternity member.

His ask may seem absurd if it wasn't so common.

Perusing Spiegel's filthy emails was like reading the unofficial minutes of my fraternity's chapter meeting minutes. Everyday banter—descriptions of "fuglies (fucking uglies)"; "butterfaces" (hot body . . . but [not] her face)—was, according to several members, G-rated compared to the vocabulary that was used when I wasn't present.

Charges of sexism were mounted against fraternities long before the arrival of the Internet, but the case against the group has undoubtedly been strengthened by the rise of raunchy "bro humor" sites like Old Row, BroBible, Barstool Sports, and Total Frat Move (TFM). In a crowded and ruthlessly competitive digital universe, these sites and their spin-offs enjoyed (and some still enjoy) remarkably long and influential lives. TFM's nine-year run (2010–19) overlapped with the college years of hundreds of thousands of young men and women, making this site's signature content—snaps, memes, and photos of fraternity men doing and saying stupid, offensive, and vile things (often about and to women)—culturally significant.[76]

What happens when the long and rich culture of fraternal misogyny has a romantic affair with the sexist corner of the Internet marketed to collegiate men? One of the monstrous offspring produced by this unholy union is a "brocabulary" that will make even the most hardened souls wince. Some men show up to fraternity recruitment events already well versed in sexist speech and rattle it off unprompted and with ease. For others, the experience marks the first time that they've heard the words and phrases they've read online vocalized in person by another human being. In 2021, A.J., a first-year student at Morehead State University who was raised by a single mother, was taken aback by how fraternity members at his school talked about women. "Let's put it this way," he told me a week after Bid Day, "I joined the only fraternity that didn't refer to them as 'bitches.'" A Villanova senior named Damian told me that his fraternity hosts recruitment-week parties for PNMs during which fraternity members ask the men to name the hottest girl on campus. Then they provide the men with a chair and say, "This chair is [the woman]. Show me how you would do her." Another activity is an adapted party game that involves providing the names of three sorority "groupies" and asking PNMs to specify which one they would fuck, which one they would marry, and which one they would kill. There is a method to the madness, Damien insisted. "How they answer the question says something about their personality. If a guy says, 'I would never answer that, I like those girls too much,' that says something."

"Does it say something good?" I asked hopefully.

Maybe Damian didn't hear my question because he didn't answer it. If a PNM refused to answer the question, he continued, the fraternity members would continue to badger him until he did: "Fine. If you were *forced* to pick, who would you fuck, who would you marry, and who would you kill?"

The members of Damian's fraternity aren't the only men on campus who imagine murdering sorority women. Several years earlier, a twenty-two-year-old Santa Barbara City College student named Elliot Rodger sat in his apartment and drew up a list of sorority women he would like to kill. "Alpha Phi is full of hot, beautiful blonde girls," he wrote, "the kind of girls I've always desired but was never able to have because they all looked down on me. They are all spoiled, heartless wicked bitches."[77]

Elliot wasn't a member of a fraternity, but he had something in common with the men cited above who are: he used the same vocabulary to describe women. I use the past tense to refer to Elliot because he's dead. On the evening of May 23, 2014, Elliot stabbed his three roommates to death before making his way to the Alpha Phi sorority house at the University of California, Santa Barbara (UCSB). He pounded on the front door of the mansion but after no one answered, turned his gun instead on a group of passersby, killing Tri Delt sorority sisters Veronika Weiss and Katherine Cooper. Over the next fifteen minutes, Elliot shot and killed another UCSB student and injured fourteen others before turning his gun on himself.[78]

Putting fraternity "brocabulary" alongside the hate-filled proclamation of a mass murderer may seem like a stretch; after all, most men who call women "bitches" talk about sex with them as a form of entitlement and fantasize about killing them do not end up shooting them at close range. While most fraternity men don't grow up to kill women, *Time* reporter Eliana Dockterman reminds us that fraternity men do grow up to run tech companies that create "the apps and devices we use and that shape our society."[79]

In her critically acclaimed book *Down Girl*, Cornell philosophy professor Kate Manne persuasively argues that the mainstream and right-wing commentators who refused to take Elliot's screed against women at face value are deniers of what really lies at the core of his murderous rampage: misogyny.[80] According to Manne, the reluctance to see Elliot's actions as anything more than a product of mental illness caused by social isolation, depression, and sexual frustration stems from the misconception that desire and hatred can't occur simultaneously. It's impossible for us to fathom, in other words, how someone like Elliott, who had such an intense desire to be loved by women and have sex with them, could also despise them with an equal intensity. Jane Ward crystalizes this so-called misogyny paradox in her most recent book, *The Tragedy of Heterosexuality*. "If you have experienced life as a girl or woman, you know the misogyny paradox all too well," she writes. "Men shout 'compliments' about girls' and women's bodies on public streets ('You are looking mighty fine today!' or 'You're a beautiful woman. Why don't you smile?') and then, a moment later, when they are not met with a response, hurl violent and misogynistic threats ('Fuck you bitch!')."[81]

Taken together, Manne's and Ward's conceptualization of misogyny redraws the boundaries that define the contours of the term. Our culture's current definition of a misogynist is a person who hates women, but when we define a person as a mysogynist if that person hates *all* women, we end up excluding almost everyone from being considered one. Manne argues instead that "misogynists can love their mothers—not to mention their sisters, daughters, wives, girlfriends, and secretaries. They need not hate women universally, or even very generally. They tend to hate women who are outspoken, among other things."[82]

If Elliot Rodger's hatred of the type of women who he perceived would reject him made him one of the faces of misogyny on campus, the fraternity member who talks about the women with whom he parties, socializes, and has sex is another. What Amanda Bennett said in a *Washington Post* op-ed about Spiegel's emails can be broadened to include all sexist parts of the fraternal brocabulary:

> So now that you are back, I would ask you to consider: Are these just words? Clearly there is a lot of hormonal prancing there. Yet, given what we know about binge drinking on campus, I think we all know that the references to blackouts are real. Aren't the references to sexual domination and contempt real, too? And if we long ago acknowledged that what we now only coyly refer to as the N-word is a real word with real powers to hurt, then why do we feel differently about allowing ourselves, our daughters, our sisters to be called bitches and whores as if it were funny?[83]

Spiegel's emails illuminate how misogyny is so embedded within fraternity culture writ large that even those who document it with a critical lens start to appropriate some of its main moves. This is the compassionate explanation of what Andrew Moisey did or, rather, didn't do in *The American Fraternity*. In addition to men pictured in compromising positions, Moisey's book also contains similar photographs of women. In one photo, for example, a woman has lifted her blouse to expose her bare breasts; in another, a sleeping or passed-out woman lies face up on a bed. She is fully clothed, but her legs are splayed open toward the camera. Moisey obscures the faces of his eighteen female subjects, but some of the women featured say that their identities are still recognizable.

More problematic is that while Moisey secured permission from the fraternity men to publish their photos, he admitted that he did not seek the same consent from all the women.[84] Alexis Schrader attended UC-Berkeley while Moisey was photographing and knows some of his female subjects. Writing in *Bust*, she says, "Moisey may not have set out to say anything about consent with his book, but, as far as women pictured in the book are concerned, he says a lot about what their consent means to him."[85] On his Indiegogo page (a kind of Kickstarter for artists), Moisey writes that "*American Fraternity* arrives as we ponder the rise of Trump and the fall of Harvey Weinstein and others, and wonder why so many male leaders have such reckless and chauvinistic behavior in their past."[86] One can't help but look at the photos of the women in Moisey's book—which have now been splashed all over the Internet and circulated in social media—and not put him into the same category of men he critiques. What is the difference, except in mode and semantics, between a group email that refers to female party guests as "sororisluts" and a snap of a woman in a compromised position, and a private Facebook page that includes homemade sex videos published without the female participant's consent and an art book that monetizes sexually suggestive images of college women, also taken and published without their permission?[87] Because technology makes it easier than ever to violate women's bodies, sorority sisters are charged with an additional task beyond helping their friends secure hookup partners: they also have to keep them safe from some of them. This is especially true when alcohol and drugs are in the mix.

THREE

Hooking Up
Hammered and High

It was supposed to be a night of fun and celebration, but everyone was, as one partygoer put it, "in a mood." The cause of the collective grumpiness for the fifty-four smartly dressed fraternity men and sorority women seated around me didn't have anything to do with the party to which they were in route, but rather the speed of the charter bus on which we were traveling. After biting their tongues for what felt like an eternity, the passengers had had enough. Emeline, a willowy brunette dressed in a strapless dress and four-inch heels acted on behalf of the group when she leaned into the aisle and cupped her hands around her mouth.

"Um, excuse me? Mr. Bus Driver?"

After making eye contact with the man in the bus's rearview mirror, Emeline made a heartfelt but pointed plea. "Can you *please* drive a little faster?"

The urgency of Emeline's request was grounded in the legitimate fear that the bus transporting the other half of the partygoers would beat ours to the venue. Despite the bus driver's order to stay seated, the bus occupants catapulted themselves out of their seats and pressed their bodies up against the bus doors. The instant that the doors swung open, bodies toppled out onto the pavement, pushed and shoved their way into the venue, and headed straight to the bar.

In *Beer and Circus*, Murray Sperber calls cheap beer "the oxygen of the Greek system."[1] The almost primal way in which the fraternity and sorority members at my school sought out and laid first claim to the proverbial life source illustrates why the Greek community unabashedly serves as the mascot of binge drinking in popular culture. Caitlin Flanagan's 2013 cover story in the *Atlantic* on the dangers of fraternity culture further codified the Greek community's reputation as filled with out-of-control party animals through its cover art portraying two fraternity men enthusiastically chest bumping each other. The stylized photo captures the moment of bodily contact and its inevitable consequence: namely, beer overflows from the red Solo cups that the fraternity brothers hold in their hands, sloshes out of their rims, and sails wildly into the air.[2]

There is truth in Flanagan's representation. While fraternity and sorority members aren't the only people on campus who imbibe alcoholic beverages by a long shot, just about every study of drinking on college campuses shows that fraternity members drink more heavily and more frequently than their fellow students.[3] Fraternity and sorority members also use cigarettes, waterpipes, and electronic cigarettes at higher rates than unaffiliated college students.[4]

There are a myriad of reasons why college students drink alcohol, and when they do, frequently drink it in excess. Included among the list of motives cited by researchers, clinicians, and the drinkers themselves are a cheap and convenient way to have fun and relieve stress, regulate emotions, and "enhance social experiences."[5]

In addition to livening up the campus fraternity party, alcohol also makes its existence possible. Alcohol is mobilized as a social lubricant in a range of settings but is most notably and visibly employed as a matchmaking tool. As fun and liberating as a casual hookup may be, it is still hard to communicate sexual interest to someone you barely know or don't know at all, and even more awkward and difficult to act on it without a little liquid courage. For this reason, the results of a massive social survey directed by New York University's Paula England aren't at all surprising. England's data—collected from over 25,000 college students between 2005 and 2011—reveal that the average male and female student drink 5.46 and 3.73 drinks, respectively, before hooking up.[6]

The perception that alcohol is a kind of one-size-fits-all liquid wingman or wingwoman that facilitates romantic encounters by helping individuals get out of their own way is buttressed by the fact that using alcohol as an aphrodisiac is a self-fulfilling prophecy. Research shows that people who think they will take sexual risks while drinking usually do.[7]

Hooking Up Hammered and High

Being inebriated is a requisite condition for having sex for many of the fraternity and sorority members with which I worked. A 2021 study of roughly 200 college students at a large university in the South (77 percent of whom were members of Greek life) revealed similar findings: students believed it was possible to consent to sexual activity after drinking and, for some, alcohol makes consent more likely.[8] By making drunk or at least tipsy sex the norm, hookup culture turns sober sex into something strange and rare, and largely reserved for committed relationships.[9] In the social circle in which my charges run, sobriety is a frequently used litmus test of a hookup partner's feelings. "If he likes me," more than one woman has told me, "he'll hook up with me again—sober." If the only way that individuals can participate in hookup culture without their actions being misread as representations of feelings they don't have is to drink before sexual encounters, then individuals who shouldn't drink find themselves caught between a rock and a hard place.

When Bars Cross Paths with Bars

At his high school in upstate New York, Cole was a high-achieving, standout athlete. On the outside, everything was going right in his life. Inside? Not so much. Plagued by emotional ups and downs since middle school, Cole felt like his brain was on a roller coaster. The symptoms that he and his parents attributed to typical teenage growing pains and the combined stress of competitive sports and rigorous high school coursework, however, didn't go away when Cole's baseball career ended, and he was accepted to Rollins. Instead, they intensified. After struggling for a year, Cole finally got up the nerve to go see someone. His psychiatrist prescribed him Klonopin, an antianxiety drug used to treat panic attacks and insomnia.

When Cole went to the pharmacy, he wasn't the only college student picking up a similar prescription. College students are seeking treatment for anxiety and depression in record number.[10] According to the 2018 National College Health Assessment Survey, 22 percent had been diagnosed with or treated for anxiety by a professional within the past twelve months.[11] While not all students who seek help for anxiety are on prescription medication, antidepressants are one of the most common types of drugs prescribed by many campus health clinics.[12]

Life was miserable for Cole at the time of his diagnosis. Indeed, one of the only bright spots was his fraternity, which he described as keeping him busy and "out of his own head." Since Klonopin and alcohol are both sedatives, mixing the two is incredibly dangerous. Cole didn't notice any ill effects when he drank moderately and took his medication as prescribed. But one particularly rough day he popped an extra pill before meeting up with friends at a local bar, and that extra Klonopin mixed with tequila shots made him "feel all sorts of amazing."

According to Cole and other fraternity and sorority women, there are two reasons why people mix alcohol with antianxiety drugs like Klonopin and its faster-acting and more popular sibling, Xanax: 1) the combination "fucks you up" quicker and for longer than alcohol alone, and 2) it's cheaper and less fattening than drinking alcohol all by itself. Rising bar prices mean that even moderate drinkers can easily drop fifty dollars or more on alcohol over the course of a night out. A QB (quarter bar of Xanax) combined with a few shots, by contrast, can produce the same effect at a fraction of the cost and without the extra calories.

The wide-ranging benefits conferred by benzodiazepines explains why Klonopin and Xanax are among the most popular party drugs on American college campuses.[13] While all corners of campus are prone to substance abuse problems, Xanax and Adderall (a stimulant traditionally used to treat ADHD patients) share the title of drug of choice for this generation of fraternity members largely because getting access to both simply requires a visit to one's family doctor, campus wellness center, or fraternity brother's medicine cabinet. Cole estimates that about 30 percent of his fraternity chapter are prescribed antianxiety drugs for legitimate medical reasons. Because of the social bonds of fictive brotherhood, fraternity brothers are taught to share the wealth. While no one is going to come after your prescription fungal cream or antidiarrheal pills, all manner of uppers and downers fall into the category of what's mine is yours and yours is mine.[14] Cole gave some to his Klonopin to fraternity brothers, and they, in turn, gave some of their Xanax to him.

Over time, Cole's generosity and overindulgence came with a cost: he ran through pills at a much faster rate than prescribed. He ingeniously solved this problem by visiting multiple doctors and getting multiple prescriptions filled by multiple pharmacies at the same time. While Cole and his fraternity brothers mobilized their creativity to fuel their own chapter's drug habit, a group of fraternity men at Eastern Carolina University (ECU) saw the entrepreneurial potential of dealing prescription sedatives on a larger scale. All was going swimmingly for the men of Phi Kappa Tau until their fraternity house was raided and authorities seized 2,500 bars of Xanax and arrested four of its members.[15]

While ECU's Phi Kappa Tau fraternity house had enough Xanax on hand to put its whole campus to sleep, recreational users of the drug typically take it not to check out of social situations but rather to participate in them. As Cole explained, "If you take a little bit, you can talk the talk and walk the walk. All the anxiety and anything you worry about is gone. Feel fat and overweight? Gone. Have a paper due the next day? Gone."

Cole used supersized doses of his antianxiety medication to help him talk to women. A natural but alarming outgrowth of other fraternity members' use of similar drugs is the inability to even talk about their social anxiety with a third party without also being drunk or high or both.

Case in point: I was in the middle of waging siege warfare against my fifth grader over incomplete math homework one evening when my cell phone lit up. The text, from a fraternity member, went straight to the point: he said he needed to talk to me ASAP. The situation was delicate in my kitchen at that moment—my son was weighing the costs and benefits of hurling his pencil across the room in frustration—so I opted not to respond to the text. A few minutes later, another text came in. Then the fraternity man tried calling, then FaceTiming. Then another text in all caps: "EMERGENCY."

The man answered my call by launching into a story about how a woman with whom he had been hooking up and really liked had just ghosted him. He wanted answers from the woman but didn't know what to say to her or how. But before he gave me the floor, he said that he needed a minute to get himself together. There was a pause on the other end of the line, followed by a gurgling sound, followed by a swish. "Are you drinking alcohol and smoking weed right now?" I asked incredulously.

I spent the rest of the evening scratching my head over what I had just experienced. In the process, I found myself mentally joining the ranks of those who long nostalgically for the good old days when people had enough confidence in their social skills that they didn't feel the need to pregame before calling their professors.

Except that this era never existed.

A Brief History of Lush Campuses

One doesn't have to pry open the vaults of history very far to see that alcohol was used as a social lubricant long before smart phones and college students came into existence. Initially, we imbibed alcohol because we had no other choice. Contaminated by pollutants and disease-carrying microbes, free-flowing water was largely unsafe to consume, leaving fermented liquids like alcohol among the only potable beverages available. However, as historians curiously have pointed out, we have kept drinking alcohol—and lots of it—long after it was medically necessary. One of the reasons why alcohol has remained a staple feature of our diets is that interpersonal communication skills have never been our strong suit.

While it's never been easy to talk to one another, our social awkwardness became glaringly obvious during Prohibition. Alcohol consumption didn't come to a screeching halt during this dry decade, but the Volstead Act made it a punishable crime to be publicly under the influence. Overnight, many Americans were asked to do something that up until this point was largely unimaginable: socialize with others while sober. This proved to be an immensely daunting and scary task. Fortunately, while Prohibition outlawed the production and distribution of liquor in public places, a caveat allowed for the legal consumption of alcohol that was produced before the law went into effect and within the privacy of one's home. The spatial sequestering of alcohol did not as much reduce the number of people who drank as much as transplanted drinking culture from public spaces likes pubs, bars, and saloons to private locales including personal residences, underground speakeasies, and fraternal clubs.

The shifting spatial contours of drinking culture in America coincided with the proliferation of Greek letter housing in the 1920s. While new fraternity houses helped ameliorate the on-campus housing crunch, these privately owned off-campus residential facilities also lay strategically outside the supervision and jurisdiction of the institution. During Prohibition, they emerged as natural sites for covert drinking and partying. Social archeologist Laurie A. Wilkie of the University of California, Berkeley, found evidence of this when she conducted an archeological dig of the area on her campus where a Prohibition-era fraternity house once stood. Included among the curiosities unearthed in the excavation was a large pit filled with an assortment of wine bottles, whiskey flasks, beer bottles, and a stoneware bottle that once held Amsterdam gin.[16] The walls of other fraternity houses constructed during the same era tell similar stories, at least according to their current inhabitants. According to one Cornell University Alpha Delta Phi member, the black-tie casino night event hosted at his chapter's fraternity house every year pays homage to the decade when the structure doubled as a speakeasy.[17]

Their location wasn't the only reason why fraternity houses were safe places to drink during Prohibition. Underlying the broader temperance movement of the late nineteenth and early twentieth centuries was a festering anxiety about the social "problems" introduced by immigration—labor conflicts, shifting gender roles, and racial, ethnic, and religious diversity. While the Eighteenth Amendment identified alcohol as the source of societal woes, its passing was, as Harvard historian Lisa McGirr bluntly puts it, "a broad assault on the 'enemies' of white Protestant nationalism."[18] Given Prohibition's secret targets, it should come as no surprise that the Volstead Act was selectively enforced. One can imagine that the same motivation driving the heavy policing of immigrant and African American communities across the country also caused authorities to look the other way when they saw white, wealthy college men belonging to organizations that prohibit Catholics, Jews, and racial minorities from joining their ranks, stumbling around with bottles in their hands.

Fraternity row may have been the drinking headquarters on campus during Prohibition, but fraternities themselves didn't bring alcohol to the campus; drinking has always been an institutionalized part of all stages of academic life. Susan Cheever notes that in the 1820s, elementary school students started their day with a sippy cup filled with a mix of grain alcohol and fruit juice. Children also took swigs of beer at recess and guzzled wine and other alcoholic concoctions at lunch.[19] University students in this era and the ones that preceded it likely were just as drunk, as evidenced by the number of bars that existed in university towns. A stock-taking document from September 1311, for example, reveals that there were at least 199 places in the famed university town of Oxford, England, where beer was served.[20]

Likewise, the origin story of many of America's colleges and universities wasn't forged in a classroom but in local taverns. Rutgers University held its first classes at the Sign of the Red Lion, a popular pub in Revolutionary-era New Brunswick.[21] The elite academic honor society Phi Beta Kappa was founded at the College of William and Mary in 1776 but held its meetings at a local bar.[22] College students roamed around campus with open containers and freely imbibed before, during, and after class all the way up until Prohibition, when the taps were abruptly turned off. After the Volstead Act was repealed in 1933, each state established a minimum legal drinking age, which, for the most part, was twenty-one. Four decades later, the legal drinking age was negotiated back down to eighteen, thanks to the Vietnam War. The logic used to push the measure through the courts was that those who were old enough to fight certainly were old enough to drink as well. A decade later, we changed our minds again and hiked the legal drinking age back up to twenty-one, where it has been officially ever since.

I say "officially" because, given the number of times that we have flip flopped over the past century, we can't help but communicate the message that the number that we have settled on for the moment is arbitrary and likely to change. Colleges and universities' response to the back-and-forth is to simultaneously shake their fists at underage drinking and openly encourage drinking culture. Like every other college in the country, Rollins bans underage drinking and routinely sends sweepers through dorm rooms looking for contraband booze. Yet it also has a fully stocked pub in the basement of its student center.[23]

Rollins isn't the only college to boast a campus bar. Georgetown University has one too, as does the University of Southern California and the College of Wooster.[24] Many other campuses have pubs directly adjacent to them that are as old (or nearly as old) as the universities themselves. When the All-American Rathskeller at Penn State University opened as a beer garden in 1933, students were issued college meal tickets for food and beer; fast-forward about eighty years, and it's the oldest continuously operating bar in the state.[25] Oklahoma State partners with Stillwater's Eskimo Joe's bar. On football game days, one can rub shoulders both with the bar's mascots (a plucky Joe and his canine sidekick, Buffy) alongside the school's gunslinging cowboy mascot named Pistol Pete.[26] Until its closure in 2021, patrons at UC-Berkeley's Albatross could play board games, eat pizza, and otherwise relax and unwind. The bar self-consciously fashioned itself as an alternative student center by once calling itself a "community center that happens to sell alcohol."[27] As an aficionado of pub grub, I will be the first to confess that I am grateful for the presence of my college's on-campus beer garden. But in an era where colleges and universities prize inclusivity above nearly all other virtues, it also strikes me as strange that so many institutions would dedicate so many resources and space to an enterprise that legally can serve only about 25 percent of the traditional undergraduate population. Put another way, it is hard to imagine proposing the construction and maintenance of a classroom or other campus amenity that excludes 75 percent of the undergraduate student population from its use—that is, until you realize that many of these same institutions also house fraternities and sororities.

On-campus bars exist (and exist in abundance) in part because of a logic of resigned acceptance and appeal to perceptions of safety. Not all students drink, but if they are going to, proponents argue, then it's better and safer for them to do it on campus than off. There's also a component of social mentoring at play in the decision to build a bar on campus. When my colleagues talk about our campus bar, many of them portray it as a kind of classroom, a place where they can show of-age undergraduates how to drink responsibly by drinking with them. A third factor informing the decision to allow legal drinking on campus has to do with the role that culture and tradition play in the construction of institutional identity. Simply put, alcohol is, for better and worse, a legitimizing agent of membership within a collegiate community.

The extent to which alcohol informs and defines the American college experience is marked both by the extent to which it shows up where you expect it—at colleges known for their beer pong tournaments, "drinking weeks," and tradition of dressing up as Solo cups for Halloween—as well as its presence in places where it unequivocally doesn't belong, like my alma mater. Located in Provo, Utah, Mormon-run Brigham Young University (BYU) is known nationally for lots of things, but drinking is not one of them. For twenty-two years running, BYU has topped Princeton Review's list of "Stone-Cold Sober Schools," a title that this teetotaling university wears with tremendous pride.[28] Alcohol consumption is prohibited for members of the Mormon faith and thus is a blacklisted activity for all BYU students, with grounds of censure that run all the way up to expulsion if violated. The success of BYU's long-standing prohibition act is reflected in part by the dearth of drinking establishments in Provo, a phenomenon that was highlighted when University of Wisconsin football fans flooded the city in September 2017 to watch the Badgers square off against the Cougars and discovered—much to their confusion and horror—that the city of over 100,000 residents had only two licensed bars.[29]

Given the energy that Mormons put into avoiding both the consumption of alcohol and the appearance of being associated with it in any way, shape, or form, you can imagine my surprise when I recently sauntered into BYU's student center and discovered a full-fledged sports bar—or at least an establishment that masquerades as one. The Wall, as it's called, boasts lounge seating, nine big screen televisions, and a full stage where local bands perform live concerts on the weekends. All of these features circle the room's main attraction: a wrap-around bar with a glass-backed liquor shelf stocked with cocktail glasses and the ingredients that go into making the establishment's specialty house drinks, including Brigham's Brew, Cougar's Blood, and Y-Life.[30] No one raised an eyebrow when I ordered a round of the latter for me and my four underage kids because instead of vodka, gin, and tequila, all of this bar's mixed drinks are made with soda water and flavored syrup. If you visit the campus in October, the drink menu expands beyond faux highbrow cocktails to include chocolate milk. The university's annual "Milktoberfest," described in advertising materials as "the holiday where you do homework and drink milk," includes sanctioned binge drinking events hosted by the library, in which students are given free rein over an open chocolate milk bar.[31] One promotional video for the event features a woman surrounded by nine empty milk bottles. For a religious university whose unofficial mantra is to produce individuals who are "in the world, but not of it," the irony that is the Wall and Milktoberfest illuminates how even the staunchest opponent to collegiate drinking culture cannot conceive of a student social sphere that doesn't include at least the specter of alcohol.

The centrality of the bar to the field of social commerce on American college campuses illuminates how and why the fraternity house has held so much sway in the social life of college students. Legally barred from adult social milieus because of their age, under twenty-one college students find in the fraternity house both a holding pen and training ground for their social life after they are legal. In addition to developing and honing the definition of "fun," fraternity drinking culture also plays a critical role in the construction of white American masculinity. One can say that the fraternity member's drink of choice—domestic beer—is a racialized class marker in the sense that its most common brands—Coors, Budweiser, Michelob Ultra, and Miller Lite—have long been marketed to middle-class white Americans. According to sociologists Nathaniel Chapman and David Brunsma, the cheap beer of fraternity parties naturally serves as a kind of gateway drink to craft beer, a beverage associated closely in contemporary culture with college-educated white men with high incomes.[32]

As the unconscious nurseries of tap rooms and local microbreweries, fraternity parties play a pivotal role in constructing where white men drink and what they drink. Anointing eighteen-to-twenty-two-year-old men as the governors of collegiate social life also goes a long way in explaining how quickly it can get out of control. The clichéd portrait of fraternity life portrayed in the 1978 cult classic film *Animal House* may have been an exaggerated representation of real life, but according to the Fraternal Information and Programming Group, a risk-management organization formed in the late 1980s by national Greek leaders, the film didn't stretch the truth by all that much. The salient features of the fraternity experience thirty-odd years ago was defined by one member as "kegs, party balls, beer trucks with a dozen taps along the sides, kegerators, fifty-five-gallon drums filled with a mixture of liquor and Kool-Aid, ad infinitum."[33]

If the college fraternity solidifies alcohol as a requisite feature of American party culture, it also bequeaths and inherits the dangers that are linked to its overconsumption. The fraternity house didn't become a site of societal contempt because it is the locus of underage drinking. The haphazard way in which underage drinking is enforced on and off college campuses (i.e., the embarrassingly lenient sentencing for DUIs) means that as a society we don't really care all that much about this issue. Once you peel back the layers of the onion, you find that society's antifraternal attitude doesn't revolve around fraternity culture's promotion of underage drinking but does include a harsh condemnation of what some men who attend fraternity parties do to women when they are drunk.

Fictive Families and Sexual Assault

On a chilly fall morning in November 2014, Abby Honold donned maroon-and-gold-striped bibbed overalls and joined hundreds of other similarly clad classmates for a pre–football game tailgate party on the University of Minnesota's (UM) Greek row. The third-year elementary education major was drinking and socializing outside the Sigma Phi Epsilon house when a friend introduced her to one of the fraternity chapter's most prominent members: twenty-one-year-old senior Daniel Drill-Mellum. A few minutes after meeting, Daniel asked Abby for help. The party's alcohol supply was running dangerously low, and he needed assistance retrieving some reserves from his apartment, which was located across the street. Once inside the apartment, Drill-Mellum allegedly raped Honold twice, leaving claw marks on her body and bite marks on her breast. He had also shoved his fist so far into her mouth that he tore open part of her tongue.[34]

Less than two months later, two Stanford University graduate students were riding their bikes past the Kappa Alpha fraternity house late one night when they caught sight of Brock Turner, a first-year student and member of the school's swim team, lying on top of an unconscious woman.[35] When Chanel Miller woke up in the emergency room, she learned that Turner, who she had met at the fraternity party, had thrust his fingers into her vagina.[36] During the closing arguments of the trial that followed, the prosecutor showed a photo of Chanel shortly after the attack. In the photo, she is lying on a clump of pine needles, her clothing half off and her hair in wild disarray. She is passed out.

Journalists and academics long have been beating the same drum about the terrible things that can and do happen in and around fraternity houses.

However, the most recent data indicates that the most dangerous place on campus, statistically speaking, is not the fraternity house but the dorm room, followed by other residence halls and off-campus apartments.[37] Before fraternities start throwing themselves a ticker tape parade, however, it is important to remember that there is a mountain of evidence piled up against them. As many have shown, fraternity members aren't the only men committing sexual assaults on campus, but they are part of a community that actively fosters and promotes a version of rape *culture* where the fraternity house is allowed to be a place where men's desire is privileged over women's wishes.[38]

According to Jennifer S. Hirsch and Shamus Khan's 2020 landmark study of sex, power, and sexual assault on Columbia University's campus, sexual outcomes are intimately linked to the spaces and settings where they occur. For these researchers, space isn't just a backdrop or a stage, but "a central dimension of institutional power" and agent that actively influences behaviors and interactions[39] A fraternity man would never dream of putting his hands down the pants of a random girl he encounters sleeping on a library sofa, but he might make a different choice if he encountered the same woman sleeping in his bed or on his fraternity house couch. If Daniel Drill-Mellum embodies the gross entitlement of the fraternity man to lay claim to and take whatever he wants from anyone who enters his domain, Brock Turner, who wasn't a fraternity member, illustrates how that privilege is extended to any man who steps foot into a fraternity house.

Sorority women aren't stupid; they know that fraternity houses are places where unequal power relations make them inherently vulnerable. One would think that all the warning bells and red flags would galvanize the sorority community against fraternity rape culture. Indeed, in isolated incidents, this has happened. At UM, sorority women did band together— not to defend Abby Honold, but her assailant. There were lots of people, including many sorority women, who saw Abby running out of Drill-Mellum's apartment, crying and bleeding. They heard her call 911 and watched as an ambulance picked her up and took her to the hospital. Yet Abby told me that none of these women publicly came to her defense when other members of the campus fraternity and sorority community started calling her a liar, a slut, and worse. There are many reasons why sorority women don't stand up to fraternity sexual assault, but one of them is not that they don't believe that it doesn't happen. I haven't talked to the women who harassed Abby, so I don't know why they didn't believe her story, but one of the things I've learned from working with sorority women for so long is that many struggle to believe stories like Abby's because what happened to her isn't usually how it happens to them.

A more relatable story of sexual assault for sorority women involves a case that is currently making its way through California's legal system. Thanks to court records from Finn Wolff's preliminary hearing and the detailed reporting of Berkeleyside's Emilie Raguso, we have a fairly clear picture of what a UC-Berkeley sorority member (given the pseudonym Jane Doe in public records) says happened to her.

The eponymous Jane Doe and Finn were both first-year students and new members of their respective Greek letter organizations at the elite northern California university when they met for the first time on a harbor cruise date party sponsored by their organizations. Following tradition, older fraternity and sorority members set up their new members on blind dates. Jane noticed some red flags in Finn's behavior on the boat, but nothing that would give her any indication of what was to come. Once the boat returned to the dock, the party continued back at the Phi Psi house. Jane said that she and Finn were talking in a crowded room when he began trying to remove her dress.

She said that she was open to hooking up with him in part because to do anything else would be to break with the social script. "This is what you do, you hook up with your date after a date party," she testified. Had she refused, she said, "I don't know what people would have thought of me." The next thing she knew, the room was empty, and she and Finn were alone. Over the next two and a half hours, she claimed, Finn aggressively groped and grabbed her, despite her repeatedly telling him that he was hurting her, and she wanted him to take a different approach. Eventually, she relented to his persistent advances, saying, "I'll let you have sex with me if you stop hurting me," adding that her motivation for saying this stemmed from fatigue. "I felt like he would get what he wanted. . . . I just, at that point, wanted it to be over." They tried to have sex multiple times, but Finn was unable to maintain an erection. When they finally left the room, Jane reported there were male students sitting in the hallway outside. They clapped as she and Finn walked past them.[40]

One of the things that this case illustrates is that no matter how innocuous their packaging, fraternity parties are structurally designed to strip guests of their agency. As the party hosts, fraternity men decide how many people and of what gender attend their parties. They also determine what kind and how much alcohol is served and to whom. In addition, they often control the transportation to and from the venue.[41] In the case of formals (overnight prom-like date parties often held at hotels in cities several hours driving distance away), fraternity members cover all the previously mentioned expenses, plus the cost of the hotel room. Within this context, it's easy to see how some fraternity men expect women to feel grateful for the entertainment and alcohol provided to them and present sex as a form of entitlement, compensation, or kind of fair exchange.[42] Historian Moira Weigel calls the transactional nature of contemporary romance "a kind of prostitution complex."[43] Women may not be forcibly held down, but, like Jane, lots of sorority women are put into positions where they either feel like they can't say no, or don't know how to.[44]

What I am going to say next seems so simple and self-evident that it does not seem worth articulating: hookups don't have to end in sexual assault. Most of them don't. By allowing nonconsensual sexual encounters to stand as a possible casualty of fraternity party attendance, however, fraternities teach young women and men that they are a normal and expected component of hookup culture.[45]

If the fraternity community is guilty of allowing hookups to swim in the same water as rape and sexual assault even when they don't belong there, it is also guilty of violating the sacred bonds of family. This is, at least, the sentiment expressed by Finn's second accuser. Roughly eighteen months after Jane Doe 1 said she was assaulted by Finn, Jane Doe 2 was hanging out with Finn and some other friends at the fraternity man's house when she ended up alone on a balcony with him. According to this woman's preliminary hearing testimony, Finn pushed her into a corner and started touching and grabbing her. After repeatedly telling him that she wasn't interested, she finally pushed him away. That's when she said Finn punched her in the eye and side. "I felt like I was in a position that I wasn't going to escape," she told the courtroom. "I saw an enemy. I saw someone who wanted to hurt me." She then said that Finn grabbed her hair in his hands, forced her onto her knees, and forced her to perform oral sex on him. "I went into survival mode and just decided not to fight back," she said. After a few seconds, she said, she was able to push him away and crawl to the door that led into the house. Crying hysterically, she called a friend to pick her up. She told the judge: "I thought we were good friends. I didn't think he would put me in that situation."

One could write a whole book on this episode, and it's precisely because so many others have recently grappled with the subject at hand—consent—in such eloquent and nuanced ways that I'll focus my attention on Jane 2's reaction to the whole ordeal.[46] It is reasonable to assume that

Jane experienced a wide range of emotions as she sat on the stand and told her story of that night, but the one that bubbled to the surface and spilled out was betrayal. Specifically, Jane 2 never imagined Finn would sexually assault her because he was her ex-boyfriend's best friend and a member of her friend group. But by virtue of their shared affiliation with the Greek community and the rhetoric that goes along with it, Finn was more than just a friend—he was also a brother, and the fictive filial bonds of Greek letter membership dictate that fraternity and sorority members are supposed to help and protect one another because that's what families do.

The idea that the boundary between friend and family member can be blurred beyond distinction is one that carries so much allure because it is pitched to an audience that is primed to receive it. Offered up at a time in their lives when they are physically separated from their biological families, college students find in the sorority and fraternity community a kind of replacement family. As cognitive linguists George Lakoff and Mark Johnson and philosopher J. L. Austin collectively remind us, metaphors are not just words that describe concepts; they also construct them through their very articulation. Thus, calling someone a brother or sister invents a conceptual framework for viewing the relationship in this way.[47]

What makes this metaphor so powerful for those who take it seriously is also what makes it so dangerous. As rhetorician Leigh Ann Jones has shown in her recent analysis of fraternal vocabulary, "brotherhood" is a sweeping term that "tap[s] into cultural commonplaces that lack a precise meaning but carry great symbolic weight."[48] The vagueness of the term and its relatives—family, brother, sister, sibling—means that individuals must bring their own interpretations to bear, and that is where and why things get messy. Sorority women and fraternity men who take seriously the idea that their fictive siblings are their sisters and brothers also expect them to act like their biological ones. No family is perfect, of course, and even the closest of brothers and sisters occasionally take jabs at one another. However, they don't occasionally have casual sex with one another. The romantic relationship that currently exists between members of sororities and fraternities makes the metaphor of family not only highly flawed but also highly creepy. At the same time as the Greek letter community wants to broaden the parameters of what is acceptable for fictive sisters and brothers to do consensually with each together in the bedroom, it also wants to hold the line in its condemnation of sexual assault. Given that there is no justification for sexual assault, this strikes me as a reasonable request. However, one of the consequences of allowing fictive siblings to sleep with one other is that when things do go slightly or horribly awry, the metaphor of family becomes even more dysfunctional than it already is. While all forms of sexual assault are deplorable, the perversion and violation of the sacred tenets of family makes fraternity-on-sorority sexual assault a particularly heinous strain.

The tight-knit and interwoven social bonds between assailant and victim also make the decision on what to do after an assault incredibly complicated. Jane Doe 1 didn't know how to describe what happened to her until several months later when she was at a sorority workshop on sexual assault, and she finally had a name for it: rape. Instead of reporting the assault to the police or campus Title IX office, Jane decided that the best way to prevent Finn from striking again was to get him kicked out of his fraternity. It was only after failing to talk the chapter president into taking any action and learning about the existence of Jane Doe 2 that she reported the incident to authorities.

Jane Doe 1's attempt to handle things on her own isn't unique; it's the norm. A 2019 Association of American Universities survey found that fewer than 30 percent of the women who were assaulted by force (or when they were unable to consent) reported the incident or sought counseling help from their institutions. The top reasons women gave for not reporting their assault to authorities (respondents were allowed to select more than one response) include the decision to handle the situation themselves (48.8 percent); the belief that the incident wasn't serious enough to report (47.4 percent); the individual felt embarrassed, ashamed, or that it would be too emotionally difficult to report (41.7 percent); the individual didn't believe that support resources could help them (21.9 percent); and they didn't want to get the perpetrator in trouble (24.5 percent).[49]

Veering from the story of consensual sex causes problems beyond one's immediate social circle. The bigger risk is getting frozen out of the broader friend group. Casting a shadow over a particular hookup brings negative attention to the fraternity member as well as to the larger fraternity and sorority group of which the accused is a part. Sorority squads work hard to make a connection between groups, and no one wants to be the one to tear at its seams. Indeed, the price for those who do so is significant.[50]

After reporting her physical and sexual assault to the police, one of Jane Doe 2's friends texted her with the possible intention of trying to get her to change her narrative. When that didn't work, Jane said that her friend accused her of lying. Abby Honold, the woman who was brutally raped at the UM fraternity tailgate party, said that the same thing happened to her.

Hooking Up Hammered and High

Abby's assault coincided with the peak popularity of Yik Yak, a social media app that allows college students to send anonymous texts to all Yik Yak app users at that school. In the weeks and months following her rape, Abby said that people published her name and phone number on the app and called her a liar and worse.

In addition to these and other casual and sporadic forms of harassment, Abby said she also experienced more structured forms of harassment. After spending over eleven hours in the emergency room on the day she was raped, Abby reported that she returned home to discover a voicemail from a fraternity member friend that said, simply, "Answer your phone, ho." Abby assumed that her friend didn't know what had happened to her and was just trying to be funny. When she called the man back, it became very apparent that he was aware of the situation. "I was on speakerphone," she said, "and all of his friends were laughing and calling me a slut."

To add insult to injury, the white Greek letter organizations at UM allegedly banned her from attending any fraternity- and sorority-sponsored events. Friends who were members of these organizations were instructed to unfollow her on Instagram, she said, and not communicate with her because she was dubbed dangerous and a false accuser. Sorority members either refused to work with her on class-assigned group projects or gave her the silent treatment.

The fraternity and sorority community at UM allegedly turned its back on Abby and, in doing so, made her a pariah within her social group on campus. As is often the case, what the Greek letter organizations did to Abby wasn't directed out of any personal malice: they could and would have publicly hung up any woman in the town square. Stripping Abby of her good name and ostracizing her from her friend group was meant to serve as a clear warning to others: if you come after one of us, all of us will come after you.

"Why didn't sorority women stand up for you?" I asked. I was especially perplexed by the silence of those who were at the party when Abby was assaulted and saw her in its immediate aftermath. Abby paused and sighed. "The most insight I got from my sorority friends who still privately communicated with me," she said, "was that they would have lost everything—their friends, their house." What sorority members stood to lose seems trivial to those of us occupying the other side of young adulthood. Yet, for eighteen-to-twenty-two-year-olds, friendship not only is *an* important thing; it is often viewed as the *most* important thing.[51]

If, for a myriad of complex social reasons, reporting one's sexual assault isn't an option, the best choice left on the table is not to get yourself into a "bad situation" in the first place. Enter the buddy system.

Friends and Near-Rape Experiences

Gender violence and prevention expert Jackson Katz travels the country giving presentations about sexual assault to college students. He begins many of his sessions by drawing a line down the middle of a chalkboard and marking one side with the male symbol and the other with the female. Then he asks the men in the audience a simple question: "What steps do you guys take, on a daily basis, to prevent yourselves from being sexually assaulted?"[52] He stands at the board, chalk in hand, ready to document the responses—that don't come. After doing this exercise hundreds of times, Katz says that the reaction is the same: nervous laughter gives way to the admission that most men don't do anything to prevent themselves from being sexually assaulted. In fact, they don't even think about it.

Katz then turns to the women in the audience and asks them the same question: "What steps do you take on a daily basis to prevent yourselves from being sexually assaulted?" Hands shoot in the air, and Katz can't write fast enough. The list of some of the most frequent answers went viral on social media during the peak of the #MeToo movement in 2018: park in well-lit areas, carry mace or pepper spray, have an unlisted phone number, make sure you see your drink being poured, and "always go out in groups."[53]

In addition to illuminating the vast difference between how men and women approach the task of personal safety (literally nothing stacked up against a list of twenty or more), the exercise highlights the centrality of the buddy system to this strategy. The guiding premise is that there is safety in numbers. The rules of the buddy system are outlined in mandatory sexual assault and safety learning modules (requisite components of first-year student orientation) and preached everywhere online:

- "You are responsible for each other and can help make sure that the other is safe and gets home okay."[54]
- "Use a buddy system, have each other's backs, and never leave your friends alone."[55]
- "Be a Bitch. Even if a friend wants to hop into a car with a guy she just met, let her be mad at you. She'll thank you when she sobers up."[56]

Hooking Up Hammered and High

There are good reasons why the buddy system is so widely and enthusiastically endorsed. Campus sexual assault is a huge problem in America.[57] As others have pointed out, defining the contours of the problem beyond this sweeping statement is tricky, in part because the definitions of "sexual assault" and "rape" have multiplied, making it unclear sometimes exactly what we are talking about.

Of course, one of the easiest and most obvious ways to actively prevent sorority women from being sexually assaulted at and after fraternity parties—at least in theory—is to rove around in packs. As journalist John Hechinger notes, "For young women, the fraternity party has an unspoken set of rules: Stay with friends you trust, especially if you're drinking; beware the mystery punch in the cooler; watch as your new buddy, the friendly guy at the bar, pours you a drink; and never let that red Solo cup out of your sight to avoid 'date rape drugs,' often reported as slipped into drinks, though rarely proven."[58]

Testimonies of buddy system success stories abound within the sorority community and become urban legends that are held up in their telling and retelling as examples of paradigmatic sisterhood in action. While there is lots of literature about how sorority women are victimized, there isn't much in the way of how saving sisters from a dangerous situation serves as a bonding mechanism. Just as women are the historic enemies to college men—their sudden arrival served as a catalyst for men's bonding—fraternity rape culture gives sorority women a common adversary. In the next section, we will see how the social bond formed between sorority sisters isn't contingent upon the buddy system working. It also works just as well, and maybe even better, when it fails.

When the Buddy System Breaks Down

Victoria's twenty-first birthday fell on a Sunday. The celebration kicked off around eight on Saturday night at a local bar with Victoria paying her last respects to her fake ID, which had served her well during her first two and half years of college. By ten, she and her crew of five sorority sisters were back at the sorority house to touch up their makeup and take a few more rounds before heading out for the evening. By the time that the clock struck midnight, Victoria was, by her own admission, well on her way to becoming blackout drunk. The group spent the next few hours bar hopping around historic Church Street, Orlando's nightlife district. Sporting a glittery birthday crown and "birthday girl" sash for the special occasion, Victoria was treated to free drinks and copious amounts of flirting by other bar patrons.

When the bar closed, Victoria's friends called an Uber. Victoria was deep in conversation with a handsome man she didn't know—a guy in his mid-twenties—and eager to take him up on the invitation to continue the festivities at another bar across the street. Her friends pulled her aside and told her gently, and then, when she resisted, more forcefully, that it was time to go home, and that she was coming with them. They proposed a compromise: Victoria could get the man's number and text him when she sobered up.

Additional pressure was put on the negotiations when the Uber arrived. Victoria's sorority sisters dragged her outside and insisted that she get in the car. Victoria got upset and told them that she was an adult and that she could do what she wanted. The word "bitch" was flung back and forth. The Uber driver gave the women a thirty-second warning. Victoria waved them off. The man assured the women that Victoria would be fine. He was a college graduate and had a good job. He said that he had sisters and was raised to respect women. He swore that he would have Victoria back at the sorority house within an hour. Victoria's sorority sisters got into the Uber, reluctantly. The next morning, Victoria woke up in a strange bed, naked from the waist down.

I know all of this because Victoria showed up to my class five hours later visibly teary-eyed. I pulled her into my office right afterward and asked her what was up. There was lots going through her mind at that moment, and none of the thoughts were good. In the hours and days that followed—which included visits to the Title IX office, the school's counseling center, local police station, and sexual assault student support group—Victoria was understandably looking for someone to blame. Everyone had some culpability, she reasoned. The man shouldn't have taken advantage of her (her terms at the time). She shouldn't have left the bar with him. Her sorority sisters shouldn't have left her. Over time, the amount of blame placed on each party shifted. In the immediate aftermath of the incident, however, Victoria directed the overwhelming bulk of her rage toward her friends.

Victoria's instinctive reaction—to harbor more anger toward her friends than the assailant—isn't just an isolated case but is reflective of nearly every case that has walked through my door over the past decade. Cassidy had the same response to what she euphemistically called her "bad night." Early one morning, she texted me this: "I had sex last night but was too drunk to consent/don't remember it. No condom. I'm so upset." The night before,

Cassidy reported, she went to dinner with her sorority sister named Rachel and the woman's regular hookup partner. To Cassidy's surprise, the couple showed up at the restaurant accompanied by the man's cousin. The cousin attended a large public university in the Northeast and was visiting for the weekend. The group drank their way through dinner and afterward went back to Rachel's apartment. Walking into her friend's house was the last thing that Cassidy remembered about the evening—a petite brunette who weighs all of a hundred pounds, it didn't take much to get her drunk. The rest of the night's events were filled in by Rachel. Evidently, the group continued drinking. At some point, Cassidy went into Rachel's bedroom to change her clothes, and the cousin followed her. She woke up the next morning with a throbbing and swollen vagina.

"Girl I was with is a fucking idiot," she told me via text. "I called her this morning & [was] like WHY DIDNT U STOP THIS & she's like 'you weren't acting drunk at all.'"

Rachel elaborated that before Cassidy announced that she was going to change, she had been sitting on the sofa "more or less comatose" while the man kissed her. "I'm like Rachel 1. That is weird as fuck 2. Why didn't u do ANYTHING. Like it isn't her responsibility but when any of my friends have been drinking. I ALWAYS make sure that they want to do what they're doing."

Holding one's friends in any way responsible for one's sexual assault follows a logic that at first glance seems ludicrous. But there is a method to the madness. Casting blame on one's friends sets in motion a choreographed sequence of exchanges that culminates in the performance or genuine feeling of guilt and a formal apology. The process is initiated by an angry early morning phone call (Cassidy) or group text (Victoria). After the friends explain their side of the story, the sexual assault victims articulate their grievances, accuse their sorority sisters of being "shitty friends," and demonstrate via a tearful in-person breakdown or digital silent treatment that their inaction inflicted serious harm. The reconciliation process consists of a flood of apology texts, interventions from other sorority sisters who testify that the friends' guilt and shame is genuine, tears, and begging for forgiveness.

One of the reasons why this pageantry garners such appeal for college-aged women is because it has a predictable and prescribed outcome, one that contrasts wildly with what they encounter after they report the assault to the Title IX office and police. The history of sexual assault reporting in our nation sends a clear message that the judicial process doesn't usually ameliorate feelings of shame but rather exacerbates them. We need only look at the outcomes of recent campus assault cases as representative illustrations. Brock Turner, the Stanford first-year student who was convicted of assaulting Chanel Miller outside a fraternity house, faced up to six years in prison, but was sentenced to a paltry six months and released after three.[59] In 2016, a Baylor student known in court records as Donna Doe drank some punch at a fraternity party and immediately began to feel woozy. That's when the chapter president, Jacob Walter Anderson, allegedly took the woman to the backyard and raped her. He received a $400 fine and deferred probation.[60]

While the justice system is predictably unpredictable in its meting out of punishments, sorority sisters are socially contracted to provide the sexual assault victim with what her assailant or the machinery of the broader community and legal support system likely will not ever offer: an unconditional admission of guilt and a heartfelt apology.

This ritual of blaming and forgiveness plays a pivotal role in how sorority women perceive sexual assault, and what they do about it. Hirsch and Khan reported similar coping strategies in their research.[61] Many young adults care about their friends more than just about any other individual or entity. For lots of eighteen-to-twenty-two-year-olds, the size of the tear in a relationship of such importance constitutes an emergency more pressing than just about anything else—including reporting the assault to the police or the campus Title IX office. The apology and "closure" that individuals receive from their sorority sisters negates, in their minds, the need to report the assault to the police or Title IX office. After much prodding and encouragement from multiple individuals, Victoria reluctantly reported her assault to the local police and Title IX office but refused to press charges. Based on my experience, Cassidy's course of action was more typical: she initially agreed to go to a local rape crisis center but changed her mind after her friend apologized. She refused to contact the police and turned down the school's free counseling and Title IX services.

From the perspective of a sorority advisor and college professor who cares deeply about the physical and emotional safety of all my students, there is another hidden peril of being part of a community that puts the buddy system on such a high pedestal: namely, it's a model of risk management that in certain circumstances is set up to fail. The first semester of college is called the "red zone" in higher education lingo because of the inherent dangers that often accompany choices made by teenagers with newly acquired freedom. Holding sorority recruitment before the start of the academic year serves as an indirect strategy of mitigating the risks of binge drinking

Hooking Up Hammered and High

and sexual assault by providing incoming first-year students with built-in buddy systems in the form of pledge classes. But because pledge classes are comprised of women who are the same age and, thus, have similar life experience, it's less of a follow-the-leader model of risk management than an instance of the blind leading the blind.

The rhetoric of sisterhood compounds the danger to new sorority women by portraying group members as intimate when they are really strangers. Even though a sorority woman is told that her fictive family members will care for and protect her with the same passion and vigilance as the parents, siblings, and extended kinship group with whom she was raised, it doesn't mean that these individuals are equipped to keep that promise. Simply being a teenager with all its inherent cognitive limitations and deficiencies (immaturity and impulsivity being chief among them) is one obstacle. Another is technology. Many college campuses have bars within easy walking distance. For those that don't, ridesharing apps have made getting to and from parties infinitely more convenient and much safer, but they also have profoundly changed the dynamics of the buddy system. In the past, one person in the group had to stay sober because she had to drive the group home. Now that the burden of transportation has been lifted (or, in the case of campuses with an adjacent bar scene, never existed in the first place), the designated "sober sister" is something of a misnomer, as it often refers to the woman who is on the spectrum of intoxication but just less drunk than the friends she is supposed to be monitoring.

Despite having the deck stacked against its success, the fictive family unit not only persists but also serves as the nucleus of the sorority same-sex relationship model. Blurring the line between friend and family has lots of benefits, but within the context of sexual violence within the sorority community, the culture and vocabulary of sisterhood reframes sexual assault from a violation of a woman's body to the violation of a friendship code that resulted in the violation of a woman's body. The distinction is as important as it is horrifying. In this formulation, the sorority sister (not the male assailant) is charged with causing the bigger hurt.

While the ideology and rhetoric of fraternity and sorority culture makes this logic possible, hookup culture portrays it as normal. As sociologist Lisa Wade persuasively argues in *American Hookup*, collegiate hookup culture makes the argument that sex is meaningless. "In this topsy-turvy world," she writes, "you have sex with people you don't like and don't have sex with people you do."[62] Intimacy is reserved for individuals with whom sex is delayed or, by extension, don't have it at all. Platonic women friends fall into the latter category. If sexless relationships are the most prized form of human relations, then the betrayals made by platonic same-sex friends are those that cut the deepest. This goes a long way in explaining why the ritual of joining a sorority models itself after courtship and marriage.

FOUR

Going After Girls

. . . .

It was ten degrees above freezing, but, thanks to the blistering wind chill, it felt about ten below. Despite being bundled up in a winter jacket, scarf, and gloves, my nose was running like a faucet, and half of my extremities were numb. As cold and uncomfortable as I was at the moment, I couldn't imagine how *they* were feeling. By *they*, I mean the roughly 550 potential new sorority members (PNMs) around me who were shivering in miniskirts and sleeveless dresses whose hemlines barely skimmed their buttocks. Women who normally wouldn't be budging from their beds for another four hours (the spring 2016 semester wasn't scheduled to start until the following week) looked like they had been getting ready for at least that amount of time. Hair curled, coifed, and otherwise shellacked into place? Check. Sticky bra and Spanx in working order? Sunless tanner and makeup evenly applied? Double check.

Welcome to sorority recruitment at Southern Methodist University (SMU). The women were divided into groups and lined up single file outside one of the university's eight sorority houses, waiting for the mansions' doors to open. Contrary to popular culture's portrayal of sorority recruitment—which often is reduced to a snapshot of this moment—joining a sorority involves more than just standing around looking pretty. In order to join a National Panhellenic Conference (NPC) sorority, women at most colleges and universities must go through a grueling multiday boot camp comprised of open houses, philanthropy presentations, meet and greets, and dry cocktail hours.

And those are just the events that are formally recognized and sanctioned. As a 2021 *Fortune* article illustrates, the process of joining a sorority for many women in the South begins at the same time as they are putting the finishing touches on their college applications.[1] Throughout their last year of high school, many PNMs begin conducting research on the sorority chapters located on their college campuses of choice. In addition to perusing official sorority websites and following individual chapters and their members on social media, PNMs pore over sorority blogs and message boards and watch individual chapters' professionally made recruitment videos on YouTube. In the spring or summer before they enroll in college, they put together a recruitment packet, which includes a résumé, tailored cover letter, standardized test scores, an academic transcript, and three photos: a head shot, full body, and three-quarter view. Copies of this packet are sent to local alumnae or alumnae boards of each sorority. After reviewing the packets, these women interview PNMs and write them letters of recommendation. The most dedicated PNMs go as far as to enlist the help of professional recruitment coaches. In addition to helping sorority hopefuls compile their recruitment materials, these hybrid guidance counselors/beauty pageant consultants help women pick out their outfits and advise them on what to do and say during recruitment.

In many cases, the conversations that PNMs and sorority women have during recruitment week are unnecessary because the sorority women already have conducted CIA-like reconnaissance missions on PNMs. In addition to studying the social media accounts of incoming first-year students, sorority women attending schools with deferred recruitment (i.e., that which takes place after the start of the school year) also compile extensive field notes on the sorority hopefuls whom they encounter in class or at parties, clubs, and other off-campus hangouts.

In the weeks leading up to SMU's sorority recruitment, which takes place during the school break in between the fall and spring semesters, each sorority gathers its members together for a marathon "PNM review meeting." I didn't have the opportunity to shadow any such meetings at SMU, but I was able to sit in on two chapters' review meetings at another institution. In both meetings, each PNM's headshot, biographical information, and GPA was displayed in sequence on a large overhead screen. After providing a quick summary introduction of the profiled PNM (i.e., "This is Mary. She's from Atlanta and is planning to major in anthropology. She has a 3.7 GPA and was on student government in high school"), the chapter's women were asked to provide positive and negative feedback on the individual. One of the chapters that I observed (Sorority A) solicited such commentary privately from each member via an online survey app; the other (Sorority B) invited women to vocalize their views of PNMs publicly in the chapter room. The rules of engagement were supposed to be clear cut—firsthand observations about how PNMs conducted themselves in class, in social settings, or on social media were welcome; rumor and hearsay were not. In practice, things were fuzzier. A PNM was given a low ranking for allegedly hooking up with sorority members' ex-hookup partners, for being a sloppy drunk, or for having a reputation of "being a bitch."

After the chapter members had the opportunity to offer feedback on each PNM, a small group of sorority women met to review the chapter members' assessments of the PNMs, weighed this information against chapter recruitment goals (i.e., Sorority A was looking to boost its overall GPA and thus privileged PNM GPAs over anything else; Sorority B had an eagle eye out for past leadership experience) and then used this information to compile a provisional list of desirable PNMs on which they would focus their recruitment energies. While I witnessed sororities using qualitative measures to determine PNMs' initial rankings—without debate, Sorority A put a conventionally beautiful woman with a low GPA at the bottom of their list—sorority recruitment teams also didn't hesitate to downgrade a PNM because an existing woman in the chapter had an unspecified "issue" with her. "It's definitely not fair," a member of the chapter's sorority recruitment team told me. "But we aren't going to invite drama into the house. Our loyalty will always lie with a sister over a PNM."

In addition to assessing the pool of PNMs, sorority chapters spend months planning for recruitment week itself. This process begins with the election of a vice president of recruitment. This woman is charged with the combined tasks of working out the logistics of the week's events and conducting dozens of prerecruitment practice sessions, where current sorority members are taught songs, chants, and dance routines; hone their conversational skill sets; and clarify and edit their recruitment wardrobes. A sizeable portion of every sorority's operating budget is dedicated to the production of recruitment-related decorations, props, videos, food, and party favors. Katie Buenneke, a former vice president of recruitment at the University of Southern California, wrote in the *Atlantic* that her recruitment budget was capped at $15,000, but confessed that "many, if not most houses spend far more than that—and conveniently forget to report their actual expenses to the campus Panhellenic."[2]

If joining a sorority seems like a big deal, it is. From the outside looking in, it's hard not to be struck by the fact that many college students invest way more time, money, and energy choosing friends than sexual partners. In addition to the obvious question—why is this the case?—standing in the midst of 550 scantily clad, half-frozen sorority PNMs raised a related one: Why in the world were they dressed like that in such cold weather? Science and common sense offer up an answer to both. Viewed from the lens of evolutionary biology, the women were wearing things and doing things that in mixed company would signal their desire to mate.[3] While sorority recruitment isn't an *Animal Planet* special, and these ladies weren't dressed up to garner the attention of men, they were braving the elements and risking frostbite to impress more coveted and often longer-lasting partners: other women.

The Homoerotics of Sorority Recruitment: A Case Study

SMU was founded in the early twentieth century as a joint collective by Dallas civic leaders and the Methodist Church with the intent of turning what was then a rural prairie outpost into a modern metropolis with industry and amenities to rival that of big cities on the East Coast.[4] Modern architects and designers kept the colonial-meets-frontier aesthetic going when they paired SMU's campus buildings—which are modeled after Ivy League campus architecture—with a statue portraying a trio of stampeding mustangs. Wander onto the campus on any given day and you will feel like you have been dropped into the middle of a Fourth of July parade: everyone, it seems, is wearing some combination of the school's official colors (red, white, and blue). Stick around long enough to enjoy the community tailgate party thrown for every home football game (a tradition called "boulevarding") and you'll encounter thousands of cowboy-boot-wearing SMU students sipping beer and spiked lemonade, grilling up burgers, and playing beanbag toss games from the back of pickup trucks and the trunks of BMWs.

Given the self-consciousness with which SMU blurs the distinction between school spirit and national pride, it is both natural and expected that the university should be home to the most quintessential of American collegial student groups. Greek letter organizations have long served as the nucleus of SMU's social scene, a fact that consistently earns the university a place in the yearly rankings of the best schools for Greek life.[5] Sororities and fraternities don't just live large in ethos at SMU; they have a significant numeric presence as well. According to a 2015 *U.S. News* survey, about 12 percent of female college students nationwide were members of sororities.[6] By contrast, roughly 43 percent of SMU students are members of Greek organizations.[7] Peruse the archives of the SMU student newspaper from the 1930s and 1940s and you will be assaulted with advertisements for recruitment clothing, Greek letter merchandise, tuxedo rentals, and "sorority specials."[8] After taking the pulse of the campus during my visits in 2016 and 2017, it seems like not much had changed. "It's possible to have a social life without being in a Greek letter organization," one sorority woman told me. "But you have to work at it." The prominence and pervasiveness of Greek culture is so strong that even students who consciously steer clear of the entire fraternity and sorority community are defined by their relationship to it. At SMU, you are either a member of a sorority or fraternity, or you are a "GDI," slang for "God Damn Independent."

SMU is home to one of the most storied Greek letter communities in the country, but also one of the most controversial. In the late 1970s and early 1980s, SMU rose to national prominence when it became a cast member of the cult primetime soap opera *Dallas*. In addition to filming several scenes on the campus, one of the show's main characters, Lucy Ewing, was a SMU student. Rebellious, promiscuous, and filthy rich, Ewing served as a fictive embodiment of oil-rich Texas—and, by extension, the United States—in the booming economy that was the early years of the Reagan administration. In addition to serving as a symbol of economic excess, the blonde-haired, blue-eyed, boy-crazy Ewing also helped construct popular culture's stereotype of the gorgeous but vapid southern sorority girl.

The legacy of *Dallas* is that it turned SMU into a representative of the typical American university. The nation was keeping weekly tabs on SMU's social scene via their television sets when the university seemingly confirmed that everything being played out in *Dallas* episodes was modeled on real life. In 1987, the tabloids hit pay dirt when word of a school scandal came to light that involved society's three favorite guilty obsessions: sorority women, football players, and prostitution. "Ponytail Gate," as it was dubbed by the media, revolved around lurid reports that SMU sorority women were paid by university boosters to seduce and have sex with football recruits.[9]

SMU was still struggling to recover from one sorority public relations nightmare, when, in the mid-2000s, it found itself mired in another. Sorority and fraternity recruitment activities aren't open to the public, which is why a twenty-something investigative journalist named Alexandra Robbins decided to go undercover to get the inside scoop.[10] Robbins spent part of a year at an unnamed university (which was quickly outed as SMU) posing as a student. While Robbins didn't officially join a sorority, she did socialize a lot with sorority women. Her published account of what went on behind the scenes at sorority recruitment and in the months afterward—much of which she gleaned from thirdhand accounts—is less than flattering. And that's putting it mildly. According to her exposé *Pledged: The Secret Life of Sororities*, the typical sorority house at SMU circa 2004 was a veritable house of horrors.[11] In addition to harboring a generalized attitude of self-entitlement and privilege, the sorority women with whom Robbins engaged spent the bulk of their time either orchestrating petty acts of cruelty against their sisters or plotting acts of revenge against them. Body- and slut-shaming were facts of daily life in the sorority house, as were catfights, verbal spats, and squabbles over men.

While Robbins has been accused of cherry-picking her anecdotes to portray sorority life as being one-dimensional, one thing is undisputable: after its publication, *Pledged* became the public narrative about contemporary fraternity and sorority life (FSL) culture in America. In a 2015 interview with the *Wall Street Journal*, Robbins argued that fraternities "represent a dominant and dangerous social culture that needs to be removed from universities."[12] The same year, Robbins published an article in *Marie Claire* in which she asserted that not only had nothing of substance changed in sorority culture since her publication of *Pledged* a decade earlier, but it actually had gotten much worse.[13]

Given that the media-appointed spokesperson for the fraternity and sorority community in America wrote a damning exposé about it, it wasn't shocking to discover that sororities and fraternities are leery of people who want to watch them in action. Following the fallout caused by the release of *Pledged*, the NPC battened down its hatches. The primary strategy for dealing with journalists and academics who wanted to examine fraternities and sororities with a critical eye was simply to not engage with them.

I arrived onto the scene just as the national Greek letter community was beginning to question whether a book written when current sorority members were in preschool should still be speaking for them. While individual organizations were starting to see the media as a partner instead of an enemy, some of the schools where they operate were eager to push this relationship along. SMU is one of them. In the years since *Pledged* was published, the university revamped its sorority and fraternity recruitment processes, upped its level of institutional oversight of Greek letter organizations, and instituted more serious punishments for violators of the community's code of conduct. While SMU's current FSL community isn't perfect by any means, it doesn't have anything to hide either.

In an unprecedented move, the campus administration at the time granted me full access to SMU's sorority recruitment. I could move around the campus freely and initiate a conversation with anyone during the multiday event, with one exception. To preserve PNMs' privacy and reduce the stress caused by journalistic surveillance, I was allowed to observe sorority recruits, but I couldn't talk to or directly engage with any of them. I could, however, pester the next best thing: the group of upper-class sorority women who volunteered to serve as the PNMs' mentors. In addition to shuttling their charges between sorority houses, these so-called Rho Gamma recruitment counselors were tasked with providing emotional support to PNMs throughout the week. A tall blonde with a nametag that read "Kelsey" caught me watching her from the check-in desk. "Are you a PNM's mom?" she asked suspiciously. Her two coleaders—Jo, a business major from New York City, and Madyson, a biology major from Atlanta—made similar assumptions. Unlike Alexandra Robbins, I couldn't go incognito at SMU even if I tried.

All three women volunteered to be recruitment counselors because they loved being in a sorority, but also because they wanted to be on the front lines of diversifying its population to include more women of color. While playing the part of a contestant on the friendship version of *The Bachelor* feels familiar for members of their generation, it doesn't mean that they have to like it. Privately, Jo didn't pull any punches in her evaluation of the sorority recruitment process, likening it to a form of first-world torture. In conversations with her charges, however, Jo and her co-counselors were more diplomatic in their critique of the ritual, calling it something that "you just have to get through" and reasserting over and over—as they took attendance, marched their charges over to Greek row, lined them up alphabetically in front of the first sorority house they would visit, and then took attendance again—that what you experience during recruitment is not reflective of what membership in a sorority is actually like.

These were comforting words but also necessary ones, given what happened next. After the eight rotation groups were lined up outside each of the eight sorority houses (two rotation groups sit out each round), a recruitment counselor from each group approached the house in front of her and, on cue, knocked on the front door. In unison, each sorority responded by swinging open their door to reveal a mass of sorority members wearing matching outfits and sporting professional manicures and blowouts.

The women in front of the Kappa Kappa Gamma house poured onto the front porch and packed the doorway while they performed the traditional sorority greeting to their guests: a synchronized chant. Like their generic relatives (the campfire song and high school cheerleader cheer) these chants are meant to be accompanied by clapping, foot stomping, hip wiggling, and other simple dance moves:

Hoo-rah for Kappa,
Hoo-rah for Kappa,
Someone in the house say, "Hoo-rah for Kappa."
1-2-3-4.
Kappa! That's hoo-rah, rah, rah.

The spectacle was both overwhelming and, just as Jo, Kelsey, and Madyson predicted, awkward. Fortunately, the women had coached their PNMs in advance on how to respond ("Stand there and smile until your mouth hurts even if inside you are like, 'What the fuck?'"). After several rounds of chanting, sorority women peeled off from the mass, linked arms with PNMs, and led them inside the house. Kelsey nudged me forward with her elbow. "Quick! Go!" I fell in line behind the last PNM and slipped inside just before the front door to the sorority mansion latched shut.

The song-and-dance routine that took place outside of the sorority house was a teaser for the dramatic performance that the sorority women would perform for the PNMs later in the week. The interaction that took place between the groups at the beginning of recruitment, however, assumed the form of a social practice that was equally choreographed: speed dating. Designed to introduce individuals to large numbers of potential romantic partners in a short period of time, speed dating takes seriously the results of a 2005 University of Pennsylvania study that found that most individuals determine their level of romantic interest in others within three seconds of meeting.[14] Speed dating events give people a little more time to pass judgment on potential partners—but not much. The structure of speed dating events varies, but generally include some form of round-robin pairing system, where participants engage in a brief three-to-five-minute conversation before switching partners. At the end of the event, the participants formulate lists of people with whom they would like to meet up with again and for a longer period. If there is a match, contact information is exchanged.

In the sorority recruitment version of speed dating, male suitors are replaced with all-women "bump groups." After leading a PNM into the chapter house, a small group of sorority women ask hopefuls the same list of questions that one would expect to encounter on a blind date: Where are you from? What is your major and what do you hope to do with it? What are your hobbies, talents, and interests? After about five minutes, two or three other sorority women join the conversation, and the PNM's initial conversation partner rotates out of the group and joins another.

In the same way that participants rate and rank their "dates" at the end of speed dating events, sorority members and PNMs do the same. To curtail the effects of peer pressure and group think, PNMs rank the chapters immediately after the last event of the day and without consulting with anyone other than their recruitment counselor. On the sorority side, decisions about who to invite back to the house each day are made collectively and are sometimes the product of heated discussion and debate.

Once the PNMs and sororities both have submitted their rankings and preferences, a complicated computer algorithm developed by the Massachusetts Institute of Technology plays matchmaker.[15] The system is devised to maximize inclusivity: PNMs may not get invited back to their first-choice house, but historically speaking, 98 percent of women who complete the entire recruitment process at SMU will get a bid from at least one organization.[16]

Just as the first day of sorority recruitment closely mirrors the form and structure of a speed date, the awkward middle stage that follows is where both parties simultaneously try to impress the other while knowing that their relationship isn't exclusive, and both are seeing other people. At SMU, the PNMs' time in the chapter house on the second day was split between learning about the sorority's philanthropic partner and more bump group rotations. By the third day, the rotation groups had dwindled in size (thanks to two rounds of cuts), and the number of PNMs visiting each house was noticeably smaller. At this point, all the PNMs still visiting a specific chapter were women whom the organization would be delighted to have as members. And so, with the supply and demand scale tipped in the opposite direction, the sorority's attention shifted from weeding out PNMs in whom they aren't interested to trying to keep hold of the ones they have ranked the highest. For generations, the standard mechanism by which individual chapters made the case for their exceptionalism was a twenty-minute-long themed skit. My visit to SMU coincided with the last year that the skit was included in the recruitment process. The NPC eliminated the skit from the recruitment event calendar starting in the fall of 2016 because they were laborious to produce and their function largely had been replaced by the skit's digital heir, otherwise known as the sorority recruitment video.

Porn for White First-Year College Women

Initially produced by tech-savvy sorority members on personal laptops, the sorority recruitment video is now a media genre in its own right. Set to music and filmed by Go-Pros, drones, and professional film crews, the most extravagant version of these productions could, according to *Teen Vogue*, pass for a slick EDM music video.[17] The specimen produced by the University of Miami's Delta Gamma chapter in 2016 went viral in part because of what *Elle* estimated to be its production cost: a whopping $200,000–$400,000.[18] The three-minute commercial—typically released a few months before recruitment—features members of its chapter sunbathing on the deck of a massive yacht, cruising around the harbor on a luxury sailboat, and frolicking around the grounds of a beachfront resort. Coming in second in The Cut's snarky "Sorority Recruitment Video Olympics" was Arizona State's equally extravagant Alpha Phi video, which features sorority women dressed in athleisure wear riding through stunning red rock canyons in off-road Jeeps, soaring above the campus in a hot air balloon, and flying around in a helicopter.[19] If the trend in outrageous, over-the-top sorority videos continues to grow (and by all accounts it will), commentators jokingly predict a future for this genre that includes "Oscar-worthy performances" and "Michael Bay–esque levels of production."[20]

While sorority videos make headlines in the mainstream media in part for their portrayal of sorority life as a wealthy white woman's paradise, they make the rounds on the straight men's media circuit for a different reason.[21] Many men's magazines talk about the videos as if they are trailers to soft core porn flicks. A pair of 2016 and 2017 sorority video-themed feature articles in *Maxim* found titillating not only the abundance of women but also what these women were wearing and doing: prancing on the beach in thong bikinis (or splashing each other in the campus water fountain if a body of open water was not available), dancing with each other in sundresses (and, in the case of Alpha Phi's University of Southern California chapter, cheerleading skirts), and jumping, running, or doing other physical activities in cutoff shorts, tank tops, and skin-tight yoga pants.[22]

It's no accident that many straight men find sorority recruitment videos to be sexy and provocative, as sororities themselves admit that they are made to be that way. Critics raise valid points about the seemingly backward self-portrayal, with one going as far as to claim that Alabama's video was "worse for women than Donald Trump."[23] However, in focusing on the ways in which the videos cater to straight men's desire and reinforce sexist and racist stereotypes, they run the risk of failing to consider that the ways in which the videos are mobilized by sororities make the opposite also true: that the sorority video's titillation of men isn't the primary objective of the video but rather is a tool used to lure and attract women. The University of Alabama's 2015 Alpha Phi recruitment video was viewed over a half a million times in the first week of its release, and that was before it was unwittingly vaunted into the national spotlight.[24] The video circulated all over social media but attracted the particular attention of men's websites and blogs. The popularity of this video among straight men serves as a twisted but effective way of proving to PNMs that the members of this organization know how to attract the attention of an increasingly scarce commodity, and are effective at doing it.

Beyond serving as a marketing tool used by sorority women to make the case that they have privileged access to men, women's sexuality also does double duty as an effective strategy to seduce other women. This is at least what is possible to read between the lines in the response given by the University of Arizona's Alpha Phi chapter to the negative backlash it received from its recruitment video. In a letter to *Arizona Republic* reporter Kaila White, then executive director of the Alpha Phi International Fraternity Linda Kahangi wrote, "The chapter's marketing team, all college undergraduates, planned and produced the video using their own market research on what would appeal to incoming freshman women."[25] Stephanie Petit, an alumna sorority member and reporter for College Candy, echoes this claim about the University of Alabama video:

> Let's think of the audience to this video. It wasn't meant to be seen by 50-year-old men who have nothing better to do than look at sorority videos on YouTube. It was meant for potential new members (PNMs) thinking about joining their sorority. When you are 18 years old and entering college, you're looking for a social life as well as an educational experience. Who would want to watch a five-minute video of a bunch of girls studying in the library or sitting in class? What the PNMs will think when they watch this video is not "Wow, these girls don't do anything of substance." They will see a group of women who love to spend time together and can have a good laugh (even when they've probably been filming this video for hours).[26]

A 2021 study of the 100 most-viewed NPC sorority recruitment videos in 2017 similarly observed that these videos willfully exclude the "business side" of sorority membership, such as required chapter meetings, committee work, and philanthropic and community service, in the interest of promoting a perception that sororities are playgrounds for conventionally attractive, privileged white women.[27] If sorority recruitment videos are, as critics argue, a fantasy of the sorority experience, then that experience is characterized as being exceptionally touchy-feely and highly erotic.

The hokey, low-budget version of the sorority recruitment video—the sorority skit—dramatized this in striking ways. Like its high-tech offspring, the sorority skits that I viewed at SMU were designed for and by women. The overarching claim made by the performances was that sororities can fulfill all their members' social needs, especially those typically provided by men. Chi Omega's skit explicitly drew attention to the shallow dating pool on the 40:60 campus, arguing (via sorority members who pranced around the stage in hoodies, saggy pants, fake mustaches, and fanny packs) that sorority women serve as surrogates for absent or undesirable men. Delta Gamma's skit elaborated on what a single-sex social life would look like via a song and dance routine where sorority women promised PNMs that they all would have a good time together whether they "go out or stay in, watching *Frozen*, or just hanging out."

In addition to presenting themselves as viable replacements for men, the performers in SMU's sorority skits also treated PNMs as if they were men. Specifically, they employed the same tools and strategies of seduction with women that they use to attract and seduce members of the opposite sex. The members of Pi Phi greeted their PNMs at the door wearing slinky iridescent angel costumes and halos. Their skit ended with half a dozen costumed angels (inexplicably) roller skating around the stage while singing a lyrically altered version of the 80s J. Geils Band pop song made famous by the refrain "My angel is the centerfold." The sorority members not on wheels sang along and gyrated their hips in the corner. Kappa Kappa Gamma's skit was a play on *The Wizard of Oz*, with the sorority playing the part of the home that Dorothy was trying to find. The G-rated plotline took a decidedly erotic turn, however, when the woman playing Dorothy pranced on stage in a skintight "sexy Dorothy" Halloween costume. Her attire paved the way for Glinda the Good Witch to show up wearing a sequined minidress. Instead of running into a lion, scarecrow, and tin man on the yellow brick road, Dorothy encountered two cowgirls wearing cutoff denim shorts and plaid shirts tied up around their exposed bellies. As it turned out, the cowgirls preferred giving lap dances to women in the audience over trekking toward Oz.

Sorority recruitment videos and skits unabashedly masquerade as kinds of foreplay in which women signal their desire to enter into platonic friendships with other women through sexual innuendo and what anthropologist Helen Fisher calls "the copulatory gaze."[28] The metaphor of friendship making as a kind of mating is extended in the sorority recruitment process to include the defining rituals and customs of straight coupling. The penultimate day of sorority recruitment is called "preference" because, at this point, the process of mutual selection has whittled down the number of sororities for which each PNM is vying to two. Both sororities that the PNM visit this day have consistently ranked the PNM high enough that they would be happy to have her join their group. PNMs go into preference day with the added confidence that they will receive a bid from one of these two chapters. Mindful that the ball is in the PNMs' court at this point, sororities self-consciously design an event that clearly communicates their attachment to their PNMs and desire for them to pick their chapter over the competition.

The form that this event takes in many sorority houses borrows heavily from the staging and script of a fantasy marriage proposal worthy of *The Bachelor* franchise. Kappa Alpha Theta rented an enormous white wedding tent for the occasion and filled it with high-top tables, a battery-powered water fountain, rose-filled vases, and hundreds of candles. I trailed a group of PNMs into the tent through a double row of softly singing sorority women wearing coordinating white dresses. Once inside the tent, the PNMs were directed to sit in white, slipcovered chairs that circled the perimeter of the makeshift room. While some of the sorority women busied themselves serving the PNMs sparkling cider in fluted champagne glasses, others knelt on the overstuffed pillows that were strategically placed at the PNMs' feet. The PNM closest to me—a willowy brunette dressed in a sparkly cocktail dress—was visibly overwhelmed by the scene.

"It's okay," cooed the sorority woman (who I'll call Bella) kneeling before her. "It's going to be all right." After the PNM took a deep breath and pulled herself together, Bella got right down to business. Taking the PNM's hand in hers, she looked deep into the woman's eyes. "I felt a connection with you the moment I first met you, you know? It was like we knew each other in a previous life." Bella paused a moment to giggle nervously and wipe the tears from her eyes. "That sounds weird, I know, but it's really true." All around the room, similar conversations were taking place. "You have a tough choice to make," another sorority woman told her PNM. "But I know this is where you belong. I love you so much. We all love you."

By the end of this interlude, most of the PNMs were crying. Those who were not moved to tears were given one more chance to get their tear ducts flowing. The so-called preference ceremony transitioned into a video slide show that honored the chapter's graduating seniors by showing photos of them having fun with their sorority sisters over the past four years. By the fourth slide, over a dozen women in the room were loudly sobbing. Other sorority women immediately moved in to comfort their crying friends, which initiated a domino reaction that resulted in more crying, along with hugging, back patting, and shoulder rubbing.

Research has shown that emotion is highly contagious, and humans are prone to synchronize their response to stimuli with those who are around them.[29] Trapped in a tent with dozens of weeping women, the PNMs didn't stand a chance. Having been fully primed, the PNMs were ready for the last part of the preference ceremony, in which each was presented with a long-stemmed rose. Traditionally, the gift was interpreted to be a temporary placeholder for a bid card. In the era of *The Bachelor*, however, the flower takes on the symbolic weight of the "final rose."

While Kappa Alpha Theta's preference ceremony reimagined a *Bachelor*-esque marriage proposal as a ritual of friendship formation, another sorority bypassed the proposal narrative altogether in favor of escorting their PNMs straight to the altar. Delta Gamma converted their spacious living room into a mock wedding chapel, complete with a nave (filled with rented chairs with satin ribbons tied around their backs) divided by a center aisle. One by one, PNMs were called from their seats and asked to the walk down the center aisle like a bride. Waiting for them at the end of the walkway was a gigantic ice sculpture chiseled into the shape of the sorority's logo (an anchor). The PNMs were then invited to take a Hawaiian lei—whose intertwining flowers, they were told, represented the bundled lives of sorority members—and put the object around the ice anchor. The ceremony ended with the chapter's current sorority members circling the PNMs and serenading them: "We got along without you / Before we met you," the song began, "but sure can't do it now."

Pi Beta Phi's (Pi Phi) preference ceremony pushed the marriage metaphor even further by skipping the wedding ceremony and heading straight to the honeymoon suite. The chapter's living room walls were draped in white bedsheets, and the space was filled with elaborate floral arrangements and hundreds of electronic candles. The PNMs entered the room while being serenaded by sorority women wearing short white dresses and singing the lyrics of Bryan Adams's 1980s megahit "Heaven." The innocuous messaging—that this chapter house is a kind of celestial paradise—turned homoerotic when a senior named Abbie stood up before the group and told the story of how she was "led into heaven" by an older sorority woman. Abbie tearfully confessed that she didn't mean to fall in love with a Pi Phi, and, in fact, doing so was against how she had been raised. As a triple legacy of another house (her mother, grandmother, and great-grandmother were all members of a different sorority), she was expected to choose that chapter. But when Abbie's favorite Pi Phi "preffed" her with a white long-stemmed rose, she took it as a sign: "It was as if my mom was saying, 'It's OK to go to another house.'" With her mother's mystical consent and blessing, Abbie followed her heart and joined Pi Phi.

The conflation of romantic and platonic matchmaking rituals figures the process of joining a sorority as a quasi-sexual act. It may seem like this is the moment where the metaphor jumps the shark, but history reminds us that what I witnessed on SMU's sorority row isn't a new thing. The culture of intense romantic friendships among women, as it turns out, has a long and rich history.

Romantic Friendship

In her examination of hundreds of letters penned by eighteenth- and nineteenth-century American women and addressed to other women, historian Carroll Smith-Rosenberg found an intricate "world of intimacy, love, and erotic passion."[30] Bound by uniquely feminine experiences, rituals, duties, and rites of passage, some friendships between women were so intimate that the most appropriate vocabulary to express the depth of emotions and strength of the bond was through sensual language.[31]

For turn-of-the-twentieth-century young women, college—and particularly the women's college—naturally emerged as the nucleus of erotic same-sex friendships. A 1904 issue of *Ladies' Home Journal* describes these friendships as compulsive and instinctual: "As a rule, this malady affects the new girls in its most severe form. The first homesickness is an awful feeling, and the next natural step is to grasp the nearest object at hand to fill up the aching void. This object is generally a girl."[32]

In her comprehensive study of the origins and early years of women's colleges, Helen Lefkowitz Horowitz notes that one college tradition included lower-class students forming erotic attachments to upper-class students. These crushes or "smashes" often involved younger women sending flowers, treats, and romantic letters to their admirers.[33] Many women's colleges had all-women's dances, and, at Smith, these were occasions where the roles were reversed. At the annual "Freshman Frolic," for instance, second-year students dressed up as men and assumed the roles traditionally assigned to straight men by inviting a first-year on a date, sending her flowers, picking her up, filling out her dance card, introducing her to dance partners, and taking her out to dinner afterward.[34] Similarly, at Vassar's annual Halloween dance, senior women dressed up as farmers and cowboys and spent the evening fawning over their "sweethearts."[35] For Horowitz, such instances of cross-dressing and role-playing was more than just a product of necessity, it was a way of reimagining traditional gender roles. Specifically, the animation of the social roles of men and women "encouraged the development of the forcefulness and direct stance of men rather than the tilts and smiles that marked female subordination. Buildings designed to protect femininity became places where women learned to act as men."[36]

While late eighteenth- and nineteenth-century women's friendships may have taken on many of the symbolic and real attributes of romantic relationships, they also borrowed heavily from the discourse of religion. Fraternity and sorority rituals are products of their time, and many of the organizations were founded by self-identifying Christians (and later Jews) and intended for audiences who shared the same beliefs. Even though white sororities and fraternities today are open to members of all faiths and creeds, many organizations' rituals still preserve the language penned by their founders. The inclusion of the Lord's Prayer, bible passages, and Christian iconography add heft to the already symbolically charged relationship between group members by conflating the vows and promises made to God and the church with those that they make to each other and their organization.

While nineteenth- and early twentieth-century college women may have used sororities as laboratories to challenge and revise gender roles, the rise of Freudianism and subsequent doubling down on the puritanical attitudes toward homosexuality turned the tide of public opinion against romantic friendships.[37] Just a few years earlier, women's magazines put sentimental relationships between women on a pedestal; now they railed against them. In an op-ed published in *Ladies' Home Journal* in 1907 titled "The Evils of Girls' Secret Societies," Grace Latimer Jones acknowledges that hero worship and crushes among schoolgirls can have their upside, but the intimacy of sorority friendships creates an environment conducive to abuse in which "one girl of evil mind and wrong habits may exert a powerful influence over another, and that she may even vitiate a whole group."[38] Women have the capacity to lead other women down a pathway to all sorts of sins and vulgarities including gossip, idleness, and misplaced priorities. Hovering just below the surface of these articulated concerns, of course, is the anxiety that sorority girl crushes might turn sexual. Where once the sorority house was a sanctuary from sex, now the implication was that the space has the potential to turn into a den of same-sex seduction.

While women's sexuality emerged as a particularly pressing anxiety and fear for campus moralists in the nineteenth and early twentieth centuries, all-women residential communities have held a starring role in the straight man's fantasy for centuries. Throughout the Middle Ages, nuns and other cloistered holy women lived under a perpetual veil of suspicion for homoerotic behavior. The oft-discussed "nunsploitation" porn fetish of the 1970s illuminates the long-held assumption that any group of women living together must also secretly be having sex with one another.[39] For their part, contemporary culture's portrayal of college coeds don't do much to dispel this rumor. A staple feature of MTV's annual coverage of the collegiate pseudoholiday known as spring break are wet T-shirt contests and girl-on-girl lap dances.[40] The notorious *Girls Gone Wild* franchise of the 2000s rose to prominence as a producer of spring break amateur erotic videos that include college girls flashing their breasts and groping each other in front of the camera. Sorority women—one of the permanent cast members of spring break and primary suspects of homoerotic activity—fuel the fire through their racy recruitment videos and virtual house tours.

A campus version spin-off of MTV's *Cribs* (a voyeuristic reality television series described by the network as "the only place where you can get a tour of your favorite celeb's pad and be jealous of everything they have!")—*Trending Houses* was a popular 2015–17 series on the College Weekly channel on You-Tube that showcased the interior of fraternity and sorority houses around the country. A requisite stop on a *Cribs*'s tour of a celebrity's mansion is the master bedroom, where the homeowner makes a predictably cryptic comment about the kinds of activities that take place in the space. Sorority women simultaneously parody and pay homage to this scene in their own virtual house tours. The scantily clad tour guides of Florida State University's Delta Gamma chapter house, for example, show off a bedroom that is shared by two women but includes only one bed "because," as one of the women coyly puts it, "we don't like to be apart."[41] The shared bed also takes center stage in the virtual tour of Indiana University's Delta Zeta chapter. The scene begins with the collegiate tour guides opening the bedroom door. "This is a typical bedroom," says the narrator. "Every bedroom has two desks, two closets, and two beds, and we push them close together because we love to snuggle."[42]

This type of posturing doesn't just happen online and on cue. During my visit to SMU, a member of one sorority's executive board gave me an impromptu tour of her chapter house. Emma, who hails from Connecticut, insisted that joining a sorority was never on her radar when she was growing up. All of that changed, however, when she got to SMU. After parading me in and out of the public areas of her sorority house, she led me through the building's internal organs, which included the bedrooms and communal bathrooms. Pausing in the latter, Emma told me that before she joined a sorority, she heard lots of rumors about the showers. "People told me that girls would totally get in there with you," she said. "And they totally do. It's actually awesome."

As sororities have become painfully aware, self-eroticization treads a thin line in contemporary culture between being seen as a symbol of women's empowerment and a shackle that makes one hostage to cliché. You don't have to be in a sorority to kiss another woman on a dance floor, but this behavior was an unstated requirement of many of the sorority formals I attended.

Public make-out sessions between straight women in these kinds of contexts rankle some scholars, and for good reason. For Laura Hamilton, this faux lesbianism—which she identifies as being endemic to but not exclusive to sorority culture—is both offensive and damaging to the LGBTQ+ community. Specifically, she claims that acts of "lesbian tourism" marginalize homosexuality by oversexualizing it and in doing so, claim it as part of the heterosexual domain.[43] For Hamilton, the consequence of appropriating same-sex eroticism as a heterosexual practice is that "heterosexual women made lesbian desire invisible and reconfigured it as a performance for men."[44] As a result, she writes, "many lesbians face a dilemma: they can make their lesbian identity visible and face social invisibility or struggle with the invisibility of their sexual identity but benefit from social inclusion. Women's homophobia thus relies on heteronormative understandings of sexuality to keep lesbians marginalized."[45]

As Hamilton notes, women's same-sex eroticism is tolerated within fraternity and sorority culture when it is mobilized directly or indirectly in the service of straight male desire.[46] The implicit notion is that homoerotic behavior will stop either when men show up or will be placed under men's jurisdiction and control. Problems arise, however, when women don't play by the rules and engage in erotic behavior with each other when men aren't around or are in ample supply. A few hours after I left Kappa Kappa Gamma's 2016 Bid Day festivities at SMU, some of the graduating sorority women took off their clothes and performed a topless dance routine while singing Carrie Underwood's "Cowboy Casanova" for their new recruits. All hell broke loose when word got out that security camera footage of the event was leaked to the sorority's national headquarters. As the media reported, sorority executives allegedly attempted to blackmail the SMU chapter members by threatening to release the footage to the university if the sorority women didn't identify the women in the video and turn them over to sorority officials for questioning and possible sanctions.[47]

The public discussion about the incident pivoted between the privacy rights of the sorority members and the appropriateness of their behavior. Citing an anonymous commenter, the *New York Daily News* summed up a popular opinion: "There should not have been a secret videotape of senior members dancing semi-naked in [the] chapter room on bid night, but [the] incident should NOT have happened in the first place."[48] Some take issue with the circumstances of the performance and claim that subjecting new sorority members to a seminude dance routine is a form of hazing. If the accusations of the lawsuit filed against Kappa Kappa Gamma by one of the SMU sorority members involved can be believed, then what upset the sorority headquarters most about the striptease itself was its potential to incite scandal.[49] From the perspective of straight gender relations, the striptease is problematic because it is nongenerative. Specifically, the provocative dance served as a form of sexual foreplay that ended not with intercourse but with the women putting their clothes back on. It's this culture of erotic wastefulness that the college sorority mobilizes so successfully as a vehicle to figure the chapter house both as a sexless sanctuary and as a place where gender and sexuality are redefined and transformed into a new model of social relations. Specifically, joining a sorority and moving into a chapter house today seems to be a ritual that prepares eighteen-to-twenty-two-year-old women less for a life with a husband than a future spent in the company of other women.

Playing House

America has long had a "weird, enduring love affair" with houses."[50] So wrote Derek Thompson in a 2014 piece in the *Atlantic*. The single-family home is one of if not *the* most iconic and enduring images of American culture and values. The rise of the house as a mode of self-conscious cultural transmission of the American dream and national identity dates back to the Industrial Revolution, when the locus of labor shifted from the farm to the city, making the house a haven from work rather than center of it. This was especially true for the middle and upper classes. As lower-class women filed into the textile mills, the factory became, by default, the designated sphere of working-class women. Excluded from such milieus, wealthy women conducted their own land grab by laying claim to the space where they had access: the family's living quarters.[51]

The increased attentiveness to the ideology of the home spawned the so-called cult of domesticity. As architectural historian Gwendolyn Wright has shown, much of the antebellum era was dedicated to promoting the virtues of the well-kept home. Ministers, schoolteachers, physicians, and jurists joined the crusade, thus making good housekeeping a moral, religious, medical, and educational necessity.[52] Once the ideology of the perfect home had taken shape, society turned its attention to the design and building of that structure. The nation's obsession with domestic architecture in the second half of the nineteenth century is reflected in the fact that a staple feature of women's magazines from that era include model home designs and floor plans. The most prolific distributor of these architectural templates—*Godey's Lady's Book*—published over 450 model home designs between 1846 and 1898.[53] Historians estimate that these designs served as the basis for over 4,000 homes built within a single decade.[54]

The rise of the "model home" in its philosophical and embodied forms converted the house from a physical structure that served the utilitarian purpose of sheltering its occupants from the elements to an entity endowed with the power to speak for the people who lived inside of it. Just as one's outward appearance (e.g., clothing and facial features) were viewed as kinds of windows into the human soul in the nineteenth century, so the house was seen as a lens through which the morality and values of its inhabitants could be examined and judged. "A house is the shape which a man's thoughts take who imagines how he should like to live. Its interior is the measure of social and domestic," wrote one believer in the 1850s.[55] In addition to serving as a public reflection of a private life, houses also were vehicles of individual and communal rehabilitation and mobility. Citing a late nineteenth-century moralist, Clifford E. Clark writes that the house has the capacity to "not only cure the vices of the individual, but they would also reform and uplift society itself."[56]

The protective and therapeutic qualities of the house extended beyond family homes to include structures that housed fictive families like fraternities and sororities. Writing in the early twentieth century, Edward S. Parsons argues passionately in a popular educational trade publication that single-sex housing is a crucial requisite for the preservation of women's morality and "is of the utmost importance in the character development of the young woman."[57] The construction of the first sorority houses were justified on the grounds that they served practical and moral purposes: they provided housing to an underserved population at the same time as they shielded that population from external negative influences.[58] In her *Sorority Handbook* (ca. 1931), Tri Delta founder Sarah Ida Shaw extols the benefits of sorority house living, writing that "in taking a girl out of the crowd and making her a permanent member of a small group, the sorority is rendering her an inestimable service. It is providing her during her college course with family affiliations and with the essential elements of a home—sympathetic interest, wise supervision, disinterested advice."[59]

As havens of morality, early sorority houses were designed to look like the single-family homes in the neighborhoods that surrounded them. Cruise down the Greek row of any college town and you'll likely encounter brick-and-mortar artifacts of the residential housing trends from the past century. Many of the University of Washington's and the University of North Dakota's turn-of-the-century stone gabled sorority houses are worthy of being listed on local historic registries.[60] The Alpha Phi house at the University of Arizona takes its design cues from Spanish colonial revival architecture.[61] Similarly, the University of New Mexico's circa-1966 Kappa Kappa Gamma house is predictably mid-century modern.[62] This phenomenon also explains why so many southern sorority houses look like they are ripped from the pages of *Gone with the Wind*.[63] While many of these structures have since been expanded or completely rebuilt, many of their originals were constructed around the same time that pattern books and residential housing trends favored the Georgian, colonial, and Greek Revival styles.

Gleaming white multistory mansions whose front entryways boast columns, porticos, porches, and window pediments pervade southern campuses. Because of their size, number, and sheer grandeur, these structures have become iconic representations of Greek letter housing in America. Popular media both reflects and promotes this architectural style as the ideal. Recent rankings of the "best" sorority houses published in *Cosmopolitan* and *Teen Vogue* overwhelmingly feature houses at universities and colleges located below the Mason-Dixon Line.[64] One of the effects of privileging this aesthetic is that prospective sorority women in other parts of the country see images of Greek Revival sorority mansions and come to expect sorority houses in their own states to look the same. Examples of exported or retrofitted southern sorority (and, by extension, fraternity) houses abound and include the Kappa Kappa Gamma houses at the University of Michigan, the University of Southern California, the University of Montana, and the University of Idaho; the Delta Gamma and Kappa Alpha Theta houses at the University of Oregon; and the Alpha Xi house at the University of South Dakota.[65] There is no denying that these houses are breathtakingly beautiful, but when viewed within the context of surrounding architecture, they are also strikingly out of place. If their construction reflects the modern American woman's appreciation for contemporary trends, it also, as Freeman notes, allows "the sorority woman to position herself as the guardian of a sacred past and as purveyor of its lessons to the new generation of members."[66]

Arguably the most peculiar manifestation of fraternity and sorority life's architectural embodiment of American housing trends isn't found in a college town, but rather in the bustling Indianapolis suburb of Carmel. One chilly spring morning, I had the surreal experience of driving down a street that was clearly suffering from an identity crisis. Interspersed among the industrial warehouses, medical offices, and other places of business were an assortment of colonial and Greek Revival mansions with perfectly manicured lawns. The former housed an eclectic range of professional enterprises including a title company, landscape design firm, and employment recruiting agency. The latter housed the headquarters of five white sororities and fraternities. The stark mix of industrial and domestic architecture was so jarring that it was the first thing that I brought up with the woman who greeted me at the front door of the Kappa Alpha Theta headquarters house.

Noraleen Young is the sorority's archivist. She wasn't a member of Kappa Alpha Theta (or any other sorority, for that matter) when she was a college undergraduate but developed an affinity for single-sex organizations during her youth spent as a Girl Scout. For her master's thesis, she researched and wrote about the history of Girl Scouts in central Indiana. Noraleen's passion for excavating and preserving women's culture made the transition to working for a national sorority after graduation easy.

Like all special topic historians, Noraleen is a walking Wikipedia of all things sorority. The thoroughness with which she gathers, catalogs, and curates sorority artifacts has earned her something of celebrity status within the fraternity and sorority world. The headquarters of most Greek letter organizations are designed to look like a sorority or fraternity house that one might encounter on a college campus, she told me. "They function like office buildings," she said, "but we call them homes."

Just as my visit to Founders Lane served as a material illustration of how sororities and fraternities are businesses and that what they are selling is the idea and feeling of home—and particularly the southern home—my tour of several of the homes/office buildings on the street also served as a poignant reminder that sorority houses have, since the beginning of their existence, served as models of the aspirational family home. By virtue of their paradigmatic status, they also promote the values of "home," whatever that means in the era of one's membership. In the dating-based culture of the nineteenth and early twentieth centuries, the sorority house was envisioned to be an exaggerated version of the structure that a woman would one day inhabit with her future husband and children. A 1906 issue of Kappa Alpha Theta's magazine openly promotes sorority membership as a kind of playing house. Author Lily Bess Campbell reported on the status of the house at Simpson College: "We have found that our chapter house is the best kind of domestic science training school. The younger girls, under the older ones, order meals and go over the bills. Each has some work to do in the house and is to some extent responsible for the entertaining of guests. Furthermore, they are early trained in the chafing-dish and salad-compounding arts."[67] In Campbell's world, the tasks and activities that take place in the sorority house are performed by women but orchestrated by the needs and desires of absent men. Mastery over the chafing dish (the cultural forbearer of the crock pot) facilitated one's relationship with same-sex friends but was a virtual requisite of a good wife. Freeman notes that when postwar culture repopularized the notion that women's place was in the home, sororities reinforced "the idea that women should prepare themselves for middle-to-upper-class homemaking."[68] Sorority tea parties and luncheons were seen as dry runs for the dinner parties that a member would be hosting just a few years later for her husband's business partners and colleagues.

If, in earlier decades, the sorority house was the home of the future wife, its contemporary analogue is a place where men are not welcome. I mean this literally in the sense that, according to Panhellenic policy, men are forbidden from most parts of sorority houses. They are allowed in common areas, but only at certain times, and always under watchful supervision. Needless to say, stepping foot in a sorority house is not for the faint of heart. In fact, several fraternity men with whom I spoke described sorority houses as stressful, anxiety-producing, and downright scary places to visit. Other than the rules and regulations, what makes sorority houses so terrifying for the straight college man?

The decor.

Step foot inside some of the nation's largest and most elaborately appointed chapter houses and you might think you've just entered a life-sized Barbie Dream House. Grand staircases, crystal chandeliers, baby grand pianos, wraparound porches, and inlaid marble flooring are all standard features in these stunning abodes. And for good reason: the professionally decorated mansions are decked out with furniture and decorative accessories that can be described using one or more of the following adjectives: pastel, metallic, glitter, faux fur, Old World, and French Country.

Fortunately, you don't have to be in a sorority to get inside their houses. *Trending Houses* offers YouTube viewers a tour of select college sorority and fraternity houses. The Delta Zeta house at the University of Tennessee at Knoxville features a sitting area with upholstered Queen Anne–style chairs and a collection of butterfly prints; a parlor room with equally opulent furnishings; and a so-called spa room, which looks a lot like a public restroom, albeit one with chandeliers and fruit-scented hand soap.[69] In a performance that simultaneously makes and mocks the sorority's claim to exceptionalism, the virtual tour pans across a perfectly manicured patio—manned by "Chef Bob" slaving away on the grill—and equally well-styled living room, with a college-aged man playing background music on a baby grand piano.[70]

That sorority houses are meant to appeal not just to current college students but also to women of all ages is reflected in the kinds of places where photographs of sorority houses pop up. A corner of the popular home design website Houzz is filled with them. *Town & Country* and *Southern Living* conduct regular rankings of their favorites.[71] The latter even includes an accompanying video that highlights the houses' unique and special features (think a specially designed staircase banister than can support 200 women leaning over it at the same).[72] A 2021 photo essay on *House Beautiful*'s website is dedicated exclusively to showcasing the fifteen most stunning sorority houses at the University of Alabama.[73]

If, by virtue of being featured on websites and lifestyle magazines whose regular content includes profiles and photographs of traditional nuclear family residences, sorority houses are embedded within traditional notions of domesticity, then the messages they communicate about women's roles are deeply conservative. By shifting the long-standing decorating trope of the "dream home" from being exclusively a single-family residence shared by a wife and husband to a mansion occupied by a group of women, sorority houses also represent its opposite. This is a sentiment reflected by alumnae sorority women who fantasize in online forums and blog posts about leaving their current living conditions and returning to life in their chapter houses. On the collegiate website Unigo, college graduate Melissa Pope lamented that "moving back in with my parents after living in a huge, beautiful house with all my friends was kind of a buzz-kill."[74] Cornell student

Amanda First described moving into the sorority house as akin to "entering an alternate-universe girl world" and moving out of it nine months later as being ripped violently away from her "home away from home."[75] Lacy, a sorority alumna in her thirties whom I met up with in Dallas, went as far as to say that being in a sorority at Louisiana State University was the best four years of her life. When I gestured to her wedding ring and jokingly asked if her time living "in house" (as she called it) trumped married life, she didn't hesitate: "100 percent."

If the sorority house fashions an alternative model of social relations by creating a micro society where heterosexual women live without men—and enjoy it—it is not a paradigm generated by evolutionary progress as much as it is a return to lives fashioned by many sorority alumnae in the nineteenth century. The first generations of sorority women were career-minded and ambitious.[76] With limited employment opportunities available to women, it's not surprising that women's college graduates at the time took a direct route leading from the university sorority house to all-women urban settlement houses. Serving the same function as a domestic peace corps, these community and social service–based organizations aimed to increase access to the poor and disenfranchised by having their aid providers live among them.

The rise and perseverance of sororities by other names goes hand in hand with the cultural redefinition of the single woman. Turk notes that many first-generation sorority women, like their nonaffiliated college-educated peers, either chose not to marry, did not marry, or married later in life than non-college-educated women. Citing a 1916 survey conducted by Kappa Alpha Theta, more than 30 percent of respondents who were initiated before 1900 reported that they had never married. The figure was even higher—55 percent—for women who were initiated between 1910 and 1916, though Turk notes that this figure is likely skewed, as it doesn't account for young survey takers who may have subsequently married.[77]

Fond memories of collegiate years in the sorority house were cited as part of the reason why Kappa Kappa Gamma constructed the organization's first alumnae clubhouse in Winter Park, Florida. Located within walking distance of Rollins, the Boyd Hearthstone was hailed as a "home where Kappa Standards may be shared by those who seek them when the years have left them lonely."[78]

Defenders of single womanhood have always existed, but the drumbeat didn't really get loud enough to hear until the women's rights era. The explosion of books and articles celebrating life as a single woman published over the past decade add to the chorus. What books like *Spinster*, *Going Solo*, *All the Single Ladies*, and *The End of Men* have in common is the argument that the constellation of reasons why women are single (e.g., shortage of qualified men, personal preference) often obscures their happiness with staying this way.[79] For all of these authors, close relationships with men and women aren't mutually exclusive, but single-sex friend groups have the capacity to provide all of the essential requisites of an intimate relationship in contemporary society. While men aren't rendered irrelevant, for straight women who prefer the company of other straight women, they are relegated to the status of what a Rollins sorority woman described as sexual takeout: "Why would I buy a penis," she said, referring to marriage, "when I just can rent one when needed?"

Discussions about the merits of single life and single-sex communities are timely, given the current demographics of the United States. The year 2014 was a watershed moment in that it marked the first time in our nation's history where the population scale tipped in favor of those who are unmarried. According to the Bureau of Labor and Statistics, about 50.2 percent of, or 124.6 million, American adults are single. It might be a bit early to say, as Public Radio International did, that "singles are taking over."[80] But the shifting census forces us to take seriously the influence of single-sex communities on the emerging social, political, economic, and cultural landscapes. Greek letter sororities are among the nation's oldest continuous single-sex communities, and with approximately 415,000 active and over 5 million alumnae or former collegiate members, they also are by far the largest.[81] As "being single" increasingly shifts from a brief stage in life to a viable long-term or even permanent option, sororities function not only as stepping stones to straight, married life but also as training grounds for living alone and spending long stretches of one's life in same-sex housing.

At hundreds of colleges and universities around the country, women express their enthusiasm for the opportunity to live with other women by literally running into each other's arms. This choreographed event—called Bid Day—marks the culmination of the sorority recruitment process. On a frigid January afternoon, I joined 500-plus SMU sorority hopefuls in the campus center ballroom. Hip-hop music was blaring from a sound system in the front of the room, but the attempt to lighten the mood was about as successful as a test proctor telling jokes right before administering the SAT. The women in the room were visibly nervous, as demonstrated by the number of them I caught wiping their sweaty palms on the carpet floor or subtly airing out their armpits. After a string of announcements, instructions, and other prefatory hoopla that dragged on forever and only served to heighten the tension in the room, members of the college's Panhellenic council handed each woman an identical manila envelope with her name printed across the front. Inside each envelope was a bid card, or formal invitation to join a specific sorority. The jittery silence that followed reminded me of the moment before the Powerball numbers are drawn on live TV. Because everyone in the room was a winner in the sorority lottery (the few women who were not matched with an organization were informed of the bad news in advance), the Panhellenic council members decided that a formal countdown was the best way to get the party started. At "zero," the room erupted into a deafening cacophony of paper ripping, followed by loud squeals of jubilation. Waving their bid cards above their heads, women ran around the room like frenzied animals in heat looking for a mate. When they found someone holding a bid card embossed on the same sorority stationary as their own, they let out loud whoops and vaulted themselves into each other's arms, in one case with such force that both bodies toppled backward onto the hard ground. Mosh pits, dogpiles, and massive group hugs eventually gave way to selfie taking, calling parents, and posting the news to social media.

Once these compulsory rituals of celebration were completed, there was nothing left to do but open the ballroom doors. During Alexandria Robbins's time at SMU in the early 2000s, newly minted sorority women stampeded out of the room and sprinted across campus to Greek row. Lining the sidewalks of their journey were fraternity men armed with water balloons, eggs, and Super Soakers filled with beer. The spectacle came to be known colloquially as the "Pig Run," presumably because of the loud squealing noises that the women would make when they were hit by these projectiles.[82]

When the same doors swung open during my visit, the newest batch of SMU sorority women were greeted by stony-faced security guards and campus police officers who stood ready to apprehend anyone who impeded their journey across campus. Waiting eagerly on the other side of campus were these women's new sorority sisters, who welcomed the running throng with loud cheers, bear hugs, balloons, sorority logo tank tops, and other celebratory gifts. Professional DJs set up shop on the front lawns of each of the houses, blaring dance music.

Sorority women—old and new—spent the next few hours taking photos in front of their houses with various props (feather boas, costume jewelry, animal ear headbands, plastic angel wings, faux fur vests), drinking "punch" out of covered coffee cups and insulated water bottles, munching on cookies baked into the shape of sorority mascots (owls, kites, turtles), and, in the case of one group, riding a gigantic mechanical bull. All the while, fraternity men roamed around sorority row in packs, making repeated and increasingly desperate efforts to join the fun while under the watchful eye of the campus police officers and security guards. The women graciously allowed themselves to be congratulated by the men, but otherwise treated fraternity members as walking coat hangers and cell phone holders. When one man asked if he could have a turn on the mechanical bull, the sorority woman manning the on/off switch flashed him a toothy smile and handed him her purse. "Sorry, no," she replied in thick Texas drawl. "But you can hold this for a few minutes."

When the wind picked up, the sororities moved their respective parties indoors. Bid Night festivities are closed-door, women-only affairs. The purpose of these bonding events is to get to know the new pledges and introduce them to their instant older sisters. Thanks to leaked security camera footage, we know that the senior class members of the Kappa Kappa Gamma chapter welcomed their new members by performing a topless striptease.[83] Other chapters reported spending the night engaged in more PG-rated activities: one played icebreaking games and gorged themselves on cake and ice cream. Others went out to dinner. Remember the large white wedding tent that earlier in the day served as the site of Kappa Alpha Theta's proposal-themed preference ceremony? It was converted into a kind of single-sex nightclub where the women spent the evening dancing with each other, taking more selfies, and otherwise having the time of their lives.

Despite the fact that all of the women had retreated into their sororal mansions, a surprising number of fraternity men were lurking around sorority row as dusk transitioned into dark. A small group of them paused outside the white tent to watch the silhouettes of the sorority women dancing inside. Somehow the women were made aware of their presence, and a few leaned against the tarp walls to talk with them for a few minutes before returning to the party. The men had no choice but to shuffle away into the darkness, as they were never invited inside.

FIVE

The Sorority Superchapter and the End of the Best Friend

The latest national data shows that more Americans are graduating from high school than ever before, but fewer of these individuals are going to college.[1] While the shrinking applicant pool is good news for prospective applicants, it also is forcing many colleges and universities to cast their recruiting nets wider and with more urgency.[2] Where schools once could fill their seats with students from local zip codes, many are now forced to engage in brazen poaching expeditions across state lines.[3]

One of the institutions that is winning the nonresident admissions game would be hard-pressed to make anyone's list of likely suspects. The university may have stellar academic and sports programs, but counteracting these selling points is the fact that the school is located in the state affectionately dubbed the armpit of America by bloggers because of its high poverty and crime rate and low overall quality of life.[4] Despite its lack of conventional sex appeal, out-of-state students are flocking in record number to attend . . . the University of Arkansas at Fayetteville (UA).

Between 2002 and 2012, UA added more than 7,000 students to its campus, increasing its total student body by over 50 percent.[5] And the numbers keep rising. In 2014, the *Chronicle of Higher Education* ranked UA one of the fastest-growing public research universities in the country.[6] Just two years later, enrollment hit 27,000 students.[7] Despite the challenges incurred by a global pandemic, a record-setting 29,000 students were enrolled at the university in 2021, a little less than half of which were from out of state.[8]

Why are so many college students from Texas, Oklahoma, Missouri, and Tennessee clamoring to be a Razorback?[9] A generous tuition discount offered to individuals from these and other border states puts UA in the running of a race in which it might not otherwise be in contention.[10] But as other states that offer similar recruitment incentives know, a few discounted math classes usually isn't enough to lure large quantities of teenagers to your state. For that, you need football, or a thriving fraternity and sorority culture. UA has both.

It was a balmy spring morning when I joined a mix of prospective students and new admits for an admissions-office-led tour of the UA Fayetteville campus. Our guide was a well-trained and energetic third-year student named Courtney who hailed from Waco, Texas. As she deftly wove our group through a maze of manicured quads, she told us that 30 percent of the students at UA—roughly three times the national average—are involved in fraternity and sorority life.[11] When you look around, it feels like a lot more. It seemed like every cisgender female student was wearing the unofficial sorority uniform: a triple extra-large sorority T-shirt paired with leggings or athletic shorts. In addition, there were groups of them tabling outside the student center, studying in clumps in the library, and sunbathing on the grassy Old Main quad. Fraternity members, also dressed in their letters, roved around campus in equally visible packs.

It's not just the members of fraternities and sororities whose presence is noticeable on campus: it's also the places where they live. Throughout the tour, Courtney drew our attention to many of the university's unique and historic architectural buildings: Peabody Hall, Ella Cornell Hall, the Old Chemistry building. But as impressive as these structures are, they can't help but look shabby and small compared to the hulking and glittery mansions that are located directly across the street. Greek row at UA is less of a strip of fraternity and sorority houses than a phalanx of mansions that rim half the campus, and soon to be more. The massive fraternity and sorority house-building project that currently is underway involves the expansion of existing structures and the construction of several new ones. The Pi Kappa Alpha house was one of the first fraternal abodes to get a multi-million-dollar facelift. To emphasize the scope and scale of the renovations, a contributor for Total Frat Move wrote, "This isn't like buying your girlfriend a pair of full C-cups to match the rest of her already great body. This is a complete, head-to-toe reconstructive overhaul—from lazy-eyed Jessica in your bio lab to Jessica Biel."[12]

Not to be outdone by their male counterparts, nearly all the sororities have suited up for battle in their own housing war. Kappa Kappa Gamma got a new house in 2013, at the cost of a cool $7 million. At 46,350 square feet, it's currently the largest sorority house in the nation.[13] Pi Beta Phi's original house was demolished and replaced with a significantly larger one on the same lot. Chi Omega upped the ante by renovating their existing house with a two-story addition that includes a coed study room, a quiet study room, and several new bedrooms.[14] Between 2017 and 2019, UA's Greek row added several new houses and completed renovations on at least one other: Alpha Chi Omega's new house reportedly cost $10 million and Phi Mu and Delta Gammas' houses each were budgeted for roughly $12.5 million, making them among the most expensive sorority houses in the nation to date.[15]

For Arkansonians who have mixed feelings about the news that their flagship state school is breaking records and making headlines for having the biggest and most expensive sorority houses in the nation, the university is quick to point out that taxpayers aren't footing the bill for the luxurious digs—all the houses are funded in their entirety by Greek housing corporations and alumni groups. While it may be true that UA isn't spending any of its own money to build and maintain these megamansions, the university quietly contributes something even more valuable to the equation: real estate. Allowing sororities and fraternities to build on school property necessitates the relocation of academic buildings and campus support services, but that is a sacrifice that is well worth making. UA fraternity and sorority life officials declined repeated requests to speak with me, but it doesn't take an email from the Office of Student Affairs to see that a robust fraternity and sorority life (FSL) program is good for the university's bottom line. UA's Greek housing boom supports national data showing that college students who are members of fraternities and sororities have much higher rates of alumni giving than their unaffiliated peers.[16]

In addition to being big contributors to university endowments, fraternity and sorority networks also serve as unofficial but highly effective admission recruiting pipelines. Anecdotal evidence from my visit to UA seemed to back this up. On the second evening that I was in town, I attended a philanthropy event held at a National Panhellenic Conference (NPC) sorority house. The chapter was raising money for their organization's designated charity by selling what one sorority member affectionately called "diabetes in a bowl." For a small donation, guests were presented with a Krispy Kreme doughnut topped with ice cream, fudge sauce, whipped cream, and sprinkles. Joining the hundreds of sorority members in attendance were fraternity and sorority members from nearly all the other white chapters on campus. As I weaved my way through the mass of bodies, balloons, and Styrofoam bowls overflowing with empty calories, I tried not to look as out of place as I felt. But I needn't have worried: I was surrounded by women who had long perfected the art of southern hospitality. When I reached the end of the buffet line, I looked up from my sundae to see a group of women scrutinizing me from afar. A petite redhead in the group smiled and waved me over. "Come sit over here!"

The common denominator in the conversation that followed was the answer to my introductory question: "Where are you guys from?" Notably, no one said "Arkansas." The story of how these women got to Fayetteville from Dallas, Plano, Tulsa, St. Louis, Memphis, and El Paso usually included a friend or relative who is or was a former fraternity or sorority member at UA. Sara (from Memphis) followed in her older sister's footsteps and enrolled at UA and joined the same sorority because "it made everything easy." If it wasn't a personal connection that drew students to UA, it was the university's FSL culture. Mallory (from Grapevine, Texas) transferred to UA from another university after her first year because she wanted a more traditional sorority experience, which for her included living in a sorority mansion. What did it in for her previous school? Sororities at this institution don't have individual houses, but rather, each has a designated meeting room in the university's campus center. Krista (from Southlake, Texas) chose UA over Texas Tech and Texas A&M because she was a legacy of a sorority that she knew she wouldn't get a bid from at these schools. She explained that the sorority chapter of her choosing at UA was filled with people who were more like her. These students approached the college application process through the lens that all college educations are more or less created equal. What made UA stand out—on social media, on online message boards, and during campus visits—was its Greek-driven social scene.

In addition to huge houses, what fraternity and sorority culture dominance looks like is the garnering of national attention. For three years running, UA has been ranked as one of the top-ten best universities for Greek life by student-generated publications.[17] All the publicity that UA's fraternity and sorority community is generating only makes Greek life more popular. Indeed, its rapid expansion is a classic example of the chicken-or-the-egg question in that it is both a result of increasing student enrollment and a source of it. With numbers like these, UA is inching up quickly on its

Southeast Conference rival and undisputed fraternity and sorority power-house: the University of Alabama (Alabama).

Tuscaloosa: The Sorority and Fraternity Capital of the World

The University of Alabama has the largest Greek letter population in the nation.[18] Like UA, it also is one of the country's fastest growing. Between 2005 and 2017, the university's FSL population more than doubled in size, from 4,014 to 10,942.[19] More than half of the members of its Greek community are out-of-state students.[20]

In a 2012 interview with PhiredUp, a fraternity and sorority consulting firm, the university shared that representatives from the office of fraternity and sorority life accompany university officers on the admissions campaign trail and collectively stump for the University of Alabama at out-of-state recruitment events and college fairs in Texas, Florida, and Georgia. When regional recruiters learn that prospective students are interested in Greek life, they connect them with a so-called Greek ambassador, or member of the current fraternity and sorority community who gives VIP tours of Greek housing and offers up insiders' views of the recruitment process. The line between university admissions and Greek community recruiting becomes even more blurry at Greek Preview Day, an annual springtime extravaganza where admitted students and their parents are invited to campus to experience a weekend full of "house tours, meals, information sharing, and building relationships."[21]

Although Alabama deserves kudos for its creative and savvy approach to out-of-state recruiting, it is also equally deserving of the recent criticism levied against the practice. A 2019 study conducted by researchers at the University of California, Los Angeles, and the University of Arizona tracked the out-of-state high schools with which Alabama focuses its recruiting efforts and found that a disproportionate number of these institutions are located in wealthy and largely white neighborhoods.[22] Josh Mitchell's 2021 *The Debt Trap* similarly uses the University of Alabama as a representative case of how American universities lure lower- and middle-class out-of-state students to their campuses with upscale amenities and the promise of a fun-filled social life (sororities and fraternities are not explicitly implicated in this study but certainly contribute to the party atmosphere that sells the school) and then saddle them with a cumbersome student loan debt that many struggle to pay off.[23]

Mobilizing fraternities and sororities to help close the deal with this demographic makes sense since most members of Greek letter organizations are white and come to school with enough expendable income to cover membership fees and other related costs. Carly, a third-year Alabama sorority member from North Carolina, acknowledged that she comes from a privileged background but described Alabama's fraternity and sorority scene as a whole different world. "A lot of people have a lot of money and it becomes very clear," she told me. "There is a look here that everyone goes for, and it is expensive."

The university's aggressive marketing of its Greek community and co-branding (fraternity and sorority life is so deeply entrenched within campus culture that it can be argued that it *is* the defining culture of the institution) has paid off in the form of unprecedented growth in the fraternity and sorority community. And, like all communities that get an influx of new residents very quickly, one of the most pressing questions is where to put them all. The university's answer consists of a village of newly constructed megamansions. Between 2005 and 2019, the university built twenty-one new fraternity and sorority houses and renovated ten others, for a total estimated cost of over $202 million.[24]

At the same time that Alabama's Greek Village is expanding through the addition of several new houses to its neighborhood, it also is growing the other way as well. To say that these houses are large is an understatement. Most of the new sorority houses average about 40,000 square feet, while the fraternity houses come in at around 27,000.[25] While these structures are jaw-droppingly beautiful in the quality of their construction and design, the fact that they are built on the same size lots that housed their previous structures but are much, much larger makes Greek row look like a parody of suburban America.

If the university's fraternity and sorority houses are absurdly and comedically large, their size is an evil dictated by their membership numbers. In 2012, the average number of members in each Interfraternity Council (IFC) fraternity was 109, while the average sorority chapter size that year was 267.[26] Flash forward to 2018, where the average NPC sorority chapter size was over 400.[27] UA sported similar numbers. Chi Omega's former chapter house was designed to serve about 75 members.[28] In 2018 its chapter had over 400.[29] Phi Mu had 439 members and Alpha Chi Omega was close behind with 396.[30]

Of course, not all sorority chapters are supersized. The sorority superchapter is a small but growing phenomena, one that you'll most likely to encounter at large universities with prominent Greek life campus cultures. Not surprisingly, flagship state schools south of the Mason-Dixon Line (Louisiana State University, the University of Texas at Austin, Mississippi State, the University of Oklahoma, and the University of Missouri) lead the pack of schools whose sorority chapters routinely exceed 200 members.[31] The rise of the so-called sorority superchapter speaks to the popularity of these social groups, as well as these organizations' willingness to meet the demand for membership in them. While women are clamoring to join superchapters, research conducted by Oxford University evolutionary anthropologist Robin Dunbar suggests that the sorority superchapter also threatens the foundational principles upon which these organizations are based.

Too Many Friends

What Dunbar discovered almost thirty years ago bears crucially both on the definition of friendship and the form that it takes. Like many scientists in his field, Dunbar's work is based on primates. It's long been recognized that, as highly social creatures, primates consciously forge and maintain bonds with other members of their social group. Scientists also observed that the number of group members with which a primate can forge meaningful social bonds seems to be limited by the size of the brain's neocortex, the part responsible for conscious thought and language.

In the early 1990s, Dunbar applied the governing logic of this observation—the bigger the primate brain, the more relationships it can manage—to develop a formula that could determine the cognitive limit of a human's social network. What does Dunbar mean by "social network"? Dunbar himself aptly summed it up "as the set of people who, if you saw them in the transit lounge during a 3am stopover at Hong Kong airport, you wouldn't feel embarrassed about going up to them and saying: 'Hi! How are you? Haven't seen you in ages!' In fact, they would probably be miffed if you didn't."[32] Based on the math, Dunbar calculated that humans could maintain about 150 of these relationships.[33]

History offers up compelling evidence to buttress this figure. Archeological finds from early hunter-gatherer communities and Neolithic farming villages suggest that our ancestors lived in villages comprised of about 150 people. Contemporary examples of what has come to be known as "Dunbar's number" or "the 150 rule" in action include army platoons, many church congregations, factory production teams, and corporate divisions and departments.[34] Even our pre-texting personal lives seem to have been governed by this principle. In 2016, a team of researchers (including Dunbar) looked at the phone data of 6 billion calls made by 35 million people across Europe. They found that individuals made reciprocal phone calls to about 100 to 150 people.[35]

According to Dunbar, there are cognitive and logistical reasons why 150 is friendship's magic number. No one denies that living in larger groups confers numerous benefits, including a diverse mating pool and increased security and protection from external threats. However, living with other people also generates internal competition—for food, social status, and access to mates. When the size of the group inches over the 150 mark, relationships start to collapse under their own weight.

Viewed through the lens of Dunbar's number, not only is the formation of large social groups like sorority superchapters unwise, but it is also, by superchapters' very constitution, unnatural. The existence of these groups also raises a pressing question: What happens when the number of your friends exceeds that which your brain allows you to maintain? This isn't just an issue for sorority sisters to ponder; it is relevant to anyone who has more than 150 "friends" on Facebook, which, according to a Pew Research Foundation survey, is most of us.[36]

Having too many friends was never a problem for previous generations. For most of human civilization, one's social network by default was comprised of the people who lived close by. The advent of technology that first enabled us frequently to travel to and then stay in constant communication with people who live outside our hometowns fundamentally altered the contours of friendship. Where once it might have been reasonable to expect the average person to have as many friends as he did fingers, social media platforms like Facebook, Twitter, Snapchat, and Instagram now enable us to keep in contact with a larger number of people than we ever have in the past. Physical proximity is no longer a requisite for a close relationship.

The upside of this is that it allows us to keep track of people in our lives who would otherwise essentially disappear and provides us with a means to slow the decay of friendship brought about by physical distance. The downside of crowding our social orbits is that we run the risk of getting spread too thin. As Fordham Law School professor Ethan Lieb notes, "Intimacy suffers at the hands of the need to keep in touch with so many, diluting our ability for focused engagement."[37] As a result, acquaintances—people who we may or may not know in real life—are intruding on the terrain once inhabited by the friend. Indeed, one of the central criticisms of Facebook and its relatives is that these platforms promote and reward casual, surface-level interpersonal interactions. The time we spend tracking and responding to the daily movements of 300 people comes at the expense of the time and energy that we could invest in forging and maintaining deeper connections with a smaller group of people. Maria Konnikova examines the effects of such divestment in her 2014 *New Yorker* article on the topic. Specifically, she explains that we traditionally spend more time with individuals with whom we interact in person than online. Social networks are flipping the script and, "in the process, reversing that balance."[38] The underlying concern for Konnikova and Lieb is what the latter refers to as a kind of "nipple confusion," or the notion that contact with our pseudofriends will pacify us with a kind of fake intimacy "and keep us from seeking out the real thing."[39]

If one school of thought holds that social media dilutes the definition of "the friend," the opposite dangles forth the tantalizing possibility that social media allows us to outwit our genes, thus rendering Dunbar's number irrelevant. Specifically, this camp argues that Dunbar's number is based on two assumptions that no longer hold: first, that people value face-to-face relationships more than those which are filtered through social media; and, second, that all of the friends in our social networks are equally valued.[40] Katie Stroud and others have pointed out that we all live in a number of layered social worlds. We have our family and our close friends, but we also have the groups of people we know as part of different aspects of our lives— like work, a place of worship, athletic involvement, or professional-interest clubs."[41] We might not communicate with our colleagues or neighbors as often as members of our immediate family, but that doesn't mean that those relationships aren't deeply meaningful and valid.

It is still early days in the field of social media studies, and there is certainly some merit to the claim that social media has the capacity to stretch our capacity to form and maintain meaningful relationships with more people than we are independently capable. However, several studies have made a compelling claim for tempering the enthusiasm over the idea that technology has leapfrogged over a few million years of evolution. In a recent study of Twitter, a team of researchers analyzed over 380 million tweets comprising 25 million conversations and determined that microblogging facilitates our communication with more individuals but does not expand the number of relationships we can manage.[42] User data from other social media platforms also support the validity of Dunbar's number. A 2015 survey of American Instagram users revealed that the average teen had 150 followers.[43] Similarly, while over half of Facebook users have 500 friends, the average number of friends is somewhere between 150 and 200 (different sources cite different numbers). Sarah Knapton of the *Telegraph* summed up the implications when she said that our legions of Facebook friends "should be seen more like a 'village' of casual acquaintances rather than a close network of allies."[44]

The second generation of research on Dunbar's number has revealed that 150 people isn't the numerical sweet spot for social groups but, rather, constitutes the ceiling. Historically, groups that reached this size did so out of necessity (caused by limited resources, external threats, or other forms of duress), and not out of desire. Most individuals prefer and thus naturally gravitate toward living and working in small groups comprised of about fifteen members.[45] According to Felix Reed-Tsochas, a professor at the Saïd Business School at the University of Oxford, an even smaller social ring is reserved for an even more select number of individuals—typically between five and eight. "Our capacity for maintaining emotionally close relationships is finite," he said, so that the development of new friendships comes "at the expense of 'relegating' existing friends."[46] As *Bloomberg* journalist Drake Bennett succinctly put it, "We live on an increasingly urban, crowded planet, but we have Stone Age capabilities."[47]

While social media may have been unsuccessful in debunking Dunbar's number thus far, the sorority superchapter may be the best test yet in that many of its group members are not floating around abstractly in cyberspace but are living together in the same house and sharing the same meals. Each of the white sorority chapters at UA have roughly 400 members, and the easiest albeit unscientific way for me to test Dunbar's number is to ask the women who live in these houses if they know all their sisters.

"What do you mean by 'know'?" a second-year named Peyton pressed. Further conversation revealed that Peyton knew all her sorority sisters, if knowing meant recognizing the women's faces when she encountered them on campus, but not knowing all their names. "How do you feel about having sisters who are veritable strangers?" I asked. Peyton squirmed in her seat until the woman sitting across from her—a brunette third-year student named Lila Grace—told me this was an unfair question since it was all that she and everyone else knew.

Fair enough. Many of the sorority women considered the benefits of being part of a superchapter as "always having someone around" and always having something to do and someone to do it with. They similarly took comfort in the knowledge that they could approach a woman wearing the same sorority T-shirt in the library or a classroom and know that even if she had no idea who she was, she'd let you sit next to her and lend you a pencil.

At the same time, many women also confessed that their sorority experience wasn't exactly bad, but it wasn't all that it was built up to be either. Sororities market themselves as surrogate families, but what "family" means depends largely on the size of the chapter. In smaller groups, you can develop sibling-like relationships with your sorority sisters. In superchapters, the hundreds of women roaming around your mansion are more like distant relatives. You may share the same DNA, but don't have any relationship to one another beyond that.

A few years ago, FSL professionals Gentry McCreary, Josh Schutts, and Sarah Cohen devised a research project to evaluate the impact of chapter size on sorority women's perceptions of sisterhood. For their purposes, they broke sisterhood down into five categories: sisterhood based on shared social experiences (having fun together); encouragement and support; belonging (being appreciated despite one's flaws); accountability (sisters make one another better women by maintaining higher standards based on shared expectations); and common purpose (sisterhood is something that transcends the chapter). The team subjected its raw data to statistical analysis, which revealed marked decreases in the last two categories (accountability and common purpose) when chapter size hit a specific number. I'll bet you'll never guess what that number is. In a blog post summarizing his research, McCreary wrote:

> When a sorority becomes larger than 150 members, it becomes much more difficult for members to transcend from selfish levels of sisterhood into the more evolved, selfless levels of sisterhood. In those chapters, most women remain stuck in a place where they see their sisters as a source of fun, encouragement, and support, remaining largely oblivious to the more advanced notions of Accountability and Common Purpose. That is not to say that chapters over 150 cannot achieve a place where most members transcend to higher levels of sisterhood, but the data do suggest that as a chapter grows beyond 150, that task becomes increasingly more difficult.[48]

A past director of Greek affairs at the University of Alabama and former associate dean of students at the University of West Florida, McCreary now runs a consulting firm that helps fraternities and sororities evaluate and assess chapter culture. Over the past five years, he's partnered with dozens of organizations and engaged directly and indirectly with thousands of fraternity and sorority members. I reached out to him in late 2020 to see if his earlier findings still hold. In short: they do. McCreary's latest research is client funded and thus confidential, but what he told me is that the most successful groups—those whose members report the highest levels of belonging and connection—are those that focus on mentorship and intergenerational relationships. Assuming that McCreary is right, the sorority superchapter is, through its very existence, promoting the proverbial girl squad. Applying the same logic, the superchapter is also killing the best friend.

The End of the Best Friend

Taylor Swift may be known for being perpetually unlucky in love, but, according to the international popstar's Instagram feed circa 2015, Swift's life has been an embarrassment of riches when it comes to female friends. Around the same time as her *1989* album dropped, Swift began compiling a celebrity entourage that included supermodels Karlie Kloss and Gigi Hadid, actresses Lena Dunham and Blake Lively, and fellow musicians Selena Gomez and Lorde. When Swift wasn't parading her friends onstage during live performances or snapping photos with them at awards shows, you could find her and her gaggle of girlfriends lounging on yachts in Hawaii, lunching in New York, or baking Christmas cookies together in her kitchen.

While Swift's much-publicized "girlfriend collection," as Buzzfeed's Anne Helen Petersen once called it, has reduced in size over the years, the singer's obsession with her friends had a huge cultural impact in that it cast the single-sex friend group as not only desirable but also preferable over the solitary best friend.[49] The social media universe responded to the rise of the girl squad movement by making "#squadgoals" one of its most popular hashtags during the summer of 2015.[50] Since then, Swift's unadulterated praise of single-sex friendship groups has been enthusiastically embraced by parents and grade school teachers who see the best friend pair as both morally problematic and a public menace. As Hilary Stout reported in the *New York Times*, contemporary society has become invested in the policing and severing of traditional best friend bonds between children and teenagers because this type of relationship has the propensity to foster the very things to which it stridently opposes—namely, cliques, bullying, and exclusivity.[51]

Given the extent to which the public imagination has esteemed the friend group above the figure of the solitary best friend, it's no wonder that kids who grow up hanging out in herds end up gravitating toward them when they enter college. Structurally as well as ideologically, Swift's so-called girl squad is a sorority by another name in that both groups present an aspirational model of women's friendship—one devoid of cattiness and competition and characterized by an abundance of generosity, encouragement, and support. But while the celebrity girl squad popularizes the sorority's model of social relations, importantly, it does not democratize it. Pan out from the carefully curated selfies and we see that, like college sororities, Taylor Swift's friend group is disproportionately comprised of rich, white, skinny women. And while the jury is out on whether the best friend figure is justifiably maligned, one would be hard-pressed to find anyone with a sound mind who would claim that having lots of friends who are mirrors of oneself makes one a better person and a more productive and engaged citizen of the world.

For all its benefits, one of the problems of the kind of girlfriend-group culture that Taylor Swift and college sororities inherently embody is that they promote superficial bonds that are held together mostly by one's identity as a member of that group. The flimsiness of this bond is illustrated in situations where individuals try and fail to hang out independently of the group itself. The difficulty of finding common ground among group members outside of their shared affiliation with the group is only compounded the larger that the group is.

At the same time as the sorority superchapter supports the gigantic girl squad—at the theoretical expense of the best friend—there is evidence within some of these chapters to suggest the presence of evolutionary adaptations to the violation of Dunbar's number. The supersized chapters at UA translated into 2016 pledge classes that ranged between 110 and 165 members. When I talked with members of these chapters about their friendships within them, the women unanimously identified the members of their pledge classes as being their closest friends. This gels with what Ohio State University researchers discovered: subgroups of sorority women who spend the most time with one another inside the sorority house and go out together to places outside of it articulate the strongest sense of group belonging and loyalty.[52]

By contrast, the nature of smaller chapters allows, and even demands, that its members form horizontal and vertical relationships. In these chapters, it isn't uncommon to find seniors hanging out with first- and second-year students. The same principle of Dunbar's number that makes it possible for members of smaller chapters to include all its members within one's social network also makes it difficult for women in larger chapters to forge relationships with older and younger women. The notable exception is the Big/Little relationship, in which an upper-class sorority member takes on the role of a formal mentor to a new member. While the Big/Little relationship provides some opportunities for intergenerational bonding, the structure of the sorority orientation program makes it difficult to expand the scope of one's friendship circle beyond the women who are joining the organization at the same time as you. New sorority members spend much of the first formative months with each other going to special classes where they learn about the history, values, and rules of the organization. For many chapters at UA and other places, it is culturally normative for a sorority pledge class to spend their second year living together in the sorority house while other classes live in apartments scattered in the neighborhoods that surround campus.

The bonds that women form during this time means that they cling together. The rule of Dunbar's number means that pledge classes numbering around 150 women don't have much choice. Fellow pledges fill up all the open friendship slots in one's brain, leaving little if any room for anyone else. Mallory, the transfer student we met earlier, joined a sorority at another institution during her first year, and then transferred her membership to the affiliate chapter at UA at the beginning of her second year. While Mallory wasn't exactly ignored by her new sisters at UA, she wasn't embraced by them either. She twirled strands of hair around her fingers as she talked with me. "Coming here was a lot harder than I thought it would be," she reminisced. "I had a hard time clicking with my [pledge] class because everyone had already found their group." Three years later and on the cusp of graduation, Mallory insisted that it all worked out, largely because of the generosity of the pledge class below her. "I started in the chapter at the same time as the new pledge class did," she explained, "so I just fell in with them."

Like Mallory, members of all superchapters learn to become experts at managing horizontal relationships. In doing so, sorority house relations both reflect contemporary social mores and reinforce them. According to the 2018 American Time Use Survey, individuals between eighteen and twenty-four spent more time in their day socializing than any other demographic.[53]

Needless to say, these individuals aren't Snapchatting their grandparents or texting with their parents for hours on end but, rather, are hanging out virtually with their friends. As author Mark Bauerlein told *Time* journalist Joel Stein, "Never before in history have people been able to grow up and reach age twenty-three so dominated by peers."[54] It's not just American

The Sorority Superchapter and the End of the Best Friend

youth who are emerging into adulthood this way. Stein points out that it is a global phenomenon: "At 80 million strong, they are the biggest age grouping in American history. Each country's millennials are different, but because of globalization, social media, the exporting of Western culture and the speed of change, millennials worldwide are more similar to one another than to older generations within their nations."[55]

The college experience doesn't profess to produce graduates who are adept at forging intergenerational relationships. Our student bodies are getting more diverse in terms of age as time goes on, but the residential college campus is still largely the domain of the eighteen-to-twenty-two-year-old set. Specifically, the demographics of the campus community means that, by default, most students will spend the bulk of their time interacting with people who were born a few years before or after them. According to Bauerlein, this isn't necessarily a good thing: "To develop intellectually you've got to relate to older people, older things," he told Stein. "Seventeen-year-olds never grow up if they're just hanging around other seventeen-year-olds."[56]

Bauerlein's Peter Pan and Lost Boys argument speaks to the limitations of relationships with same-aged peers. A 10,000-foot view of college students may not distinguish much difference between an eighteen-year-old first-year student and a twenty-two-year-old graduating senior, but for those living within this demographic window, the separation between the two feels vast. Even though the journey through the undergraduate experience is short—or perhaps because it is—those who have just boarded the train are set up to see those who are about to hop off as seasoned travelers.

Sororities are designed to create a community within a community that allows for vertical relationships that are hard to forge on one's own. Yet, because of chapter size or culture, new members' interactions with older sorority sisters might be superficial and limited. And, in this way, sororities are failing to deliver the very thing they promise. But just because many sorority women don't have close relationships with older sorority sisters doesn't make the interaction that they do have with them inconsequential. It's precisely the attributes of rarity and distance that make vertical sorority relationships so powerful and, in some instances, so problematic.

The Power and Perils of Horizontal Friendships

Rollins is one of many colleges and universities across the country that holds fraternity and sorority recruitment in the beginning of the spring semester (January) instead of the beginning of the fall (August or September), meaning that first-year students have a whole semester to learn about the fraternity and sorority community at their institution before joining a specific organization. Delayed recruitment similarly benefits individual chapters by giving them ample time to scope out potential new members and formulate strategies for how to recruit the most desirable. In the weeks leading up to a recent sorority recruitment week at my college, a conventionally beautiful first-year student named Cassidy came to my office with a statement of fact and a dilemma: while much of her future was up in the air (she had yet to declare a major and had "no clue" what she wanted to do with her life), she knew one thing with certainty: she could join whatever sorority on campus that she wanted. I raised my eyebrow. "Oh?" I asked, surprised by her confidence. Even though the match rate for sorority recruitment is upward of 98 percent, most of the first-year women I encounter openly wring their hands in worry that they will be among the 2 percent who are dropped by all the chapters. Cassidy explained that her confidence came from the positive interactions that she had with multiple sorority women from different organizations over the past few months. "I've been dirty rushed by all of them," she said, referring to the "top three" chapters on campus.

The NPC sets strict rules for recruitment that explicitly prohibit socializing with potential new members (PNMs) before recruitment, but chapters are often willing to break the rules because so much is at stake. As we have seen, sorority women form sororal teams whose job is to love, support, and serve one another in all milieus, including and especially the romantic marketplace. The identity and social status of many sorority chapters at Rollins isn't powered by their popularity with fraternity chapters, but for those that are (frequently but not always the self-professed "upper-tier" organizations) replenishing their ranks with "a good class" (which is sorority code for a new crop of glamorous and gorgeous first-year students) is critical to preserving their social capital and signaling superiority over rival sorority groups.

The small category of women-who-could-be-supermodels of which Cassidy is a part are the beneficiaries of a social privilege bequeathed by a combination of wealth and genetics. But it's not just the Cassidys of the world who join a sorority feeling like they are doing the organization a favor by accepting their invitation to join. First-year women are the newest members of the straight campus dating arena, and their novelty and newness make them objects of intense romantic interest by all grade levels of men. While the flurry of attention is flattering, it's also dangerous because it gives eighteen-year-old women the impression that they control the dating script, when, in reality, at 40:60 institutions, it is the other way around. The same carryover cultural norms from high school that make it socially acceptable for older men to hook up with younger women frowns upon older women doing the same with younger men. Thus, while college women's romantic capital diminishes over time, their male classmates' romantic prospects are most limited during their first year of college and increase as they age. In this way, sorority recruitment at Rollins differs from fraternity recruitment: the former recruit women based on their current value while the latter recruit based on potential. Because straight first-year men occupy the lowest rungs on the social totem pole, they go into fraternity recruitment with something to prove. Highly touted women like Cassidy, on the other hand, come to sorority recruitment knowing what they are worth. As a senior, Cassidy reflected back on her first-year self and spoke for her cohort when she said, "I thought I was hot shit."

No one can blame older sorority women for bristling a bit when Cassidy and her friends waltzed into the sorority house on Bid Day 9 and acted like they owned the place. "We needed to be knocked down a peg or two," Cassidy told me. For some sorority chapters around the country, this is accomplished through formal group hazing. Let me be clear: many sorority chapters don't haze. During my research, I talked with dozens of women from an equal number of chapters who swore they would have left their organization and reported their chapters if they were hazed—and I believe them, because these women are also those who reported sorority sisters for honor code and community standards violations. I also believe that sorority hazing is underreported in part because of the codes of secrecy that govern the practice and, in part, because the definition of hazing is so broad and capacious that many sorority women don't recognize it as such. Such was the case of the second Rollins sorority chapter for which I served as a faculty advisor. I was brought on board when the chapter was in active freefall. The women understood how accusations of forced drinking and drug use on Bid Day was a form of hazing, but they couldn't see how making their pledge class clean up after a fraternity party, proposing marriage (with a candy ring) to their crushes, or serving as designated drivers for older sorority women were violations of the policy. In their minds, these activities were examples of civic responsibility, clean fun, and community service.

Illicit Bid Day drinking is a frequent form of group hazing. The Tri Delta chapter at the University of Georgia was suspended in 2019 after allegations surfaced of Bid Day hazing activities, and sorority chapters at the University of Central Florida (UCF) and Eastern Carolina University received three-year suspensions for the same reason.[57] UCF's Pi Beta Phi chapter was suspended in 2019 after reports surfaced that some chapter members were forcing others to drink and do drugs.[58]

But of course, it's not the only form in which it appears. In an op-ed for *Cosmopolitan* that defended the practice of hazing, former sorority woman Tess Koman tells how she and her forty-two pledge class sisters were forced to dance provocatively to sexually explicit songs in front of fraternity members, were locked in the sorority basement overnight, and were made to stand under a spotlight while their older sisters critiqued their appearance.[59] In 2018, the Alpha Chi Omega chapter received a two-year suspension from Lehigh University after details of its annual scavenger hunt—which included tasks such as drinking bong water, hooking up with an Uber driver, and having a threesome—went public.[60]

While group hazing is an integral part of the culture of some chapters, informal hazing is a part of many others. A recent study of fraternity and sorority members revealed that women were more likely than men to believe that pledging should be a positive experience.[61] Because women are embracing a new attitude toward pledging, some chapters have moved from a universal to an opt-in practice.[62] Such is the case with two recent "top-tier" sorority chapters at Rollins. Shortly after graduation, I reached out to and talked with multiple members of the same pledge class of Chapter A. Some of the women confessed to being hazed as first-year students (mostly through forced drinking by select older women in the chapter) or said that they heard rumors that others were hazed but that they weren't. When I asked those who weren't hazed why they felt like they were spared, the answer was quick and universal: "Because everyone knows that I would report it."

The same phenomenon existed in Chapter B. In this chapter, hazing allegedly occurred within "families" and almost always took the form of Big sisters forcing Little sisters to drink. Cassidy told me a memorable story from her first year on campus when she was at a bar and her Big delivered four shots to her table and said, "They're all for you, drink up." A few weeks later, the same woman and a group of her friends got drunk with their Littles (voluntarily) and then came up with the bright idea of herding them into the chapter courtyard, where they forced them (involuntarily) to remove their clothing and sing the sorority's drinking song at the top of their lungs.

Cassidy's voice drops as she finishes the tale. "How did these incidents impact your relationship with your Big?" I asked. Cassidy quickly assured me that she loved her Big, and these events made for funny stories, but in the same breath she also acknowledged that they were less about bonding than about "hierarchy and control." The message communicated to Cassidy and her similarly hazed pledge sisters was loud and clear: you may be at the top of the social ladder outside of the sorority house, but inside you're at the bottom. According to researchers at Colgate University, using hazing to establish and reinforce social rank is common.[63] There is no better example of this than weekly chapter meetings, which take place in a room where there is not enough seating for all the sisters. It is an unwritten rule that seniors get the chairs and everyone else sits on the floor beneath them. Cassidy recalled a time as a first-year student when one of her pledge sisters sat in a chair during a chapter meeting: "A senior came up to her said, without batting an eye, 'Get out of that seat. Now.'" Cassidy sighed wistfully. "It sounds mean, and it was. But in that moment, I wanted to be just like her." I pressed her. What about the senior's actions or words were commendable? "That she has the nerve to be that ballsy, that direct. They all [the seniors] are badasses. They are so intimidating and sure of themselves, which is everything that you aren't as a freshman." Cassidy searched for a metaphor to best describe how she felt about older sorority women and finally landed on this: "It's like the popular girls in high school that you wanted to be like so badly but couldn't because they are untouchable. But being in the same sorority with them and knowing that you will be in their shoes one day gives you a vision of what you'll become." As a senior, Cassidy admitted to treating younger women the same way that she had been treated. The behavior that Cassidy describes as "tough love" is done with good intentions. Older sorority women may be modeling the kind of self-determination, entitlement, and authoritative decision-making that will serve them well in their professional lives after graduation, but they are also promoting and legitimizing bullying and hazing.

The modus operandi of hazing for sorority chapters like Cassidy's isn't just to shape new members into strong professional women but also to shape them into team players who, through their popularity with fraternity men, will elevate the chapter brand. Being known as someone who is pretty and "classy" but also knows how to have a good time is good for the brand. According to Cassidy and her friends, being that girl who is "chronically blackout drunk" and who sleeps with "anyone with a dick" isn't. The ideal sorority woman will land on the former end of the spectrum, but because the line between classy and trashy isn't fixed, classification is both inconsistent and subjective.

A 2014 research study examined the motivations behind so-called slut-shaming (deriding women for their real or imagined sexual activity) on a particular college campus and found that high-status (white, heterosexual, largely Greek letter) women employ slut discourse to assert class advantage over women of color and members of the LGBTQ+ community by figuring their definition of femininity and approach to sexuality as classy instead of trashy.[64] Slut discourse isn't just mobilized by sorority women against nonsorority women but is also a vocabulary used by older sorority women against younger women within the same organization. "The most poignant lesson that I learned from older sorority women," Cassidy told me, "is that they will ruin you."

Cassidy went on to tell me a version of the story that Lisbeth Berbary writes about and I have heard dozens of times before by sorority women in other chapters and at other universities: a new member is a sloppy drunk at a social event or posts racy photos of herself on social media. Depending on the offense, the woman is either reprimanded informally by older women via text or in person, or the woman is called into Standards (the sorority chapter's student-run judicial board).[65] The woman is given the opportunity to express remorse and pay for her sins (either via a monetary fine or withholding of social privileges). If she repeats the offense or anything like unto it, she risks being subjected to the silent treatment, deleted off text chains, blocked on social media, permanently excluded from social events, and kicked out of the sorority.

This moral policing isn't just confined to sorority women's sexual behavior, of course. As Lucy Taylor recounts in the first season of her 2020 six-part podcast series *Snapped*, it also extends to the photos that sorority women post of themselves on their personal social media accounts. The day after accepting a bid from a top-tier sorority, Lucy's "pledge mom" (the upper-class sorority woman responsible for shepherding the chapter's new recruits through the new member education process and teaching them the norms and rules of sorority behavior) asked her to remove four "inappropriate" photos from her Instagram account.[66] Lucy struggled to understand what was problematic about the photos in question, but, being new in the organization and eager to please, she complied with the request. A few months later, when she was on vacation in Italy, she posted a photo of her and her friend wearing "cheeky" bikini bottoms at the beach. The next time she checked her phone, she said she discovered a stream of texts and DMs (direct messages) from her sorority sisters back home instructing her to remove the photo by using the code word "snap." In addition to these private reprimands, Lucy also reported that a member of her sorority sent this email to the whole chapter:

Hi hi, with the start of the semester just one month away (yay!), PNMs [potential new members] are beginning to check us out to get an idea of what our sorority is really like. That being said, now is the time where it is really important to be keeping our image up and constantly sharing posts that are an appropriate portrayal of our chapter. Everyone needs to be mindful of the photos they are posting on social media and remember that your pictures are not only representing you as an individual but the chapter as a whole. Love the beach pics but let's try to keep the booties tucked away from here on out [smiley face]. With this in mind, remember that part of being in [blah blah blah—the sorority name] is holding each other accountable, so remember to use "snap" if you think you see something that might not be the best image of our chapter. And, of course, if you are ever unsure about a post or a photo, don't hesitate to reach out and get a second opinion. XOXO.[67]

Several things bothered Lucy about this email, but chief among them was that her sorority sister was slut-shaming her and encouraging other sisters to do the same. Lucy's bikini represents one of the many contradictions within her sorority experience. She reported that she and other members of her pledge class were given champagne at their first social event but then were lectured the next day by sorority women for drinking too much; were ordered to stay at fraternity parties until midnight but cautioned against sending nudes to a fraternity man lest he circulate the images and make the whole chapter look bad; were taught a drinking chant by older sisters that talked about "sucking cocks and fucking guys" but then were chastised for posting photos of themselves to social media that included visible cleavage and butt cheeks.[68] "It seemed like they wanted us to come off like these dainty, conservative virgins but perform sexually like the sluts that they've shamed us to be," she continued. "It was one large contradiction."[69]

As Lucy's story illustrates, slut-shaming is alive and well within contemporary sorority culture; so is the practice of women calling other women "crazy." During the #MeToo movement, writers called out men for using the term in the same way that Victorians did with the word's synonym "hysterical"—that is, as a catch-all descriptor of women's behavior that might otherwise be labeled as assertive, mean, noncompliant, demanding, needy, aggressive, and/or feisty.[70] As Sady Doyle deftly illustrates in her 2016 feminist manifesto *Trainwreck*, if the sexist term started out as part of men's vocabulary to describe women, it's evolved into a word used by women to describe other women who act in ways—sexual and otherwise—that are outside the socially and culturally prescribed bounds.[71] It's not just sorority women who call each other crazy, of course, but, because of the community's insularity and culture of self-policing, its usage and effects are both pronounced. If sororities mirror the kind of power hierarchies of society at large, then what older sorority women do is craft a uniform model of behavior for younger new members that privileges a conservative, heteronormative vision of femininity through shaming any deviations from it—actions and perspectives that they themselves often tentatively explored or provisionally held when they were the same age. Viewed from this lens, the purpose of "Big" sisters and other vertical relationships within the chapter isn't to shepherd and cultivate diversity in its new members but, rather, to strip them of it.

This view aligns with hazing expert Stephen Sweet's take on the overarching purpose of sorority and fraternity initiation processes. Applying symbolic interactionist theory to these groups, Sweet argues that material paraphernalia—pledge pins, T-shirts, hats, and other logo-imprinted objects—gifted to pledges serves as a new "identity kit" that encourages people to privilege conformity to group aesthetics over individual style.[72] This principle is reinforced and expanded through the pledging process, which is designed to isolate new members from external friend groups and restrict their social relationships to members of that sorority and fraternity.[73] Groupthink isn't just a problem plaguing vertical relationships in some sorority chapters. What happens when you leave a hundred or so male college students unattended in a fraternity house together? What hangs in the balance in these situations is something bigger than the definition and model of friendship. What stands to be lost is nothing short of life itself.

SIX

Playing War and the Case for Fraternity Hazing

Most people of sound mind would go out of their way to avoid eating their friends' feces and allowing their buttocks to be branded with a hot iron hanger.[1] Yet every year thousands of otherwise sane college students clamor for the opportunity to do these things, and other things like it. In 2012, five fraternity pledges at Boston University agreed to strip down to their underwear, be duct taped to each other, and smeared with condiments.[2] The same year, pledges at Salisbury University gussied themselves up in dresses and high heels and then presented their rear ends to upperclassmen, who took turns smacking them with wooden paddles.[3] New recruits at one University of Tennessee fraternity signed up to have alcohol-filled enemas squirted up their rectums in a practice known as "butt chugging."[4] Fraternity hopefuls at Clemson allegedly dunked their heads in a cooler filled with a mixture of water, phlegm, pubic hair, and urine.[5] Pledges at Ohio University were routinely taken to the "fun room" in their fraternity house, where they were beaten with belts, pelted with eggs, and forced to drink a gallon of alcohol in an hour.[6] Not to be outdone, the brothers of Tulane University's Pi Kappa Alpha chapter welcomed new members into their fold by boiling up vats of water containing pepper spray, cayenne pepper, and "crab boil" seasoning and then pouring the mixture down pledges' backs. The fun ended after one recruit suffered second- and third-degree burns to his genitals and had to be admitted to a hospital burn unit.[7]

The formal recruitment process ends with fraternity chapters extending invitations or bids to individuals to join their organizations. Before pledges become full-fledged members, they go through a probationary period that lasts anywhere from a few weeks to a few months. Officially, this period is dedicated to educating new members about the organization's history and learning about its values. Since fraternity membership can't be swapped or exchanged (if you join one fraternity you are barred from ever joining another) and, like marriage, is cast as a lifelong commitment, organizations want to make sure that new members know what they are getting themselves into and give them the opportunity to opt out if they decide that membership isn't for them. Somewhere along the way to the altar, fraternity members decided that asking their pledges to read biographies about their organization's founding fathers and complete workbook pages designed to increase one's leadership IQ were neither glamorous nor particularly effective ways of forging deep bonds between existing and new members. For some chapters, water torture, exercise gauntlets, and sodomy with foreign objects emerged as more desirable alternatives.

Why do fraternities haze, and why do aspiring members allow themselves to be subjected to hazing? These are the million-dollar questions that have plagued the fraternity and sorority life (FSL) community for over a century. Anti-hazing watchdog and research institute StopHazing.org defines the practice as "any activity expected of someone joining or participating in a group that humiliates, degrades, abuses, or endangers them regardless of a person's willingness to participate."[8] University of Maine researchers Elizabeth Allan and Mary Madden report that 73 percent of fraternity and sorority members have been hazed at least once.[9] Over the past decade, enormous amounts of money have been thrown at hazing education and prevention. It's the subject of hundreds of combined books, journal articles, documentaries, podcasts, and webinars. Whole academic conferences and expensive week-long summer institutes are dedicated to identifying its forms and discussing its effects. Saunter onto any campus during the third week of September (i.e., National Hazing Prevention Week), and you'll be bombarded with anti-hazing posters and billboards as well as invitations to attend hazing prevention workshops, lectures, and seminars. The force of the anti-hazing crusade gains both momentum and increased manpower with each passing year, and its influence is registered in the number of anti-hazing laws currently in existence. As of 2019, forty-four states have passed anti-hazing legislation, and in eleven hazing is a prosecutable crime.[10]

The combined effect of the education about and legislation passed against hazing has ingrained its risk into the psyche of every college student in America. One would be hard-pressed to find a fraternity or sorority member who hasn't heard about hazing or been told by multiple sources that the practice is dangerous, cruel, and against the law. Unfortunately, many of these warnings seem to have fallen on deaf ears. In September 2016, I shadowed fraternity members at Florida State University (FSU) as they went through their university's National Hazing Prevention Week programming. Even after receiving rigorous in-person and online training and one-on-one chapter counseling from one of the nation's leading hazing experts, FSU's fraternity community would still go on to haze one of its members to death the following year.

Scholars attribute the reasons why college students sign up to be on both the giving and receiving ends of hazing rituals to a myriad of factors including but not limited to groupthink, peer pressure, and the need for acceptance.[11] In addition to all of these causal factors, there is another more fundamental reason why some of the most severe and violent forms of hazing persists within college fraternities: because they work.

The Pleasure of Pain

Tall and broad-shouldered with a chiseled physique earned through years of playing competitive sports, twenty-year-old Andrew Coffey may have cast an imposing presence, but, according to Andrew's former high school guidance counselor Kathy Fish, "he was the type of person you wanted to know. Whether you were a kid or an adult, he just had that personality that drew you in."[12] Given that Andrew was neither a novice drinker nor a pushover, what would compel this new transfer to FSU to guzzle an entire bottle of Wild Turkey 101-proof bourbon at a fraternity initiation event? Two mid-century Stanford University psychologists would say that Andrew drank himself far beyond the limits of what was pleasurable for the same reason that prudish college girls more than half a century ago suffered through membership in a soft-core pornography book club.

In 1959, Drs. Elliot Aronson and Judson Mills approached female students with a tantalizing invitation: a student group that met regularly to discuss the provocative topic of sex recently had lost a member. Would the student like to fill the vacant spot? Each of the sixty-three women who accepted the invitation were placed in one of three initiation groups: the first was required to engage with what the researchers called "embarrassing" and sexually explicit material before being allowed to join the group. This material included reading aloud both a list of obscene words like "fuck" and "screw" and vivid sex scenes from steamy romance novels. The second group was required to read a milder version of this material. The third "control" group wasn't required to read anything before gaining membership. After successfully completing the initiation process, each of the new group members listened to the same audio recording of the supposed group's meeting-in-progress. The conversation—which took the form of a stilted and dry academic discussion on the less-than-titillating topic of secondary mating characteristics of animals—intentionally was designed to be, as the researchers put it, "one of the most worthless and uninteresting discussions imaginable."[13] In addition to the dry subject matter, the planted discussion participants spoke haltingly, mumbled their responses, didn't finish sentences, and otherwise did everything within their power to make the conversation as disjointed and noncaptivating as humanly possible. After listening to the recording, the women were then asked to evaluate different aspects of the discussion. The mild initiation group rated it accurately—they found the participants to be uninspiring and the conversation itself to be mind-numbingly boring. The severe initiation group, on the other hand, rated the discussion and its participants far more favorably.[14]

In the decades since its enactment, Aronson and Mills's experiment stands within the field of psychology as a classic illustration of the power of cognitive dissonance. This theory holds that no matter how appealing a group is to an individual, membership within that group is rarely completely positive. There are always things about the group that the individual is bound not to like or about which they disagree. An individual who goes through unpleasant initiation rituals in order to join a group with which they are not totally in love has two options when it comes to reconciling their continued membership: 1) they can rewrite the narrative of their initiation in a way that minimizes or elides completely the psychological or physical injury it caused them; or 2) they can exaggerate the positive attributes and attractiveness of the group.[15] "It is a frequent observation," Mills and Aronson concluded, "that persons who go through a great deal of trouble or pain to attain something tend to value it more highly than persons who attain the same thing with a minimum of effort."[16]

If the Mills and Aronson experiment showed that intense, painful, or embarrassing initiation experiences make individuals more enamored with and thus committed to the groups they are joining, subsequent research has revealed that the same sentiment also carries over to the group members

Playing War and the Case for Fraternity Hazing

themselves.[17] Like other fraternity pledges across the country, Andrew Coffey was conditioned to believe that the tightest bonds of friendship can only be formed through trauma and suffering. Zooming out from both the college campus and the contemporary world beyond, we see that this form and function of hazing is not unique to modern society. Rather, it is a practice that seems to have been integral to our understanding of "friendship" and "community" since the dawn of civilization.

Friends by Near-Death Experience

Our Neanderthal ancestors lived in nomadic tribes where collective survival depended on all group members pulling their weight. While we don't know if early humans utilized formal initiation rituals as pathways to membership in their groups, we do know that the rigors and demands imposed by daily life served as de facto tests of one's competence and thus utility to the whole. The history of Western civilization reminds us that it wasn't until very recently (the past hundred years or so) that everyday life for just about everyone was punctuated by constant injury, illness, and accidental death. Perhaps more than anything else, what characterized the societies that came before us was the shared experience of suffering and pain.

If the rise of autonomy and self-sufficiency are two of modernity's crowning achievements, they come at the cost of upending the way that social bonds are formed and maintained. Today's closest relative to the ancient bands of hunter-gatherers may be military units. At least that's the case that award-winning war journalist and *Restrepo* director Sebastian Junger makes in his 2016 book *Tribe: On Homecoming and Belonging*. Through shadowing combat battalions during the Balkan Wars in the early 2000s, and more recently in Afghanistan, Junger came to see war and other disasters as correctives to nature. "What catastrophes seem to do—sometimes in the span of a few minutes—is turn back the clock on ten thousand years of social evolution," he writes. "Self-interest gets subsumed into group interest because there is no survival outside group survival, and that creates a social bond that many people sorely miss."[18]

Of course, the contemporary college campus is not an active combat zone in the literal sense, and fraternity members are not real soldiers, but it makes sense that fraternity hazing should mimic the horrors of war, given the culture of American masculinity in the era of these organizations' founding and growth. The first collegiate Greek letter fraternal organization, Phi Beta Kappa, was founded as a kind of intellectual social club at the College of William and Mary on December 5, 1776, just a few weeks before George Washington famously crossed the Delaware River during the Revolutionary War. The war shuttered the college's chapter just six years later but survived in the form of three colony chapters—at Harvard, Yale, and Dartmouth. The organization dropped its requirement for secrecy and transitioned into an academic honor society around the same time as Greek letter social fraternities were beginning to come on the scene. Several of these social fraternities were founded in the decades leading up the Civil War, but interest in them didn't really start gaining momentum until the last quarter of the nineteenth century.[19]

The members of social fraternities in the 1870s, 1880s, and 1890s grew up in cultural proximity to the Civil War but were a generation or more removed from its horrors. While history has always been kind to rich white men, the late nineteenth century was an undeniably good time to be a middle- or upper-class Protestant man of Anglo-Saxon heritage in America. The economy was booming, and a rapid fire of emergent medical discoveries (germ theory, vaccines) and technological inventions (lightbulb, telephone, internal combustion engine) made it possible to do just about everything better, faster, or longer. While the world was the white man's oyster, there was at least one thing that got harder for this figure in the age of industrialization: forging deep and meaningful friendships with other white men.

In his seminal history of American masculinity, E. Anthony Rotundo illustrates how violence was a key component of boy culture throughout the nineteenth century. Young boys and teens who sparred with each other through the staging of mock battles, wrestling matches, debates, and testing-of-wit challenges stayed together.[20] An unfortunate byproduct of growing up and not having an outlet to act like a soldier was that individuals were deprived of the circumstances to bond like one. One of the solutions to this problem was as ingenious as it was simple: they could manufacture it.

In the late nineteenth century, the primary manifestation of this outgrowth of boy culture came in the form of single-sex clubs and organizations. In 1896, approximately one in five to eight men in the United States were members of a secret fraternal order.[21] The actual number is significantly higher if you count the members of labor organizations, secret military clubs, college fraternities, and formal branches of the military—the latter of which itself exceeded 250,000 members at the time.[22] Because fraternal orders served as unconscious proxies for military platoons, it's no surprise that many of these organizations adopted the names of real and fictive military groups. Men looking to join a fraternal order could choose between the

Playing War and the Case for Fraternity Hazing

Knights of Labor, Patrons of Husbandry, Benevolent and Protective Order of Elks, Grand Army of the Republic, Ancient Order of Foresters, Knights of Columbus, Loyal Order of Moose, and the Independent Order of Good Templars, among others.[23]

With the absence of any recent or impending wars from which to draw inspiration for initiation rituals, many of these fraternal orders mined military history. Some organizations reenacted generic horrors endemic to all wars. Part of the Masonic ritual of initiation was rumored to have members pretend to slit an initiate's throat from ear to ear.[24] One of the rituals of a Chicago-based chapter of the Onward Christian Soldiers club included blindfolding initiates and pulling the triggers of revolvers in their faces multiple times.[25] The Order of the Oddfellows—which, at its turn-of-the-century heyday, was the most popular fraternity in the nation, with over a million registered members—welcomed new members by treating them like prisoners of war. After being blindfolded and bound in chains, they were jostled around the lodge house until they reached an open coffin that contained a life-sized skeleton, which hooded and masked men identified as a foreshadowing of the fate of the initiate.[26]

If war and combat were popular tropes of the initiation rituals of adult fraternal orders in the late nineteenth century, college students were well prepared to participate in these rituals by the time of their graduation in large part because they had spent their collegiate years converting their campuses into virtual battlefields. At Yale, students from northern and southern states waged what historian David Allmendinger calls "miniature civil wars" on campus quads, whose outcomes frequently resulted in injury and sometimes even death.[27] Class warfare was rife within this period, with the most heated rivalries existing between first- and second-year students. Both populations attended class at their own risk, as evidenced by the sheer number of kidnappings, ambushes, and muggings that were reported during this period. At Cornell in 1905, a three-day class battle ended after both sides had kidnapped several of their opponents and subjected their hostages to humiliating treatments, including being "painted up" and dressed in ridiculous clothes.[28] At Rutgers, first- and second-year students held contests to see which group could trap the most members of the other class and tie them up with rope.[29]

According to Nicholas Syrett, fraternity hazing can be seen as an outgrowth of the hazing inflicted upon incoming freshmen by upperclassmen. As college populations ballooned and allegiance to one's class decreased, fraternities appropriated class-related hazing and applied it on a smaller scale within their chapters. Fraternity hazing increased in the 1860s and by 1894 was pervasive enough that one fraternity addressed the problem at its national convention.[30]

Twentieth-century college fraternities not only embraced these traditions but, in many cases, expanded them. Some of our culture's most deeply entrenched and pervasive hazing rituals are borrowed from military training exercises and are designed to mimic wartime tasks and duties. In addition to lining up, standing in formation, and participating in group runs and choreographed calisthenics, a sociologist studying post–World War II chapters observed new initiates being instructed by their pledge trainer how to properly conduct a "raid." Instead of sneaking into enemy terrain to steal top secret documents or rescue POWs, however, new members were ordered to break into a fraternity house and snatch and grab specific high-value items.[31]

Today's fraternity members still use war to forge and deepen social bonds. The advent of digital technology in recent decades has further expanded the geography of the mock battlefield to include virtual terrain. The focal piece of every contemporary fraternity house—at least in the cultural imagination—is the big screen television and attached video game console. The screen is the social hub of the house not only because it is where fraternity members watch each other play against the computer but also because it is where they play against and with each other. Video gaming is enormously popular among young adults in America—a 2018 Pew Research survey reports that 68 percent of eighteen-to-twenty-nine-year-olds own a console—and some of the most popular games for this demographic are violent shooting games.[32]

An activity that is embedded within fraternity culture because of the demographic makeup of its members became institutionalized when, amid the 2020 global pandemic, the international headquarters of Phi Delta Theta posted on its website a list of ideas to keep the chapter going while its members were attending school remotely. Included among the recommendations were "playing Call of Duty: Modern Warfare" with one's fraternity brothers—a game in which each player logs in from their home and communicates with each other via headset. For fraternity members who aren't into playing video games themselves, an alternative offered was to watch their friends play them via live streaming platforms like Twitch.[33] As social distancing regulations stretched into the 2020–21 and 2021–22 academic years, some members of the fraternity community began to advocate for the use of video games as a recruiting tool. Nick Koulogeoge of the website Fraternity Man argues that playing video games remotely with potential new

Playing War and the Case for Fraternity Hazing

members enables fraternity members to evaluate the same things that they would in person, including individuals' attitude toward teamwork and their ability to adhere to specialized roles and functions.[34]

Viewed through the historical prism of fraternity culture and campus/organizational violence, today's in-person fraternity hazing is what you get when you ask predominantly white and wealthy eighteen-to-twenty-two-year-old veterans of multiple video game wars but participants in no actual ones to replicate the spirit and comradery forged through real battle. Without access to grenades, land mines, and IEDs, they create surrogate weapons of warfare from materials that are readily available in college dorms—namely, turds, body fluids, and whatever rotten leftovers happen to be lurking in the back of community refrigerators. In the absence of any actual enemies to fight, fraternity members take on these roles themselves.

For the brothers of the Delta Tau Delta chapter at Miami University (Ohio), the process of playing war during the 2019 initiation season allegedly included blindfolding their pledges and taking them into the "war room," where they were hit with paddles, kicked, spit on, and forced to guzzle a six-pack of Smirnoff Ice.[35] The pledge educator at Louisiana State University's Phi Delta Theta chapter allegedly prepared his 2017 charges for the physical rigors of "bible study"—a verbal quiz where new members were forced to drink hard liquor every time they missed a question about their fraternity's history—by shooting them with airsoft gun pellets.[36]

Perhaps nothing illuminates the notion that fraternity hazing is a form of playing war more, however, than a photograph posted to Total Frat Move (TFM). The image features four newly minted soldiers dressed in U.S. combat fatigues posing in front of a tank. In one hand each man is holding an assault rifle, and in the other, a corner of the Kappa Sigma fraternity flag. The caption of the photo reads: "Started out hazing pledges, now we're off to haze ISIS."[37] Several responses posted in the comments section of the post further collapse the discourses of fraternity hazing and combat by portraying the acts as interchangeable. "This is one of those rare times when you hope hazing leads to death," writes ProudToBe270.[38] "Stay safe down range fellas," writes another. "And remember it's better to be judged by 12 than carried by 6. Shoot 'me [sic] and let God sort 'em out."[39]

It's not just active fraternity members and recent alumni who collapse the distinction between campus hazing rituals and acts of war. The late conservative journalist Rush Limbaugh ignited a firestorm of criticism in 2004 when he compared the photographs taken of tortured inmates at Abu Ghraib by American military police to the hazing rituals of collegiate secret societies: "This is no different than what happens at the Skull and Bones initiation, and we're going to ruin people's lives over it, and we're going to hamper our military effort, and then we are going to really hammer them because they had a good time. You know, these people are being fired at every day. I'm talking about people having a good time, these people, you ever heard of emotional release? You [ever] heard of the need to blow some steam off?"[40] The fraternity brothers of the Sigma Pi chapter at Hofstra University likely didn't know about Limbaugh's metaphor when, in 2016, they dressed up their fraternity house like a POW camp and took photographs of their pledges in similarly demeaning poses.[41] In one grainy photograph, a row of men lie prostrate on the cement floor covered in flour; another photo shows one man crouching inside a small metal dog cage. A third takes the form of a close up of a row of shirtless and blindfolded men, who are kneeling—with their hands bound behind their backs—in front of a dirty and punched-out wall. A large swastika is inexplicably duct taped to the remaining drywall fragment behind them.[42] A writer for TFM argues that it looks worse than it is; the fact that there is pictorial evidence of these ordeals, he argues, suggests that the spectacle was more about the photo op than about suffering. Even if the writer's theory held water, he was right to acknowledge that the photographs weren't going to be read that way by the viewing public: "People are going to look at it like it's Abu Ghraib."[43]

The notion of hazing as a kind of combat is more than just a superficial metaphor employed by fraternity chapters because of its convenience. The result of recent research conducted by Gentry McCreary and Joshua Shutts reinforces what hazing expert Hank Nuwer has been saying for decades: that the relationship penetrates the ideological core of some chapters.[44] McCreary and Shutts asked active fraternity members to define brotherhood and describe how it differed from friendship. After compiling and coding the responses, the duo discovered that fraternity members' conceptions of brotherhood adhered to four broad schemas: solidarity, or the notion that "I've got your back, you've got mine"; shared social experiences; belonging; and accountability.[45] The research team then devised a survey instrument to evaluate these schemas and determine which were the more dominant. The survey was completed by 301 fraternity members across nineteen different institutions, and it revealed that most fraternity members defined and understood brotherhood primarily through the notions of shared social experiences and the commitment to mutual assistance.[46]

What does "mutual assistance" translate to in contemporary fraternity speak? The most succinct answer I got came from Dylan, a first-year medical student who, just five months earlier, was an active and well-respected member of a top-tier campus fraternity. While we consumed gritty sandwiches purchased in his medical school's cafeteria, Dylan flipped through his phone and showed me photos of his college-age self. He landed on a photo taken of him and his fraternity brothers. "Never fuck a brother," he told me. "That's the cardinal rule." According to Dylan, there are three main ways that you can do this: 1) publicly admit that you have eyes for any fraternity brother's fuck buddy; 2) publicly critique or disparage a fraternity brother; or 3) "not have a fraternity brother's back" or otherwise do something that privileges your individual needs and desires over those of your brothers.

While Dylan described his fraternity days as some of the best and most defining years of his young life, he also didn't put his organization on a pedestal, or consider its secrets and rituals too precious, at least not anymore. "The minute you graduate and get into the real world, it all seems kind of silly," he confessed. "But at the time you're going through it, it feels huge." Dylan's willingness to talk candidly with me about his fraternity's hazing practices created a hairline fracture in his fraternity chapter's code of silence that eventually split wide open. Two years after I started interviewing Dylan, the organization's national headquarters shuttered the chapter for an accumulation of violations and dangerous behavior that included rumored acts of hazing. When the chapter was still active, Dylan's fraternity brothers kept their mouths clamped shut, refusing to corroborate Dylan's stories beyond admitting a generalized acknowledgment of the existence of hazing practices within the university's FSL community (e.g., "Everyone does it"; "It's definitely a thing"). Once the fraternity was kicked off campus, however, its active and alumni members reasoned that they had nothing to lose by talking with me. Their only request was that I anonymize their identities as well as that of their chapter and school.

Many of what I'll call Chapter X's hazing rituals were designed to reinforce the value of mutual assistance, or "not fucking over your brother." One beloved tradition masqueraded as a new member scavenger hunt. What the pledges didn't know was that by design, the activity was doomed to fail.[47] After dividing the pledge class into four groups, the pledge master gave each group a list of items to locate and bring back to the fraternity house within thirty minutes. When the proverbial starting gun went off, the groups hastily shot off in all directions. Upon their return, the pledges discovered, much to their collective horror, one of their fraternity brothers sitting on a trashcan surrounded by all the chapter's active members. "Here's this guy, a big burly dude, a member of the lacrosse team," Dylan remembered. "I've never seen anyone looking so dejected in my life. They had covered him with eggs, sour milk, and other stuff. He was miserable." Instead of congratulating the pledges on the success of their mission, the older fraternity members lit them up. Dylan continued: "They were screaming at us, 'How did you not know that one of your pledge brothers was pulled out of the group and left here? You need to know where *all* of your brothers are at all times. Never leave *anyone* behind!'"

The mantra "Leave no man behind" is, of course, borrowed from American military culture. Paul Springer, a military studies professor at the Air Command and Staff College, told Mashable in 2014 that the phrase is rooted in the familial-like contract forged between volunteer servicemen and the government: "You promise to serve us, we promise not to leave you."[48] The sacralization of the principles of solidarity and mutual assistance plays into and off of traditional conceptions of masculinity that may find its most dramatic illustration in contemporary military culture but, as Junger points out, is not unique to it. All American men, he reminds us, are bred to be heroes and conditioned from an early age that their designated role in life-threatening situations is to rescue and to save others. Statistically, most of the people that able-bodied adult men save are women, the elderly, and children. The problem with this model of social relations is that it is lopsided. Men do all the saving, but Junger argues that they themselves "have to wait, on average, until age seventy-five before they can expect the same kind of assistance in a life-threatening situation that women get their whole lives."[49] What Junger intimates but doesn't come right out and say is that if men are culturally programmed to be rescuers, then they also share with the rest of humankind a need also to be saved and rescued by others. The conditions of war shorten the wait that time and age impose on men by allowing them, at different turns in their prime of their lives, to take up the roles of rescuer and the person in need of saving. One way of seeing hazing is as a practice that does the same thing.

Saving Men with Cinderblocks

The 2003 comedy *Old School* chronicles a trio of thirty-something-year-old men as they attempt simultaneously to stave off midlife crises and relive the glory days of their undergraduate years by starting a campus fraternity. While the film's many spot-on parodies of fraternity culture inspire guffaws and giggles, there is one scene that viewers can't watch without wincing. In what affectionately has come to be known as the "cinderblock scene," a

Playing War and the Case for Fraternity Hazing

group of prospective fraternity members are lined up on the roof of a campus building. The men are naked from the waist down, and each is holding a large cinderblock. Wrapped around the cinderblock is a rope. Attached to the other end of the rope is the pledge's penis. The point of the hazing ritual is to test the initiate's commitment to the organization. If they want in bad enough, they will accept the consequence of what will happen to their genitals when they throw their respective cinderblock over the ledge.[50]

Depending on who you ask, the cinderblock trust throw is either a gross exaggeration of a specific brand of ritualistic hazing or an accurate reflection of it.[51] Sighing in irritation when I asked him to weigh in on the debate, Dylan made his views clear. "Please," he replied. "That was a *movie*." The consensus of all the fraternity men from Chapter X was that there is a vast and impregnable difference between cinematic hazing rituals like those portrayed in *Animal House* (1978), *Neighbors* (2014), *Goat* (2016), and *Alpha Class* (2017), and those in which they participated in in real life. Specifically, the latter involved a cinderblock tied not to your genitals but to your hands. Here's Dylan again, describing his personal hazing experience:

> So first they blindfold you and shove you in cars and drive you around like crazy for about a half hour. The music is blaring, the heater is blasting as high as it will go. You can't see or hear anything, and you have no idea where you are or where you are going. And you are sweating. It's all very disorienting. When they stop and pull you out of the car, they tell you that you are at the edge of a cliff in the middle of nowhere but really you are in someone's backyard with a swimming pool. Then they call you up and tie a cinderblock to your hands and say, "Do you trust us?" After you say, "OK," they tell you that the bluff is about four feet away and that it's time to run and jump. When they say, "Go," you run and think you are running off a cliff but what really happens is that two guys catch you and one puts his hand over your mouth. At the same time, another brother jumps in the pool. And then one or two minutes later two other brothers jump in the water to make it sound like you are getting saved.

The suicidal act of jumping into a swimming pool with a cinderblock belted to one's waist signals the surrender of the individual's body to his friends in that the latter literally holds his life in their hands (or so he thinks). For blindfolded pledge brothers who are lined up nearby and listening to what's going on but can't see anything, it sounds like their pledge brother jumped into the pool and was saved from drowning by his fraternity brothers. The revelation that it was all just an elaborate farce communicates two messages. The first is that when you are in danger, your fraternity brothers will always protect you. The second is that even when you think you are in danger, you really aren't.

Instilling belief in the expectation of injury and the possibility of death has long been a common theme in fraternity hazing rituals. An unofficial handbook to the college fraternity pledging process that was written by a self-professed fraternity member in 1963 called *Fraternity Row* describes a variation of the cinderblock challenge that readers of the book might participate in as fraternity pledges. After being awakened in the middle of the night, the pledge is blindfolded and hauled to what he is told is the precipice of a high cliff:

> By this time, you realize that you and your pledge brothers are walking toward a high cliff and that you are all going to have to jump off of it, blindfolded. Soon you are all told to walk more slowly and you know you must be nearing the cliff. A couple of actives take you by the arm and guide you up to the edge of the cliff. You can feel the edge under your feet but you don't know how far you're going to have to fall. When the word is given, you and your pledge brothers jump.
>
> Now you learn the truth. You and your pledge brothers were not jumping off a high cliff. You were jumping, blindfolded, into a shallow ditch, but some of the pledges learned too late.[52]

Fake-out hazing rituals extend beyond the genre of trust jumps and falls to include a broad range of other activities that are designed to scare pledges but, in reality, amount to little more than smoke and mirrors. According to court documents, one of the rituals that Greg Rizzo and his pledge brothers allegedly participated in during their initiation into Beta Theta Pi fraternity at Pennsylvania State University (Penn State) in 2016 began with a sort of trust walk where pledges (whose heads were covered by pillowcases) were asked to walk barefoot over shards of glass, only to discover in the process that they were really walking over potato chips. They were then asked to drink the blood and urine of their brothers, which turned out to be tomato juice spiked with Tabasco sauce and Gatorade, respectively. Finally, the pledges were asked if they were willing to take a "hit" for their brothers. After answering in the affirmative, they weren't shot with a gun but whacked twice with a wooden paddle.[53]

The promise that the violence isn't real—that hazing may leave you a little bit roughed up, but that you will never be put in any actual life-threatening danger—is the reason why pledges participate in these initiation rituals. The assertion that hazing is mostly just illusion, however, is a product of over-confidence and a claim premised on false logic. *Old School* calls out fraterni-ties at the moment in the scene when, on command, the pledges nervously drop their cinderblocks off the roof. Much to the pledges' relief, the length of the rope attaching their penises to the object is longer than the height of the building. At the same time as the strategic thinking and benevolence of the fraternity brothers is displayed, so is their inability to anticipate and prepare for every calamity that may occur. The consequence of their cocky shortsightedness is exposed when one of the fraternity members drops his cinderblock and it breaks through the cover of a storm drain, pulling the man by his penis through the exposed hole and into the belowground sewer. The message that the clip comically but pointedly elucidates is that fraternity brothers don't intentionally break promises, but they aren't always equipped to keep some of the promises that they make. This is especially true when alcohol is in the mix.

Drunk Support

Alcohol and hazing are the conjoined twins of fraternity and sorority cul-ture: where you find one, you almost always find the other. The results of the Harvard School of Public Health's 2001 alcohol survey revealed that the single strongest predictor of binge drinking in college is fraternity or sorority membership.[54] The intimacy of the relationship between initiation rites and alcohol makes sense, given alcohol's special talent for lowering the drinker's inhibitions and thus making them more likely to do things that they wouldn't do when they are sober. In her history of American drinking culture, Susan Cheever notes that both the Revolutionary and the Civil Wars were waged by soldiers who were always at least a little buzzed.[55] In the same way that it would be difficult to get up the nerve to run headfirst into a pha-lanx of bayonets and canons without the assistance of a little liquid courage, it is equally hard to head into a hazing ritual without first pregaming away one's fear and anxiety.

According to researchers, alcohol consumption not only makes it eas-ier for men to suit up for real and fictional battles but also functions as a critical tool in attracting and retaining the affections of other men. In his 1969 groundbreaking work on men's initiation rites, Lionel Tiger showed that straight men's romantic and platonic preferences are the same; that is, they prefer their lovers and their same-sex friends to both be attractive and socially engaging.[56] Alcohol facilitates male bonding by loosening the lips—most productively, it seems, when women are not around. In 2014, a team of university researchers discovered that men smiled, laughed, and told more jokes when they were drinking in the company of other men. Men who drank in mixed company, however, displayed much lower signs of social bonding.[57]

The broader idea that the presence of women stymies the ability of men to pursue other men finds support in the work of Lois West, who, in 2001, conducted a comparative study of drinking cultures within college fraternities and military platoons. What he discovered surprised exactly no one: that people who are close choose to drink together.[58] Follow-up studies both confirm this finding and elaborate on its significance by showing that friends who drink together often perceive their relationships to be more intimate than the relationships of individuals who don't.[59]

Because of its combined competence at doing its job and ease of accessibility, alcohol is on the permanent guest list of fraternity social events, including and especially those involving the initiation of new members. From the outside looking in, competitive drinking games and contests where pledges are compelled to drink excessive amounts of alcohol constitutes a form of torture. In this view, requiring assistance is an unintended consequence of overconsumption and the people doing the assisting—the drunk individual's fraternity brothers—are an unwelcome burden and nuisance.

Sometimes this form of what anthropologist Thomas Vander Ven calls "drunk support" does take on this cast.[60] However, one of the things that we have been overlooking in our study of the landscape of undergraduate drinking culture is the way that college students and young adults of similar age binge drink not with the hope that they will defy the odds and avoid needing help from their friends, but, rather, precisely in order to seek it out.[61]

This peculiar phenomenon is on display all over campus but arguably is most pervasive within fraternity and sorority culture. To "have too much to drink" in the company of one's fraternity brothers or sorority sisters is, in its most basic sense, an explicit act of submission in that the drinker literally relinquishes their body to the care of friends for safekeeping. By allowing their friend to reach a state of inebriation that requires intervention and assistance, the individual's friends implicitly accept responsibility for the two-part task of tending to the incapacitated body and restoring it to its pre-drunken condition. The assumption of both the role of rescuer and person needing rescuing functions as an embodied performance of the defining

Playing War and the Case for Fraternity Hazing

principles of fraternal brotherhood and, by extension, sisterhood: solidarity and mutual assistance.

In the course of my fraternity and sorority advisory work and research for this book, I have witnessed firsthand multiple times the performance of the scripted drama that is triggered by the act of binge drinking. In one representative case in point, I watched as an inebriated fraternity member stumbled out of a downtown nightclub where his fraternity semiformal was being held and into the attached garden patio, where he proceeded to distribute the contents of his stomach all over the grass and bushes. Almost immediately, a small herd of fraternity men congregated around their friend, sat him down, and busied themselves with the tasks of cleaning up both the man and the area surrounding him. The drunk man's slurred insistence that he only needed one helper evolved into a heated squabble— not over who *had* to take care of him but rather who *got* to. Each fraternity brother made the case for his qualifications for the job: "I'm his Big." "I'm less drunk than you." "I'm his roommate." "I helped him out last time and know what to do." Later, I asked some of the men why they wanted to spend their evening disposing of barf bags and hand-feeding their friend saltines instead of partying with their other friends. They looked at me like I was the village idiot. "It's what brothers do," they told me.

The competition for playing rescuer in the fraternity house speaks to both the function and prestige of the roles of both the rescuer and person being rescued. Within the context of men's friendship, binge drinking accomplishes the same thing as trench warfare in that it creates a stage upon which individuals can alternately play both the role of the rescuer and the person needing to be rescued, often in quick rotation. Following the logic that practice makes perfect, the best soldiers and fraternity brothers are those men who have the most experience playing each role. By extension, bad brothers are those who either don't do their jobs well, or don't do them at all.

The Social Benefits of Other People's Dead Friends

Thanks to court records, we know a lot about what happened at the FSU Pi Kappa Phi party on the night of November 2, 2017.[62] The chapter's twenty-one-member pledge class had been under a strict liquor ban for weeks, but that night was a special occasion. It was Big Brother Night, the evening where each pledge brother would finally meet the older fraternity member designated to serve as his mentor, advocate, and go-to person for the duration of his fraternity experience. To celebrate outside the watchful eye of the university and their national headquarters, the chapter's executive council (i.e., the chapter president and other elected leaders) arranged for the pledges to be taken by Uber and Lyft from the fraternity house to a private residence located two and a half miles away. There, each pledge was given a bottle of alcohol hand-picked by his new Big brother. Andrew Coffey's Big brother—twenty-year-old Connor Ravelo—gifted Coffey a bottle of Wild Turkey 101 Bourbon. Several fraternity members later told investigators that a tradition called the Family Bottle dictated that pledges were expected to consume the entire content of their bottles that night.[63] After downing as much booze as he could, Coffey passed out on a futon on the house's front porch. Three fraternity members, including Ravelo, moved Coffey inside and laid him on his side on a couch. Several hours later, another pledge found Coffey unresponsive.[64] During the 911 call, someone can be heard saying, "We had a party last night and my friend passed out on the couch on his side and his lips are purple. His body is extremely stiff, and I can't wake him up, and, honestly, I don't feel a pulse."[65]

If the circumstances surrounding Coffey's death sound eerily familiar, it's because they echo in striking detail the story of what happened to a Penn State Beta Theta Pi pledge named Timothy Piazza exactly nine months earlier. Caitlin Flanagan and others have elegantly stitched together the horrifying sequence of events that led to Piazza's tragic end.[66] As part of a hazing ritual called the Gauntlet, Piazza and his fellow pledge brothers ran through an obstacle course that included three drinking stations. At the first, the pledges chugged from a bottle of vodka; at the second, they drank beer; and they finished off the course by drinking from a bag of wine. The rapid consumption of so much alcohol within such a short period of time impaired Piazza's motor skills so dramatically that he slipped while descending the staircase to the fraternity house's basement. The initial fall knocked him unconscious, and he had to be carried upstairs by four fraternity members. Despite noticing a large bruise on his left abdomen, the fraternity brothers did not seek professional medical assistance for their injured fraternity brother but instead tried to revive him by slapping him in the face, punching his stomach, and pouring beer on him. Security footage shows Piazza regaining consciousness in the early morning hours but falling twice more in his attempt to get to the front door. When the brothers of Beta Theta Pi finally called for an ambulance some twelve hours after Piazza's initial fall, Piazza's limbs were rigid, his face was gray, and, according to a text message

Playing War and the Case for Fraternity Hazing

sent by one fraternity member who witnessed the scene, "he looked fucking dead."[67] At the hospital, it was revealed that Piazza had sustained a traumatic brain injury and ruptured spleen. He died the next day.

For the families of Andrew Coffey and Tim Piazza, a single incident of fraternity hazing upended everything in their lives. If the past is any indicator of the future, however, their sons' deaths are not likely to radically change national fraternity hazing culture. In fact, there is an argument to be made that the way that these and other fraternity hazing death cases make the whole situation worse. A year before Coffey's death, I asked FSU fraternity men to describe their organizations and identify where they felt their chapter ranked in relation to other campus chapters in terms of prestige and reputation. "My fraternity is struggling," said exactly no one, even those from chapters that struggled to recruit and retain members. What I did hear throughout my interviews at FSU and everywhere else, however, were a lot of superlatives: "My fraternity is the best"; "We're top tier"; "We're definitely number one." The same principle of exceptionalism that enables fraternity members of all chapters to see themselves as exemplary specimens of their kind also justifies the violence and severity of their hazing rituals. As Dylan, the recent fraternity alum, aptly put it, "You can't just *get* the name. You have to earn it."

What it takes to "earn" one's letters varies depending on the chapter, but the fact that fraternity men elsewhere are dying in the attempt both validates the rigor of the activity (binge drinking, in the cases of Piazza and Coffey) and reaffirms the superiority of one's own chapter. Other fraternity chapters let their brothers die; we protect ours. Peruse the comment sections of news reports about Piazza's case on fraternity-themed websites like BroBible and Total Frat Move and you'll notice a common thread: respondents place blame for Piazza's death squarely and almost exclusively on Piazza's fraternity brothers. What happened to Piazza isn't the result of a cultural cancer within fraternity life, but the failure of individual soldiers who shirked their moral and physical duties by leaving a man behind:

> What happened here? The so called "men of principle" at this frat
> didn't give a shit about their new "brother," they were only worried
> about their own selves. They never called for help. They could have
> called his roommates to get him, they could have dropped him at the
> hospital, they could have even taken him 100 ft. down to the corner
> and made an anonymous 911 call, but they didn't.[68]

I'm an active member of my fraternity, and to say I would ever let one of my own brothers DIE for the sake of ensuring the future of my chapter is fucking disgusting.[69]

The same hierarchy of blame also surfaces in the margins of the Coffey case. While nine of Coffey's fraternity brothers were criminally charged in his death (basically everyone who held leadership positions in the chapter and Ravelo, who provided Coffey with the alcohol), Ravelo was singled by the grand jury for particular rebuke: "The last observations of him [Coffey] alive were during the late-night hours while other partygoers played pool. He was heard 'snoring loudly' on a couch in the living room. His Big Brother left him there and went home."[70] Of all of the balls that were dropped that evening, the grand jury deemed that Ravelo's abandonment of Coffey was the worst. In accusing Ravelo of privileging his own desires over the safety and well-being of his fraternity brother, the grand jury endorsed the same "bro code" that it professed to condemn.

Proving that history tends to repeat itself, the exact same thing happened in the Max Gruver case. Six weeks before Andrew Coffey died at FSU, the Louisiana State University (LSU) first-year Phi Delta Theta pledge was forced to drink himself to death. In a rare break in solidarity, the chapter's fraternity members assigned sole blame for Gruver's death to one of their own: Matthew Naquin. Chapter members and graduates testified in court that they told the twenty-one-year-old pledge educator to reduce the severity of the hazing rituals (evidently, they were OK with the practice continuing), but that their counsel fell on deaf ears. "It only takes one kid to bring down the fraternity," Phillip Clark testified. "One bad apple can ruin everything."[71] Like the juries that preceded them, the one in Baton Rouge largely let the group off the hook by coming down hard on one individual. In July 2019, they convicted Naquin of negligent homicide.

The bad apple argument is not without flaws, but, when you look at the numbers, it also has some merit. There are roughly 380,000 active members of Interfraternity Council (IFC) fraternities at any given time on college campuses, and thousands of members of independent and culturally based fraternities.[72] Even the most conservative of estimates puts the number of individuals who have passed through the four-year revolving door of collegiate fraternity membership in the millions over the past twenty years. The data isn't precise, but, applying the widest definition of a hazing death calculated by Hank Nuwer, about sixty fraternity men have died from hazing-related activities since 2000. Given the senselessness and ease of its prevention,

Playing War and the Case for Fraternity Hazing

that is sixty deaths too many.[73] But that number also is dwarfed when put in context of all the causes of death for college students in the United States every year. Car accidents comprise the leading cause of death for college students (about half of which are alcohol-related) by a big margin. Roughly 1,100 college students commit suicide every year in America.[74] By contrast, seven fraternity members died from hazing in 2017, including Coffey and Piazza.[75]

No one advertises that hazing isn't the mass killer that it's portrayed to be, in part because it's not in anyone's interest to do so. Universities, the professional anti-hazing industry, and the media all benefit from keeping this narrative alive. Portraying fraternity hazing deaths as a national "epidemic" or in other synonyms of crisis as the media has been wont to do certainly is helpful in captivating public interest and injecting urgency into proposals for tougher laws against the practice.[76] But at the same time as we champion and celebrate the successes achieved by mobilizing dead fraternity members as public service announcements and agents of institutional and cultural change, we may find it valuable to weigh these successes against the benefits accrued by fraternity men by holding to the narrative that joining a fraternity means putting one's life at serious risk.

It's long been recognized that one of the biggest appeals of secret societies is the risk factor that accompanies membership in them. There is a strong correlation between high-risk fraternity chapters (i.e., those with more conduct and alcohol and drug violations) and campus popularity. The chapters that have the longest list of infractions are perceived to have the most fun and thus, have the most competitive admissions processes. Just as the continued appeal of these chapters depends on them having a lengthy and varied rap sheet, so the appeal of fraternity membership more broadly depends on preserving the illusion of a high body count.

What's true about individual chapters also seems to hold for broader fraternity membership as well. As part of the preliminaries to his initiation into Cornell's chapter of Kappa Alpha in 1873, a pledge named Mortimer Leggett was blindfolded and transported several miles into the country, at which point he was dropped off and instructed to find his way back to the chapter house. After stumbling around in the darkness for a few minutes, Mortimer was "rescued" by two fellow chapter members, who, following custom, took him by the arm with the aim of escorting him back to campus. In the process of groping their way home, the disoriented men slipped over a thirty-seven-foot cliff.[77] The incident—the first reported fraternity hazing death in the country—made national headlines and caused such a public uproar that it prompted one prominent journalist to predict that it "is likely to wound fatally the system."[78]

Of course, it didn't. Over the subsequent century, the college's Greek letter community flourished until history repeated itself in October 2019 when another Cornell first-year student met his tragic end in an eerily similar way. Antonio Tsialas was last seen alive at an unregistered "dirty rush" Phi Kappa Psi party where, according to a police statement, attendees were encouraged to participate in a variety of drinking games. His body was discovered at the bottom of a nearby gorge two days later.[79]

The successive hazing deaths of Piazza, Gruver, and Coffey in 2017 sent similar shock waves through the national Greek community and reignited the public's war cry against fraternities. Given all the bad press—and there was a lot of it—one would think that incoming first-year students would shy away from these organizations. Instead, the exact opposite has happened: more students than ever are clamoring to join them.[80] A year after Antonio Tsialas's death (which was ruled an accident), Cornell permanently banned Phi Kappa Psi from campus.[81] What about the college's other sorority and fraternity chapters? Twenty-eight of the thirty chapters voluntarily banned all chapter activities for the remainder of the fall semester, but, as the *Chronicle of Higher Education* reporter Wesley Jenkins mused at the time, the move ended up being largely symbolic.[82] Just three months later, the Greek letter community at Cornell was up and running again. By dedicating its fall 2020 Hazing Prevention Week activities to Tsialas, the college all but admitted that the man's accidental death was helped along by fraternity hazing. The dark shadow that this admission cast on the community, however, was replaced in the same press release by the announcement of a new scholarship named in Tsialas's honor.[83]

While no charges have been filed in the Tsialas case to date, the hazing death trials of Piazza and Coffey resulted in misdemeanor convictions (mere slaps on the wrist, in the views of family members and anti-hazing advocates).[84] Naquin's trial for Gruver's death at LSU, by contrast, yielded an unprecedented result in the form of a felony conviction. The sentence, which was handed down in July 2019, was supposed to send a clear message to the entire fraternity community: that the "boys will be boys" excuse isn't going to cut it anymore in the court of law.[85] Unfortunately, the warning went in one ear and out the other, since, just three months later, a new Phi Kappa Psi member was forced to drink himself nearly to death during a pledging activity. If LSU's fraternity community is revealing itself to be a slow learner, the local legal system is, so far, standing its ground; the pledge's twenty-one-year-old new member educator was arrested and charged with one count of felony hazing.[86]

Will upping the consequences for hazing reduce its severity or, in the most optimistic of worlds, eliminate it completely? It's way too early to tell. While everyone hopes it turns the tide one way, there is also an equal if not greater chance that further criminalizing acts of hazing will make membership in fraternity chapters that continue to haze even more dangerous and thus desirable.

While the legal system may be an unwitting promoter of hazing by clamping down on it, the governing body of college fraternities is more direct in its support of fraternity communities that haze. At the same time as the investigation into Tsialas's death was making national headlines in 2020, Cornell's Interfraternity Council was featured on the North American Interfraternity Conference's website. In the photo, two IFC representatives are tabling in a gymnasium at what appears to be a student club or fraternity information fair.[87] The decision to profile a fraternity community currently under investigation for a hazing-related death could be written off as unintentional if the North American Interfraternity Conference (NIC) wasn't so media and public relations savvy. This is an organization, after all, that exists to support and advocate for college fraternities and thus bends over backward to craft and maintain a positive narrative of its culture. The bad press from the Tsialas case should have prompted the NIC to distance itself from Cornell's fraternity community, but it's telling that in the moment when the horrifying events of that fateful night were slowly being revealed to potential and current fraternity members and the public alike, the NIC chose to indirectly promote it.

It's not just the legal system and fraternity industry that are at fault here. The public also participates in the glamorization of fraternity initiation rituals. Specifically, we help fraternities preserve their allure by keeping the narrative of their danger in constant circulation. In 2018, a research team from the University of Texas looked at fraternity-related news coverage and found empirical proof of what we already know: when fraternities make headlines, it's more often because they've done something negative than positive.[88]

If part of the popular perception of fraternities comes from biased reporting, the other part comes from us. Unlike many other forms of violent death, which are either accidental or have some real motivation (criminal or otherwise), participating in hazing rituals is, at least on the surface, voluntary and supposed to be fun. After we stop shaking our heads over the utter pointlessness of it all, however, we keep watching. As consumers of media, we get what we ask for. And what we say with our remote controls and share, link, and like buttons is that we can't get enough of dead, wealthy white boys. There is a little JonBenét Ramsey in every fraternity member who has died by hazing—their photos are paraded on the evening news for weeks at a time; their untimely deaths become the subjects of *Dateline* investigations, CNN interviews, and feature stories in smart culture magazines; and the criminal trials of their fraternity brothers receive daily coverage and commentary by national news and cable TV commentators.

As a mother of three sons, I empathize with the parents of hazing victims and admire and appreciate their attempt to mobilize their sons' stories to enact legal and cultural change. But in as much as it is possible to depersonalize fraternity hazing deaths, we see that this category of victim hogs a disproportionate amount of media limelight and, in doing so, squeezes out other stories of tragic and premature loss. What some might call this over-memorialization of the dead white fraternity member works in a backward kind of way to fuel the practice of hazing by conferring upon historically white fraternity members a scary kind of exceptionalism that says that their deaths—and, by extension, their lives—matter more than other similarly aged individuals.

The national narrative of dead fraternity members perpetuates the notion that different human bodies have different values, and, what's more, that those belonging to fraternity members are among the most precious. Hazing further reinforces the broader claim that fraternity bodies are exceptional by pronouncing upon those who make it through the initiation process a special entitlement: the right to wield control over people's bodies.

This is, in fact, the first lesson that new members learn when they join a fraternity. Prior to learning about an organization's history, values, and moral codes, pledges are taught through the violence done to their own bodies at the hands of others that the fraternity house is inherently a place where nonmembers have no agency, where pledges are "owned" by and "belong to" his brothers.

While fraternity pledges enter the fraternity house with no value, they are promised that they will acquire it at the end of the initiation process. Hazing endows pledges' bodies with value by proving through their endurance of the suffering inflicted upon them the confirming stamp that they have bodies worth saving and, equally important, that their bodies are capable of saving others. The title of full-fledged membership in a fraternal organization includes the right to lay claim to others' bodies, and to do with those

Playing War and the Case for Fraternity Hazing

bodies what they want. This is why newly minted fraternity members often and openly fantasize about hazing next year's initiates and spend much of their first year of membership reflecting on their own hazing experience and planning ways to tweak and revise the acts that they will make future pledges perform. For some chapters, these plans include beating their new friends, dousing them in hot sauce and boiling water, hitting them with paddles and sticks, and making them drink ludicrous amounts of alcohol to the point where some of them will unintentionally die. While the potential costs of hazing are high, so are the benefits from surviving it. Included among the perks that come from perfecting the art of playing the rescuer and rescued throughout college is the confidence in knowing that the broader fraternity community has your back after graduation.

If mutual assistance is code for drunk support in the fraternity house, what "never leaving a brother behind" looks like outside the campus is a powerful network of fraternity alums helping current fraternity members get prestigious internships and jobs, often at the exclusion of others.

SEVEN

Friends Who Fit

Things were going well for Brett Kavanaugh until, suddenly, they weren't. The U.S. Court of Appeals judge was gliding through his job interview for the U.S. Supreme Court in late 2018 when women from his high school and college years began emerging with disturbing tales alleging that he sexually harassed and assaulted them. While the nation remained sharply divided on how to weigh these accusations and what to do with them, there was never any question about Kavanaugh's professional qualifications for the role—he checked all the standard boxes. In addition to boasting an Ivy League law degree, prominent clerkships, and decades of public service, Kavanaugh has something else in common with most of the men who have sat on the same bench: in college, he was a member of a white fraternity. Since the early twentieth century, Greek letter members have made up 85 percent of Supreme Court justices, comprised 63 percent of all U.S. presidential cabinet members, 76 percent of U.S. senators, and 85 percent of Fortune 500 executives. Eighteen Greek letter alums (69 percent) have gone on to become U.S. presidents, including two from the same chapter (Yale's Delta Kappa Epsilon, or DKE) as Kavanaugh.[1] The perception that fraternity membership instantly slingshots individuals to the top of the socioeconomic food chain isn't a universal truth, but, as fraternity and sorority life (FSL) spokesman Kent Christopher Owen modestly puts it, fraternity alumni have "achieved affluence and prominence in dispropor-tionate numbers."[2]

The clustering of fraternity men at the top has been going on for so long that it is easy to overlook its significance. While fraternity men can be lumped into the larger category of society's movers and shakers who are the beneficiaries of white male privilege, they also comprise a special category within it. Fraternity men spend their formative college years learning about the virtues of and practicing acts of population control and mutual assistance. After graduation, it's time to get down to business—literally. The same skills honed at fraternity parties and through hazing rituals are put to use in the professional arena. Instead of rescuing each other from self-induced alcohol poisoning, they now spare each other from having to go through a different type of hell—namely, navigating the contemporary job market without any professional connections. Where once they competed against each other for social capital on campus, fraternity alums from all white chapters join forces after graduation to lay claim to and control of our nation's social, political, and economic resources. Later, we will see how they do this by creating professional pipelines from college fraternity chapters to investment banks, corporate empires, political think tanks, and other sectors of commerce and industry. Of course, keeping the right kind of people funneling through this pipeline also means keeping everyone else out. The whole system depends on it.

The Mentality of Us against Them

The social Greek letter fraternities that sprouted up in the 1820s and 1830s had been in existence for about fifty years before women started matriculating on their campuses. The first coeducational colleges were founded by groups—Quakers, abolitionists, Methodists, and Congregationalists—in the 1830s and 1840s, but the push to welcome women into the student bodies of existing colleges and universities didn't kick in until the 1870s and 1880s. By the start of the twentieth century, men still far outnumbered women on campus, but there were enough of the latter occupying the coveted first-row classroom seats, winning academic prizes, and demanding their own restroom facilities that their presence felt less like a pesky annoyance and more like a forced invasion.[3]

One of the responses to the desegregation of academic space was the flourishing of gender-segregated private spaces like men's-only clubs, masonic lodges, and college fraternities. While each type of fraternal order developed its own unique traditions and practices, social historian Mark C. Carnes notes that all the organizations shared the common purpose of effacing "religious values and emotional ties with women."[4] In his cultural study of masculinity in America, Michael Kimmel goes further, calling the fraternal lodge "the unfeminized church, devoid of clucking mother hens and effete ministers."[5]

Kavanaugh's fraternity chapter serves as a representative case in point. As one of the oldest and most prestigious chapters on Yale's campus, DKE had a long-standing reputation for throwing drunken parties and being sexually aggressive toward women. During Kavanaugh's confirmation hearings, a photograph surfaced from the school's archives that showed the judge's fraternity brothers flying a flag made from female classmates' bras and panties, items that the women say were pilfered from their rooms while they were attending class.[6] In the thirty-odd years since Kavanaugh graduated from Yale, DKE has not demonstrated that it has done much, if anything, to clean up its act. In 2010, one of the chapter's initiation rituals was secretly recorded and subsequently went viral. The grainy footage shows the chapter's fraternity members leading blindfolded pledges around the first-year dorms and women's center while the new recruits chant "No means yes / yes means anal."[7] The uproar over this incident resulted in a five-year suspension. Following its reinstatement, the chapter found itself again in hot water when, in 2017, a female Yale student accused the former president of DKE of forcing her to have nonconsensual sex at a 2016 holiday party.[8]

One would think that the public outcry over these episodes would motivate other fraternity chapters to clean up their acts, but sadly this isn't the case. The Internet is bursting at the seams with examples of fraternity behavior ranging from thoughtless and insensitive to downright repulsive. An example of all of these things combined: if you were the parent of an Old Dominion University first-year woman in the fall of 2015, you would have been greeted on campus by a trio of bedsheet welcome signs hung over the second-floor railing of the Sigma Nu house that read: "Rowdy and fun: Hope your baby girl is ready for a good time . . . ; Freshman daughter drop off (with an arrow pointing to the Sigma Nu front porch); and "Go ahead and drop off mom too."[9] The fraternity members in the state of Virginia seemingly have a short memory, because, just a year after the welcome sign incident at Old Dominion, two University of Richmond Kappa Alpha members emailed about 100 male students announcing the school year's first house party, which ended with this directive: "If you haven't started drinking already, catch up. Tonight's the type of night that makes fathers afraid to send their daughters away to school. Let's get it."[10]

That white fraternities are rooted in misogyny and derive much of their power from identifying women as an enemy to be conquered and dominated isn't a surprise to social psychologists who study group formation and be-havior. Greek letter organizations comprise quintessential examples of what they call in-and-out-group homogeneity. In-group status is constructed by individuals with shared qualities coming together to denigrate those who don't fit the mold. Women were the first so-called others to trespass on men's collegiate hallowed ground. Men who didn't fit the bill—and by that I mean those who weren't white, wealthy, and Protestant—rushed in right behind them.[11]

If some fraternity members at the beginning of the twentieth century saw their chapter houses as physical representations of white male Protes-tant privilege, then the chapter house today is the last unconquered corner of the college campus. In addition to having to rub shoulders with women, Catholics, Jews, immigrants, and members of the middle and working classes, today's fraternity members also face multiplying threats in the form of students of color, commuter students, and members of the LGBTQ+ community.[12] And the list of "others" keeps getting longer. According to the National Center for Education Statistics, the percentage of Asian/Pacific Islander, African American, Hispanic, and Indigenous college students has been steadily increasing, while the number of white students enrolled in college is declining.[13] In what is certainly bad news for white fraternities' intent on staying that way, the college student body is becoming exponen-tially more heterogeneous with each passing year.

Viewing fraternities as combatants in a turf war doesn't excuse offensive and uncouth behavior, but it does explain how fraternities became bastions of racism and sexism, and why unmooring these organizations from tra-ditional ways of thinking about and treating those who stand outside their ranks is so difficult. If we reserve some of our greatest expressions of cruelty for those by whom we feel most threatened, then today's biggest enemy (right behind women) is the category of individuals that one fraternity in the 1950s unflinchingly labeled "non-Aryans."[14]

Just Us

During her college years, Claire was an active member of her National Pan-hellenic Conference (NPC) sorority. Now in her mid-thirties, she oversees the roughly twenty chapters of her sorority located at colleges and universi-ties in the Mid-Atlantic and Southeast regions of the United States. As some-one who is in constant contact with hundreds of sorority women and their alumnae advisors, Claire has her pulse on who is joining her organization, and who isn't. While Claire doesn't know exactly how many women of color are in her ranks, she readily admits that racial and ethnic diversity is a problem in all her chapters, save those in Baltimore and Washington, D.C. While acknowledging that white sororities and fraternities have a long way to go when it comes to issues of diversity and inclusion, Claire attributes the lack of diversity to the painfully small recruiting pool from which campus FSL groups have to draw. "Universities want us to be more diverse," she explains, "but there is no diverse population to pull from." Claire didn't intend for her racial calculus to be offensive, but, through its hyperbolic erasure of existing students of color from the equation, it is. This wasn't the first time I encountered the supply chain line of reasoning; I have heard it so often during my research that it's clear that it's become something of a standard narrative. Though disparaging because of its inaccuracy, the underlying point of the argument holds: In many parts of the country, including and especially the South, colleges and universities are still predominantly white spaces.[15]

In her electric 2018 *New York Times* best seller, *So You Want to Talk About Race*, Ijeoma Oluo describes what it is like being a Black woman in a society that is structured in such a way that its social, political, and economic forms of capital are largely held and governed by rich white people. "Racism in America," she writes, "exists to exclude people of color from opportunity and progress so that there is more profit for others deemed superior. This profit itself is the greater promise for non-racialized people—*you will get more because they exist to get less*."[16] By framing the relationship between whites and everyone else in economic terms, Oluo follows the philosopher and critical race theorist Charles W. Mills, who argues that individuals who are socialized as white are conditioned by history and culture to see themselves as superior to people of color. "When white people say 'Justice,'" he writes, "they mean 'Just Us.'"[17] All fraternities in the North American Interfraternity Conference (NIC) have clauses in their bylaws expressly forbidding discrimination against nonwhite pledges and members. But a single line in a legal document doesn't mean that members of protected classes are made to feel particularly welcome in white Greek letter organizations. In an interview with a CNN reporter, sociologist Matthew Hughey described the nation's fraternity and sorority system as a form of homegrown apartheid, and it's easy to see why.[18]

Seven percent of the student body at Clemson University identifies as Black, but why would any of these individuals fork over hefty membership fees to join a white fraternity, especially after one chapter held a gang-themed "Cripmas Party" where guests were encouraged to wear bandanas, saggy pants, and T-shirts screen-printed with photos of a 1990s Black rap-per?[19] The same goes for the University of Georgia, where, up until 2015, the white fraternity and sorority community hosted several Civil War–themed events, most notably Kappa Alpha Order's (KA) Old South Week and Sigma Alpha Epsilon's (SAE) Magnolia Ball. In the case of the latter, fraternity members dressed up like plantation owners and their dates (who were al-most invariably sorority women) like Scarlett O'Hara—complete with hoop skirts and parasols.[20] In March 2019, four Tau Kappa Epsilon (TKE) mem-bers at the University of Georgia posted a video to social media where they pretended to whip each other with a belt while saying "Pick my cotton."[21] Four months later, the KA chapter at the University of Mississippi made national headlines when a photo surfaced showing three of its members posing with shotguns in front of a memorial for Emmett Till, the fourteen-year-old African American boy who was brutally beaten and killed in 1955 for allegedly flirting with a white woman.[22]

John Hechinger's 2017 book-length study of SAE notes that several of this fraternity's chapters have come under fire in recent history for unques-tionably racist behavior, suggesting that the problem isn't isolated to one chapter or geographic region but is pervasive throughout the organization itself. This notion was solidified after a leaked video surfaced showing a busload of University of Oklahoma SAE fraternity members spewing forth a racist chant, which they learned on a SAE leadership cruise.[23]

When it comes to fraternity-generated racial insensitivity and cultural appropriation, there are plenty of examples to go around—every nationality and ethnicity is a potential source of mockery in the guise of a party theme. The invitation to a 2013 Duke University Asian-themed affair opened with "Herro Nice Duke Peopre!!" and closed with "Chank You."[24] Three frater-nity chapters at California Polytechnic University joined forces to throw a "Colonial Bros and Nava-Hos" party on Thanksgiving Day the same year.[25] What would Cinco de Mayo be without a "Mexican-themed" fiesta? White fraternity members at Baylor, Randolph-Macon College, the University of Texas at Austin, and my own college dressed up as construction workers, drug runners, and border control agents.[26] In the case of the latter, the same fraternity chapter that I would go on to advise a few years later threw a Mexican-themed "Cinco de Drinko" party where guests showed up dressed as border patrol agents and wearing ponchos and sombreros.[27]

While fraternities may be the masterminds behind these offensive party themes, sorority women attend the festivities and thus are complicit in the damage they cause. Included on the list of cringeworthy examples is the

University of Maryland sorority sister who celebrated her twenty-first birthday by taking photos in front of her alcohol-themed cake that was piled high with minibottles, beer bottles, and inscribed with "Suck a nigga dick," the latter being a reference to a Three Six Mafia lyric.[28] A Kansas State sorority woman posted a selfie on social media wearing a mud mask along with the caption "Feels good to finally be a n—."[29] Harley Barber, a nineteen-year-old sorority woman at the University of Alabama celebrated Dr. Martin Luther King Jr. Day in 2018 by posting a profanity-ridden racist rant on social media. "I'm in the South now, bitch," she said in a video uploaded to her Finsta (fake Instagram) account, while surrounded by a group of friends. "So everyone can fuck off. I'm from New Jersey, so I can say n— as much as I want."[30]

Barber's homemade videos (yes, there are multiple), ignited the fury of the Internet and pronounced collective shame on the broader fraternity and sorority community. After her videos went viral, Barber made a perfunctory and entirely predictable public apology. "I did something really, really bad," she told the *New York Post*. "I don't know what to do and I feel horrible. I'm wrong and there's just no excuse for what I did."[31] Like other statements belonging to the same genre, Barber's apology doesn't make it entirely clear what she is apologizing for: her racist rant or her failure to heed her sorority sisters' advice to keep her homemade videos to herself and not post them to social media. Either way, their very public circulation worked to undermine the publicly documented strides that the university has made in recent years to make their fraternity and sorority community more racially diverse and inclusive.

Barber's excuse was that she was drunk. The fraternity members in my chapter who threw the Cinco de Mayo party acknowledged that their actions were thoughtless but weren't particularly remorseful. "You have to admit that it was funny," one of the partygoers maintained several years later. The sentiment that racism can be legitimized (and that fraternity members have the authority to legitimate it) by packaging it as a joke isn't unique to fraternity culture, of course, but it is fair to say that the average white fraternity man at Rollins is less likely to have spent his youth being educated in critical race theory than being schooled by YouTube personalities and cable comedians who make a living out of mocking protected classes. These aren't uninformed mistakes, however, but part of a larger epistemology of ignorance. The term, coined by Mills in his grounding book *The Racial Contract*, refers to the way that ignorance is structured and institutionalized in society in such a way that the dominant group (i.e., white people) can remain ignorant about their ignorance of race and racism. That many white people live in a state of willful oblivion about their own white privilege doesn't condone or excuse fraternity and sorority racist behavior of any kind, but it does help explain how the desire to be the next funny man combines with unacknowledged white supremacist beliefs to create what we see in the leaked Swarthmore Phi Psi documents.

In April 2019, an anonymous source sent the elite liberal arts college's two student newspapers, the *Phoenix* and *Voices*, copies of the fraternity chapter's meeting minutes from the spring 2013 and spring 2014 semesters.[32] Some of these documents bear a vague resemblance to what notes might look like from actual chapter meetings—there is mention of dues and philanthropy events for example. However, most of the entries take the form of painfully self-conscious comedic recaps of the week whose stated goal is to "roast" specific chapter members. That entries pay homage to and attempt to emulate stand-up sketch comedy is evidenced by an early reference to the controversial Black comedian Dave Chappelle, who is known for poking fun at just about everything and everyone, including Blacks, whites, gay and transgender rights, and the women's movement.[33]

We see white fraternity men trying to hit the mark in a photo of a fraternity member who sustained a head injury during a lacrosse game that resulted in his forehead being wrapped in a thick gauze bandage. The photo caption reads "Tupac Shakur," referring to the 90s Black hip-hop artist noted for the omnipresent bandana that he wore around his forehead who was murdered in Las Vegas at the age of twenty-five.[34] Another compares the chapter's signature party to a rival fraternity's 80s-themed party, saying that the former made the latter "look like Hilary [*sic*] Clinton's butchfest bachelorette party at the local Tilted Kilt."[35] The recap of the event includes a photo of two men—one white and another presumably not (all identifying features have been redacted by the student newspapers) covered in colored chalk powder. The caption purports to articulate "what everyone was thinking during Paint" but no one would say—namely, that no one could tell the two men apart: "They literally look the exact same." The same party is also notable because of a unique hookup that occurred: one of the fraternity members allegedly (none of the described events can be confirmed as really having happened) took a woman of color into an upstairs room, only to have another fraternity man pound on the door and demand entry on the grounds that he "wants to see some black nips!"

This isn't the first time that a fraternity's amateur comedy hour has made its way into public view. Just a year before the Swarthmore documents surfaced, the sixteen new members of Syracuse's Theta Tau, a professional engineering fraternity and non–Interfraternity Council (IFC) member, were given an hour to create and rehearse a roast of their older brothers in the style of a Comedy Central skit. What they came up with was a series of sketches that involved simulated sex acts, mimed attacks on the disabled, and the assertion that one of the members "likes black cock."[36]

In both the Syracuse and Swarthmore examples, the go-to strategy for embarrassing one's white brother is to illustrate how he looks or acts Black. The men's white superiority is affirmed by the implicit retraction of that comparison and the reassurance that the racial conflation was just temporary. The fraternity man's hookup with a woman of color was just a one-night stand; the head injury will heal, and the forehead bandage will come off; a shower is all that stands between the white man and his reclaimed racial identity; the white man isn't really gay and thus isn't interested in any penis except his own.

There is something more to it than this, though. As an English professor, what's fascinating to me about the Swarthmore entries is their attentiveness to form. Unlike the hastily cobbled together Syracuse video, these are thoughtfully constructed and fabulously creative analogies. The Tupac Shakur metaphor didn't just emerge out of nowhere. The Hillary Clinton jab required intellectual labor to generate. The deliberateness paid to the craft of writing signals a second level of critique: it's not just the subjects of the roast who are being evaluated but also the authors of the roasts themselves. If the in-group status of the former is affirmed by being a target of roasting, then the status of the latter is affirmed by the quality of their roasts. The best entries are those that approximate most closely the style, tone, and content of the standup routines performed by their named hero—Dave Chappelle.

Although the Phi Psi and Theta Tau fraternity members attend two well-regarded colleges, they fail to grasp the simple truth that they aren't Dave Chappelle or any other Comedy Central comedian. For innumerable reasons—chief among them their race, age, and socioeconomic backgrounds—white fraternity members can never craft a punch line that doesn't make them appear racist and sexist. Indeed, one of the glaring symptoms of white male privilege is the inability to recognize that you have it.

The public day of reckoning never came for the Swarthmore fraternity members: they had long graduated from the college before their "meeting minutes" were released, and because the school's newspapers redacted all identifying information from the documents, it's likely that the specific identities of the individuals will never make their way to the surface. In upstate

New York, however, it was a different story. When the video of the Syracuse fraternity members' slapstick routine surfaced and subsequently went viral, all the participants were publicly outed and summarily suspended from the university. It's only when the hammer dropped that they were forced to confront the reality that the world didn't share their sense of humor. "Looking back on it," one said, "I am upset that we thought it was OK because it was supposed to just be for the brothers." Even if this expression of remorse can be read as genuine, any teaching moment that could have been seized was quashed by the police investigator, who is on tape telling one of the pledges at the end of his investigation that the biggest mistake the group made wasn't what they said or did in the skit but rather that they recorded it on video.[37]

Friends Like Me

By the simple virtue of the historic bonds that tie them together, white fraternities and sororities reduce nonmembers to the lowest common denominator. Yet, if we look closely, we see that the organizations resort to categorization based on the crudest and least imaginative stereotypes in part because they conceive of the relationship between their own members in equally reductive terms. When I ask white fraternity men and sorority women what they are looking for in a new member of their group, they invariably pull from the same grab bag of vague descriptors. They want someone "who fits in," "who they know they will have fun with," and "who they can imagine hanging out with." More often than not, the people who have all of these attributes come from similar socioeconomic backgrounds and have the same skin color.

In *Blackballed: The Black and White Politics of Race on America's Campuses*, Lawrence Ross notes that the few men and women of color who do gain admission to white organizations usually find acceptance within the group despite their race and ethnicity because their wealth mirrors that of their fictive brothers and sisters and thus enables them to otherwise act white.[38] Such is the case, at least, with Christina Houston, a biracial sorority member at the University of Alabama in the early 2000s who grew up in the predominantly wealthy and white Chicago suburb of Naperville.[39] The same might also be said of the so-called Mexican Pi Phis at Southern Methodist University, a yearly contingent of uber-wealthy international students from Sonora who are grafted en masse into one of the university's top-tier sorority chapters.

Money can sometimes motivate white sororities and fraternities to look the other way when it comes to race. In other cases, no amount of cash will unlock the gates for racialized recruits. Charlie grew up in a suburb of New York City. He loves Southeastern Conference football and was eager to get out of the cold. The University of South Carolina checked both these boxes, plus it boasted a top-ranked engineering program. He started packing his bags midway through his senior year of high school. When Charlie got to campus, the decision to join a fraternity was easy: a self-described extrovert, he not only seeks out parties but often serves as the proverbial life of them.

The university held its 2017 fraternity recruitment a few weeks into the fall semester. As a way of leveling the playing field and encouraging new recruits to associate fraternity chapters with something other than their houses (which vary in size, condition, and amenities) the university bussed all prospective fraternity members to the city's convention center. Inside the arena, each chapter had a booth. The idea was that recruits would make their way around the room and visit each chapter. If a chapter liked you, its members would ask you to add your name to a callback list. If it didn't, they would shake your hand and wish you a good evening. As a senior reflecting back on that night, Charlie described his fraternity recruitment experience as a stream of "thanks but no thanks" handshakes. In some cases, he wasn't even extended that dignity. He told me how he walked up to booths surrounded by fraternity men, and "no one wanted to initiate conversation or attempt to initiate conversation." When he tried to get the ball rolling himself, he said he was stonewalled by polite but indifferent stares.

The unabashed way that many of the chapters signaled what Charlie described as a "severe lack of interest" in him was startling, as Charlie had never experienced anything like that before. He grew up in a wealthy and overwhelmingly (as in 93 percent) white town. His parents weren't billionaires, but they could hang with the Joneses. He was a superstar athlete in high school, and because of this and his outgoing personality, he always felt accepted by his white peers. Needless to say, the string of unexpected social rejections forced him to look at himself in a different way. When he flipped the mirror around and looked at himself through the lens of a group of white fraternity boys at a university in the South, he saw that he was no longer a multifaceted individual, but rather was simply just a Latino.

Once Charlie was alerted to the fact that his race was playing a role in his fraternity recruitment, everything clicked into place. "Kappa Alpha's founding father was Robert E. Lee," he explained with grim resignation. "You're not gonna see a person of color in that org." The other fraternity chapters who snubbed him "had been on campus since around the time of the Civil War" as well and, because of that, were too steeped in their own racist traditions (disguised as cultural legacy) to see anything but Charlie's skin color. Throughout our conversation, Charlie kept up his cordial attitude toward these chapters. He insisted that he didn't have any reason to be bitter because he ultimately was welcomed into a different chapter and went on to have a positive fraternity experience. "I'm not upset by that," he said, referencing the incident at the convention center. I let his assertion hang in the air for an instant. Before I could reply, he corrected himself. "It bothers me. I don't think people should be like that."

Charlie's story is not the only one I could recount about the value placed on race during recruitment. Time and again, individuals who betrayed any sign—however small or subtle—of embodying any racial and cultural stereotype rang their own death knell. Carsyn identifies as an African American member of a white sorority at Virginia Tech. A high-achieving economics major with lots of friends in different social groups across campus, Carsyn went back and forth between joining a Black sorority and an NPC organization but ultimately decided on the latter because she was raised in a white community, and it's what felt most natural to her at the time. Like her white friends in the dorm, she went through NPC recruitment during her first year on campus, but, unlike her white peers, she was quickly dropped from all but two of the houses. "Do you think it was because you're a person of color?" I asked. She paused for a minute before replying: "Maybe. You'd hope not. But you don't know."

I don't know either, but it certainly raises a red flag, especially when put alongside the story of what happened to Makayla Culpepper.[40] The entering first-year student who identifies as mixed race was one of the most popular Alabama sorority potential new members (PNMs) to post under the #BamaRush hashtag in August 2021. Millions watched Makayla's outfit-of-the-day videos and publicly rooted for her—that is, until Makayla revealed that she had been dropped from all seventeen NPC sororities that participated in recruitment after a video surfaced from her past in which she is accused of looking drunk. Marissa Lee, who served as the first Black president of Alabama's Phi Mu chapter in 2017–18, published a TikTok video response to the incident in which she acknowledges Makayla did some things in the past of which she isn't proud but also calls out the white Alabama sorority community for having a double standard: "We can't have this trend where if you're going to be a woman of color or if you're going to be in this environment, you have to be exceptional."[41]

My personal experience shadowing sorority recruitment hasn't left me with a lot of confidence in other white sorority and fraternity communities, including my own. Early on in my tenure as a sorority advisor at Rollins, I had the opportunity to be present when my chapter was evaluating and ranking PNMs (these meetings are notoriously private and closed to outsiders). I was told by the chapter president to stay quiet and be otherwise invisible in the back of the room throughout the process. Over the course of four hours, each PNM's photo and stats (i.e., hometown, prospective major, GPA, hobbies) were projected on an overhead screen while sorority women made the case for and against her admission to the group. Sitting through the discussion was a reminder of the arbitrary and superficial nature of the selection process. Conventionally pretty white women were given glowing reviews and passed through for being "adorable, sweet, hilarious, and fun." The language abruptly changed, however, when a Black woman's photo was displayed. The rules of engagement required that the discussion of each PNM start by listing positive attributes of the individual's candidacy. Some of the women in the room volunteered that the woman—I'll call her Sonya—was friendly and outgoing during her visit to the chapter house earlier in the day. Once these courtesies had been dispensed, other women chimed in with a list of reasons why Sonya wasn't a good fit. "She's really loud," one complained. "I've seen her get into it with someone and she can get really aggressive," volunteered another. A few other cultural euphemisms of Blackness were put forward before I broke my promise to keep my mouth shut by wondering out loud if the attributes that the women were tagging as red flags weren't actually assets to a chapter that claimed to value diversity of perspective and background. Fifty heads swiveled backward and looked in my direction. And then, without missing a beat, the group put the nail in Sonya's coffin. "I live on the same floor as her," a woman said, "and I hear her having sex all the time. It's like she *wants* people to hear."

I draw attention to this incident because it involves the same group of sorority women profiled in this book's introduction. The story with which this book opens illustrates how the women in this chapter make a big display of pausing a sorority girls' night long enough for them to have casual sex with their male hookup partners. While participation in hookup culture is both a celebrated and wholly accepted component of membership in white sororities, what is ironic about this situation is how the same expressions of women's sexuality are used as weapons against women of color. The problem with Sonya wasn't that she was a woman having sex but that she was a Black woman having sex.

While Sonya was found guilty of being Black while trying to join a white Greek letter organization, a fraternity member named Mohammed received a similar sentence after being initiated into his. Mohammed grew up in Connecticut, but his extended family hails from Saudi Arabia. He followed several of his older high school friends from an elite northeastern boarding school to Rollins and thus wasn't surprised when he received a bid to join the fraternity chapter that they had all joined. What did surprise him, though, was when all his friends started calling him "Terrorist." The first time I heard it—in the middle of a chapter meeting—I did a double take. When it popped up again, I pulled Mohammed aside. He laughed off my concern and insisted that everything was fine.

"You know you don't have to put up with that, don't you?" As the words came out of my mouth, I knew that they weren't true. Everyone in the chapter had a nickname. Even though no one else's nickname referenced anything about their ethnicity, simply having a nickname signaled acceptance within the group. To push back or suggest an alternative moniker would not only be a violation of customary practice but also constitute an insult worse, in Mohammed's view, than the racial slur itself.

I paced the halls for the next two years trying to figure out what to do about the situation. Because Mohammed insisted over and over that being called a terrorist didn't bother him and "wasn't a big deal," I didn't feel entitled to stand up in front of the group and demand that they stop. Instead, I worked behind the scenes to help Mohammed's white fraternity brothers see how that kind of language can chip away at someone, and how the mechanism by which the nickname was conferred didn't really leave Mohammed any opportunity to reject it. When they denied that "Terrorist" was an ethnic slur on the grounds that the term didn't exclusively refer to individuals of Middle Eastern descent, I shared with them Juan Cole's observation that white terrorists usually are referred to by a different name: "gunmen."[42] On a broader level, I tried to convey how such terms of endearment can actually do the opposite of their intended effect: instead of communicating their love for Mohammed, drawing attention to this ethnic difference via the most crude and offensive term possible actually signaled that while he may physically be part of the group, he could never truly be one of them. We talked about Dave Chappelle, Chris D'Elia, and Chris Rock and how they weren't any of them and shouldn't try to be them. Over time, I heard less and less "Terrorist" talk, though I suspect it continued when I wasn't around. By the time Mohammed graduated, I felt moderately proud of the gains we had made and cautiously optimistic that at least the members of his own pledge class would go forward thinking of him and other people of color differently. Two years later, I tried reaching out to Mohammed to interview him for this book. When he didn't respond, I texted one of his fraternity brothers for his new contact information. The man's response made me simultaneously cringe and sigh: "What'd that brown boy do[?]"

Diversity, Sorority and Fraternity–Style

A cluster of recent studies show that when people are left to their own devices, they feel most comfortable in the proximity of other people who look like them. The intuitive pull toward similarity explains why, as a team of researchers put it, "birds of a feather sit together" in the college classroom.[43] It also explains the crazy-but-true phenomenon that most of us are related to our friends. According to the findings of James Fowler and Nicholas Christakis of University of California San Diego and Yale, respectively, when we look across the whole genome, our friends share about 1 percent of our DNA, making them the equivalent to our fourth cousins.[44] Of course, there are evolutionary advantages to forming friendships with distant kin: such relationships increase the likelihood that individuals will trade goods and services with one another, will fight for instead of against one another, and will otherwise act in a way that is conducive to promoting each other's survival.

White people are particularly good at circling the wagons around each other. A 2013 Public Religion Research Institute study found that 91 percent of the members of an average white person's friendship group is also white.[45] *Guardian* columnist Rebecca Carroll wrote a year later that white people aren't opposed to cultivating friendships with people of other races; it just doesn't occur to them.[46] In her 2018 *New York Times* best seller *White Fragility*, critical race and social justice educator Robin DiAngelo writes that the "most profound message of racial segregation may be that the absence of people of color from our lives is no real loss. Not one person who loved me, guided me, or taught me ever conveyed that segregation deprived me of anything of value. I could live my entire life without a friend or loved one of color and not see that as a diminishment of my life."[47]

Logic holds that people who do not feel like they are missing out on anything by having a racially homogeneous friend group also don't feel particularly motivated to diversify their ranks when they have the opportunity. The sorority and fraternity chapters with which I've worked bristled at the idea of creating a strategic plan to bring women and men of color into their respective folds, arguing that they didn't need one in part because they were all color-blind. The reason why few if any people of color made it through? It had nothing to do with race or ethnicity; they wanted the *best* people and those who didn't make the cut—Black, brown, or white—just weren't up to snuff.

The insistence that all their members be exceptional isn't a new feature of sorority and fraternity recruitment practices but is an admission requisite inherited from their forefathers. In her study of Kappa Alpha Theta, historian Diana Turk notes that the sorority was picky about who it took right from the start, taking great pains to recruit only those women who were "the choicest spirits among the girls" and only the "very brightest and best of all who came."[48] While the first generation of sorority women only had other white women to choose from, the privileging of exceptionalism (recognizing that what "exceptional" means has changed over time from referring to academic excellence to something vague and amorphous at best) over other admission criteria like racial and ethnic diversity is a practice that is reproduced in white sorority and fraternity chapters today. Brian Joyce, the director of the Office of Greek Life at Dartmouth, recently interviewed fraternity members at an unnamed predominantly white university located in the southeastern United States. When asked about their recruitment practices, the men told Joyce that race wasn't an issue at all in their decision-making process and that invitations were extended to men with whom they get along, regardless of skin color or ethnicity. Did anyone wish that their chapter was more racially diverse? The fraternity men all shrugged their shoulders and said that they were content with their group the way that it was.[49]

Everyone acknowledges that "diversity" is a big word. When colleges and universities use the term, they most frequently are talking about it in respect to race, class, religion, and gender. White fraternities and sororities, however, define diversity much more broadly, to include differences in individuals' personal interests, talents, hobbies, and hair color.[50] This ideological mismatch explains how these single-sex organizations, whose members are overwhelmingly white, upper-class, and Protestant, can say with straight faces that they are plenty diverse.

The depth to which white sororities and fraternities are steeped in traditions of white supremacy and racial bias lies at the center of the mounting call to disband them. In her 2017 no-holds-barred op-ed for *Time*, sociologist Lisa Wade argues that we are long past the point where reform is possible. "Abolition is the *only* answer," she writes. "All social fraternities—alongside the sycophantic sorority life that they exploit—must go."[51] In the face of increasing external and internal pressure to solve the fraternity problem, some colleges and universities are taking it upon themselves to clear the ground of homogeneous groups whose composition and ideology is counterintuitive to the goals and mission of their institutions. Included among the targeted organizations are Greek letter sororities and fraternities. Amherst, Middlebury, Colby, Franklin and Marshall, and Williams have shuttered them completely. In 2016, Harvard followed suit. With two notable exceptions, Harvard students who were members of single-gender clubs (including all-men's "finals" clubs and Greek letter fraternities and sororities) were temporarily barred from leading campus groups or becoming captains of sports teams. The school also refused to endorse these students for prestigious fellowships, including the Rhodes and Marshall fellowships.[52]

As any college president will tell you, taking on white fraternities isn't for the faint of heart. It's well documented that former fraternity members are among many of the schools' richest alumni. And it's precisely these individuals' involvement in fraternity life during their undergraduate years that helped generate their fond feelings toward the institution and their desire to give back to it in the first place. Universities may not like the idea of fraternities, but they also are reluctant to bite the hand that feeds them. If colleges deem fraternities to be a necessary evil, then the institutions that seek to disband them are, in the minds of active fraternity members, just plain evil—and dumb. An *Inside TFM Podcast* episode put the matter bluntly: "These institutions, as much as you might as well hate them or, uh, have disdain for them . . . they are really good at pumping out successful business people that are successful at making money, that they can successfully put into your fucking university. So, I mean, if you want to cut off your own dick just to spite your own dick . . ."[53]

Harvard's decision to ban IFC and NPC organizations might have been motivated by all the right reasons, but the university's ability to even consider putting fraternities and sororities on the chopping block also illuminates the institution's privileged position within higher education. With an endowment greater than the net worth of many countries in the world, Harvard can afford to lose the patronage of fraternity and sorority alums. The university also has the privilege of not having to rely on fraternities and sororities as recruiting tools. In short, it doesn't cost Harvard much to cut the cord. Unfortunately, that's simply not the case for most other colleges and universities.

Friends Who Fit

While the nation's academic community rallied behind Harvard's decision to take on fraternities and sororities, proponents of fraternity life see membership within these groups as a constitutionally protected right and an act of individualism. "The idea that Harvard is now going to exercise the same sort of control over its student body as a strictly run middle school is deeply offensive," writes Richard Porteus Jr., a former finals club president. "It should not be up to the dean and dean alone to decide when Harvard undergraduates have recess, with whom, for how long and doing what."[54]

In 2018, a group of white fraternities, white sororities, and three students filed state and federal lawsuits against Harvard, claiming a violation of Title IX.[55] Harvard has deep pockets and wields a powerful club of social and political influence, but, as the institution quickly learned, the fraternity and sorority community is also armed. The Fraternity and Sorority Political Action Committee (or FratPAC, as it's often called) is a little-talked-about but highly influential PAC funded by fraternities and sororities (using collegiate members' dues), as well as these organizations' housing corporations, alumni, friends, and associates.[56] The purpose of this bipartisan organization is to support political candidates who either are Greek letter alums or support pro-Greek legislation. According to the Center for Responsive Politics (also known as OpenSecrets.org), a nonprofit that tracks political spending, FratPAC gave $382,500 to federal political candidates in 2019–20.[57] While I can't find any evidence that FratPAC didn't directly fund the legal fight against Harvard (and it didn't respond to my emails), it supported legislative proposals that ran parallel to the lawsuit that included the PROSPER Act, which would disqualify Harvard from receiving millions of dollars in federal research funding if it enforced its sanctions, and the Freedom of Collegiate Association Act.[58] In August 2019, a federal judge denied Harvard's request to have the suit dropped, claiming that the school's policy of sanctioning students based upon the gender of the people with whom they are associating may be a form of gender discrimination.[59] The following summer, sorority and fraternity advocates found an unlikely ally in the LGBTQ+ community when the U.S. Supreme Court ruled that federal law prevents employers from discriminating on the basis of sexual orientation or transgender status.[60] While Harvard applauded the Court's stance on LGBTQ+ rights, the ruling—whose protections have the potential to expand to include gender identity—caused Harvard to drop its sanctions against single-sex student organizations.[61] FratPAC's response to Harvard's retreat on Facebook didn't hold back any punches:

It shouldn't take the Supreme Court to get a school to understand a student's freedom of association rights don't stop when they set foot on campus. Harvard University admitted today it slept through "Freedom of Association rights" day in Constitutional Law class. After four years of trampling on student rights, including utterly decimating every single-sex women's organization on campus, and moments away from being dunked on in federal court, Harvard gave up its ludicrous policy of punishing students for associating with people of the same sex. Time for an overdue apology and more to make whole the women of Kappa Alpha Theta, Delta Gamma, Kappa Kappa Gamma, Alpha Phi, the men of Sigma Alpha Epsilon, Sigma Chi, Fly Club, the Porcellian Club, and members of numerous single-sex Finals Clubs. #HEARHERHARVARD #STANDUPTOHARVARD #DeanKStrikesOut[62]

What makes the Harvard case tricky is that while the merits and problems of gender homogeneity might be what is formally up for debate, Harvard didn't come after finals clubs and fraternities and sororities solely because they are single sex. It also came after them because these organizations are, in the college's views, inherently discriminatory. In his letter to the Harvard community, President Lawrence S. Bacow didn't use the term "race," but his plea for integration, when situated within the larger context of diversity and inclusion to which the letter repeatedly referenced, extended beyond gender to include all forms of identity.[63]

Very Distant Relatives

The first African American sororities and fraternities were created at a time when virtually no people of color attended white colleges and universities.[64] That same historical moment was also an era when Black students at historically Black colleges and universities were creating student organizations that reflected and celebrated their African American history and culture. As Lawrence Ross eloquently shows, the nine Black Greek letter organizations (BGLOs) that comprise what we refer to today as the Divine Nine differ in key structural ways from their white counterparts.[65] In addition to having a different recruiting model, these organizations' membership education and initiation processes follow a unique script. Gregory S. Parks and Matthew W. Hughey's breathtaking social history of BGLOs, *A Pledge with Purpose*, showcases the ways that Black fraternities and sororities since their inception have been inexorably bound up in the broader goal of "racial uplift" and its attendant relationships with the Black church, civil rights groups, policy makers, and community activists.[66]

While all collegiate Greek letter organizations typically are housed under the same organizational umbrella of fraternity and sorority life (FSL) and share campus administrative staff support and resources, there often isn't a lot of nonforced interaction between the Black and white sides of the house. These separate spheres of existence were drawn into stark relief wherever I visited, including North Carolina State University (NC State). It was here, on a blustery winter day in November 2019, where I met up with Shantelle. A senior applied physics major from Charlotte, Shantelle was heavily recruited by colleges out of high school because of her winning combination of brains, quick wit, and sense of humor. As she headed into the home stretch toward graduation, her popularity was proving to repeat itself with potential employers. Stretching out in the chairs of the Witherspoon Student Center lobby, we talked about the reasons why she joined her Divine Nine organization, and the specific social benefits that membership in the organization conferred upon her. Shantelle said that being separated from her family by several hundred miles was hard, and that her sorority provided a much-needed surrogate support system. It also provided her with guaranteed contact with other Black students. Just over 6 percent of NC State's students identify as Black, but the size of the campus and the student body sometimes make it feel like a lot less. Having organizations that both recognize and celebrate African American history and culture, Shantelle said, has been critical to her happiness and significantly contributed to her overall sense of belonging. When the conversation touched on the ethics of race-based student organizations, Shantelle said that she wouldn't support the dissolution of white sororities and fraternities if it also means disbanding the Divine Nine. With that being said, she also takes issue with people who think that it would be unethical to keep one and do away with the other: white sororities and fraternities were formed to repress people of color, whereas Black sororities and fraternities were created to serve, in part, as a safe haven from that repression. If protection from institutionalized and individual repression is still one of the active purposes of these organizations, then, in Shantelle's view, we have not yet advanced to a place in society where the Divine Nine are rendered unnecessary.

While social reformers may have bigger goals, Shantelle's hopes and aspirations for her Greek letter community are more modest. She just wants Black and white organizations to interact. She admits that Divine Nine chapters could always do more in extending invitations, but she also can't remember a time when an NPC or an IFC chapter invited her organization to pair up for any activity that wasn't required by the school. Sending half-hearted email party invites back and forth also doesn't do anything to fix the underlying issue driving the problem: that white organizations struggle to see Black sororities and fraternities as part of the same family tree because of an overmagnification and simultaneous disavowing of their differences.

The white sorority and fraternity members with whom I've spoken about African American organizations get caught up in the mechanics of process. Because Black and white organizations don't form parallel lines with their organizations' traditions and rituals of operation, they are often quick to dismiss Black organizations as being "a whole other ball game." Another metaphor I have heard is that Black and white sororities are like PhDs and MDs: both are doctors, but they operate in completely different arenas. As scholars of Black Greek letter organizations are the first to point out, there are really important and fundamental distinctions between the two groups, chief among them being the ideology that inspired their creation. Without dismissing this critical part of the equation, it remains that the day-to-day function of both groups is the same: to fill their members' social calendars. People are people, and Black students and white students both like to drink, dance, go paintballing, raise money for charities, flirt, and hook up, but on many campuses—including NC State—they don't do these things with each other.

To illustrate this point, Shantelle and I headed outside. The courtyard in front of the student center had been converted into a circular stage, around which were hundreds of Black men and women, and three white people: one was the FSL assistant director, and another was me. The third white person in attendance was an undergraduate passerby who was filming what was going on with her cell phone. I wandered over to her and played stupid. "What is this?" I asked, motioning toward the crowd. "I have no idea," she responded.

Several members of the crowd were holding large metallic balloons in the shape of numbers ranging from one to seventeen. A group of white students walked by, stopped, and stared. They looked at the balloons. "Happy birthday," one said to no one in particular, before moving on. Shantelle sighed in exasperation and identified what just happened as her biggest pet peeve. "I wish white people would ask questions. Instead, they just stare."

Shantelle had good reason to be irritated, as what we were all witnessing wasn't a birthday celebration, but the initiation ceremony or probate of Alpha Kappa Alpha's new members. As the seventeen women marched in, shortest to tallest, hands clutching the shoulders of the woman in front of her as a way of paying homage to the slave chain gangs, it became clear that the numbered balloons referred to the initiates' respective line numbers. The choreographed performance that followed—comprised of singing, chanting, calling, stepping, and strolling—told the story of their organization's founding and introduced the new members to the community.[67]

Unlike the initiation rituals of white Greek letter organizations, which are top secret and held in private, probates are open to the public. Attending one seems like an easy way for white sorority and fraternity members to learn about these organizations and, in the process, learn something about themselves. While white sorority and fraternity new member education programs delve into the histories of their respective organizations, they don't exactly advertise the fact that one of the motivating reasons for their founding was to insulate themselves and their resources from people of color. Witnessing a probate dramatizes the history of white Greek letter oppression and makes it difficult for even the most committed to the practice of willful ignorance to deny the legacy of racism that they promote through their very existence.

As the much larger (often by tenfold or more members) and resource-rich social organizations on campus, white sororities and fraternities could be doing a lot more to help their members increase their racial awareness and sensitivity. Partnering with Divine Nine organizations and other multicultural sororities and fraternities to cohost social events on a regular basis can't help but improve relations, and may result in the formation of genuine bonds of respect, trust, and friendship.

Instead of upping the effort to getting their respective groups together, white sororities and fraternities have taken a different approach: they want people of color to join their organizations. Daniel, a third-year student from Richmond, Virginia, is used to standing out in a crowd: in addition to being one of the only people of color in his STEM program at Purdue University, he is also one of only two Black members of his white fraternity. Daniel told me he had reservations about joining an organization with a racist history but felt like he didn't have any other option for a social life since underage drinking laws are so strictly enforced by local bars that "they make you bring three forms of identification and a birth certificate to get in." Instead of being a marginalized outcast in the broader white Greek community, Daniel was surprised to find himself a kind of celebrity. "Brothers sometimes get jealous because they can only go to parties that they host. But I can go anywhere," he told me. "Being an African American at a predominantly white school makes them [white fraternity men] scared of me. They feel like I'm from Philly or something and are afraid to trigger me. I can go to any party I want because they assume that I'm an athlete. I get mistaken for [one] every time I go out. They'll come up to me and say, 'I'm pretty sure I saw you . . . you play basketball. . . .'" Daniel laughed as he admitted feeling no shame for not correcting the mistaken identities. In his view, if white people were going to construct a narrative about him based on racist stereotypes, he was going to use that narrative to go where he wants and get what he wants: "I don't have to do anything when I go to parties—women come to me. They usually want to hook up with me for the sole purpose of hooking up with a Black man, but I don't feel objectified because I control the situation."

While Daniel tolerates racism by reimagining tokenization as a form of mutual assistance—his white Greek letter community uses him to reinforce its own superiority, and he uses it to transgress cultural codes and access places and people that are out of reach for his white fraternity brothers— he isn't ignorant of the reality that the same golden ticket that grants him passage into all campus fraternity house parties marks him as exceptional in the most offensive and heartbreaking way. The privilege of being a fraternity man who can roam freely up and down fraternity row comes with the cost of being one who is not identified and respected as a brother of a single organization.

Tokenization is something that white fraternity and sorority members inflict upon members of color, even (and arguably especially) when they say that they don't. Dara, a George Washington University (GW) first-year student whom we will encounter again in the conclusion, attends an ethnically diverse school filled with sorority women whose political views lean left and who pride themselves on being social activists. Thus, it surprised her when, during her 2021 sorority recruitment, sorority chapters paired her and other brown and Black PNMs with other racialized sorority women. While the women with whom she spoke were all perfectly lovely and nice, Dara found the matches to be profoundly insulting, adding that "the only thing I had in common with many of them was the color of my skin." By being matched with similar-looking sorority women (as opposed to women with similar skills, talents, and interests), Dara realized that, despite all the protestations to the contrary, her race was the primary—and in some cases only—lens through which many campus sororities saw her. Dara's hope of being able to be viewed more holistically was further dampened when she scrolled through the chapters' Instagram accounts and noticed that most of the photos were of white women "with a brown or Black face scattered here or there." The racial portrait painted online of these chapters didn't match up with what Dara encountered during recruitment. Instead of feeling relieved that there were "lots of women of color in sororities at GW," the difference between appearance and reality rubbed Dara the wrong way and left her feeling like the absence of women on the sorority chapters' social media was at least a thoughtless oversight and, at most, an orchestrated exclusion. Either way, it signaled that one of the most progressive Greek letter communities still has a long way to go when it comes to racial and ethnic inclusivity.

Sororities' and fraternities' push to diversify their ranks may sprout from a place of good intention, but it is also based on the false premise that simply adding a couple of people of color to a chapter composite makes the organization less racist as a whole. Stonybrook sociologist Crystal M. Fleming puts that myth to rest in *How to Be Less Stupid about Race*. What she says about interracial love applies just as well to interracial friendship. "Why oh why do people *still* believe that interracial love (or sex) can end racism when thousands of years of heterosexual love and sex have quite obviously failed to end patriarchy?" she writes. We can't "fuck our way out of racial oppression. That's not how power works."[68] Interracial love is possible, Fleming says, but it can only happen when two requirements are met. The first is that both parties must recognize that racial oppression isn't just a thing of the past but is a present reality. The second acknowledgment is that love isn't a magical antidote to racism. It's a tool for dealing with it, but not the solution itself.[69]

The idea that white sororities and fraternities are offering people of color a superficial form of love and friendship instead of the real deal is illustrated by the fact that they openly profess how badly they want students of color to go through their recruitment processes but can't be bothered to attend the activities held by the Black and multicultural organizations that are staged on their own campuses.

Applying Fleming's criteria of interracial love to the relationship between white and Black Greek letter organizations also hits a roadblock when we consider that NPC and white NIC organizations refer to themselves in conversation as *historically* white sororities and fraternities. While the qualifier technically became true the minute that the first woman and man of color joined their ranks, it would be a misrepresentation to say that their days of being majority-white organizations are behind them. Neither the NPC nor the NIC professes to keep records of the racial and ethnic demographics of their chapters, so it's impossible to measure the yearly gains in this area. There are white sorority and fraternity chapters whose membership is comprised primarily of women and men of color, but for every one of these chapters there are a multitude of sorority and fraternity composites filled with a sea of white faces.

In addition to being not quite accurate in practice, the term "historically white" also exemplifies the central problem that Fleming, Mills, and other critical race scholars say plagues contemporary society: the persistent and totally false belief that racism is a thing of the past. During the conversations that I had with multiple sorority representatives during my visit to Founder's Lane, I deliberately used the term "white sorority" to describe what these organizations were. In every instance, I was corrected with "historically white." The distance that white sororities and fraternities put between themselves and their histories is even greater online. In 2019, the NPC's website featured a four-minute video that told the story of the NPC's founding through voice-over graphics and cartoon stick figures.[70] The tale of sororities' own repression at the hands of white fraternity men was alluded to in only the vaguest of terms. The stated reason for their collective founding was that, at a time when they were demographic minorities, college women thought it would be in their best interest to band together. Given that the NPC didn't acknowledge the history of fraternity repression of sorority women, it isn't surprising that race wasn't brought to the forefront.

Because NPC and white NIC organizations are key players in the epistemology of racial ignorance (i.e., they promote a state of willful oblivion about their racist history), what they offer prospective brown and Black members isn't integration but rather assimilation. New members aren't grafted into organizations that are open to honest dialogue and meaningful change but rather are neck deep in the sandpits that they call ritual and tradition. Sororities and fraternities (at least according to their bylaws) may state that they are happy to have people of color, but that invitation is conditioned upon individuals' willingness to embrace white supremacist origin stories. With an offer like this, it's no wonder why Black students aren't leaving Divine Nine fraternities and sororities in droves and heading to the other side of Greek row. What is equally astounding is that it took so long for white sorority and fraternity members to recognize that what they are asking from their racialized peers is not only unfair but also incredibly hurtful.

Black Lives Matter and the Abolish Greek Life Movement

In the early evening hours of May 25, 2020, Minneapolis police officers arrested George Floyd, a forty-six-year-old Black man, for allegedly using a counterfeit bill. During the arrest, Floyd was handcuffed and ordered to lay face down on the ground. A white officer named Derek Chauvin then restrained Floyd by kneeling on his neck for over eight minutes. Witnesses' cell phones and nearby security cameras were rolling as the three other police officers in attendance refused to intervene and assist Floyd as he struggled to breathe and begged for help.[71]

Floyd's murder—and the deaths of Ahmaud Arbery and Breonna Taylor—triggered a season of public protests against police brutality and racism that took place in over 2,000 cities and towns across more than sixty countries.[72] In the United States, an estimated 15 to 26 million people participated in the protests, making it one of the largest protest movements in American history.[73]

The global support of the Black Lives Matter (BLM) movement combined with national shame to mount a public outcry over systemic racism in America. White sororities and fraternities joined the chorus of organizations that condemned racism by issuing statements of solidarity and support of BLM on their websites and on social media, but for five sorority women of color at Vanderbilt University, neither their chapter nor the broader Greek letter community was doing enough fast enough. At the end of May 2020, all five women resigned from their sorority, Kappa Kappa Gamma. One of the women, rising senior Taylor Thompson, attributed her decision to the generalized apathy of her sorority sisters and unwillingness to rise to the occasion and actually do something about the social issues that they professed to care so much about. "We've had countless, you know, diversity inclusion sessions and workshops," she told the *New York Times*, "and everybody is, quote unquote, trying. But the fruits of that labor don't really show up when it means the most."[74] In the weeks and months after Thompson left her sorority, students estimated that about 200 other members of the white Greek community at Vanderbilt followed suit.[75] An anonymous pop-up Instagram account started by former Vanderbilt sorority and fraternity members—@abolishvandyifcandpanhellenic—quickly amassed a following of more than 3,500 and, as of September 2021, served as a repository for over fifty testimonials penned by Vanderbilt students who left their organizations.

Vanderbilt was one of the first universities to participate in the Abolish Greek Life movement, but within weeks copycat Instagram handles sprang up at the University of Alabama, the University of Southern California, the University of Georgia, and Duke University, to name a few. As the anti–fraternity and sorority movement gained steam, some national sorority and fraternity organizations responded by unveiling plans to create diversity and inclusion commissions, to make diversity a strategic priority, and to host diversity and inclusion summits.[76]

Some organizations mobilized their quarterly magazines to perform the joint duties of damage control and narrative reframing. The cover story of Alpha Delta Pi's summer 2020 issue of the *Adelphean* fulfills its promise of "owning our past" by tracing how the sorority's membership criteria evolved over time.[77] The news that the organization's past exclusion of non-Christians, women of color, and members of the LGBTQ+ community aligned with the political, legal, and social norms of the eras in which these policies existed might have been enough to reconcile some sorority members with their organizations, but the information had the opposite effect on a Duke third-year student named Daisy.[78] Referencing the timeline of progress that runs along the article's footer, she said, "It's like they are saying, 'Look how aware we are of what we've done.' The bad is that it's also exposed how little we've come."

In Daisy's view, all collegiate student organizations—especially those with the social capital and deep pockets of sororities and fraternities—should be leading social change, not merely reflecting the status quo. She always knew in the back of her mind that white sororities and fraternities were socially conservative, but it took the BLM movement to see the chasm between her beliefs and those of her organization. Frustrated by what she perceived as her sorority's self-serving plan, including ramping up diversity education and training its current members while doing nothing to help the populations harmed by the organization's racist history and past discriminatory policies, Daisy then decided to "make a statement" and drop the sorority. She was not alone in her decision: in her estimation, about 90 percent of her chapter's members quit along with her. While the mass exodus certainly had the intended effect of drawing attention to the chapter and signaling its members' support of racial and social justice, Daisy readily acknowledged that leaving her sorority came with very little personal cost, as all her friends dropped at the same time and her campus's Greek life was basically shut down anyway because of the coronavirus pandemic. "It's easy to stand up for Black lives," she noted, "when your own life isn't impacted."

Daisy's decision to leave her sorority wasn't entirely virtuous, and neither, she insisted, were the decisions made by many of her white peers. Duke's Greek life may be large in size, but several confessed that its members aren't particularly loyal: when membership loses its utility, it's socially acceptable to walk away. In Daisy's opinion, BLM offered to Duke FSL members who were bored, ambivalent, and/or overcommitted a convenient excuse for doing what they would have done anyway.

Former Vanderbilt FSL members floated the same theory, with one white student going as far as to admit outright that the BLM protests weren't the primary motivation for dropping her sorority: "I got as much out of Greek life as I wanted to . . ." she explained, trailing off. While many of her friends dropped their sororities, Ava, a woman of color who attends a university in the South, chose to stay in hers— not because she believes that the Greek system should stay intact, but in protest of the composition of the current wrecking crew. "If it's going to go down," she argued, "it shouldn't be at the hands of people who constructed the system." During our conversation, Ava rattled off a list of FSL-related racist incidents that involved either her or one of her friends. When I furrowed my brow and confessed that I didn't remember reading any of her stories on her university's Abolish Greek Life website or Instagram feed, Ava laughed and told me that's because she didn't post any of them there. In Ava's view, the efforts of white sorority and fraternity members to dismantle their own organizations and write the scripts of their departure doesn't eliminate white power as much as it showcases how it works. The Abolish Greek Life platforms aren't where people of color are heard, she told me, but rather constitute repositories of mostly white voices where individuals signal their white privilege. "People who want to abolish FSL are not the oppressed," she continued, "but those doing the oppressing."

Ava's well-founded frustration that the repeated call to abolish white sororities and fraternities was only taken seriously when white members of the organizations themselves got on board is an illustration of the kind of selective listening that she says pervades her community. Even if racialized voices are muffled by white ones, the negative publicity generated by the Abolish Greek Life movement should have put a screeching halt to racist behavior within the broader FSL community. Unfortunately, that wasn't the case. Shortly after George Floyd's death, members of New York University's Lambda Phi Epsilon fraternity posted racist comments on their chapter's GroupMe.[79] In September 2020, fraternity members at the University of Nebraska–Lincoln were caught on surveillance cameras stealing BLM signs posted on lawns in neighborhoods surrounding the campus.[80] Arianna Mbunwe, a third-year student at the University of Georgia, authored a Twitter feed that exposed and poked fun of students who violated COVID-19 protocols.[81] After posting a photo of University of Georgia sorority women posing maskless at a local bar, Mbunwe, who is Black, became the subject of a racist group chat by members of the Lambda Chi Alpha fraternity.[82] If the summer of 2020 was supposed to constitute a bright line between *then*, when we tolerated racist behavior and language, and *now*, when we don't, the persistence of racist speech and actions suggests that we may have drawn that line in invisible ink.

EIGHT

Friends in High Places: The Fraternity Power Pipeline and Opportunity Hoarding

The evening was balmy, the temperature in the low eighties, not a cloud in the sky. While snowstorms and frigid temperatures had rendered college students in other parts of the country with few entertainment options for that particular Saturday night, anything was possible in the Sunshine State, including a white trash wedding.

The marriage that took place was of the arranged kind: a sorority woman and a fraternity man were instructed to show up to the party dressed in wedding regalia. The courtship progressed quickly from there. The bachelorette party—complete with a hired male stripper—kicked off thirty minutes later. While the stripper was putting his clothes back on, the wedding guests—who were wearing a mix of cut-off jean shorts and dress shirts, cowboy boots, white ribbed tank tops (a.k.a. "wife beaters") and Make America Great Again (MAGA) ball caps—dragged ratty sofas and lawn chairs out to the backyard and arranged them so that they formed a makeshift aisle down the middle. A minister wearing camouflage hunting overalls, an American flag shirt, and a headlamp was recruited from the group to do the honors. A parade of drunken bridesmaids, clutching red Solo cups, stumbled down the aisle, followed by the equally drunk bride. After the pseudominister pronounced the couple husband and wife, the newlyweds treated the crowd to a short public make-out session, which, as expected, sent the place into hysterics. The festivities ended with a moderate trashing of the wedding venue—half-filled Solo cups went flying, sofas were jumped on and toppled, and fake dollar bills (left over from the stripper) were tossed into the air and "made to rain."

I didn't receive an invitation to the party, but several of my students sent me videos of the event. Although the nuptials served as a blatant form of mockery, this white trash wedding didn't make national headlines or spur the ire of the Internet because the actors weren't poking fun at another race but instead were making fun of their own—*allegedly*. I say this because everything about the fraternity and sorority party scene at Rollins and elsewhere suggests that members of these organizations don't see the people who fall into the category of "white trash" (a catch-all slur for poor and working-class whites) as really belonging to the same racial category as themselves. The two groups might share the same skin color, but somewhere along the evolutionary road, the path forked, and white people went one direction, and white trash went another.

Race has always been constructed as a political category. Individual sorority and fraternity members will stridently protest the suggestion that there are two races of white people and that they are members of the group that views the other as a separate breed of whiteness not deserving of the race's full set of privileges. However, we know that they are nonetheless part of a system deeply entrenched in racism of all kinds, including prejudices that involve class. Evidence that the white fraternity and sorority community ascribes to a two-tiered intrarace system lies in the groups' party themes, which are explicitly designed to create occasions for individuals to pretend to be something that they aren't. Viewed in this way, dressing up like white trash is no different than dressing up like bikers and biker chicks; gods and goddesses; rockers and groupies; famous criminals, etc. The point of dressing up as any of these stock figures is not to pay homage to them, but, rather, to illuminate the vast difference that exists between the actor and character.

The 2016 and 2020 presidential elections may have politicized race and class to its highest level in recent memory, but, as many have noted, there has always been a stark racial and class divide in America. Books like J. D. Vance's *Hillbilly Elegy*, Nancy Isenberg's *White Trash: The 400-Year Untold History of Class in America*, and Matthew Wray's *Not Quite White* do much to illuminate the diminished social, economic, and political status of working-class whites in contemporary society at the hands of white elites.[1] As social scientist Charles Murray told the *New Yorker*: "We so obviously despise them, we so obviously condescend to them—'flyover country.' The only slur you can use at a dinner party and get away with is to call somebody a redneck—that won't give you any problems in Manhattan."[2]

The presence of the iconic MAGA hat perched on top of the head of a Rollins fraternity member reminded me of something Ta-Nehisi Coates said about Donald Trump in a powerful essay penned for the *Atlantic* shortly after the 2016 election. "The scope of Trump's commitment to whiteness," he wrote, "is matched only by the depth of popular disbelief in the power of whiteness."[3] Poking fun at working-class whites through wearing a hat that's culturally associated with Trump's voting base simultaneously marks the fraternity man as a member of the first, higher order of whites and illustrates just how oblivious the fraternity man is to the range of privileges and powers conferred through his higher-order whiteness. We have seen how racial homogeneity is one of the glues that binds fraternity members together. Now we'll explore how fraternities maintain and reproduce the privileges inherent in their members' class and gender.

Keeping It Classy

We should have seen this coming. This is how Harvard political scientist Robert Putnam's 2000 landmark book *Bowling Alone* reads today. Putnam argues that social capital (an individual's trust and confidence in someone else) has been eroding since the 1950s, and that this erosion is directly correlated to the marked rise in social and political unrest and isolationism. If America is, as Putnam argues, a low-trust society, then it makes sense that one of our prized values is homogeneity.[4] In a conversation with *Freakonomics* podcast host Stephen Dubner, Putnam and David Halperin, from the UK's Behavioral Insights Team, noted that the more racially, ethnically, and gender diverse a community is, the lower the overall social trust between its members.[5]

Utility, it seems, was the agent that bound our ancestors together. "In all cases," historian Keith Thomas writes, "friends were valued because they were useful. One did not necessarily have to like them."[6] Fast forward 2 million years, and what we find in the fraternity credo is the same model of friendship that calls itself by a different name. Instead of relationships based on utility, fraternity friendships are based on mutual assistance. If you were to pop into the meeting space of the Masons, Knights Templars, or other brotherhoods, however, you probably would not have seen a lot of mutual assisting going on, as nineteenth-century members of fraternal orders were notorious for not actually doing anything when they got together. According to Mark C. Carnes, they spent inordinate amounts of time initiating new members, and not much else.[7] The reason why individuals put up with such monotony wasn't for the thrill of dressing up in costumes. Yet there was something about the collective donning of robes, pseudo–Native American headdresses and other goofy and strange accessories that made it easier to be vulnerable in other productive ways—like proposing a business partnership, asking for a job, or soliciting a professional or personal favor.[8]

If fraternal organizations helped fuel the Industrial Revolution by linking employers with workers and men who wanted to be in business partnerships with businessmen who needed partners, the college fraternity grew up on the same street of this narrative of the American dream, and many rightly saw membership in both of these types of organizations as a vehicle of class mobility.[9] In the first part of the twentieth century, white fraternities used their newly acquired social capital to wield influence on classmates and campus culture and politics.[10] This is how a small portion of the student body came to speak for the whole. Speaking of the situation in the 1930s, one social historian wrote, "Often, many sororities and fraternities join together in what is known as a 'combine'; and by voting solidly for one candidate or one issue, they can control student opinion, for the rest of the campus has no way of organizing sentiment. Endless pork-barrel tactics are possible; so that, in return for supporting Mu Omicron Mu's candidate for honor council, Mu Omicron Mu guarantees the vote of its combine in the next election for senior class president."[11]

Fraternity members saturate some of the most influential industries and professional fields in the country. In 2013, *Bloomberg* contributors Max Abelson and Zeke Faux conducted a more granular examination of the people working on Wall Street, and what they found is evidence of a lot of fraternal nepotism. The reputation of Sigma Alpha Epsilon (SAE) for keeping it all in the family is well deserved. In one year alone, a single organization sent "almost 3,000 men into finance," according to *Bloomberg*'s analysis of résumés on LinkedIn. J. P. Morgan alone employs 140 SAE members, with only Bank of America and Wells Fargo employing more.[12]

The same applies to other industries as well. It's common practice for companies to enlist recent hires to go back to their college campuses to help recruit the next class of associates. Before heading to the campus career fair, these company representatives often make a pit stop at their former fraternity houses. Lucas, a 2019 Colgate University graduate, told me that representatives from advertising, marketing, and sales firms routinely hold private meet and greets with his fraternity chapter in advance of their public presentations. In addition to providing fraternity members with an advanced briefing of the company, these industry men navigate chapter members through the job application process and, once back on site, make sure that their résumés float to the top of the review pile. Lucas admits that this hiring process isn't exactly fair, wherein fair means that the most meritorious individual (i.e., the individual with the best GPA and work experience) gets the job offer, but he argues that a résumé isn't showing up to work every day—a person is. And, in this way, personal connections and relationships matter. Lucas all but ventriloquizes social anthropologist Lionel Tiger's assertion that fraternity members "court men" when he says, "At the end of the day, a company rep is going to advocate for the person who he feels would be the easiest and best to work with, and the fraternity brother is almost a sure bet."[13]

As powerful as the fraternity pipeline is between a chapter and a specific corporation or industry, there are only so many individuals it can move through at one time. While fraternity men enter finance fields like investment banking and finance at abnormally high rates, it is not like entire chapters are being grafted into corporations after graduation. The problem of supply and demand necessitates the construction of alternative pathways to high-paying careers in adjacent fields. The most powerful players in the college fraternity network are not always alums of the organization; sometimes, they are the parents of active fraternity members in the chapter. At Rollins and many other schools with thriving Greek letter communities, Family Weekend is less of an occasion to hang out with one's own parents than it is an opportunity to play golf with one's fraternity brothers' fathers.

During the weeks leading up to the mass parental pilgrimage to campus every year, the line outside my office is always disproportionately comprised of fraternity men who want help crafting the introduction emails that they plan to write to their fraternity brothers' relatives who are government officials, executives at Fortune 500 corporations, partners in high-profile law firms, and CEOs of multimillion-dollar companies. Parental help doesn't end with taking the meeting and passing on a résumé. Time and again I've seen fathers help their son's fraternity brothers navigate through the complex hiring process by coaching on them on what to say in interviews, how to frame past experiences on job applications, and how to prepare for and act in the office.

And it doesn't stop there. Once parents have successfully helped their son's friends get the kinds of high-profile internship experiences that are prerequisites for equally high-profile and high-paying entry-level jobs, they often further grease the wheels by assisting in the areas of free or heavily discounted room and board. Ask any fraternity member of the chapter I advised where he lived during his recent summer internship in New York City and odds are that he stayed rent-free in the spare bedroom of his fraternity brothers' family brownstone or penthouse apartment, or he couch-surfed at an older fraternity alum's apartment. The generosity of these individuals simultaneously astounds and perplexes me. Why would people spend so much time and effort helping college students who aren't even their own? The last time one of the most magnanimous parents of one of my campus's fraternity chapters was in town, I took him out to lunch. Rick started out his career on Wall Street but has spent the past decade running the international arm of a large investment firm. During the four years that his son attended Rollins, Rick helped several of his son's fraternity brothers secure internships at his company or at companies run by his friends and business associates. "We've gotten to a place [in society] where we can't hire our own kids," he told me. "But I can hire other people's." What Rick didn't say but strongly implied is that the principle of mutual assistance doesn't just apply to fraternity men, but also extends to their family members. In other words, Rick helps his son's friends get jobs with the understanding that another parent in the group will return the favor and do the same for his son.

If this story of professional networking makes you feel uncomfortable, you aren't alone. Comments to the *Bloomberg* article's anecdotes of fraternity job search stories went viral, and not because everyone found them inspirational. While fraternities may be stacking the deck, promoting members of their own friend group is far from abnormal. According to a recent report, 70 percent of jobs are acquired through networking.[14] Another recent study estimated that percentage to be as high as 85 percent.[15]

The fact that everyone is borrowing from the college fraternity playbook means that competition for elite jobs is fiercer than ever. Now that many job applicants have people working behind the scenes for them, those who want to stand out from the crowd have to mobilize the assistance of their connections earlier in the game. A few decades ago, college graduates transitioned into jobs in finance and government and other sectors with little to no work experience. Now, the new requisite for even entry-level positions is the summer internship. Fraternities use the same strategies as described above to promote the interests of their own members in such a way that, by the time a fraternity member applies for a full-time position, he has had multiple high-profile internships with prestigious corporations and thus legitimately might be the best qualified person for the job.

This was certainly the case for Lucas. Career preparation was a central part of his fraternity chapter's culture at Colgate and one of the main platforms used to recruit new members. Seniors courted prospective new members by attributing their impressive résumés and successful full-time job searches to the assistance provided by older members and alums. "There was a very strong sense from the beginning that these guys are here to help you," he reported. Throughout his tenure in the fraternity, members who were one or two steps ahead went out of their way to make sure that Lucas was equipped to follow their lead. Older brothers advised Lucas and the other members of his pledge class on what subject in which to major (economics); what classes to take, and what professors to so-licit as mentors. In addition, they provided the group with recommended reading lists on career-related topics, guided them to campus clubs and organizations that had corporate connections, and put a good word in with employers, friends, business associates, and relatives who were hiring. The beneficiary of lots of helping hands along the way meant that Lucas had, as he put it, "first pickings" among the most lucrative and prestigious jobs upon graduation.

Lucas's experience is not unique. A 2021 *Forbes* article highlighted the ways that white fraternities are keeping pace with the needs of their mem-bers and demands of the current marketplace. Sigma Chi, for example, introduced several skills- and knowledge-based certificate programs that function like grown-up Boy Scouts' merit badges that fraternity members can proverbially display on their résumés. Other fraternities are reimagin-ing their leadership development programs to include increased focus on career-ready skills.[16]

The fraternity career preparation and networking system is a classic ex-ample of what Brookings Institute scholar Richard Reeves calls "opportunity hoarding." In his book *Dream Hoarders*, Reeves argues that the widening gap between the classes in our society is caused in part by the upper mid-dle class's unwillingness to share resources in the form of internships, job opportunities, and professional networks with others. According to Reeves, this act is understandable, but selfish in that it promotes the well-being of a small group of individuals to the detriment of the whole.[17]

As the first population marginalized by fraternities in the nineteenth century, today's college women are uniquely poised to loosen men's monopoly of the most privileged corners of the labor market.[18] NPR's award-winning entrepreneurial-themed podcast *Start Up* didn't coin the term "unfair advantage" but certainly popularized it. In business terms, a company's unfair advantage is the quality that makes it unique and special and thus gives it an edge over its competitors. Within the landscape of higher education in America, women's unfair advantage is their sheer number. And sororities have access to the most privileged and well connected of this demographic.

A striking peculiarity of the contemporary fraternity and sorority community is that its members are virtually inseparable in college, but that their paths diverge so wildly afterward. During college, sorority women and fraternity men join the same extracurricular clubs and organizations. They serve on the same student councils and homecoming courts. They populate the same majors and take the same courses. They hook up with each other—and often only each other.[19] Statistically, women outperform men in school.[20] In December 2019, women hit another historic milestone. According to the Bureau of Labor Statistics, that's when they tipped the scale and held 50.4 percent of the jobs in America.[21] Taken together, college sororities have a lot of weight to throw around, and certainly enough to crack the glass ceiling if they all kicked together. So why don't they?

When There Isn't Strength in Numbers

On Halloween night 2019, my sixteen-year-old daughter texted me from school with a friendly heads-up: she was going to her friend's house to get ready for the evening's festivities and wanted to let me know that I could expect a group of eight high school girls to roll up to the house around dinnertime. It would be nice, she told me, if several pizzas were waiting for them upon arrival. The first group of trick-or-treaters had just come and gone when the group arrived. "Wanna guess what we are?" one of my daughter's friends asked. If the khaki shorts, backward baseball caps, and boat shoes weren't enough to give the group costume away, the matching T-shirts with Greek letters scrawled across the front with black Sharpies was.

Dressing up like a stereotypical southern fraternity man for Halloween has obvious appeal for middle- and upper-class straight white high school and college girls, as the occasion provides a socially sanctioned opportunity to poke fun at the group in which you have a romantic interest. My four children have grown up alongside this project and thus have spent about as much time at local fraternity and sorority events as I have. As my three teenagers headed closer to the college years, the idea that they very well might end up joining Greek letter organizations was something with which I was starting to grapple. Once I stopped laughing at my daughter and her friends' rendition of my former fraternity chapter, I immediately thought about the sad truth behind their cross-dressing. Despite dressing like high-flying, overly confident fraternity guys, none of the girls were socialized to act like them.

My daughter may not have been interested in hearing my thoughts on why all college women need to think and act more like fraternity men (at least in the area of professional networking), but I did find a more receptive audience at Rollins. A few years ago, I was asked to give a workshop on career planning for a sorority chapter. I told the women about my experience working with a campus fraternity and how I was struck by the extent to which its members helped each other secure internships and jobs. As I scanned the room, my eyes landed on the daughter of an oil executive; one whose parents owned a waste management company; and others who I knew had fathers, mothers, aunts, uncles, and family friends who were movers and shakers in the fields of medicine, banking, finance, and law. "There is just as much professional networking power in this room as there is in any fraternity chapter house," I told them. What I was there to do was help them mobilize their network into action. I moved to the whiteboard at the front of the room and asked the women to come up with a collective list of individuals from their personal networks with whom they could connect their sorority sisters. When I conducted a similar exercise with my fraternity men, I couldn't write down names fast enough. The women in the room didn't look energized by my proposal, however. They looked horrified.

I saw the same look in the eyes of another sorority woman a few weeks later. Addison, a graduating senior, expressed her desire to build on her two previous summer internships—one with a wedding magazine and another with the purchasing department of a major department store—by finding a full-time position working somewhere in the fashion industry. After scrolling through my mental Rolodex, I landed on another current student named Krissy whose father owns a successful chain of high-end clothing boutiques. I told Addison that I would be happy to make an introduction. When I mentioned Krissy by name, Addison threw back her head and laughed. "I know Krissy! She's my sorority sister and one of my best friends!" Why hadn't Addison done the obvious and talked to her friend about her professional goals and potential ways that Krissy's father might be able to help her reach them? Addison confessed that she wanted to but also didn't want to "use" her friend or put her in "a weird place."

The scenario that is women having professional connections but not feeling entitled or empowered to use them is played out in my office—and every campus's career center in America—every single day. The reluctance, which in its most extreme cases takes the form of flat-out resistance, to utilize their friends' professional networks to their own advantage is one of the most striking differences between contemporary sorority and fraternity culture and, experts would argue, between women and men more broadly.

Mallun Yen, Cisco's former vice president of Global Intellectual Property and cofounder and CEO of ChIPs Network, an organization that connects and advances women in the fields of technology, law, and public policy, says that women tend to create a "false dichotomy between personal relationships and the transactional nature of business." Citing psychologist Ronald Riggio, who claims that men's friendships are based on shared activities (i.e., fishing or drinking buddies) and reciprocating favors, women's friendships tend to be based on the sharing and exchange of feelings (i.e., a venting or ranting partner).[22] Because of these cultural differences, Yen says that "women who received an ask from a friend said they didn't expect their friends to hit them up for business and when they did, it sometimes caused an unspoken tension that dampened their enthusiasm for the relationship. Some even began to doubt the true motives behind the friendship in the first place. Others went so far as avoiding those who might ask for business later."[23]

The unfortunate reality that professional networking doesn't strengthen women's friendships as often as it strains them helps explain why so many of the sorority women with whom I've worked and spoken not only don't ask their friends for help but also serve as such rigid gatekeepers to the professional connections which they have personal access. Lucy's father, for example, is the CFO of a large insurance company headquartered in Manhattan and has lots of sorority sisters who would jump at the chance to intern at his company. When I pitched her some possible women whom she might recommend, she hemmed and hawed. "I don't know how well she'd do," she said about one. "I'm not sure she's the best fit," she said about another. When pressed, Lucy confessed that her reservations weren't based on any hard evidence of her friends' ineptitude but on the perceived social costs to her if the new relationships she would forge didn't work out. What if her friend interviewed for the job and didn't get it? The woman would be upset, and Lucy would have to manage those emotions and feel responsible for them. What if her friend did get the job but screwed it up? Lucy's professional credibility would be shot. In the end, the risk just wasn't worth any potential reward.

I am speaking in generalities here, and while I hope and believe that the scenarios that I'm describing aren't part of every Greek letter community's register, I have shadowed enough of them to confidently say that what I experience at Rollins isn't atypical. While women are reluctant to open doors for their friends (even if those friends are really great and totally qualified) because they overpersonalize the situations and worry about hurt feelings and fear of failure, the fraternity men with whom I have worked operate with the completely opposite mindset. Specifically, they bend over backward to assist every member of their chapter find and secure internships and jobs, even and especially those individuals who are at risk for not being successful in them. During the same semester that Lucy came to talk to me, a fraternity man named John also solicited my professional assistance. In addition to a fast-approaching college graduation, John had a 2.5 GPA, an arrest record, and a $50-a-week marijuana habit. While Lucy picked apart her sorority sister's qualifications for a mere introduction to her father, John's fraternity brothers didn't deem any of their friend's defining attributes to be compelling reasons to not put his name forward to their family and friends. By the time that John ambled into my office, he already had an informal job offer from the insurance firm owned by one of his fraternity brother's relatives. All he needed to make things official was a résumé, and he wanted to know if I could show him how to make one.

John admittedly is an outlier of his kind, but his case serves as a striking illustration of how professional networking is an integral part of fraternity culture and an entitlement of membership, whereas in sororities it constitutes a serious threat to the organization's relationship model. While the combined instincts of fear and self-preservation are preventing sorority women from getting out of their own way, fraternity men are capitalizing on the opportunities left open by their women friends and seizing them for themselves.

Marissa, a double major in international business and French with a copious amount of the X-factor (otherwise known as "executive presence"), came to my office one semester to debrief me on a multiday fly-back interview that she just had with a big accounting firm in New York City. After telling me how well everything went, she asked for my advice in dealing with an all-too-common dilemma. One of her fraternity member friends had caught wind of Marissa's good fortune and had repeatedly asked her to connect him with her hiring manager. She was torn about what to do. On one hand, she "worked her ass off" for this opportunity and didn't like the idea of someone else getting to bypass the extensive and laborious legwork process that it took to get her to this point. On the other hand, she didn't want to be mean. "Let me ask you this," I replied. "Have you or your sorority sisters connected this guy or any of his fraternity brothers with your family members or people you know?" She nodded vigorously. "Now has this guy or any of your other well-connected male friends ever offered to help you get an internship or job? Has any fraternity man ever invited you to have lunch with his CEO father?" Marissa's cheeks pinkened. "Well, when you put it that way . . ."

My goal wasn't to discourage Marissa from sharing the wealth with anyone as much as it was to point out that fraternities and sororities conceive of themselves as one big family, yet the principle of "mutual assistance" has an unfortunate habit of only cutting one way. Fraternity members grease the wheels for each other and mine the connections of their sorority friends but are often slow to return the favor. A huge part of the reason why is because women simply don't ask. Another, equally problematic part of this equation: after centuries of cultural conditioning, fraternity members don't think to offer.

Where Are the Sorority Boss Ladies?

As we know, professional networking has always been a central part of fraternity culture, but what we often fail to remember is that it was a defining part of early sorority culture too. Diana Turk's pioneering work on the subject illuminates how the first generation of sorority women in the 1870s and early 1880s founded their organizations with the explicit purpose of providing academic support, intellectual extracurricular activities, and career mentoring to high-achieving women students at a time when colleges and universities were not welcoming spaces for any women, especially those who were smart and ambitious and desired to construct career paths for themselves that extended beyond homemaking and teaching.[24]

While the first generation of sorority women had something to prove—namely, that women could not only keep pace with men in the classroom but also outperform them—the second generation of sorority women faced a different adversary: themselves. In 1870, about 4,600 women attended coeducational colleges and universities. By 1890, that number jumped to 39,500. By 1900, it was 61,000.[25] The flood of women into higher education put to rest the claim that women didn't belong in college and that studying the same subjects as men somehow unsexed them. As Turk masterfully shows, the acceptance of women on campus (or the resignation to their presence) coupled with the rise in amenities and support services for women and increased demand for sororities (caused by the higher women's student population) caused a monumental shift in the goals and mission of collegiate sororities. In the 1870s and 1880s, the primary focus of these organizations was literary and academic. In the 1890s and 1900s, their focus became more social.[26] In addition to hosting banquets, house parties, teas, luncheons, and other social activities for its members, chapters also began spending considerably more money and energy wooing potential recruits. In the frenzy of competition between sororities for new members, the profile of desirable women shifted from those who earned the best grades to those who were perceived to be the most fun, lively, and socially engaging.

Part of what has happened with some sorority chapters is that they have gotten stuck in a time warp, never fully keeping pace with the culture of the global marketplace and lives and ambitions of its members. Putting lists of notable fraternity and sorority alumni side by side illuminates what I mean. While fraternity websites offer up extensive lists of corporate CEOs and U.S. presidents, the lists of notable alumnae posted to most sorority websites are top-heavy with Hollywood actresses, pageant queens, first ladies, royal duchesses, and TV news anchors.[27]

In addition to being horribly stereotypical, the kinds of role models that sororities offer up on their websites are strikingly out of date. Roughly a quarter of the sorority women who Alan DeSantis interviewed for his book on Greek culture in the late 2000s said they had put themselves on the fast track to becoming suburban housewives with attractive husbands, large houses, and stashes of credit cards.[28] How quickly things have changed. None of the sorority women I interviewed for this book said they aspired to be beauty queens or members of the British royal family (i.e., Meghan Markle was a Kappa Kappa Gamma at Northwestern University). Instead, the list of career paths they rattled off were exactly the same as those offered up by fraternity members: lawyers, doctors, engineers, investment bankers, and securities traders. The problem isn't that sorority women don't go on to be titans of industry; it's just that not all of them keep their sorority membership on their résumés or want their bios posted on sorority websites.

One of the reasons why sorority alumnae go silent once they ascend the corporate ladder is because they want to be taken seriously in the workforce. If the line on the résumé denoting fraternity membership communicates professionalism, identifying oneself as a sorority woman does exactly the opposite. A former sorority woman named Nora who now works in corporate finance in New York City told me that she didn't even consider including her sorority credentials on her résumé—which included several stints in impressive leadership positions—lest she risk prospective employers thinking that she is "into hair and makeup."

The hot but vapid sorority girl archetype doesn't do real sorority women headed onto the job market any favors, as that which is superficial is also coded as expendable. In the popular genre of slasher films set on college campuses, sorority women are always the first to go. Of course, one doesn't need to go to the movie theater to find examples of sorority women who are killed for entertainment or out of misogynistic rage (one can argue that they are one in the same). Serial killer Ted Bundy famously broke into the Chi Omega sorority house at Florida State University in the early morning hours of January 15, 1978, killing two women and seriously injuring two others.[29] We heard earlier about twenty-two-year-old college dropout Elliott Rodger, who drove to the University of California, Santa Barbara's sorority row and calmly pumped bullets into nearby women, killing two members of the Tri Delta chapter.[30]

The perceived futility of erasing stubborn stereotypes and replacing them with new realities causes many sorority women to elide reference to their sorority membership on their résumés altogether. The cost of doing so is that they wipe away four years of work experience from their applications. Prospective employers don't get to hear about the leadership positions they held within their organizations or the work that they did to keep an unsteady boat afloat. They also miss out on the opportunity to convey their mastery of the kinds of attributes that all hiring managers covet and financially reward people who have them—skills like conflict resolution, negotiation, teamwork, and resilience. When all reference to sorority membership gets scrubbed from their professional portfolios, another, arguably more important, loss is inevitable: the opportunity to network with other sorority women.

As a result of this intentional omission, some sorority women find themselves in the ironic situation of hiring a "sister" without knowing it. During her years at Rollins, Katherine was an active member of a Panhellenic sorority. After graduation, she took a prestigious finance job in Chicago. A few years and an equal number of promotions later, Katherine hired a summer intern who unknowingly turned out to be a member of the same sorority at a different university. The woman didn't advertise her sorority membership in her job application materials, and Katherine never volunteered information about their shared affiliation, even after she learned about it. "We never once talked about it," Katherine told me. The urge for sorority members to repress and deny their shared affiliations in order to preserve their professionalism is just as strong as the instinct among fraternity members to share and advertise it.

I find Katherine's interaction with her intern fascinating because the situation perpetuates the exact culture that she publicly critiqued a few years earlier. During her senior year at Rollins, Katherine was interviewed by a national news magazine for an article about fraternity and sorority networking. Despite touting an impressive GPA, several prominent campus leadership positions (secured in part by her immensely likeable personality and equally laudable smarts and work ethic), and two prestigious summer internships at a large New York investment bank and hedge fund, respectively, Katherine still struggled to gain traction at any of the big financial services corporations to which she had applied. I shadowed Katherine during the semester that she was on the job market and witnessed her well-founded frustration as she tried to tap into her sorority's national professional network for postgraduation job search assistance, only to find that the well was empty. Sorority women, she learned, either couldn't or wouldn't help her.

What Katherine discovered about her sorority's relationship to the world of corporate finance parallels what other sorority women had to say about the role that their organization played in helping them land jobs in finance or politics after graduation. The women worked in a myriad of different industries ranging from finance and investment banking in New York City to asset management and mergers and acquisitions in Atlanta and Los Angeles. In almost all cases, the typical response to the question was a flummoxed "Ummm," followed by a long pause. "Do you know anyone in your chapter past or present whose sorority connections have helped her find a job?" I pressed. The answer to this question quickly became predictable. There had to be women in their chapters who tapped into alumni connections, sorority members assured me. They just couldn't think of any examples off the tops of their heads.

While most of the women said that their sorority connections didn't play any role in helping them find postgraduate employment, there are notable exceptions to the rule: Kappa Alpha Theta has a mentorship program (called Theta Connect) that pairs summer college interns who are working in Washington, D.C., with sorority alumnae who live and work in the area. Rebecca, a senior at a prestigious college in the Midwest, attended some of the program's social and networking events during her time in the city and found them to be incredibly helpful in navigating unfamiliar and dauting terrain. Similarly, Ava, an international student in a top-tier sorority at a prestigious university in the South, told me that she wouldn't have landed her postgraduate job at a top-five accounting firm without the assistance of one of her sorority chapter's alumnae members (who works at the firm). In addition to helping Ava tailor her résumé and cover letter to meet the specifications of the position, the alumna also gave Ava valuable interviewing tips and inside information about company culture.

While some sororities lack parallel networking chains that link its smartest and most capable members to alums who can fast-track their ascent to professional superstardom, what about the alumni Facebook groups that representatives from sorority headquarters talk so much about during their semester visits to campus? What about the alumni LISTSERVS that purportedly contain the contact information of thousands of alumnae members? Katherine's response pretty much sums it up: "Oh yeah. *That*." Unprompted, many women described their sorority alumni groups as being inconsequential as a professional resource. As graduation loomed, Nora scoured her sorority Facebook and LinkedIn alumni groups for job postings. "The only things I've ever seen posted," she told me, "were by people who needed a roommate." Other women cited a slightly broader range of posts, but even then the spectrum expanded only to include professional services or products peddled by group members themselves (anyone need skincare products, dietary supplements, essential oils?), offers to show newbies around a big city, or open invitations to let group members crash on their couches for a night or two.

The Internet tells the same story. While fraternity networking blog posts and testimonials are a dime a dozen, you must delve surprisingly deep into the bowels of the Internet before finding something substantive by way of similar advice targeted specifically to sorority women. What you get instead are lots of testimonials about how participating in sorority recruitment serves as a primer for company cocktail parties and how sorority alumni networks are great resources for finding new friends and boyfriends.[31] Even the most promising articles—such as ones with titles like "How to Use Your Sorority Network after College"—couldn't imagine these organizations extending beyond their social function. Citing a self-conducted survey, the article states that "almost 64% of survey participants noted that their sorority network helped them feel more comfortable in a new city or area. 81.8% noted that their sisters helped them make a new friend. Some participants even met their significant others through their sisters."[32]

Sorority Makeovers in the Era of Racial
and Social Justice Movements

So many sorority women have been killed off in horror films over the years that it's hard to imagine that there are any left to kill. In *Black Christmas*, a 2019 reboot of the 1974 cult classic of the same name, sorority women at the fictitious Hawthorne College similarly drop like flies. But what marks the surviving Greek women as a different breed from their generic ancestors is that instead of relinquishing themselves to their scripted fate, they aggressively fight against it.[33] In the process, they discover that they are targeted by demonically possessed fraternity members for being ostensibly out of line, and by that I mean that they demand accountability for sexual assault, expect equal treatment in the classroom, and insist that they stand alongside—and not behind—fraternity men as they graduate from college and go on to populate "courtrooms, boardrooms, and the halls of Congress." The women of the fictional Mu Kappa Epsilon chapter win this battle of the sexes by literally burning the fraternity house down. While that's certainly one way to clear the path forward for women, current collegiate chapters are demonstrating that it's not the only way.

In recent years, sororities have taken steps to try to improve the professional development of its undergraduate members. Most campus sorority chapters have career- and life-planning programming embedded into their organizational calendars that are mandated either by their university's fraternity and sorority life (FSL) office or the organization's national headquarters (or both). Often such programming takes the form of a one-off résumé workshop conducted by a member of the career center staff or a guest lecturer on professional branding, LinkedIn, or other job-search-related topics. Many organizations host webinars and keynote speakers featuring sorority alumnae who hold corporate leadership positions. In the fall of 2020, Delta Zeta sponsored a series of industry-specific virtual networking workshops where collegians and graduates could connect with each other and solicit advice from alumnae industry leaders.[34] Tri Delta's current networking platform, CONNECTDDD, provides a place for users to post job and internship opportunities while offering collegiate sorority members a way to reach out to alumnae for advice, informational interviews, and other resources.[35]

All these things are useful, but none of them address the underlying social and cultural issues that keep sorority professional networks largely inaccessible to its members. As two Clemson University researchers recently argued, what sorority members need more than webinars and templates for cover letters are scripts for how to ask their sisters—those in their current chapter and those who have graduated—for help getting internships and jobs, and how to respond when a sister solicits help from them.[36]

Sororities' existing professional development programming demonstrates that they have good intentions, but the difference between women's organizations and men's organizations is that the former treat professional networking as a bonus to membership, not an element that is core to their mission and high on their list of priorities. At the time of writing this chapter (early and mid-2021), career-related content is buried on the websites of many of the twenty-six Panhellenic sororities, if it appears at all.[37] The websites of many North American Interfraternity Conference (NIC) fraternities, by contrast, openly identify—often on the front page of their sites—academic-to-career-transition programming and professional networking as central components of their organizations' short- and long-term strategic plans.[38]

When I asked National Panhellenic Conference (NPC) president Dani Weatherford in early 2021 about the disparity between the career-related focus of white sororities and fraternities, she had a different explanation for why sororities lagged behind men's groups. Collegiate sororities and fraternities are classified as social clubs that hold federal tax-exempt status under Section 501 (c) (7) of the U.S. Internal Revenue Code. According to Weatherford, an industry attorney advised organizations in the 1990s to be careful about engaging with topics and hosting events whose subject material might jeopardize their tax-exempt status. It's unclear why fraternities and sororities interpreted this directive so differently, but, assuming that women's groups really restrained themselves from career programming out of legal concerns, it's safe to say that they received some really bad advice.

Frustrated by the lack of career-planning support they are receiving from their national organizations, one chapter at the University of Florida (UF) is taking matters into its own hands. In 2017, the women of this sorority created a new leadership position on its executive board. The job of the networking chair is to serve as the designated liaison between the chapter's members and the university's career- and life-planning resources. In the months leading up to the campus's annual internship and job fair, this individual organizes workshops and panels focused on résumés and cover letters, interview dos and don'ts, and professional networking.

Knowing that it's hard for even the most prepared to self-motivate, the chapter also has put into place a system to help women prepare for internship and networking opportunities. Starting in their first year, new members are assigned two "Big Sisters." One of these upper-class women is tasked with the conventional duties of all sorority "Big Sisters": namely, to look out for the social and emotional well-being of her Little. The other Big has the same or similar academic major as her Little and is assigned the more specific task of making sure that her mentee is doing all the necessary things to put her in a position to be eligible for prestigious academic opportunities (e.g., Fulbright Fellowships, Rhodes and Truman scholarships), competitive summer internships, and high-profile jobs. What this mentorship model looks like in motion depends on the individuals, of course, but, according to Ashley, it includes everything from pep talks and "talking stressed-out women off the ledge" to tailored mock interviews and, more important, introducing younger women to the professional contacts that older sisters have made during their time at UF and beyond. The chapter keeps a running spreadsheet of all its alumnae, including information about what each woman majored in at UF, where they currently work, and how to best reach them. All the current and former collegiate members of the chapter have access to this list, and undergrads are not only encouraged but expected to reach out to their proverbial older sisters for advice and assistance.

According to Ashley, the simple act of naming professional development and networking as a defining feature of the organization and a strategic priority of the chapter has had the wondrous effect of removing the awkwardness of networking with friends. "We are very up-front about the importance of networking during the recruitment process," she told me. "And so women self-select into the group knowing that we are going to expect them to professionalize and help their sisters do so as well."

Being transparent about the mission and values of the organization helps with the big-picture focus, but the chapter also makes sure that the sorority doesn't devolve into a women's networking club. They have their cake and eat it too by clearly identifying the rules of engagement for each hosted activity. During Alumni Weekend, when groups of sorority alumnae are lingering in and around the sorority house, the chapter hosts networking breakfasts and lunches, where current and alumnae women can talk business. The evening wine and cheese hours, however, are reserved exclusively for socializing.

Carving out spaces for career planning in the chapter calendar has inadvertently led to the reimagining of the look and feel of the sorority's social scene. While this chapter (and just about all sorority and fraternity chapters nationwide) has long held mandatory study halls (designated times when chapter members must do academic work), this chapter has recently made their study halls coed—and given them a purpose. Almost every night, you'll find groups of fraternity men and sorority women who are enrolled in the same classes hovered around dining room tables doing homework together and studying for exams. In addition to the academic benefits gleaned from group study, one of the surprising revelations that has emerged from these study groups is that it's possible to interact with the opposite sex outside of bars. This groundbreaking discovery has, in turn, led to the development of a whole new model of social interaction, affectionately known as the "sober social." "We've started playing laser tag with fraternity brothers. And going boating," Ashley explained, almost apologetically. "I know, it's weird."

Some of the domino effects generated through the prioritization of academic and career-related initiatives are predictable—sorority women are becoming more career-minded earlier on in college, and they have clearer pathways toward their career goals. The sorority chapter also seems to have found a way to battle the culture of women's friendship that makes it awkward and inappropriate for women friends to tap into each other's professional networks by changing the chapter's mission to include professional development as one of its overarching goals. By altering the kinds of events that it hosts and making them more transactional in nature, the sorority isn't just taking baby steps; instead, it's propelling its members forward by leaps and bounds. Forming bonds with other women based on the principle of mutual assistance is an attribute that will serve sorority women well throughout their collegiate and professional lives.

By highlighting these initiatives, I risk endorsing the same practices that I critique in fraternity culture. While I am a proponent of gender equality in the workplace, I'm also stating the obvious when I say that sorority professional development programs largely benefit privileged white women. If the changes to the sex ratio on college campuses in the late nineteenth and early twentieth centuries were indirectly responsible for the shift in sororities' role and function, one of the things largely lost in this transition was the organizations' original purpose to advocate for and uplift marginalized students. If the contingencies of place and time could only allow the members of the first generation of sororities to imagine this population to include white women, the failure of later generations of white sorority women is that they didn't open their doors to other women pioneers (women of color and members of the LGBTQ+ community). Even though women have outnumbered men on college campuses for almost thirty years, the origin story of the sorority house as a safe haven for women allows current white sorority members to still see themselves as privileged minorities. This perspective, which is grounded partly in the proven existence of ongoing gender discrimination, prevents white sorority women from recognizing their own privilege respective to others and, in doing so, releases them from the moral obligation to help and assist these individuals. To put it plainly: If many of our nation's most privileged white women are, for a range of social and cultural reasons, reluctant to help other privileged white women make professional connections, what hope do we have that they will mobilize the privileges conferred to them by their race and class to extend a helping hand to other groups of women? The same moral responsibility to lift as you climb, I argue, also lies with fraternity men.

I am not the only scholar to raise the concern that the perspectives, habits, and practices cultivated in white sorority and fraternity houses may carry over to the workplace. In 2021, Frank Samson, a senior research associate at the University of California, Los Angeles, used his scholarly platform to argue for more research into the relationship between individuals' pre-occupational membership in white fraternities and their views on ethno-racial workplace policies and culture.[39]

The potential of sorority networks to be a marketplace game changer that benefits all women is one of the things that motivates fraternity and sorority life professional Aubrey Frazier. But, like the sorority chapter at UF, she's not waiting for the NPC or its member organizations to initiate change—she's taking the reins herself. Aubrey grew up in a single-parent household in Oklahoma and attended the University of Central Oklahoma as a first-generation college student. Her collegiate sorority experience was pivotal to her success, as it put her in a company of peers who could lead by example. "I didn't know what the heck I was doing," she recalls of her early days on campus. "I needed—and found—a group of people who could show me the ropes and support me along the way." Aubrey's appreciation for her own sorority experience was so transformative that she decided to dedicate her career to helping other women like her carve an upward path through sorority membership. Between 2013 and 2016, Aubrey served as the assistant director of fraternity and sorority life at Rollins. I caught up with her five years and two institutions later. Then the director of fraternity and sorority life at the University of North Georgia (UNG), Aubrey's job was to grow her campus's Greek letter community. She did so not only in conventional ways—like exploring the possibility of adding more chapters—but also by expanding the field of eligible potential new members.

Peruse any fraternity and sorority website and you'll encounter mostly white faces, but, as Aubrey points out, faces of people who also are roughly the same age and pursuing the same degree. Most current Greek letter collegiate chapters are populated by eighteen-to-twenty-four-year-old students seeking bachelor's degrees. While this demographic profile might be the one most firmly entrenched within the popular imagination, it doesn't reflect the reality of who is actually on campus. According to 2018 government statistics, approximately 35 percent of U.S. college students attended two-year degree institutions and 7.6 million (or about two out of every five) college students were over the age of twenty-five.[40]

Because sororities have a laser focus on recruiting and retaining the first group of college students, they are missing what Aubrey calls the "huge untapped market" that is the second. What drew her to the rural mountain campus in 2016? It was the perfect time and place to run a bold experiment. Just four years earlier, the University System of Georgia's Board of Regents approved the merger of North Georgia College and State University, one of the nation's six senior military colleges, and Gainesville State College, a primarily two-year degree-granting institution with four branch campuses. UNG was the product of this merger: a public institution offering two- and four-year undergraduate degree programs across five campuses. While most of the students attending the university's largest campus in Dahlonega are between the ages of eighteen and twenty-four, 20 percent of UNG's total student population is twenty-five or older.[41]

Merging two well-established universities is like getting married later in life: for the arrangement to work, both parties must be willing to cultivate a spirit of tireless generosity and perfect the art of compromise. Aubrey was greeted into her role by a long and rich narrative of "this is how fraternity and sorority life operates here" but also, because the university was technically brand new, by a blank slate. As Aubrey toured UNG's satellite campuses—many of which offer high numbers of two-year degree programs—she thought, "Wouldn't it be great if associate degree–seeking students at those campuses could join the sororities headquartered at the Dahlonega campus?" When she sat down to make a list of compelling reasons why they couldn't, she only came up with one potential roadblock: NPC rules. What she found in this trade organization's bylaws made her heart race: membership eligibility is conditioned on the individual being enrolled at a four-year degree-granting institution. UNG checks this box: "The bylaws don't explicitly exclude individuals who are enrolled in two-year degree programs at a four-year university." Aubrey quickly decided that it was in her students' best interest to adopt a better-to-ask-forgiveness-than-permission approach to sorority recruitment, so she promptly opened up her university's Greek letter organizations to associate degree–seeking students. Aubrey identifies as a rule follower, except when the rules she's asked to follow are discriminatory. "I can't see why sororities wouldn't want good women in their ranks for two years rather than none at all," she reasoned.

However, Aubrey discovered that just because a linguistic loophole opened the door for associate degree students to join their member organizations, it didn't mean that women were granted a free and clear pass through the chapters' thresholds. Four out of the five NPC chapters at UNG don't include language in their bylaws that prevent associate degree–seeking women from joining their organizations, but one does. "I had to call women and tell them that they couldn't be considered by that chapter simply because of the degree that they were pursuing," Aubrey told me. "Those conversations were gutting." While many sororities and fraternities may not explicitly exclude two-year-degree-seeking students, they don't go out of their way to embrace them either. Over the course of the twentieth century, sororities and fraternities grew increasingly picky about where they established new chapters. In an attempt to preserve the prestige and exclusivity of membership, they focused their attention on flagship state institutions and colleges and universities with a proven track record of high academic standards and a good reputation. Amid the civil rights and women's rights movements of the 1960s and 1970s, interest in Greek letter organizations started to decline, prompting the NPC to consider expanding to newly accredited state universities, regional branch campuses of flagship universities, and community colleges. Ultimately, the NPC took a half step toward inclusivity: they decided to expand their membership eligibility to all four-year degree-granting institutions but not to allow new chapters to form at two-year community colleges.[42] Almost fifty years later, NPC rules still prevent organizations from setting up chapters at these institutions.[43]

The bypassing of this sizable student population becomes strange and notable when we consider the other groups that sororities and fraternities do allow to join their ranks. Alumnae initiate programs have existed for years, but over the past decade, they have occupied a prominent presence on organization websites. Most organizations require an alumna potential new member (PNM) to be nominated for membership by a sorority member (or chapter). While a requisite for membership is a close relationship with a member or chapter, what isn't required of alumnae initiates is a history of attending a four-year degree-granting institution. The flexibility afforded to alumnae initiates buttresses Aubrey's claim that the cultural criteria of Greek letter membership need to be dramatically revised. The

2020 fall–winter edition of Alpha Delta Pi's quarterly magazine includes a feature story about Auburn's Beta Omega chapter, which added a non-degree-seeking student with intellectual disabilities to its sisterhood, also helps to make this claim.[44]

Given the ways in which sororities and fraternities have opened their doors to nontraditional members of other types, why haven't they expanded their outreach to community colleges? It's a question that Dani Weatherford says her organization has seriously engaged with twice over the past five years. "Nothing is carved in stone for eternity," she told me in 2021. For confidentiality reasons, she wasn't able to fill me in on the specifics of the current conversation about membership eligibility expansion, but enough member organizations have expressed interest in exploring the possibility of opening their doors to community college students that in 2020 the NPC formed a community college task force, part of whose work included taking the temperature of member organizations and soliciting interest-related survey data from students currently seeking two-year degrees.[45]

While white sororities are in the early stages of examining this issue, there is nothing stopping white fraternities from forging ahead. NIC bylaws have long allowed member fraternities to be housed at community colleges, though the presence of white fraternities at two-year degree-granting institutions is few and far between.[46] The NIC doesn't keep records of this data, and I was only able to independently verify the existence of one such fraternity chapter at Miami Dade Community College from 1972 to 1997.[47] Todd Shelton, chief communication officer at the NIC, can't speak to the rationale of individual member organizations but speculates that the reasons why expansion efforts up to this point have focused almost exclusively on four-year institutions has to do with resources (the difficulty of recruiting a dedicated volunteer corps to supervise these chapters), and the challenges of developing undergraduate peer governance in a two-year or shorter experience. "Two years isn't a lot of time to develop individuals," he told me in 2021. "If you join your first year and leave your second, there's not a lot of time." Weatherford said similar things about NPC organizations. "NPC was created because organizations wanted parity amongst themselves," she said. Expanding membership to community colleges could disrupt NPC community relations by allowing sororities with the largest alumna populations and most financial resources to expand into territory where other organizations could not.

Time, resources, the quality of member experience, concerns about equality: these are all valid reasons for being hesitant to enter into the community college market. But lying just under the surface of this well-founded conservative decision-making is another unstated reason why white sororities and fraternities may be more than a little leery of targeting students at vocational schools and community colleges, and that is money. Community college students often have fewer financial resources than their four-year residential college peers and less expendable income to dedicate to luxury items like social club dues. In some cases, the cost of sorority and fraternity membership might even exceed the cost of tuition, thus making the proposition of joining one of these organizations an incredibly tough sell.

Money is something that is top of mind for Aubrey as well, since 30 percent of her students are Pell recipients.[48] "While we certainly have our fair share of wealthy students at UNG," she told me, "most are putting themselves through school." Through interviewing a dozen UNG sorority members (selected at random from all the campus chapters), I found Aubrey's assessment to be spot-on. Every single woman with whom I spoke had at least one part-time job, and many were juggling two or more. When I asked the women why they chose to attend UNG, they gave different versions of the same answer: they liked the small-campus feel of UNG and wanted to be part of a sorority community but couldn't afford to do so at a bigger school. The women were acutely aware that the larger-than-life Greek culture at Southeastern Conference (SEC) schools comes with a lot of social pressure and a big price tag that they can't afford. Sage, who hails from a small town outside of Augusta, learned this firsthand when, as a first-year student at UGA, she dropped out of sorority recruitment midway through the process. She told me that she realized pretty quickly that she didn't fit in and that continuing with recruitment would be a big mistake. Sage's response surprised me because, as a tall, willowy blonde, she was the physical embodiment of the stereotypical southern sorority girl. But then she explained that she drove a 2008 Camry and colored her own hair.

If the perception, real or imagined, that sorority membership at UGA and its sister schools is largely the domain of the 1 percent, then UNG's Greek community is the neighborhood that houses what several UNG sorority members referred to as "regular people." The no-frills Greek culture at UNG—epitomized by the lack of sorority and fraternity houses and the ban on gift-giving and expensive formals, mixers, socials, and Big/Little reveals—is what keeps dues low and makes membership possible for UNG's many budget-conscious students. Sage left UGA after her first semester and spent the next eight months working full-time at an outlet mall to save up enough to transfer to UNG. When Sage joined a top-tier sorority during her second year and moved in with a group of sorority sisters shortly thereafter, she was acutely aware of the gulf that divided what she gave up at UGA (the opportunity to live in a glittery mansion) and what she traded it in for (a shared bedroom in a rural farmhouse with well water and questionable plumbing). Despite the inconveniences of her living quarters, Sage has no regrets about her decision to transfer to UNG. She explained that she and her sorority sisters get a discount on their rent for helping to care for the farm's animals. She ticked off the members of her barnyard menagerie while scrolling through her phone's photo album. Landing on a picture of her favorite charge, a large emu named Dwayne, she warned, "He might look cute, but don't let him fool you. He's aggressive and nasty."

Top-tier sorority women (happily) earning their keep by feeding pigs and shoveling cow dung was a surprising discovery. So was the relationship between sorority chapters at the university. The absence of designated sorority and fraternity housing at UNG reduces membership expenses, but it also works to prevent the formation of cliques. The sorority women with whom I spoke were just as likely to live with women in other sororities as they were with members of their own. Elaine, a senior from Cumming, Georgia, proudly told me that she had four roommates and that each was a member of a different campus sorority. If one of the problems plaguing Greek communities at other institutions is the struggle to get sorority chapters to interact with each other, UNG struggles with keeping its FSL community members away from each other. The tight-knit nature of the community, coupled with a spirit of overly gracious southern hospitality, landed the Greek letter community in hot water with UNG's campus administrators and made national news when, in August 2020, photos and videos of a massive block party—held during COVID-19—surfaced and went viral.[49]

The COVID party gave the university a black eye, but it's the spirit of inclusivity that inspired the celebration that Rose names as the reason why, after spending four years on a navy submarine and starting UNG at age twenty-two, she signed herself up for sorority recruitment. At the time of my visit, Rose was a graduating senior and predicted that she was the oldest woman in her chapter, but she didn't really know. Half a dozen of her sorority sisters were listening in on the conversation and shrugged their shoulders. They didn't know either. The same reason why Rose's background and age didn't matter also explained why no one raised an eyebrow when Misha showed up for UNG's virtual recruitment in January 2021. The sorority women on both sides of the fence—those who were running recruitment behind the scenes and those who were meeting with and ranking PNMs—applied the same set of descriptors to Misha as they did to other PNMs: "funny," "very sweet," and "really interesting." It's only when a woman mentioned in passing that Misha was "a little bit older" that my ears perked up. Upon pressing, the woman explained that Misha belonged to a category of women defined by their indeterminate age. In other words, Misha could be anywhere between twenty-nine and forty-five.

As it turns out, Misha was a forty-one-year-old African American mother of three. She had her first daughter when she was seventeen and spent the better part of the past two decades juggling the demands of raising small children while working an assortment of jobs—including positions as a nurse's assistant, phlebotomist, and assistant manager at McDonald's—before saving enough money and carving out enough free time to go back to school. She clawed her way to an associate degree in psychology at a community college and then transferred to UNG to finish her bachelor's. When an email about sorority recruitment hit her inbox, she signed up on the spot. Misha told me that she always wanted to have a conventional "college experience" like her high school friends enjoyed, but life got in the way. Now, twenty years later, she wasn't as much trying to relive her youth as taking full advantage of everything that her campus community had to offer. "I have a sister and friends who are my age," Misha explained. "But who can I reach out to here?" In addition to wanting a group of on-campus "sisters" to whom she could turn to for assistance and support, Misha also rightly believed that she had something to offer her teenage and early-twenty-something sorority sisters in the form of wisdom that comes from lived experience. "I'm looking forward to telling them how it [life] is," she laughed. Then she got serious. "I want to share with my new sisters the importance of being comfortable with yourself and who you are—no matter what."

I talked to Misha via Zoom after she had gone through the recruitment process, including the preference ceremony, but before she received her bid. Throughout our conversation, I kept waiting for her to bring up the two giant elephants in the room—namely, her age and race—but she didn't. Curiosity finally got the best of me, and I asked her flat out what it was like to be a woman of color joining a white social organization comprised of women who were half her age. Misha paused and then furrowed her brow. "You know, I never thought about what I was doing like that," she said slowly. What Misha said next made me check my own assumptions, because it exposed my question to be a form of projected embarrassment that didn't reflect how Misha actually felt. "I'm a college student just like they are," she said matter-of-factly. "And if something is offered to me, I'm going to take it." After Misha logged off, I spent the rest of the night thinking about entitlement and how Misha brings to the white fraternity and sorority community the most virtuous form of it. Fraternities and sororities are student organizations, and Misha is a student. In her mind, membership criteria are as simple and clear-cut as that.

I don't disagree.

CONCLUSION

Preference

Approximately sixty fraternity brothers were gathered on Rollins College's main quad, tossing footballs to each other, talking sports, and otherwise passing time while they awaited the arrival of their new members. The group made for a striking sight, not only because of their number but also because of their shared aesthetic. For this group of Rollins fraternity men, the unofficial uniform included khaki shorts, boat shoes, baseball caps (turned backward), and matching Bid Day T-shirts. The yellow shirt paid homage to the chapter's founding members via a photo laser-printed on its back. In the photo, the group's members—circa 1977—are huddled around the entrance of the Spanish revival–style residence hall that would come to serve as the organization's fraternity house for the next forty-plus years.

These fraternity brothers weren't the only groups of men wearing matching outfits on campus that afternoon. Scattered around the college's grounds were members of the other four North American Interfraternity Conference (NIC) fraternities. While white sorority chapters are matched with potential new members (PNMs) by a computer algorithm in such a way that each PNM receives only one bid from a single house, NIC rules allow fraternity PNMs to receive bids from multiple fraternity chapters. The previous evening, the fraternities had extended their bids to PNMs; all the fraternity brothers could do now was wait and see who chose to "run home." "Im [sic] nervous," Andrew, the president of the above fraternity chapter, texted me. Part of his anxiety stemmed from the open worry that his chapter wouldn't get the PNMs that they really wanted, while the other part had to do with the irrational fear that they wouldn't get anyone at all.

At the exact same time as the campus's fraternity men were anxiously waiting to meet their new members, 100-plus PNMs were preparing to make their grand entrance. One by one, the PNMs signed the bid card of their choosing and, by handing it over to the Interfraternity Council (IFC) student representatives, formally accepted the invitation to join a specific fraternity. As in previous years, PNMs celebrated their decision by sprinting in the direction of their new fraternity brothers. Andrew's chapter greeted their newest members with chants and cheers, chest pumps, side hugs, and hearty handshakes. Once all the new members had been gathered and made indistinguishable from their new brothers by donning matching Bid Day T-shirts, the pack congregated in front of their fraternity house for a group photo. To fit into the frame, the fraternity members squished together, shoulder to shoulder. Following tradition, a select few scaled the stucco wall of the building and climbed up onto the second-story balcony overhang. Just like in years past, the photographer snapped the photo and, shortly thereafter, a proud member of the group posted the image to the chapter's Instagram page.

Less than twenty-four hours after that, the campus administration suspended the fraternity. "We just did what we always did," Andrew complained. He had back-to-back Zoom calls with his organization's headquarters and Rollins's administration later in the day, and he wanted my help preparing for the difficult conversations ahead. In the four years that I had known Andrew, he was nothing but a shining example of rationality, good judgment, and self-awareness. I say this because that moment was notable for Andrew's struggle to understand why everyone was up in arms. "We've been doing this for years," he said, referring to the group photo. It pained me to have to remind him that 2021 was no normal year.

The coronavirus pandemic that began sweeping across the globe in early 2020 shuttered nearly all college campuses in America. Students across the country were sent home for spring break in March 2020 and told not to return. When the first wave of campuses started to reopen in the fall of 2020, things looked very different. At Rollins, social distancing protocols necessitated that all double-occupancy dorms be reduced to singles. In order to provide enough on-campus housing for incoming first-year students, the college temporarily reclaimed all of its upper-class residence halls, including those long occupied by fraternities and sororities, in order to reassign them to new students. Fraternity and sorority members weren't pleased about being forced off campus for the year, but they took comfort in the fact that their organizations' names and letters remained affixed to the outside of the buildings. In their minds, the structures were still *their* houses; they were just on short-term loan to the first-year students.

Their enduring proprietary claim to the campus building that bears their organization's letters was cited as the main reason why the chapter members of Andrew's fraternity didn't think twice about climbing the wall of their residence hall and dangling off the balcony for their annual Bid Day photo. Of course, the first-year woman who responded to the ruckus outside her dorm room window by pulling back her curtains and subsequently coming face-to-face with a group of fraternity men standing on *her* balcony saw things a little differently.

The fraternity men's refusal to respect school property and another student's privacy was only part of the problem. The other was the photo that was taken in front of the building. The image posted to Instagram replicated with astounding accuracy the 1977 photo printed on the members' T-shirts, including the maskless faces. Andrew explained that his fraternity brothers didn't consciously remove their masks to better copy the vintage photo; it just so happened that very few people were wearing them in the first place. Like every other college campus during the 2020–21 academic year, Rollins had strict safety protocols in place, and chief among them was a campus mask mandate. Approximately ten days after fraternity recruitment ended, the campus reported a spike in COVID-19 cases. Of those positive cases, 67 percent were fraternity and sorority members. Of the students who were quarantined due to COVID exposure, 49 percent were members of Greek letter organizations.

Scan old news headlines and you'll see that Rollins's COVID violations were representative of what happened on campuses around the country in early 2021, and with particular frequency in the South, where, generally speaking, there were fewer state-mandated COVID restrictions.[1] In January 2021, the University of Miami's student newspaper published photos of fraternity and sorority members attending large maskless pool parties.[2] Similar photo evidence revealed maskless Bid Day revelers at the University of Virginia.[3] Jim Ryan, the University of Virginia's president, refused to assign sole blame to Greek letter organizations for the subsequent uptick in his campus's COVID cases, saying that policy noncompliance was widespread across the campus. In the same breath, he admitted that "there's no doubt rush contributed to this."[4]

Fraternities and sororities were in the spotlight from the beginning of the pandemic—and not in a good way. Anticipating their university's imminent closure, Vanderbilt students moved up their celebration of Saint

Patrick's Day 2020 (affectionately known as St. Fratty's Day) and, in doing so, might have contributed to the spread of the virus.[5] Around the same time, more than 100 University of Texas at Austin students, many of whom were allegedly members of Greek life, went on a spring break trip to Mexico, where a Centers for Disease Control and Prevention report shows that they infected not only one another but also other people with whom they inter- acted.[6] Throughout the summer and fall of 2020, similar reports streamed in from other institutions, many of which were profiled in this study, includ- ing the University of Arkansas, the University of Georgia, the University of Central Florida, the University of Northern Georgia, the University of North Carolina–Chapel Hill, and the University of Mississippi.[7] Following Presi- dent Ryan's reasoning, fraternity and sorority members might not have been violating social-distancing protocols any more than anyone else. However, by virtue of the size of their gatherings, there was an increased risk that fraternity and sorority parties would become super-spreader events.

Colleges and universities have long been troubled by aspects of fraternity and sorority culture, but COVID represented the first time in recent history that the concern rose to the level where it was possible to imagine this con- cern evolving into a catalyst for real change. In September 2020, sociologist Lisa Wade, author of *American Hookup* and vocal supporter of the abolition of Greek life, told Vox that COVID had the potential to place further stress on an already tenuous relationship between colleges and universities and Greek letter organizations: "We've adapted to those threats—the rise of sexual violence and physical harm to students—and have accepted them as a cost of doing business in higher ed. But COVID introduces another risk that's especially dangerous."[8]

If news reports and Zoom watercooler conversations that took place in 2020 and early 2021 served as a litmus test for where the field of higher education and society at large stood, sororities and fraternities had cause for worry. Andrew's Bid Day excuse—that, by taking a maskless group photo, his fraternity was simply doing what it has always done—could be extended to Greek letter culture writ large by making the argument that many frater- nity and sorority members also were doing the same things in 2020 and 2021 that they did in past years. The obvious difference is that socializing in large groups not only hurt themselves and irritated their neighbors but also posed a public health risk that threatened everyone.

Fair or not, fraternity and sorority noncompliance with COVID regula- tions caused them to make enemies beyond the campus community. Their "rules for thee but not for me" attitude also prompted some FSL members to turn on their own. As we saw in chapter 7, the Abolish Greek Life movement grew out of the Black Lives Matter movement, but its complaints against fraternities and sororities expanded beyond systemic racism to include white privilege and entitlement more broadly. The critique that quickly mounted against the Abolish Greek Life movement is one grounded in past experience: the call to abolish Greek life is cyclical and marked by a predictable pattern of rapid rise and equally fast fizzling out. It's true that history isn't on the side of this movement, but what made it more threatening and powerful than the ones that proceeded it is that it was attacking the white Greek letter community not at the peak of its strength and power but at a moment when it was already on its knees.

The combined labor of researching and writing this book has spanned six years. A lot has happened in our country during that time, including the tenure of a divisive and openly misogynistic president, the #MeToo and Black Lives Matter movements, the legalization of same-sex marriage, and the coronavirus pandemic. Greek letter organizations have made nominal policy changes to adapt to changing social mores, but, as a testament to Greek life's commitment to upholding tradition, the interview and field notes I gathered in sorority and fraternity chapters in 2016 and 2017 are nearly indistinguishable from those I took in 2021. Throughout this project, I intentionally avoided wading into the ongoing debate about the future of fraternities and sororities in favor of focusing on the questions that undergird it. If the fraternity and sorority industry is in the business of relationships, then what exactly are they selling? More important, what is the scope and scale of these organizations' influence on relationship culture on campus and beyond? My goal was to provide a nuanced conceptual framework for thinking about these organizations that would better inform our opinion of them and guide our answer to the question that hovers over fraternity and sorority life like a dark and ominous cloud: Should they stay, or should they go?

Just as I was patting myself on the back for positioning readers to enter into the debate, COVID came along and fundamentally changed the question. While the pandemic didn't officially shut down fraternities and sororities, it prohibited or severely restricted their ability to host large social gatherings and, in doing so, dramatically altered their visibility on campus. In the age of COVID, the question was no longer should sororities and fraternities be abolished or reformed but should we revive them and, if so, to what state. As anyone who has worked in higher education will tell you, it is difficult to uproot anything on campus, especially organizations that have been integral parts of it for so long. However, it is significantly easier not to revive something that has been dormant for a year or two (a blink of an eye for faculty and staff but one-quarter to one-half of an undergraduate's collegiate experience) or to authorize its reanimation under dramatically different terms.

In February 2021 Duke University was beginning to play out this thought experiment. The conversation about the reallocation of campus space began before the pandemic after complaints that the university's prime residence halls—those located on the main campus quad—were reserved for selective living groups including sororities and fraternities. Following the recommendations of a campus committee, the university's administration reclaimed the residence halls and pushed back fraternity and sorority recruitment to students' second year.[9] The university didn't identify it as one of its goals, but the move to delay recruitment and relocate Greek letter organizations to the peripheral parts of campus will likely decrease interest in fraternity and sorority life because, as Sara Pequeño wrote for *INDY Week*, "Once you've got a core group of friends, or inch closer to turning 21, there isn't as much of a drive to join a culture focused on getting drunk underage and finding buddies."[10]

In response to the university's mandate, nine fraternities withdrew from the campus's IFC and moved their groups off campus. While the fraternities are still affiliated with their national organizations and thus are subject to some oversight, they severed all ties with Duke and are not officially recognized by the university. For proponents of inclusive housing, the fraternities' mass exodus elucidates these groups' aggrieved sense of entitlement to the best spaces on campus. As we have seen throughout this study, white Greek letter organizations distinguish themselves and claim superiority over one another (and unaffiliated students) through the adoption of superlatives: If you don't have the best dorm (or house) on campus, you have the oldest chapter or the largest one. If you are none of these, you have the chapter with the most beautiful women or the best-looking men, the chapter with the highest GPA or the one that raised the most money for its philanthropy. There is intense pressure to preserve these titles and accrue more of them regardless of how nebulous their criteria.

When you are wearing a sparkly crown, it's hard to take it off, which is why some organizations hold on to them until they are yanked off their heads. At least this is the decision made by the top-tier fraternity chapter that I supervised. I came on board as the group's chapter advisor at a time when its members were trying to claw their way back into the good graces of the campus administration and their organization's national headquarters. I was sympathetic to their plight: they had a rap sheet filled with conduct violations, dues delinquency, and underground membership, but they were also being asked to atone for the sins of alumni who graduated before current students ever stepped foot on campus. The men who comprised the group were smart, charming, funny, and ambitious, but over time it became increasingly apparent to me that most of them were not seriously interested in making the kinds of cultural changes that were necessary to meet the minimum threshold of expectations set out for them. After three years of fits and starts and a handful of additional accusations (some of them serious), the fraternity's headquarters and the college made the joint decision to revoke the chapter's charter. Both parties asked my opinion, and I agreed with the direction in which they were leaning. The chapter was put on notice. But a few months before the final decision was made, I sat down with its members and floated the idea of resignation. It was obvious that both Rollins and their headquarters wanted them to be something that they weren't, and there was no shame in walking away. When I finished talking, every man in the room gave me death stares. Quitting was clearly not an option. Always one to press the issue, I brought up the topic later with the chapter's president. He had put his heart and soul into trying to save the chapter, and at that point he was nothing short of exhausted. If anyone could see that they were fighting a losing battle, it was him. "What's stopping you from just pulling the plug?" I asked. The man didn't even blink. "It's not going down on my watch," he stated matter-of-factly.

The desire to avoid guilt and shame is a powerful motivator in any context but particularly one where the upholding of tradition is a virtue esteemed above all others. Even though the chapter members didn't recognize or respect the authority of their national organization, I understand why they unanimously voted to keep staggering forward even after it became clear that their self-inflicted wounds were fatal. As the president reminded me, the chapter members didn't have to answer only to one another but also to the thousands of alumni who supported them financially, socially, and professionally. Even if the chain is weak, no one wants to be the one to break it.

COVID took away a lot from society, but one of its gifts was a universal fall guy. The pandemic took bolt cutters to several long-standing fraternity and sorority traditions—some of which are innocuous and some of which are not. One of my fraternity's most beloved euphemistically named "traditions" (which I learned about after the chapter was dissolved) was to kidnap pledges from their dorms, blindfold them, toss them in the back of a rented U-Haul truck, and drive them around town until they got sick from all the jostling. Needless to say, it's hard to re-create this hazing ritual over Zoom. The benefit of having an external agent end a tradition is that it absolves you of the guilt of having to do the dirty work yourself. The global pandemic, in other words, served as a scapegoat for chapters that wanted to abandon rituals and practices to which tradition held them hostage. Where much is given, much is required, however, and being the beneficiary of a gift-wrapped reason to abandon a tradition means that current sorority and fraternity members, as well as the broader community that supports them (and by "community" I mean campus administrations, current and alumni FSL members, prospective PNMs and their parents, fraternity and sorority nationals, the NIC and the NPC [National Panhellenic Conference], chapter advisors, taxpayers, and society writ large) become collectively responsible for what happens next.

There are winners and losers in the world created by COVID, and while no one in the fraternity and sorority community would wish a global pandemic on anyone, the circumstances into which the virus thrust us uniquely positioned fraternities and sororities to hit the jackpot. Physically isolated from their peers for months on end, college students were never more in need of friends than they were in 2020 and 2021. As numerous studies have revealed, loneliness and depression exploded among members of this demographic and ran alongside COVID as a kind of parallel pandemic.[11] Given the reduced opportunities for students to make friends on their own, one would expect membership numbers in fraternity and sorority recruitment during the 2020–21 school year to skyrocket. While this didn't happen, neither did its opposite.[12]

Sororities and fraternities are in the business of relationships, and while in-person connections might be more desirable, many existing sorority and fraternity practices and procedures are portable. When COVID shuttered college campuses, the NPC moved its 2020–21 recruitment process online. I spent five days at the University of North Georgia (UNG) in January 2021 shadowing this process. While all the events were held virtually, most of the sorority women and PNMs were living on campus. During my visit, I had the opportunity to speak with over two dozen sorority women about their experiences selecting new pledge classes out of a group of women they'd never physically laid eyes on. The women's responses aligned with what I heard from sorority women at other institutions and others reported online.[13] While Zoom conversations were inherently awkward, women on both sides of the screen enjoyed being able to talk one-on-one with each other without the noise and distraction of a room filled with people. They liked how the online format eliminated the gossipy and often disparaging chatter about low-tier sororities that taints some in-person recruitment groups. They also liked participating in the process in the privacy and comfort of their own personal spaces, and without the pressure to "dress to impress" (at least from the waist down). In these ways and others, COVID has helped unmoor white sorority culture from traditions that reproduce class and social hierarchies.

If the pandemic gave us a window into a world of what a new and arguably improved sorority recruitment might look like, COVID's long reach has also elucidated the capacity of the broader Greek letter community to evolve and change. Because of COVID restrictions barring large in-person gatherings, sororities and fraternities had to reimagine what the membership experience looks like. In the fall of 2020, chapters swapped out weekly in-house chapter meetings for virtual events, held Big/Little celebrations via Zoom, and ran philanthropy drives on social media. The process wasn't without hiccups, but it was impressive how many in-person experiences they were able to move online. It is perhaps because organizations were so successful at delivering the programming advertised on their websites that many felt justified in charging the same membership fees as they did in nonpandemic years.

Individuals who joined Greek letter organizations for their educational, leadership, and philanthropic programming were likely satisfied with their pandemic Greek life experience. For those who saw these events as the price you had to pay to party, the driving question became: What exactly am I paying for?[14] When sorority and fraternity programming perseveres but the sanctioned parties disappear, the disconnect between organizational goals and some members' priorities became a glaring eyesore. A FSL professional put it best in the description of their campus's COVID-era fraternity recruitment: "For the IFC, it is a complete eye opener that they have nothing substantial to offer other than a party. The groups that were successful in recruitment could actually identify why new members should join other than to party. Unfortunately, that was not the mainstream and most fraternities just sat on their hands for the fall because they didn't know how to recruit without a party and alcohol."[15] Sorority and fraternity members were not shy about lamenting what they missed out on in a year without formals, mixers, date parties, and giant weekend keggers. However, I would be remiss if I didn't point out the upside of the muted party scene: binge drinking rates went down and 2020 was the first year since 1959 where there were no reported college fraternity or sorority hazing deaths.[16] This was one broken tradition that undeniably needed to stay broken. Unfortunately, the respite was short lived. Despite all the COVID-related challenges to hazing, the fraternity community still managed to kill two of their own in the spring of 2021. On February 26, Virginia Commonwealth University (VCU) freshman and pledge Adam Oakes allegedly attended a party where he was blindfolded and given hard alcohol to drink. Witnesses allegedly told Adam's cousin that at some point, Adam hit his head on a tree and was placed on a couch on his side. He was found dead the next morning.[17] Five days later, twenty-year-old Bowling Green State University second-year student Stone Foltz was hospitalized after an alleged alcohol-related hazing incident at Pi Kappa Alpha. He was kept on life support long enough to harvest his organs for donation and then died on March 7.[18]

The heartache of this particular tragedy is compounded by the fact that its alleged perpetrators aren't ignorant of life's fragility. Even if the prevaccine pandemic largely spared the young and healthy, the virus's scope and scale have had a humbling effect on everyone, including those who might otherwise feel invincible.

While VCU's DKE fraternity members may not have applied COVID's lessons to their chapter's practices, other events gave some members of the Greek letter community pause for thought. Claire, a self-described "brown" woman, came into the NPC sorority recruitment process at George Washington University with deep reservations. Three years earlier, on the eve of Black History Month, a racially insensitive photo surfaced showing a white sorority woman holding up a banana peel with the caption that read: "Izzy: I'm 1//16th black."[19] While the banana-peel-wielding woman neither took nor posted the photo, the fact that the photo appears to have been generated in the sorority house raised a big question for Claire: "If someone is going to make an Asian joke about me, how is my chapter going to handle it?"

What ultimately convinced Claire to go through with recruitment was the overarching progressive views of her university's student body and her hope that the sentiment captured in the banana photo was a minority viewpoint held by a few narrow-minded individuals at her downtown Washington, D.C., campus, and not reflective of the whole Greek community. While this turned out to be true, something that occurred during the second day of recruitment sparked new worry. Claire was in the middle of a Zoom party with a sorority chapter when the din of chatter was disrupted by screams, shouts, and the loud wail of police sirens. When the sorority women looked out their windows, some of them could see a large mob of protestors breaching security barriers and storming the U.S. Capitol Building in an attempt to overturn Donald Trump's defeat in the 2020 presidential election. The January 6, 2021, attack on the U.S. capitol and congressional leaders animated a host of simmering national tensions having to do with race and class. Some rioters, including those donning Nazi insignia and waving Confederate flags, ransacked the inside of the building, while others fashioned a makeshift gallows in front of the building, complete with a noose.[20]

Two blocks away, against this backdrop of unprecedented violence and civil arrest, George Washington University sorority women were making small talk with PNMs. Claire was quick to note that the sorority women running recruitment offered up a blanket free pass to participate in a makeup recruitment later on if the city's lockdown made them feel anxious. She also talked about the unexpected sense of community she forged with other PNMs and sorority women through the shared experience of being together (virtually) during the riots. "Everyone felt unsafe," Claire explained, "and sorority gave you a sense of peace." Despite the comfort she received from the women, the whole situation felt comedically wrong. "We are watching our capital get torn into," she recalled, "and I have to talk to you about my hobbies."

A similar disconnect was registered at the start of the 2021–22 academic year when the University of Alabama's sorority recruitment process proverbially took over the Internet.[21] Millions of people were captivated by the short videos featuring mostly white first-year college women who posed in their "OOTD" (outfit of the day) while naming the brand of each clothing item and accessory. Twenty-nine-year-old Californian Jenn Ficcara told CNBC that she saw the videos as a temporary welcome distraction: "It's been kind of nice to forget a minute at a time that the world is ending," she said, referring to the Delta variant of COVID-19 that spread through the United States in the spring and summer of 2021.[22] If the university's decision to host in-person recruitment despite surging infection rates in the state could be seen as socially irresponsible, the amalgamation of Alabama sorority recruitment and OOTD videos came across as tone deaf.

The "show must go on at any cost" mentality of the white sorority and fraternity community is a huge part of their continued endurance over space and time. Holding sorority recruitment in the middle of a riot populated with white supremacists and a deadly pandemic serves as a powerful example of the inherent paradox of its construction: white sorority and fraternity culture insulates members from the same world that it creates. Histories of fraternity and sorority life have done a fantastic job of telling the story of how these organizations came into existence and what they used to do. This study pulls the narrative forward and connects the dots between then and now to determine the cultural impact of sororities and fraternities. When critiques of fraternity and sorority culture surface, one of the oft-articulated responses is "Greek life isn't for everyone." Truer words were never spoken. By distilling down to their core what white sororities and fraternities do and why, this book has shown how these organizations can be powerful social influencers that mobilize same-sex platonic friendships as familial surrogates that bind Greek letter members together but also buttress a culture of institutional sexism and racism.

One of the inherent pitfalls of any book that takes contemporary culture as its subject is that by the time of its publication and circulation some of the questions it poses might already be answered. Such is the case with the impact of COVID-19 on fraternity and sorority life. At the time of this writing in October 2021, the pandemic is still very much raging in the United States, especially among the unvaccinated population, where most cases causing hospitalization and death are concentrated. Even though many colleges and universities ran or plan to run sorority and fraternity recruitment this academic year, continued social distancing mandates and other restrictions on group gatherings will, by nature, impact the culture of this community. The Abolish Greek Life movement may have failed to gain enough momentum to accomplish its overarching aim, but a pandemic that has already disrupted the social and academic experiences of three classes of college students—and may impact a fourth—has the inherent potential to disrupt an entire collegiate life cycle. The governing boards of fraternities and sororities routinely close high-risk college chapters for five years and then reinstate them. The hiatus time frame isn't a number pulled at random, but a period that corresponds with the time that it will take for the most recent pledge class to graduate, with a buffer year added in for good measure. If the premise holds that it is possible for a chapter's culture to dramatically change within a single student life cycle simply by its temporary removal, then the same might also be true for a broader fraternity and sorority community that hasn't been officially abolished but has been operating in radically different form since the advent of the pandemic.

It seems both natural and appropriate to conclude a book about white Greek letter organizations with a metaphor borrowed from its culture. As we have learned, the last night of sorority recruitment is called preference because it marks the occasion when PNMs visit two sorority chapters and then decide which of them they prefer to join. The sorority members go through a parallel selection process at the same time, ranking the PNMs who visit their chapter that night from most to least preferred. The guiding principle of this process of mutual selection is that both parties have a say in what happens next. I've long been intrigued by this matchmaking system and the promise of agency that it offers to both sides. Higher education has been in a long-term relationship with sororities and fraternities, but COVID has opened up the possibility of a different future. Sororities and fraternities have articulated their preference of how they want things to go. Now it's up to us to do the same.

ACKNOWLEDGMENTS

It is fitting that a study of friendship and fictive families owes its existence to the support and generosity of a large network of colleagues, students, and loved ones. My deepest and most sincere gratitude goes to my current and former students at Rollins College, hundreds of whom tolerated my presence at their sorority and fraternity events, trusted me with their stories, and generously introduced me to their friends involved in fraternity and sorority life at other institutions. I am equally indebted to these "friends of friends" who responded to my texts and emails, agreed to speak with me, and said "yes" when a strange middle-aged woman asked to follow them around their campuses for a few days (or longer). The combined contribution of these individuals to this book is enormous.

I am incredibly proud to be part of the Rollins community and am grateful for the continued support offered up by my college's fabulous administration, faculty, and staff. Internal research grants funded some of this book's field work, and its bibliography is populated with titles secured by my college's always accommodating interlibrary loan librarian, Shannon Johnson. Several Rollins alumni (you know who you are) deserve special recognition for being thoughtful interlocutors and offering valuable insight on early- and late-stage drafts. I am particularly appreciative of the critical commentary and brutally honest feedback provided by Keisha Dawson, Katie Deisler, and Grant Gillman. Special thanks also are in order to Jake Green and Siobhan Cooney for their editorial and proofreading assistance. Amy Scott Anderson's astute observations helped me expand my argument in key places, and I am tremendously grateful for her generosity and kindness. Emily Russell's combined brilliance and trailblazing spirit would have made her an ideal first-generation sorority woman, and these same attributes make her a cherished colleague, work spouse, and friend. I couldn't have asked for better external readers than those solicited by UNC Press, and I am profoundly appreciative of their generous comments and concrete suggestions for revision. I wrote this book with a lottery hope that UNC Press would be interested, and I'm so happy that Mark Simpson-Vos was willing to look past my Duke pedigree and take a chance on the work of a crosstown rival. UNC's editorial and marketing team—which includes Dino Battista, Maria Garcia, Catherine Hodorwicz, Elizabeth Orange, and Emily Shelton—went above and beyond to ensure that this book met the highest academic standards and is ready to see the light of day, and for their patience, commitment, and faith in me, I am forever indebted.

The best friends often are those who don't seek recognition for their efforts, and to the list of individuals named above I humbly add my husband, Tim, and our four children: Camber, Kellen, Cortlen, and Cameron. The former served as my uncomplaining date to more sorority and fraternity formals than he would care to recall, and the latter spent their formative years being subjected to sideline views of recruitment activities, chapter meetings, mixers, and philanthropy events. Spending so much time in the world of fictive families has given me a deeper appreciation for my real one. To my four "Littles" who aren't so little anymore: this book is for you.

NOTES

PREFACE

1. The National Panhellenic Conference is an umbrella trade organization that currently houses twenty-six white sororities. This paragraph is adapted from my personal essay on the topic. See Mathews, "Oldest Sister."

2. "Stone-Cold Sober Schools"; Walch, "Stone-Cold Sober XXIII."

3. Frost, "Mormon Women Are Caught."

4. "*Playboy* Releases Its List."

5. The North American Interfraternity Conference is a trade organization that, as of March 2021, is comprised of fifty-eight collegiate fraternities. Not all of the fraternities are white, but most are.

6. Freeman, *Women of Discriminating Taste*, 5.

7. Turk, *Bound by a Mighty Vow*, 8; Syrett, *Company He Keeps*, 3–8.

8. C. Flanagan, "Dark Power of Fraternities."

9. Fraternity Advisor, "Greek Life Statistics."

10. Cochrane, "Why Heteronormativity Is a Bad Thing."

INTRODUCTION

1. See B. Bailey, *From Front Porch to Back Seat*, 57–60; Fass, *Damned and the Beautiful*, 260–90; and Weigel, *Labor of Love*, 83–86.

2. Sedgwick, *Tendencies*, 7.

3. Sedgwick, *Between Men*; Rich, "Compulsory Heterosexuality and Lesbian Existence," 631–60.

4. J. Ward, *Not Gay*, 7.

5. Bach, *When Men Meet*.

6. See England, Shafer, and Fogarty, "Hooking Up and Forming Relationships"; and M. Lewis et al., "What Is Hooking Up?"

7. Stepp, *Unhooked*, 24.

8. Kern and Malone, "Heirs to the Sexual Revolution."

9. See Yael, "I Was So Ashamed," and Dani, "20 Minutes of 'Please?,'" in J. Bennett and Jones, "45 Stories on Sex and Consent"; and Wade, *American Hookup*, 184–90.

10. Grigoriadis, *Blurred Lines*, 35; Orenstein, *Girls and Sex*.

11. Borzelleca, "Male-Female Ratio in College"; J. Marcus, "Degrees of Separation."

12. Schmid, "2020 Census Is Underway."

13. Rose, "Same- and Cross-Sex Friendships," 63–74.

14. Kiersz, "Here's When You're Probably Getting Married."

15. Chopik, "Associations among Relational Values," 408–22.

16. Macmillan, "Why Friends May Be More Important Than Family."

17. Dictionary.com. s.v. "play date"; Merriam-Webster.com, s.v. "playdate"; Mothering, "When Did the Word 'Playdate' Come About?"

18. Bernholdt, "Banish the Playdate."

19. Wiest, "15 Moments"; A. Fern, "48 Signs."

20. B. Cooper, *Eloquent Rage*, 21.

21. Kimmel, *Guyland*, 47.

22. "'Hooking Up'—What Does It Really Mean?"

23. "These 12 Everyday Words."

24. "Bumble for Besties?" See also Beck, "What It's Like."

25. R. Smith, "Looking for a Friend?"

26. Peyser, "10 Signs." See also Kravitz, "Your Best Friend"; and T. Anderson, "15 Reasons."

27. Brain, *Friends and Lovers*.

28. Feiler, "Should Your Spouse Be Your Best Friend?"

29. See Syrett, *Company He Keeps*; and Turk, *Bound by a Mighty Vow*.

30. See Robbins, *Pledged*; and Lohse, *Confessions of an Ivy League Frat Boy*. For self-consciously more nuanced representations of fraternity and sorority culture, see Robbins, *Fraternity*; and J. Hechinger, *True Gentlemen*.

31. Cohen, "What If Friendship."

32. Scott, "American College Sorority," 516.

33. Torbenson, "From the Beginning," 33.

34. Freeman, *Women of Discriminating Taste*, 5.

35. Freeman, 5.

36. Kendall, *Power of Good Deeds*, 97–109.

37. Syrett, *Company He Keeps*, 107.

38. Freeman, *Women of Discriminating Taste*, 70–74.

39. Freeman, 60.

40. Hogg, "Sorority Rhetoric," 444; L. Jones, *From Boys to Men*, 76–79.

41. Feher, "50 Most Stunning Sorority Houses"; Wasserman, "Most Beautiful Sorority Houses in America"; Finney and Maloney, "22 Most Over-the-Top Sorority Houses"; Rodick, "Most Beautiful Sorority Houses."

42. Chan, "Alabama Rush Videos"; Talmadge, "Sisterhood of the Exact Same Pants"; Mau, "Selling the South."

43. Sieczkowski, "Lilly Pulitzer Sorority Prints."

44. Maloney, "Jack Rogers Now Creates."

45. Shontell, "Meet the Genius Frat Dudes."

46. Shontell; Gallaga, "Debauched, Yet Self-Aware."

47. J. Gordon, "Total Frat Move"; Pierson, "Is Sexist Rhetoric a Total Frat Move?"; Thompson and Ortiz, "Frat Daddies and Sorostitutes," 1–9.

48. Rein, "U of Alabama Sorority Criticized."

49. Beaird, Mobley, and Lawrence, "'Selling Sisterhood,'" 9.

50. Rosenblatt, "University of Alabama Sorority Rush"; Jennings, "Bama Rush TikTok."

51. Lang, "RushTok."

52. Kilanski and McClendon, "Dating Across and Hooking 'Up,'" 1917–32.

53. C. Harris, "Whiteness as Property"; McIntosh, "White Privilege," 10.

54. Fleming, *How to Be Less Stupid about Race*, 45–46.

55. Park, "Clubs and the Campus Racial Climate," 652.

56. Khyati, *White Christian Privilege*.

CHAPTER 1

1. J. Marcus, "Why Men Are the New College Minority."

2. National Center for Education Statistics, "Fast Facts: Enrollment"; J. Marcus, "Why Men Are the New College Minority"; Tanzi, "Women Are Outpacing Men."

3. Synott, "Friendly Rivalry," 119.

4. Edwards, Hartman, and Fisher, *Undergraduates*, appendix.

5. Waller, "Rating and Dating Complex," 729–30.

6. Waller is critiqued for portraying Penn State's campus culture as a representation of American campus culture writ large. Michael Gordon convincingly argues that Waller's claims stretch too far. See Gordon, "Was Waller Ever Right?," 67–76.

7. Guttentag and Secord, *Too Many Women?*, 35–150.

8. See Turk, *Bound by a Mighty Vow*, 3.

9. Lopez and Gonzalez-Barrera, "Women's College Enrollment."

10. Birger, "Unequal Gender"; Birger, *Date-onomics*, 20–22.

11. Drake, "Dawgy Style." In 2017, UGA received a similar honor in a related category by making the Top 10 list of colleges for hookups. See Piña, "Top 10 Colleges for Hookups."

12. Monto and Carey, "New Standard of Sexual Behavior?," 605–15. See also England, Shafer, and Fogarty, "Hooking Up and Forming Relationships," 531–47.

13. Wade, *American Hookup*, 18–20.

14. "Students at Georgia Institute of Technology"; "Students at University of Georgia."

15. Uecker and Regnerus, "Bare Market," 409.

16. Armstrong and Hamilton, *Paying for the Party*, 89–91.

17. See, for example, Barkho, "Why Are Millenials Putting Off Marriage?"; Chu, "5 Ways the Hook-Up Culture Is Empowering."

18. See, in particular, Wade, *American Hookup*, 158–79; and Orenstein, *Girls and Sex*, 103–40.

19. For NPC data, see National Panhellenic Conference, "National Panhellenic Conference to Call for Critical Change" and "NPC Fact Sheet." NIC data was provided by Todd Shelton, in an email to the author, June 3, 2019. An important caveat to Shelton's provided number—391,824—is that NIC member fraternities include white fraternities and multicultural fraternities.

20. National Panhellenic Conference, "RFM Update 2018."

21. Center for Fraternity and Sorority Life at Washington State University, "Facts and Figures."

22. University of Georgia, "Greek Life."

23. Waller, "Rating and Dating Complex," 732.

24. Purdue University Undergraduate Admissions, "Student Enrollment, Fall 2018."

25. Rochester Institute of Technology, "Overview of RIT."

26. Duke University, "Duke Facts."

27. Haas, "Price of Sex at USC."

28. Cited in Dick, Ziering, and Matthiessen, *Hunting Ground*, 46.

29. Cited in Dick, Ziering, and Matthiessen, 47.

30. North American Interfraternity Conference, "Policy Prohibiting Alcohol."

31. Porta et al., "It Could Bring Down Greek Life," 3–5.

32. Hernandez, "Sexual Economics," 58–61.

33. Kilanski and McClendon, "Dating Across and Hooking 'Up,'" 1926.

34. Shontell, "Founder of $3 Billion Tinder."

35. Buchholz, "Most Popular Dating Apps."

36. Hakala, "This Is Why Men Outnumber Women."

37. Total Frat Move, "ΦΚΤ Member from Georgia Tech." Things went from bad to worse for the university's fraternity community when, a year later, two women filed separate lawsuits against Phi Kappa Tau, alleging that the same fraternity member raped them at different house parties. See Hess, "Two Lawsuits Allege Rape."

38. Unigo, "What Are the Most Popular Student Activities/Groups?"

39. R. Florida, "Where There Are More Single Men."

40. Sales, "Tinder and the Dawn."

41. Marinova, "How Tinder Used Greek Life."

42. Marinova; Hagan, "IPO Could Value Tinder Rival."

43. Hartmans, "Bumble"; J. Bennett, "With Her Dating App."

44. Au-Yeung, "Bumble Cofounder."

CHAPTER 2

1. "Trending Houses–Aphi."

2. Safranek, "Stanford Students."

3. Fern, "11 Things Every Girl Does."

4. Smith and Anderson, "5 Facts about Online Dating."

5. Sales, *American Girls*, 204.

6. Roberts and Dunbar, "Communication in Social Networks," 439–52; see also Sutcliff, Dunbar, Binder, and Arrow, "Relationships and the Social Brain," 149–68.

7. Handler, "In the Fraternal Sisterhood," 242.

8. Almaatouq et al., "Are You Your Friends' Friend?," 2.

9. Total Sorority Move, "6 Steps."

10. Case, Hesp, and Eberly, "Exploratory Study," 31–46; Trump and Wallace, "Gay Males in Fraternities," 8–27; Hesp and Brooks, "Heterosexism and Homophobia," 395–415; Rankin, Hesp, and Weber, "Experiences and Perceptions," 570–90.

11. IPOSOS, "IPSOS MORI Almanac," 98.

12. Gyee, "Five College of Charleston Fraternities."

13. Bird, "Gay Student Assaulted."

14. Stafford, "College Students Say They Were Kicked Out."

15. Focus group interviews conducted of fifty fraternity members of an unnamed organization reveal that, in its paradigmatic form, a fraternity chapter can be a welcoming place for gay men. See Harris and Harper, "Beyond Bad Behaving Brothers," 714–15.

16. Neumann, Kretovics, and Roccoforte, "Attitudes and Beliefs of Heterosexual Sorority Women," 12.

17. Clemens, "Gay and Greek"; Hesp and Brooks, "Heterosexism and Homophobia," 408.

18. Reddit, "Any Gay Frat Guys?"

19. Johnny_Fratkins, comment on the post "Any Gay Frat Guys?"

20. PingPongx, comment on the post "Any Gay Frat Guys?"

21. Reddit, comment on the post "Any Gay Frat Guys?," April 21, 2018, 1:38 A.M. GMT.

22. Taylor and Jeff, "Coming Out in the South."

23. Taylor and Jeff.

24. Baker-Jordan, "My Fraternity Years."

25. Roche, "Pike Might Be Able to Blacklist Me."

26. Dean, *Straights*, 55–56; Jonathan Ned Katz, *Invention of Heterosexuality*, 19–32.

27. Syrett, *Company He Keeps*, 203, 206.

28. Juzwiak, "That's Not How Dicks Work"; Ward, *Not Gay*, 8.

29. J. Ward, *Not Gay*, 8.

30. Moisey, *American Fraternity*.

31. For digital images of the photographs to which I refer, see Sanchez, "15 Dark and Disturbing Pictures."

32. Fishbein, "Cornell Fraternity Kicked Off Campus."

33. McQuade, "Cops Called After 20 Dudes Streak."

34. NBC, "21 SUNY Students Charged."

35. Burnell, "UI Greek Members Danced Naked."

36. Salo, "Frat Accused."

37. Ward, *Not Gay*, 156.

38. Carrillo and Hoffman, "'Straight with a Pinch of Bi,'" 90–108.

39. Silva and Whaley, "Bud-Sex, Dude-Sex," 438.

40. Lehman, "Brief History of Fraternity/Sorority Paddles."

41. Drouin, Coupe, and Temple, "Is Sexting Good for Your Relationship?," 749–56.

42. Garcia et al., "Sexting among Singles," 428–35.

43. "2019 SKYN Condoms Sex & Intimacy Survey."

44. Young, "Social Psychology of the Naked Selfie."

45. Bath, "How to Take the Perfect Nude Selfie"; T. Horn, "7 Tips"; Zaydenberg, "7 Things to Know."

46. Biddle, "How to Take Flawless Phone Pics."

47. Griffis, "Have You Been Frexting?"

48. Jerkovich, "Chrissy Teigen Posts."

49. Marquina, "Chelsea Handler Posts Nude Mirror Selfie."

50. Levinson, "Girl, Send Me a Frext."

51. Setty, "Frexting." See also Setty, *Risk and Harm in Youth Sexting*, 54.

52. Stover, "Selfie That Dares to Go There"; Reid, "Why Are Women Sending Nudes?"; Yagoda, "Satisfying Joy."

53. Grimm, "'Frexts' Is a Thing Now."

54. Burkett, "Sex(t) Talk," 846–47.

55. Lavender, "I Took My First Nudes."

56. Nelson, *Frientimacy*.

57. Communication professor Amy Adele Hasinoff explains how sexting serves as a form of creative media production and thus is akin to other talents and hobbies. See *Sexting Panic*, 116–18. See also Wang, "10 Women Share."

58. Narins, "30 Fitness Stars."

59. See Fardouly, Willburger, and Vartanian, "Instagram Use and Young Women's Body Image"; Feltman and Szymanski, "Instagram Use and Self-Objectification"; and Reade, "Keeping It Raw."

60. Crane, "Florida International University Fraternity Suspended"; Fernández, "Leaked Chat."

61. Reddy, "Students React to Fraternity Suspension."

62. See entry for April 8, 2013, in Phi Psi, "Redacted_Phi_Psi_1. pdf," in Wagner et al., "Cult of Misogyny."

63. Emelianchik-Key, Byrd, and Gill, "Dating Violence."

64. Maas et al., "Slutpage Use," 2210.

65. *Kathryn Novak v. Brandon Simpson*; see also Romero and Giambruno, "Lawsuit Accuses Frat Brothers"; and Victor, "Florida Fraternity Sued."

66. *Kathryn Novak v. Brandon Simpson*, 4.

67. *Kathryn Novak v. Brandon Simpson*, 5.

68. *Kathryn Novak v. Brandon Simpson*, 6.

69. Techno FAQ, "How Porn Drove Innovation."

70. Gallagher, "How Reggie Brown Invented Snapchat."

71. Biddle, "'Fuck Bitches Get Leid.'"

72. Dave, "How Snapchat Began."

73. Biddle, "'Fuck Bitches Get Leid.'"

74. Gross and Griggs, "Snapchat CEO 'Mortified.'"

75. Statt, "Former Snap Employee"; Adam Smith, "Snapchat Investigating Itself"; Shah, "Is Snapchat Sexist?"; Kosoff, "People Are Going to Make Mistakes.'"

76. J. Gordon, "Total Frat Move"; Pierson, "Is Sexist Rhetoric a Total Frat Move?"

77. Rodger, "My Twisted World," 132.

78. Serna, "Elliot Rodger."

79. Dockterman, "Imagine If Half of All Tech Inventions."

80. Manne, *Down Girl*, 36–41.

81. J. Ward, *Tragedy of Heterosexuality*, 27. See also Manne, *Entitled*.

82. Manne, *Down Girl*, 52.

83. A. Bennett, "Snapchat CEO's Emails."

84. Flaherty, "Consent Matters for Photos, Too."

85. Schrader, "Art Book *The American Fraternity*."

86. Moisey, "American Fraternity."

87. For "sororisluts," see Biddle, "'Fuck Bitches Get Leid.'"

CHAPTER 3

1. Sperber, *Beer and Circus*, 151.

2. C. Flanagan, "Dark Power of Fraternities."

3. Fairlie et al., "Fraternity and Sorority Leaders," 187–93; Fuentes and Hoffman, "Alcohol Consumption and Abuse," 236–40; Wechsler, Kuh, and Davenport, "Fraternities, Sororities," 395–416.

4. Soule et al., "Cigarette, Waterpipe."

5. Norberg et al., "Social Anxiety," 555–66; Aurora and Klanecky, "Drinking Motives," 341–42; Hamilton and DeHart, "Drinking to Belong," 1–15.

6. England, Online College Life Social Survey.

7. Walsh, Carey, and Carey, "Alcohol and Marijuana Use," 145–58; Dvorak et al., "Drinking Motives Associated with Sexual 'Hookups,'" 133–38.

8. Marcantonio and Jozkowski, "Do College Students Feel Confident," 5.

9. N. Clark, "How to Have a Good Hookup"; Fielder and Carey, "Prevalence and Characteristics," 346–59; Fielder and Carey, "Predictors and Consequences," 1105–19; Vrangalova, "In Hookups."

10. Reilly, "Record Numbers of College Students."

11. American College Health Association, American College Health Association—National College Health Assessment.

12. Jackson, "Campuses."

13. Murdoch, "Xanax"; Anness, "Dealing (with) Xanax on Campus."

14. Skene, "At LSU"; "Rutgers Fraternity Accused of Spiking Punch"; "10 People Indicted."

15. "ECU Fraternity Shut Down."

16. Wilkie, *Lost Boys of Zeta Psi*, 77.

17. BroBible, "30 Best Frat Houses."

18. McGirr, *War on Alcohol*, xx.

19. Cheever, *Drinking in America*, 7.

20. Pedersen, *First Universities*, 230.

21. Rutgers University, "Rutgers through the Years."

22. Cheever, *Drinking in America*, 7.

23. Rollins College, "Dave's Boathouse."

24. Georgetown University, "Bulldog Tavern"; University of Southern California, "Traditions"; College of Wooster, "College Underground."

25. All-American Rathskellar, "Skellar through the Years."

26. "More Than Cheese Fries."

27. Adams, "America's Best College Bars."

28. C. Anderson, "BYU Ranks No. 1."

29. S. Cooper, "Provo Bar Had 'Biggest Day Ever.'"

30. The Wall, "Our Menu."

31. Brigham Young University, "Milktoberfest 2019"; see also Caffier, "Inside Milktoberfest."

32. Chapman and Brunsma, *Beer and Racism*, 94.

33. McMurtie, "Fraternity Problem," A16–21.

34. Hagerty, "Campus Rapist."

35. M. Miller, "All-American Swimmer Found Guilty."

36. C. Miller, *Know My Name*.

37. Cantor et al., "Report on the AAU Campus Climate Survey."

38. Sanday, *Fraternity Gang Rape*, 23–37; Seabrook, McMahon, and O'Connor, "Longitudinal Study of Interest," 510–18; P. Martin, "Rape Prone Culture."

39. Hirsch and Khan, *Sexual Citizens*, xx.

40. Raguso, "UC Berkeley Student Charged with Rape"; Raguso, "UC Berkeley Student Charged with Sexual Assaults; "1st of 2 UC Berkeley Students Testifies."

41. See Bowell and Spade, "Fraternities and College Rape Culture," 137.

42. See Armstrong and Hamilton, *Paying for the Party*, 85–92; and Canan, Jazkowski, and Crawford, "Sexual Assault Supportive Attitudes," 3502–30.

43. Weigel, *Labor of Love*, 22.

44. I'm hardly the first one to make this assertion. See Kipnis, *Unwanted Advances*, 197; and Grigoriadis, *Blurred Lines*, 35.

45. Ortiz and Thompson, "Risky Recruitment"; Canan, Jozkowski, and Crawford, "Sexual Assault Supportive Attitudes"; Minow and Einolf, "Sorority Participation and Sexual Assault Risks."

46. See Frietas, *Consent on Campus*; Friedersdorf, "How Does Hookup Culture Affect Sexual Assault?"; Hess, "How Drunk Is Too Drunk?"; Kulbaga and Spencer, *Campuses of Consent*; and Sanday, *Fraternity Gang Rape*.

47. Lakoff and Johnson, *Metaphors We Live By*, 7; Austin, *How to Do Things with Words*, 1975.

48. L. Jones, *From Boys to Men*, 71.

49. Cantor et al., "Report on the AAU Campus Climate Survey," 30–31.

50. See Germain, *Campus Sexual Assault*, 40–45.

51. *Relentless with Kate Snow*.

52. Jackson Katz, *Macho Paradox*, 2.

53. Jackson Katz, 2.

54. Chesnasis, "12 Tips."

55. Wallace, "17 Things."

56. "Buddy System."

57. While there is no denying that campus sexual assault is a huge problem, getting a full picture of its scope and magnitude is tricky because of underreporting and iffy math. One of the frequent (and horrifying) campus sexual assault statistics appears on the first page of the 2014 White House Task Force to Protect Students from Sexual Assault report: that one in five women are sexually assaulted while in college. As Christopher Krebs and Christine Lundquist, senior researchers at RTI International (an independent nonprofit research institute) and codirectors of a 2007 Campus Sexual Assault Study funded by the U.S. Department of Justice from which this number was derived, reported in *Time*, the one-in-five number is problematic on several grounds: it was culled from a survey with a low participation rate conducted at only two universities; it includes acts spanning the gamut from forced kissing to rape; and it doesn't include acts that were attempted and not completed. See U.S. White House–Office of the Press Secretary, "Fact Sheet"; and "Setting the Record Straight on '1 in 5.'" See also Parry's deconstruction of campus rape statistics in Parry, "Behind the Statistics," 1.

58. J. Hechinger, *True Gentlemen*, 77.

59. Grinberg and Shoichet, "Brock Turner Released from Jail."

60. Rosenberg and Phillips, "Accused of Rape."

61. Hirsch and Khan, *Sexual Citizens*, 190–91.

62. Wade, *American Hookup*, 137.

CHAPTER 4

1. Lake, "Southern Sorority Recruitment."

2. Buenneke, "Outfits Aren't the Biggest Problem."

3. H. Fisher, *Anatomy of Love*, 20–21.

4. Marshall, *From High on the Hilltop*, 3–10.

5. "Top Greek Schools."

6. Powell, "10 Universities."

7. Southern Methodist University Student Affairs, "Fraternity and Sorority Life."

8. A representative ad from 1931 features an illustrated drawing of two coeds who are on their way to fall rush parties dressed in their new dresses purchased at Volk Department Store. "Betty would make any important club in this dress!" the ad boasts. See "Betty and Babs," 5.

9. See "SMU Allegedly Provided Sex"; and Whitford, *Payroll to Meet*.

10. Robbins wasn't the first journalist to profile SMU's cutthroat sorority culture. See Peterson, "Battle of the Big Three."

11. Robbins, *Pledged*.

12. Robbins and Martin, "Should Colleges Get Rid of Fraternities?"

13. Robbins, "Sorority Secrets."

14. Kurzban and Weeden, "HurryDate," 240.

15. Mongell and Roth, "Sorority Rush as a Two-Sided Matching Mechanism," 441–64.

16. Southern Methodist University Student Affairs, "Frequently Asked Questions."

17. C. Lewis, "This Ridiculous Sorority Recruitment Video."

18. Artec Media, "Delta Gamma | University of Miami—2016"; Harman, "What It Costs."

19. Artec Media, "Alpha Phi | Arizona State University—Recruitment 2016"; Paiella, "These Are the Winners."

20. Wenerd, "Arizona State's Alpha Phi Sorority Recruitment Video."

21. K. White, "ASU Sorority."

22. "USC Alpha Phi 2016"; Yenisey, "5 Sorority Recruitment Videos"; Maxim, "This University of Florida Sorority Video." See also "Hottest Sorority Recruiting Videos 2018."

23. A. Bailey, "'Bama Sorority Video."

24. "Alabama Alpha Phi 2015 Recruitment Video."

25. K. White, "ASU Sorority."

26. Petit, "Why Everyone Needs to Back Off."

27. Beaird, Mobley, and Lawrence, "'Selling Sisterhood,'" 10.

28. Fisher, *Anatomy of Love*, 21.

29. Howell, "Why Are Emotions Contagious?"

30. Smith-Rosenberg, *Disorderly Conduct*, 28. This chapter is based on Rosenberg's watershed article "Female World of Love and Ritual," 1–29.

31. Smith-Rosenberg, *Disorderly Conduct*, 53–76.

32. E. Walker, "Pretty Girl Papers IV," 21.

33. Horowitz, *Campus Life*, 166.

34. Horowitz, 162.

35. Horowitz, 162.

36. Horowitz, 169.

37. Fass, *Damned and the Beautiful*, 260.

38. G. Jones, "Evil of Girls' Secret Societies," 26.

39. Shelton, "Nunsploitation and the Figure of the Naughty Nun."

40. L. Horn, "MTV Spring Break Used to Rule"; Clem, "MTV Is Bringing Back 'Spring Break.'"

41. "Delta Gamma–Florida State University."

42. "Delta Zeta–Indiana University."

43. L. Hamilton, "Trading on Heterosexuality," 167–68.

44. L. Hamilton, 168.

45. L. Hamilton, 169.

46. L. Hamilton, 150.

47. Hacker, "Topless Dancing at SMU Sorority"; Dunn, "SMU Student Sues."

48. Salinger, "Texas Sorority Members' Topless Dancing."

49. Salinger.

50. D. Thompson, "America's Weird, Enduring Love Affair."

51. C. Clark, "Domestic Architecture," 50.

52. G. Wright, *Building the Dream*, 75.

53. G. Wright, 82.

54. G. Wright, 82; Hershey, "Godey's Choice," 105.

55. C. Clark, "Domestic Architecture," 57.

56. C. Clark, 47.

57. Parsons, "Social Life of the Coeducational College," 385.

58. See Turk, *Bound by a Mighty Vow*, 129–31.

59. S. Martin, *Sorority Handbook*, 41–42.

60. See Johnston, "Row Show"; Dorpat, "Delta Gamma Helped Pave the Way"; Grand Forks Historical Preservation Commission, "University of North Dakota Historic District."

61. Monroe, "Sorority House Tour!!"

62. Kappa Kappa Gamma, "The University of New Mexico."

63. D. Roberts, "Black, White & Greek."

64. Rodick, "Most Beautiful Sorority Houses"; Feher, "50 Most Stunning Sorority Houses."

65. Kappa Kappa Gamma–University of Michigan, "Fraternity and Sorority Life"; Kappa Kappa Gamma–University of Southern California, "Our House"; Kappa Kappa Gamma—University of Montana, "Our House"; Kappa Kappa Gamma—University of Idaho, "Our House"; Delta Gamma—University of Oregon, "Our House"; Kappa Alpha Theta, "Alpha Xi Oregon"; Alpha Xi Delta, "Epsilon at University of South Dakota."

66. Freeman, *Women of Discriminating Taste*, 66.

67. Lily Bess Campbell, "Alpha Theta's House Management," 4.

68. Freeman, *Women of Discriminating Taste*, 50.

69. "Delta Zeta–University of Tennessee."

70. Artec Media, "Alpha Phi | University of Arizona."

71. Finney and Maloney, "22 Most Over-the-Top Sorority Houses."

72. "You've Never Seen Sorority Houses Like These."

73. Mahtani, "15 Most Outrageous University of Alabama Sorority Houses."

74. Pope, "Greek Life."

75. First, "What I Learned."

76. See Turk, *Bound by a Mighty Vow*, 13–41.

77. Turk, 147.

78. Kappa Kappa Gamma, "Build a Home Where Kappa Standards," 367. See also Freeman, *Women of Discriminating Taste*, 64; and K. Smith, "We Should Live Together."

79. See Bolick, *Spinster*; Klinenberg, *Going Solo*; Traister, *All the Single Ladies*; and Rosin, *End of Men*.

80. Rao and Raphael, "Singles Now Outnumber."

81. National Panhellenic Conference, "2016–2017 Annual Survey Highlights."

82. Rogers, "First Person."

83. Hacker, "Topless Dancing at SMU Sorority."

CHAPTER 5

1. The reasons why fewer high school graduates are matriculating into college are complex, but significant factors include the rising cost of college tuition and lower national birth rate. Related to the latter, Carleton College economist Nathan D. Grawe notes that the Great Recession triggered a dramatic drop (12 percent) in the national birth rate, and the numbers have stayed more or less static ever since. This means that, starting in 2026, the number of native-born children reaching college age will be on the decline. See Grawe, *Demographics and the Demand*, 6. For further discussion, see McGee, *Breakpoint*, 23–24; Wong, "Where Are All the High-School Grads Going?"; and Hechinger Report Contributor, "Colleges Set to Fight."

2. Wong, "Where Are All the High-School Grads Going?"

3. Han, Jaquette, and Salazar, "Recruiting the Out-of-State University"; Burd, "Out-of-State-Arms Race"; Saul, "Public Colleges Chase Out-of-State Students."

4. Arkansas was ranked 49 out of 50 in Gallup's 2019 National Health and Well-Being Index in 2019, beating only West Virginia, which has been at the bottom of the barrel for the past decade. See Witters, "Hawaii Tops U.S. in Wellbeing." The state has fared equally poorly in other rankings and reports. In 2016, CNBC named it the worst state to live in. See Cohn, "America's 10 Worst States to Live In." The same organization awarded the state with the dubious distinction of having the worst quality of life in 2018.

5. University of Arkansas, "University of Arkansas Enrollment Reaches Record High"; University of Arkansas, "University of Arkansas Enrollment Grows by 5.8 Percent."

6. University of Arkansas, "U of A Ranked."

7. University of Arkansas, "Fall 2016 11th Day Enrollment Report."

8. University of Arkansas, "University of Arkansas Enrollment Hitting Record Highs."

9. If enrollment trends continue, reporters estimate that more Texans will be attending the University of Arkansas than residents of Arkansas in 2022. See "Woo Horns Sooiree!"

10. University of Arkansas, "New Arkansan Non-Resident Tuition Award"; for information on the program that this replaced, see Brantley, "University of Arkansas Adds."

11. In 2018–19, 31 percent of the UA student body were members of a Greek letter organization. This includes historically white fraternities and sororities as well as multicultural organizations. See University of Arkansas, "Welcome to Greek Life!"

12. Cheverere, "Pike House at U of Arkansas." Lambda Chi also completed a renovation. See Hollis, "Greek Members Expect Renovations."

13. "7 Largest Sorority Houses."

14. Chi Omega Psi, "Sweet Home Chi Omega."

15. Adame, "UA Gets Two New Sorority Houses."

16. University of Arkansas, "Welcome to Greek Life!"; Biddix, "Sorority Membership and Educational Outcomes: Results from a National Survey."

17. UA was ranked number eighteen for Best Greek Life Colleges by Niche in 2019, number 9 by Total Frat Move in 2016, and number six by TSM in 2016. See "2019 Best Greek Life Colleges"; H. Lee, "TFM's 10 Best Universities"; and Montemayor, "Top 25 Best Universities."

18. University of Alabama, "Fraternity and Sorority Life."

19. University of Alabama, "Define Your Experience."

20. University of Alabama, 7.

21. Orendi, "New #1."

22. Han, Jaquette, and Salazar, "Recruiting the Out-of-State University," 4. The study's authors admit that the University of Alabama is an outlier in its recruiting strategies and doesn't represent the norm. See Koplowitz, "UA Is 'Extreme Case.'"

23. Mitchell, *Debt Trap*, 167–87.

24. University of Alabama, "Greek Housing"; B. Flanagan, "Alabama Sorority Row 2016."

25. Orendi, "New #1."

26. Orendi.

27. University of Alabama, "University of Alabama Interfraternity Council"; University of Alabama, "University of Alabama Panhellenic Association."

28. WER Architects/Planners, "Chi Omega House."

29. Chi Omega Psi, "Sweet Home Chi Omega."

30. Adame, "UA Gets Two New Sorority Houses."

31. Louisiana State University Greek Life, "Annual Report 2016–2017"; University of Texas at Austin Panhellenic Council, "Discover Sorority Life"; Mississippi State Panhellenic Council, "Mississippi State University Panhellenic Council Chapter Score Card 2019"; University of Oklahoma Office of Student Life, "University of Oklahoma Panhellenic Association Recruitment Look Book 2019"; University of Missouri, "Greek Statistics."

32. Dunbar, *How Many Friends?*, 28.

33. Dunbar, "Neocortex Size as a Constraint," 469–93; Dunbar, "Coevolution of Neocortical Size," 681–735.

34. Dunbar, *Human Evolution*, 70. Dunbar identifies Gore-Tex's factory unit size as a representative illustration of the law of 150 in action in contemporary commerce. Malcolm Gladwell made this example famous by discussing it at length in *Tipping Point*, 169–92.

35. MacCarron, Kaski, and Dunbar, "Calling Dunbar's Numbers," 151–55.

36. Aaron Smith, "What People Like and Dislike." Dunbar and his team got very different results in their survey of Facebook users, finding that the average person surveyed had 155 friends. For a summary of Dunbar's argument, see Knapton, "Facebook Users Have 155 Friends."

37. Lieb, *Friend v. Friend*, 2.

38. Konnikova, "Limits of Friendship."

39. Lieb, *Friend v. Friend*, 31.

40. De Ruiter, Weston, and Lyon, "Dunbar's Number," 557–68.

41. Stroud, "Social Learning and Dunbar's Number."

42. Gonçalves, Perra, and Vespignani, "Modeling Users' Activity," 1–5.

43. Statista, "Average U.S. Teen Instagram Follower."

44. Knapton, "Facebook Users Have 155 Friends."

45. Dunbar, *Human Evolution*, 82.

46. "1 In, 1 Out"; see also Reed-Tsochas, "Science May Explain Why." For the complete study results, see Saramäki et al., "Persistence of Social Signatures," 942–47.

47. D. Bennett, "Dunbar Number."

48. McCreary, "How Big Is Too Big?"

49. Petersen, "Genius of Taylor Swift's Girlfriend Collection."

50. Garber, "Summer of the #Squad."

51. Stout, "Best Friend?"; Emery, "Is My Best Friend Toxic?"

52. Paxton and Moody, "Structure and Sentiment," 45.

53. United States Bureau of Labor Statistics, "Table 11A."

54. Stein, "Millennials."

55. Stein.

56. Stein.

57. Sicurella, "UGA Tri Delta Chapter"; Stancill, "ECU Sorority Suspended."

58. A. Martin, "UCF Suspends Sorority."

59. Koman, "Getting Hazed by My Sorority."

60. "Revealed: Threesomes."

61. Tingley et al., "Sorority and Fraternity Attitudes," 55.

62. For "opt out" sorority hazing, see Véliz-Calderón and Allan, "Defining Hazing," 19–20.

63. Keating et al., "Going to College," 107.

64. Armstrong et al., "'Good Girls,'" 100–122.

65. Berbary, "'Don't Be a Whore,'" 606–25.

66. Taylor, "2: Meet the Greeks."

67. Taylor, "3: Crash."

68. Taylor, "2: Meet the Greeks"; Taylor, "2: Crash."

69. Taylor, "3: Crash."

70. Fialka, "It's Time to Stop Calling Women 'Crazy'"; J. Wright, "Women Aren't Crazy."

71. Doyle, *Trainwreck*, xv–xxi.

72. Sweet, "Understanding Fraternity Hazing," 1, 6.

73. Sweet, 7.

CHAPTER 6

1. "Frat Dudes Make Pledges"; Netter, "Texas Fraternity Brother Branded"; H. Lee, "Video Surfaces."

2. Rocheleau, "BU Suspends Fraternity."

3. Simpson, "What Hazing Is Like."

4. Kingkade, "'Butt Chugging' Allegations."

5. For a detailed account of hazing at Clemson in the 1990s, see Brad Land's memoir, *Goat*, and the 2016 film of the same name.

6. Carter, "Wrongful Death Lawsuit."

7. "Boiling Water, Pepper Used."

8. "Hazing Defined."

9. Allan and Madden, "Hazing in View," 16.

10. At the time of writing, several states were considering either adding anti-hazing laws to the ballot or bolstering existing laws. See "States with Anti-Hazing Laws."

On July 1, 2019, Senate Bill 1008, otherwise known as "Andrew's Law" (after Florida State University hazing victim Andrew Coffey), came into effect in the state of Florida. This bill added muscle to the existing law by making hazing a third degree felony (at least). See Dobson, "Gov. DeSantis Signs 'Andrew's Law.'"

11. The literature on hazing is vast. For recent and influential studies on the need for acceptance, see Cimino, "Evolution of Hazing"; McCreary, Bray, and Thoma, "Bad Apples or Bad Barrels?"; and Sweet, "Understanding Fraternity Hazing." On peer pressure and groupthink, see Janis, "Groupthink"; and, on underestimating the coercive powers of groups, see Cimino and Delton, "On the Perception of Newcomers"; and Roosevelt, "Deconflating Buffoonery and Hazing."

12. Velzer, "FSU Student Who Died."

13. Aronson and Mills, "Effect of Severity of Initiation," 179.

14. Aronson and Mills, 179–80.

15. Aronson and Mills, 177.

16. Aronson and Mills, 177.

17. Schlenker, "Liking for a Group," 99–118.

18. Junger, *Tribe*, 66.

19. Sanua, *Going Greek*, 492.

20. Rotundo, *American Manhood*, 62–74.

21. Harwood, "Secret Societies in America," 617.

22. Harwood, 618.

23. Gray, "Fraternalism in America."

24. Burt, "Mysteries of the Masons."

25. "Lodge Initiates Man; Kills Him," 1.

26. Carnes, *Secret Ritual and Manhood in Victorian America*, 20–21.

27. Allmendinger, *Paupers and Scholars*, 108.

28. "Cornell Sophomores Win," 9.

29. Newman, "Rutgers Has a Rope Rush," 20.

30. Syrett, *Company He Keeps*, 151–52.

31. Leemon, *Rites of Passage*, 77.

32. Perrin, "5 Facts about Americans."

33. Simmons, "Virtual Brotherhood Building Ideas."

34. Koulogeoge, "Video Games."

35. BieryGolick, "Miami University Hazing Case."

36. Gyan, "Days before Max Gruver Died."

37. Animal Mother, "Started Out Hazing Pledges."

38. "ProudToBe270," comment on article by Animal Mother, "Started Out Hazing Pledges."

39. "ChristianPKP," comment on article by Animal Mother, "Started Out Hazing Pledges."

40. Meyer, "Rush: MPs Just 'Blowing Off Steam.'"

41. M. Ortiz, "Alleged Sigma Pi Hazing."

42. M. Ortiz.

43. Fox, "Some Pretty Bad Hazing Photos."

44. See Nuwer, *Broken Pledges* and *Wrongs of Passage*.

45. McCreary and Schutts, "Toward a Broader Understanding of Fraternity," 33.

46. Velzer, "FSU Student Who Died."

47. Anthropologist Aldo Cimino makes a compelling argument about hazing activities and planned failure in Cimino, "Fraternity Hazing," 214–36.

48. Daileda, "Military History of 'Leave No Man Behind.'"

49. Junger, *Tribe*, 56.

50 *"Old School* (7/9) Movie Clip."

51. This hazing ritual is also described in Michael Kimmel's *Guyland*, 96–97.

52. Johnson, *Fraternity Row*, 83–84.

53. "'He Died in a Room Full of People,'" 24.

54. Wechsler and Wuethrich, *Dying to Drink*, 35.

55. Cheever, *Drinking in America*, 65, 110–16.

56. Tiger, "Males Courting Males," 14.

57. Fairbairn et al., "Alcohol and Emotional Contagion," 686–701.

58. In 2001, Lois West conducted a comparative study of drinking cultures within college fraternities and military platoons and discovered essentially that friends that drink together in these contexts tend to stay together. See West, "Negotiating Masculinities," 371–92.

59. Boman, Stogner, and Miller, "Binge Drinking," 220; Iwamoto, Corbin, Lejuez, and MacPherson, "College Men and Alcohol Use," 29–39.

60. Vander Ven, *Getting Wasted*, 87–94.

61. MacLean, "Alcohol and the Constitution of Friendships," 99.

62. "'He Died in a Room Full of People.'"

63. "Coffey Family Calls for 'Accountability and Education'"; Karma, "5 Plead Guilty."

64. Levenson, "FSU Fraternity Pledge Died."

65. Etters, "911 Tape."

66. C. Flanagan, "Death at a Penn State Fraternity"; Gass-Poore, "They're Going to Get Me F***ed Up"; Roebuck, "Security Footage."

67. Ruland, "Messages from the Night."

68. Tmaddog, comment on Jared Borislow, "Penn State Has Indefinitely Banned Alcohol."

69. fratcock_12, "When You Wait."

70. Levenson, "FSU Fraternity Pledge Died."

71. Gyan, "Days before Max Gruver Died."

72. North American Interfraternity Conference, "Member Fraternities."

73. Nuwer, "Hazing Deaths."

74. Wilcox et al., "Prevalence and Predictors," 287–94.

75. Nuwer, "Hazing Deaths."

76. Bruckner, "Students Fall Victim," 459–93; K. Thompson, "Moral Crisis"; Higgins, "Experts on Hazing."

77. Gesensway, "Sad Tale of Mortimer Leggett"; Kellogg, *College Secret Societies*, 51–66.

78. This citation is found in the preface to Kellogg, *College Secret Societies*.

79. Robinson, "Private Investigators Focused on Frat Party."

80. Gajilan, "Greek Life More Popular Than Ever."

81. Sykes, "No Charges in Death of Cornell Freshman"; Steecker, "Cornell Bans Phi Kappa Psi."

82. Jenkins, "After a Freshman's Death."

83. Lefkowitz, "Anti-Hazing Efforts."

84. Allen, "5 Plead Guilty"; Holcombe, "3 Fraternity Brothers Sentenced."

85. Gallo, "Matthew Naquin's Felony Conviction."

86. Burnside and Levinson, "LSU Fraternity Member Charged."

87. North American Interfraternity Council, "About Interfraternity Council."

88. Taylor et al., "Positive Spin on a Negative Narrative," 51.

CHAPTER 7

1. "Greek Life Statistics"; Dukcevich, "Best Fraternities for Future CEOs."

2. The lopsided representation of fraternity and sorority members in these milieus is emblematic of the relationship between men and women in the contemporary labor market more broadly. *Elle*'s 2015 #MoreWomen Campaign—where an artist photoshopped men out of photos of White House cabinet meetings, UN councils, newsrooms, and the like—reveals just how outnumbered women are in these environments—comes to mind. See Lindig, "This Video Shows What History Would Look Like."

3. See Syrett, *Company He Keeps*, 129, 185–86.

4. Carnes, *Secret Ritual and Manhood*, 115.

5. Kimmel, *Manhood in America*, 126.

6. Ferner and Schulberg, "Here's What Yale Was Like."

7. Ofosu, "Brett Kavanaugh."

8. Tian, "Yale's Fraternities Enter National Spotlight."

9. New, "Common Sign."

10. Hatch, "Read the Sexist Email."

11. See Syrett, *Company He Keeps*, 67–78.

12. For example, see Sanua, *Going Greek*; Ross, *Divine Nine*; Parks and Hughey, *Pledge with Purpose*; and Whaley, *Disciplining Women*.

13. National Center for Education Statistics, "Fast Facts: Degrees Conferred by Race and Sex."

14. Lee, *Fraternities without Brotherhood*, 3.

15. Universities in Louisiana, Arkansas, North Carolina, South Carolina, and Kentucky hover near the bottom of at least one national ethnic diversity ranking. See *U.S. News & World Report*, "Campus Ethnic Diversity." See also C. Parks, "With White Students."

16. Oluo, *So You Want to Talk about Race*, 12.

17. Mills, *Racial Contract*, 110.

18. Sutter, "Are Frats 'a Form of American Apartheid'?" See also Fausset and Robertson, "Beyond College Campuses."

19. R. Ward, "Fraternity Grounded."

20. Dries, "Backlash Comes over UGA's Ban."

21. S. Garcia, "'Pick My Cotton.'"

22. Chavez and Lynch, "3 College Students."

23. Muskal, "Racist Chant Taught."

24. Zucchino, "Duke Protests Frat Party."

25. Gold, "6 Disturbingly Racist and Sexist Frat Party Themes."

26. Nashrulla, "This Fraternity Held a 'Mexican-Themed' Party"; Schallhorn, "Virginia College Students"; Smothers, "UT Fraternity"; A. Jones, "Child's Treasury."

27. Fadel, "Cultural Appropriation."

28. Hathaway, "Sorority Girl Celebrates 21st Birthday."

29. Bacon, "K-State Disavows Student's Racist Snapchat."

30. J. Miller, "Sorority Sister Speaks Out."

31. J. Miller.

32. Pizarro, Wang, and Robbins, "'Phi Psi Historical Archives' Leaked"; Wagner et al., "Cult of Misogyny."

33. Baker, "We Need the Shock."

34. Phi Psi, "Redacted_Phi_Psi_1. pdf."

35. Phi Psi.

36. Ogozalek, "Second Theta Tau Video."

37. McMahon, "Syracuse Theta Tau Brothers."

38. Sanders, "UA Sophomore Says."

39. Sanders.

40. O'Connor, "Truth about Bama Rush"; Lang, "RushTok."

41. "No One Can Dim the Light Within."

42. Cole, "Top Ten Differences."

43. Mackinnon, Jordan, and Wilson, "Birds of a Feather."

44. Christakis and Fowler, "Friendship and Natural Selection."

45. Friedman, "Importance of Friendship Diversity."

46. Carroll, "Do White People Really Know"; Eligon, "'Some of My Best Friends Are Black' Defense."

47. DiAngelo, *White Fragility*, 67–68.

48. Turk, *Bound by a Mighty Vow*, 26.

49. Joyce, "Perceptions of Race and Fit," 35.

50. Morgan et al., "Stick with Yourselves"; Zimmerman, Morgan, and Terrell, "Are We Really?'"

51. Wade, "Why Colleges Should Get Rid of Fraternities."

52. The two single-sex sororities and fraternities not subject to administrative censure are Alpha Phi Alpha, a fraternity targeted to African American men, and Alpha Kappa Alpha, a sorority targeted to African American women. Because Harvard no longer recognizes single-sex student organizations, these groups can't tap into school funds or hold meetings or events on school property. Their members were allowed to keep their membership active because of their blended population. While the membership of white sororities and fraternities at Harvard was comprised exclusively of Harvard students, the Alpha Phi Alpha and Alpha Kappa Alpha chapters opened up their membership to students in neighboring schools as well. See Engelmayer, "'Cultural' Fraternities and Sororities"; Bauer-Wolf, "Fraternities, Sororities Sue."

53. Freid, "69: The Future of Greek Life."

54. Schuster, "Inside the Harvard Clubs."

55. Field, "Fraternities and Sororities Sue Harvard."

56. Bump, "Meet FratPAC."

57. "PAC Profile."

58. Engelmayer and Xie, "Pro-Greek Life PAC Fights"; H.R.4508–Propser Act; H.R.3128–Collegiate Freedom of Association Act.

59. Bauer-Wolf, "Title IX Lawsuit against Harvard." See also S. Cobb, "State Court Denies Harvard Motion."

60. Totenberg, "Supreme Court Delivers Major Victory."

61. Knieriem and Schumer, "Harvard Drops Social Group Sanctions"; "Will Supreme Court Ruling Mean More."

62. Fraternity and Sorority Political Action Committee, "It Shouldn't Take the Supreme Court."

63. Harvard University, "Policy on Unrecognized Single-Gender Social Organizations."

64. Washington and Nuñez, "Education, Racial Uplift," 141–82.

65. Ross, *Divine Nine*, 5–6.

66. Parks and Hughey, *Pledge with Purpose*, 4.

67. Dickinson, "Pledged to Remember," 9–32.

68. Fleming, *How to Be Less Stupid about Race*, 156.

69. Fleming, 158–59.

70. National Panhellenic Conference, "Our Story." As of September 2021, the video is disabled.

71. Newman, "What We Know about the Death of George Floyd."

72. Westerman, Benk, and Greene, "In 2020, Protests Spread"; Shaw and Kidwai, "Global Impact."

73. Buchanan, Bui, and Patel, "Black Lives Matter."

74. E. Marcus, "War on Frats." See also Lautrup, "Abolish Greek Life?"

75. Wellemeyer, "Students at Vanderbilt Leave."

76. For an example of the formation of a diversity and inclusion commission,

see Sigma Chi, "Diversity & Inclusion." For another example, see M. Cobb, "Soul Searching," 32–33. ADPi named diversity, equity, and inclusion as a strategic priority in 2021. See Alpha Delta Pi, "Diversity, Equity, and Inclusion in Alpha Delta Pi." See also Gamma Phi Beta's BEDI (Belonging, Equity, Diversity and Inclusion) Summit in Gamma Phi Beta, "BEDI Summit."

77. Alpha Delta Pi, "Owning Our Past," 6–17.

78. Alpha Delta Pi, 14.

79. Fischetti, "Fraternity Suspended."

80. Dunker, "UNL Frat Investigated."

81. Pietsch, "Fraternity at University of Georgia."

82. Larrison Campbell, "How a Black Lesbian Took Down"; Liang, "UGA Fraternity Self Suspends."

CHAPTER 8

1. See Vance, *Hillbilly Elegy*; Isenberg, *White Trash*; and Wray, *Not Quite White*.

2. Packer, "Hillary Clinton and the Populist Revolt."

3. Coates, "First White President."

4. Putnam, *Bowling Alone*.

5. Dubner, "266: Trust Me."

6. Cited in Nehamas, *On Friendship*, 40.

7. Carnes, "Middle-Class Men," 39.

8. Carnes, *Secret Ritual and Manhood*, 18–21.

9. Lee, *Fraternities without Brotherhood*, 106.

10. See Syrett, *Company He Keeps*, 121–33.

11. Eldridge, *Co-EDiquette*, 45.

12. Abelson and Faux, "Secret Handshakes."

13. Tiger, *Men in Groups*, 144.

14. J. Fisher, "How to Get a Job."

15. Belli, "How Many Jobs"; Adler, "New Survey Reveals."

16. Busteed, "From Beers to Careers."

17. Reeves, *Dream Hoarders*.

18. Fry, "U.S. Women Near Milestone."

19. Scott, "American College Sorority," 525.

20. Tanzi, "Women Are Outpacing Men."

21. Law, "Women Are Now the Majority."

22. Riggio, "How Are Men's Friendships Different?"

23. Yen, "How Friendship Holds Women Back."

24. Turk, *Bound by a Mighty Vow*, 13–41.

25. Newcomer, *Century of Higher Education*, 49.

26. Turk, *Bound by a Mighty Vow*, 43–79.

27. See, for example, Kappa Kappa Delta, "Meet Some Notable Kappa Deltas." Given Kappa Alpha Theta's investment in archiving its organization's history, it is not surprising that this sorority's website profiles alumnae who represent a much wider range of fields and critical interests. See Kappa Alpha Theta, "Notable Thetas."

28. DeSantis, *Inside Greek U*, 193–95.

29. Newman, "40 Years Ago."

30. Winton, Xia, and Lin, "Isla Vista Shooting."

31. Levo League, "Networking, Sorority Style."

32. S. White, "How to Use Your Sorority Network."

33. Kelley, "'Black Christmas'"; Harnish, "Horror of Being a Woman."

34. Delta Zeta, "Truly Connected Nights."

35. Tri Delta, "Preparing Our Members."

36. K. Walker and Havice, "Student Affairs Practitioners' Perceptions," 27.

37. As a representative case in point, the only place where a career-related topic is mentioned on Pi Beta Phi's website is in the site's description of its password-protected alumnae search portal. Specifically, the portal is described as a place for "building relationships for career opportunities." See Pi Beta Phi, "Stay Connected with Pi Beta Phi." Similarly, the "Career Opportunities" page of Alpha Gamma Delta's website only includes information about volunteer opportunities (with the sorority) and information about how to apply to work at the AGD headquarters. See Alpha Gamma Delta, "Alpha Gamma Delta International Headquarters." Phi Mu's "Jobs" page similarly focuses its attention on information about its one-year postgraduate "leadership consultant" positions.

38. See, for example, Phi Delta Theta's strategic plan on Phi Delta Theta, "Phi Delt 2020." See also Pi Kappa Phi, "Alumni Engagement"; and Tau Kappa Epsilon, "Goal Two."

39. Samson, "Fraternity Membership," 24.

40. Husser, "Condition of Education 2020," 131; National Center for Education Statistics, "Digest of Education Statistics"; Nadworny, "I Need a Degree."

41. College Factual, "Review Age Diversity."

42. See Freeman, *Women of Discriminating Taste*, 182–83.

43. National Panhellenic Conference, "Extension Information for College Panhellenics."

44. Ethridge and Milton, "Eagle Becomes a Lion," 10–11.

45. National Panhellenic Conference, "NPC Community College Task Force Survey."

46. Sigma Pi was founded in 1897 at Vincennes University, which was, at the time, a two-year institution. The chapter closed in 1911 due to low enrollment. When the fraternity petitioned to reopen the chapter in 1965, it had to receive a special dispensation from NIC to do so because at that time NIC prohibited member organizations from operating at two-year colleges. See Sigma Pi, "Our Chapter."

47. North American Interfraternity Conference, "Constitution of the North American Interfraternity Conference," 9.

48. University of North Georgia, "Quick Facts."

49. O'Kane, "Georgia College Students Throw Massive Party."

CONCLUSION

1. Fraternity parties have been linked to COVID-19 outbreaks across the United States. See, for example, Sheridan, "Coronavirus Outbreak"; Meyerhofer and Hamer, "UW-Madison Orders"; and McEvoy, "Outbreaks Hit Fraternities, Sororities." COVID policies are not static, but, as of January 2021, all but two southern states (North

Carolina and Texas) ranked in the Top 25 of Wallet Hub's least-restrictive COVID restrictions. See McCann, "States with the Fewest Coronavirus Restrictions."

2. Lieberman, "Fraternities Host Massive Pool Parties."

3. "UVA Confirms COVID-19 Violations."

4. McKenzie, "Watch Now."

5. Irrera, "Exclusive."

6. Cabe, "Spring Breakers"; Lewis et al., "COVID-19 Outbreak," 830–35.

7. Vang et al., "Participation in Fraternity and Sorority Activities," 20–23; Van Beusekom, "In-Person Classes"; Kenney, "Parties Don't Stop"; Kelly and DeMarco, "UCF Suspends Fraternity"; O'Kane, "Georgia College Students Throw Massive Party"; Harmon, Robles, Blinder, and Fuller, "'Frats Are Being Frats.'"

8. Nguyen, "Why It's So Difficult."

9. Forinash, "Duke to Create 'Residential Community.'"

10. Pequeño, "Report."

11. G. Anderson, "Mental Health Needs Rise"; Son et al., "Effects of COVID-19 on College Students' Mental Health," e21279; Gupta, "COVID-19 Pandemic."

12. Phired Up, "Fraternity & Sorority Will Endure."

13. See, for example, Poindexter, "Members of Greek Life Reflect"; J. Clark, "LSU Sorority Members Reflect"; and Zhu, "Virtual Sorority Recruitment."

14. See Humphries, "College Freshman Paid $1000."

15. Coffey-Melchiorre, "Student Survey."

16. Bonar et al., "Binge Drinking"; Nuwer, "Hazing Deaths."

17. Hauser, "Virginia Fraternity Is Suspended."

18. Perricone, "BGSU Sophomore Dies."

19. Konneker, "University 'Looking Into' Racist Snapchat Post."

20. Evon, "Was a Noose Hung?"; Shinkman, "Prosecutors"; Bendix, "Harrowing Photo."

21. A. Jones, "#BamaRush, Explained."

22. Rosenblatt, "University of Alabama Sorority Rush."

BIBLIOGRAPHY

Abelson, Max, and Zeke Faux. "Secret Handshakes Greet Frat Brothers on Wall Street." *Bloomberg*, December 23, 2013. www.bloomberg.com/news/articles/2013-12-23/secret-handshakes-greet-frat-brothers-on-wall-street/.

Adame, Jaime. "UA Gets Two New Sorority Houses; Campus 'Greek' Life Is on Upswing." *Arkansas Democrat Gazette*, August 12, 2018. www.arkansasonline.com/news/2018/aug/12/ua-gets-two-new-sorority-houses-2018081/.

Adams, Jenny. "America's Best College Bars." *Travel + Leisure*, March 29, 2013. www.travelandleisure.com/culture-design/americas-best-college-bars/.

Adler, Lou. "New Survey Reveals 85% of All Jobs Are Filled via Networking." LinkedIn, February 29, 2016. www.linkedin.com/pulse/new-survey-reveals-85-all-jobs-filled-via-networking-lou-adler/.

"Alabama Alpha Phi 2015 Recruitment Video." WKRG/CBS News, YouTube video, 4:13, August 17, 2015. www.youtube.com/watch?v=KudwS5U9ouA/.

The All-American Rathskellar. "The Skellar through the Years." Accessed December 14, 2019. https://theskeller.com/skeller-history/.

Allan, Elizabeth J., and Mary Madden. "Hazing in View: College Students at Risk." StopHazing.org, March 11, 2008. www.stophazing.org/wp-content/uploads/2014/06/hazing_in_view_web1.pdf/.

Allmendinger, David F. *Paupers and Scholars: The Transformation of Student Life in Nineteenth-Century New England*. New York: St. Martin's, 1975.

Almaatouq, Abdullah, Laura Radaelli, Alex Pentland, and Erez Shmueli. "Are You Your Friends' Friend? Poor Perception of Friendship Ties Limits the Ability to Promote Behavioral Change." *PLOS ONE* (2016): 1–13.

Alpha Delta Pi. "Diversity, Equity, and Inclusion in Alpha Delta Pi." Accessed March 12, 2021. https://alphadeltapi.org/news/newsitem/?ni=958201/.

———. "Owning Our Past: An Exploration of Membership Selection in Alpha Delta Pi's History." *Adelphean* (Summer 2020): 6–19.

Alpha Gamma Delta. "Alpha Gamma Delta International Headquarters." Accessed January 14, 2021. https://alphagammadelta.org/about/careers/.

Alpha Xi Delta. "Epsilon at University of South Dakota." Accessed February 4, 2021. http://usd.alphaxidelta.org/index/.

American College Health Association. "American College Health Association—National College Health Assessment II: Reference Group Executive Summary." Fall 2018.

Accessed November 19, 2021. www.acha.org/documents/ncha/NCHA-II_Fall_2018
_Reference_Group_Executive_Summary.pdf.

Anderson, Colton. "BYU Ranks No. 1 'Stone-Cold Sober School' for 22nd Straight
Year." *Daily Universe*, August 12, 2019. https://universe.byu.edu/2019/08/12
/byu-ranks-no-1-stone-cold-sober-school-for-its-22nd-year/.

Anderson, Greta. "Mental Health Needs Rise with Pandemic." Inside Higher Ed,
September 11, 2020. www.insidehighered.com/news/2020/09/11
/students-great-need-mental-health-support-during-pandemic/.

Anderson, Taylor. "15 Reasons Your Best Friends Are Better than Partners." *Cosmopolitan*, February 14, 2017. www.cosmopolitan.com/uk/love-sex/relationships/a33630
/best-friends-are-better-than-boyfriends/.

Animal Mother. "ChristianPKP." Comment on "Started Out Hazing Pledges, Now We're
Off to Haze ISIS." Total Frat Move. Accessed May 17, 2017. https://totalfratmove
.com/started-out-hazing-pledges-now-were-off-to-haze-isis/.

———. "ProudToBe270." Comment on "Started Out Hazing Pledges, Now We're Off
to Haze ISIS." Total Frat Move. Accessed May 17, 2017. https://totalfratmove.com
/started-out-hazing-pledges-now-were-off-to-haze-isis/.

———. "Started Out Hazing Pledges, Now We're Off to Haze ISIS." Total Frat Move.
Accessed May 17, 2017. https://totalfratmove.com/started-out-hazing
-pledges-now-were-off-to-haze-isis/.

Anness, Emily. "Dealing (with) Xanax on Campus." *Sandspur*, March 29, 2018.
www.thesandspur.org/dealing-xanax-campus/.

Armstrong Elizabeth A., and Laura T. Hamilton. *Paying for the Party: How College Maintains Inequality*. Cambridge, Mass.: Harvard University Press, 2013.

Armstrong, Elizabeth A., Laura T. Hamilton, Elizabeth M. Armstrong, and J. Lotus
Seeley. "'Good Girls': Gender, Social Class, and Slut Discourse on Campus." *Social
Psychology Quarterly* 77, no. 2 (2014): 100–122.

Aronson, Elliot, and Judson Mills. "The Effect of Severity of Initiation on Liking for a
Group." *Journal of Abnormal and Social Psychology* 59, no. 1 (1959): 177–81.

Artec Media. "Alpha Phi | Arizona State University—Recruitment 2016." YouTube
video, 3:32, August 1, 2016. www.youtube.com/watch?v=Pr4USQjr9is%2C/.

———. "Delta Gamma | University of Miami—2016." YouTube video, 4:16, January 6,
2016. www.youtube.com/watch?v=tpBzmdj3G_0/.

Aurora, Pallavi, and Alicia K. Klanecky. "Drinking Motives Mediate Emotion Regulation
Difficulties and Problem Drinking in College Students." *American Journal of Drug &
Alcohol Abuse* 42, no. 3 (May 2016): 341–50.

Austin, J. L. *How to Do Things with Words: The William James Lectures*. 2nd ed. Edited by
J. O. Urmson and Marina Sbisà. Cambridge, Mass.: Harvard University Press, 1975.

Au-Yeung, Angel. "Bumble Cofounder Becomes World's Youngest Self-Made Woman
Billionaire, Thanks to IPO." *Forbes*, February 11, 2021. www.forbes.com/sites
/angelauyeung/2021/02/11/bumble-founder-whitney-wolfe-herds-fortune-rockets
-past-1-billion-as-dating-app-goes-public/?sh=410d076578d9/.

Bach, Henning. *When Men Meet: Homosexuality and Modernity*. Cambridge: Polity, 1997.

Bacon, John. "K-State Disavows Student's Racist Snapchat." *USA Today*, September 15,
2016. www.usatoday.com/story/news/2016/09/15/k-state-disavows-students
-racist-snapchat/90417654/.

Bailey, A. L. "'Bama Sorority Video Worse for Women Than Donald Trump." AL.com, August 14, 2015. https://www.al.com/opinion/2015/08/bama_sorority_video_worse _for.html/.

Bailey, Beth L. *From Front Porch to Back Seat: Courtship in Twentieth-Century America.* Baltimore, Md.: Johns Hopkins University Press, 1988.

Baker, Gerard. "We Need the Shock of Dave Chappelle's Comedy." *Wall Street Journal,* September 6, 2019. www.wsj.com/articles/we-need-the-shock-of-dave-chappelles -comedy-11567787318/.

Baker-Jordan, Skylar. "My Fraternity Years as an Out Gay Man." Salon, January 12, 2015. www.salon.com/2015/01/11/my_fraternity_years_as_an_out_gay_man/.

Barkho, Gabriela. "Why Are Millennials Putting Off Marriage? Let Me Count the Ways." *Washington Post,* June 2, 2016. www.washingtonpost.com/news/soloish/wp /2016/06/06/why-are-millennials-putting-off-marriage-let-me-count-the-ways /?utm_term=.a3a23cda430a/.

Bath, Elsie. "How to Take the Perfect Nude Selfie, According to a Photographer." VICE, May 23, 2017. www.vice.com/en_us/article/j5epv8/how-to-take-the-perfect -nude-selfie-according-to-a-photographer/.

Bauer-Wolf, Jeremy. "Fraternities, Sororities Sue over Harvard Single-Sex Club Rule." Inside Higher Ed, December 4, 2018. www.insidehighered.com/quicktakes /2018/12/04/fraternities-sororities-sue-over-harvard-single-sex-club-rule/.

———. "Title IX Lawsuit against Harvard Will Move Forward." Inside Higher Ed, August 16, 2019. www.insidehighered.com/quicktakes/2019/08/16/title-ix-lawsuit -against-harvard-will-move-forward/.

Beaird, Kaitlynn, Steve D. Mobley, Jr., and ShirDonna Y. Lawrence. "'Selling Sisterhood': (Re)Viewing White Women's Self-Portrayals in Recruitment Videos." *Oracle: The Research Journal of the Association of Fraternity/Sorority Advisors* 16, no. 1 (2021): 1–18.

Beck, Julie. "What It's Like to Make a Friend of Bumble BFF." *Atlantic,* February 15, 2019. www.theatlantic.com/family/archive/2019/02/friendship-files-meeting -bumble-bff/581575/.

Belli, Gina. "How Many Jobs Are Found through Networking, Really?" Payscale, April 6, 2017. www.payscale.com/career-news/2017/04/many-jobs-found-networking/.

Bendix, Aria. "A Harrowing Photo Shows a Trump Supporter Carrying a Confederate Flag inside the U.S. Capitol, Flanked by Portraits of Civil War–Era Figures." Business Insider, January 6, 2021. www.businessinsider.com/photo-trump -supporter-riot-confederate-flag-us-capitol-2021-1/.

Bennett, Amanda. "Snapchat CEO's Emails Show Need to Confront Misogyny." *Washington Post,* June 1, 2014. www.washingtonpost.com/opinions/snapchat-ceos-e mails-shows-need-to-confront-misogyny/2014/06/01/fd32cc36-c816-11c3-afc6 -a1dd9407abcf_story.html/.

Bennett, Drake. "The Dunbar Number: From the Guru of Social Networks." *Bloomberg,* January 11, 2013. www.bloomberg.com/news/articles/2013-01-10/the-dunbar -number-from-the-guru-of-social-networks/.

Bennett, Jessica. "With Her Dating App, More Women Are in Control." *New York Times,* March 18, 2017. www.nytimes.com/2017/03/18/fashion/bumble-feminist-dating -app-whitney-wolfe.html/.

Bennett, Jessica, and Daniel Jones. "45 Stories on Sex and Consent on Campus." *New York Times*, May 10, 2018. www.nytimes.com/interactive/2018/05/10/style/sexual -consent-college-campus.html/.

Berbary, Lisbeth A. "'Don't Be a Whore, That's Not Ladylike': Discursive Discipline and Sorority Women's Gendered Subjectivity." *Qualitative Inquiry* 18, no. 7 (2012): 606–25.

Bernholdt, Chris. "Banish the Playdate." Huffington Post, December 7, 2017. www .huffingtonpost.com/chris-bernholdt/banish-the-playdate_b_5577558.html/.

"Betty and Babs Go Back to School by the Volk Way of Smartness and Style." *S.M.U. Campus*, September 1, 1931. http://digitalcollections.smu.edu/cdm/ref/collection /stud/id/230/.

Biddix, J. Patrick. "Sorority Membership and Educational Outcomes: Results from a National Survey." National Panhellenic Conference, October 2014. Accessed November 19, 2021. www.npcwomen.org/wp-content/uploads/sites/2037 /2017/10/Retention-Research-Results-2014.pdf.

Biddle, Sam. "'Fuck Bitches Get Leid': The Sleazy Frat Emails of Snapchat's CEO." Valleywag, May 28, 2014. http://valleywag.gawker.com/fuck-bitches-get-leid-the -sleazy-frat-emails-of-snap-1582604137/.

———. "How to Take Flawless Phone Pics of Your Naked Body." Gizmodo, July 25, 2013. https://gizmodo.com/how-to-take-flawless-phone-pics-of-your-naked-body- 5893968/.

BieryGolick, Keith. "Miami University Hazing Case: 'Please Do Not Say Anything That Would Threaten the Future of the Fraternity.'" *Cincinnati Enquirer*, June 27, 2019. www.cincinnati.com/story/news/2019/06/27/miami-university-delta-tau-delta -hazing-case/1569018001/.

Bird, Grace. "Gay Student Assaulted at Delaware Fraternity." Inside Higher Ed, April 23, 2018. www.insidehighered.com/quicktakes/2018/04/23/gay-student-assaulted -delaware-fraternity/.

Birger, Jon. *Date-onomics: How Dating Became a Lopsided Numbers Game.* New York: Workman, 2015.

———. "Unequal Gender Ratios at Colleges Are Driving Hookup Culture." *Money*, October 15, 2015. https://money.com/college-gender-ratios-dating-hook-up-culture/.

Blackout B. "6 Steps to Being the Ultimate Wingwoman." Total Sorority Move, October 14, 2016. https://totalsororitymove.com/6-key-steps-to-being-the-ultimate -wingwoman/.

"Boiling Water, Pepper Used in Hazing, Police Say." CNN, May 7, 2008. http://edition .cnn.com/2008/CRIME/05/07/tulane.hazing/.

Bolick, Kate. *Spinster: Making a Life of One's Own.* New York: Broadway, 2016.

Boman, John H., John Stogner, and Bryan Lee Miller. "Binge Drinking, Marijuana Use, and Friendships: The Relationship between Similar and Dissimilar Usage and Friendship Quality." *Journal of Psychoactive Drugs* 45, no. 3 (July–August 2013): 218–26.

Bonar, Erin E., Michael J. Parks, Meredith Gunlicks-Stoessel, Grace R. Lyden, Christo- pher J. Mehus, Nichole Morrell, and Megan E. Patrick. "Binge Drinking before and after COVID-19 Campus Closure among First-Year College Students." *Addictive Be- haviors* 118 (2021): n.p.

Borzelleca, Daniel. "The Male-Female Ratio in College." *Forbes*, February 16, 2012. www.forbes.com/sites/ccap/2012/02/16/the-male-female-ratio-in-college /#52586927fa52/.

Bowell, Ayres A., and Joan Z. Spade. "Fraternities and College Rape Culture: Why Are Some Fraternities More Dangerous Places for Women?" *Gender and Society* 10, no. 2 (April 1996): 133–47.

Brain, Robert. *Friends and Lovers*. New York: Paladin, 1977.

Brantley, Max. "University of Arkansas Adds to 'Border State' Tuition Break Program." *Arkansas Times*, September 11, 2015. https://arktimes.com/arkansas-blog/2015/09 /11/university-of-arkansas-adds-to-border-state-tutition-break-program.

Brigham Young University. "Milktoberfest 2019." Accessed November 19, 2021. https://calendar.byu.edu/student-life/milktoberfest-2019-10-03/.

BroBible. "The 30 Best Frat Houses in the United States." Accessed December 14, 2019. http://brobible.com/college/article/30-best-frat-houses-united-states/.

Bruckner, Helene. "Students Fall Victim to Hazing Epidemic: Unity at What Cost?" *Touro Law Review* 34, no. 2 (2018): 459–93.

Buchanan, Larry, Quoctrung Bui, and Jugal K. Patel. "Black Lives Matter May Be the Largest Movement in U.S. History." *New York Times*, July 3, 2020. www.nytimes .com/interactive/2020/07/03/us/george-floyd-protests-crowd-size.html/.

"The Buddy System That Can Save Your Life." *Cosmopolitan*, February 23, 2009. www.cosmopolitan.com/lifestyle/advice/a2843/The-Buddy-System-That-Can -Save-Your-Life/.

Buchholz, Katharina. "The Most Popular Dating Apps in the U.S." Statista, March 12, 2021. www.statista.com/chart/24404/most-popular-dating-apps-us/.

Buenneke, Kate. "Outfits Aren't the Biggest Problem with Sorority Recruitments." *Atlantic*, February 18, 2015. www.theatlantic.com/education/archive/2015/02 /outfits-arent-the-biggest-problem-with-sorority-recruitment/385583/.

"Bumble for Besties? Yes!" Bumble. Accessed May 17, 2020. https://bumble.com /the-buzz/what-exactly-is-bumble-bff/.

Bump, Philip. "Meet FratPAC, the Group Advocating Greek Causes on Capitol Hill." *Atlantic*, July 24, 2013. www.theatlantic.com/politics/archive/2013/07 /meet-fratpac-group-advocating-greek-causes-capitol-hill/312949/.

Burd, Stephen. "The Out-of-State-Arms Race: How Public Universities Use Merit Aid to Recruit Nonresident Students." New America, May 2015. Accessed November 19, 2021. www.chronicle.com/blogs/ticker/files/2015/05/OutOfStateArmsRace.pdf.

Burkett, Melissa. "Sex(t) Talk: A Qualitative Analysis of Young Adults' Negotiations of the Pleasures and Perils of Sexting." *Sexuality & Culture* 19 (2015): 835–63.

Burnell, Ellamae. "UI Greek Members Danced Naked, Records Show." *University of Idaho Argonaut*, November 28, 2018. www.uiargonaut.com/2018/11/28 /ui-greek-members-danced-naked-records-show/.

Burnside, Tina, and Eric Levenson. "LSU Fraternity Member Charged with Felony Hazing after Student with Alcohol Poisoning Put on Life Support." CNN, November 3, 2020. www.cnn.com/2020/11/03/us/lsu-student-arrest-hazing/index.html/.

Burt, Andrew. "The Mysteries of the Masons." *Slate*, May 15, 2015. https://slate.com /news-and-politics/2015/05/masons-and-american-history-the-1826-kidnapping -allegedly-by-freemasons-that-changed-american-politics-forever.html/.

Busteed, Brandon. "From Beers to Careers: The New Value Proposition of Fraternity." *Forbes*, January 16, 2021. www.forbes.com/sites/brandonbusteed/2021/01/16/from-beers-to-careers-the-new-value-proposition-of-fraternity/?sh=59de7a11431f/.

Cabe, Caroline. "The Spring Breakers That Broke West Campus: Behind the Infamous Cabo Spring Break Trip." *Texas Orator*, February 26, 2021. https://thetexasorator.com/2020/05/15/the-spring-breakers-that-broke-west-campus-behind-the-infamous-cabo-spring-break-trip/.

Caffier, Justin. "Inside Milktoberfest: The Mormon Alternative to Oktoberfest." VICE, October 6, 2017. www.vice.com/en_us/article/xwgp3q/inside-milktoberfest-the-mormon-alternative-to-oktoberfest/.

Campbell, Larrison. "How a Black Lesbian Took Down a Racist, Pandemic-Partying Fraternity in the Deep South." Daily Beast, October 1, 2020, updated October 2, 2020. www.thedailybeast.com/how-arianna-mbunwe-took-down-a-pandemic-partying-lambda-chi-alpha-frat-at-the-university-of-georgia/.

Campbell, Lily Bess. "Alpha Theta's House Management." *Kappa Alpha Theta Magazine*, November 1, 1906.

"Campus Ethnic Diversity." *U.S. News and World Report*. Accessed March 2, 2021. www.usnews.com/best-colleges/rankings/national-universities/campus-ethnic-diversity/.

Canan, Sasha N., Kristen N. Jazkowski, and Brandon L. Crawford. "Sexual Assault Supportive Attitudes: Rape Myth Acceptance and Token Resistance in Greek and Non-Greek College Students from Two University Samples in the United States." *Journal of Interpersonal Violence* 33, no. 22 (November 2018): 3502–30.

Cantor, David, Bonnie Fisher, Susan Chibnall, Shauna Harps, Reanne Townsend, Gail Thomas, and Hyunshik Lee. "Report on the AAU Campus Climate Survey on Sexual Assault and Misconduct," October 15, 2019. www.aau.edu/sites/default/files/AAU-Files/Key-Issues/Campus-Safety/FULL_2019_Campus_Climate_Survey.pdf.

Carroll, Rebecca. "Do White People Really Know How to Have More Than One Black Friend?" *Guardian*, September 3, 2014. www.theguardian.com/commentisfree/2014/sep/03/white-people-one-black-friend/.

Carnes, Mark C. "Middle-Class Men and the Solace of Fraternal Ritual." In *Meanings for Manhood: Constructions of Masculinity in Victorian America*, edited by Mark C. Carnes and Clyde Griffen, 37–52. Chicago: University of Chicago Press, 1990.

———. *Secret Ritual and Manhood in Victorian America*. New Haven, Conn.: Yale University Press, 1989.

Carrillo, Héctor, and Amanda Hoffman. "'Straight with a pinch of bi': The Construction of Heterosexuality as an Elastic Category among Adult U.S. Men." *Sexualities* 21, no. 1–2 (2017): 90–108.

Carter, Tyler. "Wrongful Death Lawsuit Filed against Ohio University Fraternity." NBC4i, February 14, 2019. www.nbc4i.com/news/local-news/wrongful-death-lawsuit-filed-against-ohio-university-fraternity/.

Case, Douglas N., Grahaeme A. Hesp, and Charles G. Eberly. "An Exploratory Study of the Experiences of Gay, Lesbian, and Bisexual Fraternity and Sorority Members Revisited." *Oracle: The Research Journal of the Association of Fraternity/Sorority Advisors* 1, no. 1 (2005): 31–46.

Center for Fraternity and Sorority Life at Washington State University. "Facts and Figures." Accessed May 25, 2019. https://gogreek.wsu.edu/our-community/facts -and-figures/. Website is no longer active as of September 1, 2021.

Chan, Jennifer. "Alabama Rush Videos Are Going Viral on TikTok, but You Can Shop the Southern Sorority Girl Look at Any Age." *People*, August 16, 2021. https://people .com/fashion/alabama-sorority-recruitment-tiktok-outfits/.

Chapman, Nathaniel G., and David L. Brunsma. *Beer and Racism: How Beer Became White, Why It Matters, and the Movements to Change It.* Bristol: Bristol University Press, 2020.

Chavez, Nicole, and Jamiel Lynch. "3 College Students Posed with Guns by the Emmett Till Memorial. The Justice Department May Investigate." CNN, July 26, 2019. www .cnn.com/2019/07/25/us/emmett-till-marker-mississippi-students-suspended/.

Cheever, Susan. *Drinking in America: Our Secret History.* New York: Twelve, 2015.

Chesnasis, Alexandra. "12 Tips for Staying Safe at College Parties." Society 19, July 19, 2017. www.society19.com/tips-staying-safe-at-college-parties/.

Cheverere, Dillon. "PIKE House at U of Arkansas to Undergo Ridiculous $6.9 Million Renovation." Total Frat Move, October 10, 2013. http://totalfratmove.com/pike -house-at-u-of-arkansas-to-undergo-ridiculous-6–9-million-renovation-video/.

Chi Omega Psi. "Sweet Home Chi Omega." Accessed June 22, 2019. http://chiomegapsi .com/sweet-home-chi-omega/.

Chopik, William J. "Associations among Relational Values, Support, Health, and Well-Being across the Adult Lifespan." *Personal Relationships* 24 (2017): 408–22.

Christakis, Nicholas A., and James H. Fowler. "Friendship and Natural Selection." *Proceedings of the National Academy of Sciences of the United States of America* 111 (July 23, 2014): 10796–801.

Chu, Tiffany. "5 Ways the Hook-Up Culture Is Empowering This Generation of Women." Elite Daily, September 26, 2014. www.elitedaily.com/women/5-ways-hook-culture -empower-women/756789/.

Cimino, Aldo. "The Evolution of Hazing: Motivational Mechanisms and the Abuse of Newcomers." *Journal of Cognition and Culture* 11, no. 1 (2011): 241–67.

———. "Fraternity Hazing and the Process of Planned Failure." *Journal of American Studies* 52, no. 1 (February 2018): 214–36.

Cimino, Aldo, and Andrew W. Delton. "On the Perception of Newcomers: Toward an Evolved Psychology of Intergenerational Coalitions." *Human Nature* 21, no. 2 (June 2010): 186–202.

Circuit Court of the Second Judicial Circuit in and for Leon County, Florida. "Andrew Coffey Grand Jury Presentment." December 19, 2017. www.documentcloud.org /documents/4333367-Document-Andrew-Coffey-grand-jury-presentment.html/.

Clark, Clifford E., Jr. "Domestic Architecture as an Index to Social History: The Romantic Revival and the Cult of Domesticity in America." *Journal of Interdisciplinary History* 7, no. 1 (Summer 1976): 1840–70.

Clark, Joanna. "LSU Sorority Members Reflect on Virtual Recruitment Experiences." Reveille, September 24, 2020. www.lsureveille.com/news/lsu-sorority-members -reflect-on-virtual-recruitment-experiences/article_abbefe6a-eaf0–11ea-aca6 -afec471935ad.html/.

Clark, Nicole. "How to Have a Good Hookup in College." VICE, September 11, 2018. www.vice.com/en_us/article/59az4z/how-to-have-a-good-hookup-in-college-vgtl/.

Clem. "MTV Is Bringing Back 'Spring Break,' So Let's Relive Some of the Show's Greatest Moments." Barstool Sports, November 14, 2018. www.barstoolsports.com/newyork/mtv-is-bringing-back-spring-break-so-lets-relive-some-of-the-shows-greatest-moments.

Clemens, Anthony. "Gay and Greek: The Deployment of Gender by Gay Men in Fraternity and Sorority Life." Honors project, Grand Valley State University, 2015. Accessed November 19, 2021. https://scholarworks.gvsu.edu/honorsprojects/413/.

Coates, Ta-Nehisi. "The First White President." *Atlantic*, October 2017. Accessed December 14, 2021. www.theatlantic.com/magazine/archive/2017/10/the-first-white-president-ta-nehisi-coates/537909/.

Cobb, Martin. "Soul Searching." *Beta: The Beta Theta Pi Magazine* (Fall 2020): 32–35. https://issuu.com/betathetapiao/docs/beta_magazine_-_fall_2020_final/.

Cobb, Sydnie M. "State Court Denies Harvard Motion to Dismiss Sanctions Lawsuit." *Harvard Crimson*, January 18, 2020. www.thecrimson.com/article/2020/1/18/state-sanctions-lawsuit-dismiss-denied/.

Cochrane, Kristen. "Why Heteronormativity Is a Bad Thing." *Teen Vogue*, September 1, 2016. www.teenvogue.com/story/heteronormativity-gender-identity-sexual-orientation.

"Coffey Family Calls for 'Accountability and Education' after Hazing Death." WCTV-CBS News, March 13, 2018. www.wctv.tv/content/news/Coffey-family-calls-for-accountability-and-education-after-hazing-death-476655843.html/.

Coffey-Melchiorre, Colleen. "Student Survey: Introduction and New Member Responses." In "Survey Results: The Impact of COVID-19 on Fraternity/Sorority Growth in Fall 2020." PhiredUp, December 1, 2020. www.surveymonkey.com/stories/SM-VL3DP8HY/ http://blog.phiredup.com/fall2020survey/.

Cohen, Rhaina. "What If Friendship, Not Marriage, Was at the Center of Life?" *Atlantic*, October 2020. Accessed December 14, 2021. www.theatlantic.com/family/archive/2020/10/people-who-prioritize-friendship-over-romance/616779/.

Cohn, Scott. "America's 10 Worst States to Live in 2016." CNBC, July 12, 2016. www.cnbc.com/2016/07/12/americas-10-worst-states-to-live-in-2016.html?slide=11/.

———. "America's 10 Worst States to Live in 2018." CNBC, July 10, 2018. www.cnbc.com/2018/06/28/americas-worst-states-to-live-in-2018.html/.

Cole, Juan. "Top Ten Differences between White Terrorists and Others." Informed Comment, August 9, 2012. www.juancole.com/2012/08/top-ten-differences-between-white-terrorists-and-others.html/.

College Factual. "Review Age Diversity at University of North Georgia." Accessed January 15, 2021. www.collegefactual.com/colleges/university-of-north-georgia/student-life/diversity/#secAge/.

College of Wooster. "The College Underground." Accessed December 14, 2019. www.wooster.edu/offices/underground/.

Cooper, Brittney. *Eloquent Rage: A Black Feminist Discovers Her Superpower*. New York: St. Martin's, 2018.

Cooper, Sam. "Provo Bar Had 'Biggest Day Ever' Financially with Wisconsin Fans in Town." *Yahoo! Sports*, September 19, 2017. www.yahoo.com/sports/provo-bar -biggest-day-ever-financially-wisconsin-fans-town-140705804.html/.

"Cornell Sophomores Win: Defeat Freshmen in Annual Battle—Fighting Three Days." Special to the *New York Times* (1857–1922), March 12, 1905, 9, ProQuest Historical Newspapers.

Crane, Emily. "Florida International University Fraternity Suspended after Leaked Group Chat Revealed Rape Jokes, Anti-Semitic Memes, and Nude Photos of Female Students." *Daily Mail*, October 30, 2017. www.dailymail.co.uk/news/article-5033041 /Florida-fraternity-suspended-leaked-group-chat.html/.

Daileda, Colin. "The Military History of 'Leave No Man Behind.'" Mashable, June 14, 2014. https://mashable.com/2014/06/14/bowe-bergdahl-are-american-military -soldiers-ever-left-behind/.

Dave, Paresh. "How Snapchat Began." *Los Angeles Times*, February 3, 2017. www.latimes .com/business/la-fi-live-updates-snap-ipo-how-snapchat-1486133618-htmlstory .html/.

Dean, James Joseph. *Straights: Heterosexuality in Post-Closeted Culture*. New York: New York University Press, 2014.

"Delta Gamma–Florida State University." *Trending Houses*, YouTube video, 2:35, October 10, 2016. www.youtube.com/watch?v=nOW7xnzrL-E/.

Delta Gamma-University of Oregon. "The House." Accessed February 4, 2021. http:// uoregon.deltagamma.org/the-house/.

Delta Zeta. "Truly Connected Nights." Accessed January 12, 2021. www.deltazeta.org /about-us/truly-connected-conference/truly-connected-networking-nights/.

"Delta Zeta–Indiana University." *Trending Houses*, YouTube video, 2:58, November 7, 2016. www.youtube.com/watch?v=LsnCw3Vn5js/.

"Delta Zeta–University of Tennessee." *Trending Houses*, YouTube video, 2.37, October 25, 2016. http://collegeweekly.com/shows/trending-houses/.

de Ruiter, Jan, Gavin Weston, and Stephen M. Lyon. "Dunbar's Number: Group Size and Brain Physiology in Humans Reexamined." *American Anthropologist* 113, no. 4 (2011): 557–68.

DeSantis, Alan D. *Inside Greek U: Fraternities, Sororities, and the Pursuit of Pleasure, Power, and Prestige*. Lexington: University of Kentucky Press, 2007.

DiAngelo, Robin. *White Fragility: Why It's So Hard for White People to Talk about Racism*. Boston: Beacon, 2018.

Dick, Kirby, Amy Ziering, and Constance Matthiessen. *The Hunting Ground: The Inside Story of Sexual Assault on American College Campuses*. New York: Hot Books, 2016.

Dickinson, Gloria Harper. "Pledged to Remember: Africa in the Life and Lore of Black Greek–Letter Organizations." In *African American Fraternities and Sororities: The Legacy and the Vision*, edited by Tamara L. Brown, Gregory S. Parks, and Clarenda M. Phillips, 9–32. Lexington: University Press of Kentucky, 2012.

Dictionary.com. s.v. "play date." Accessed October 1, 2018. www.dictionary.com/browse /play-date.

Dobson, Byron. "Gov. DeSantis Signs 'Andrew's Law', Enacts Tougher Hazing Mea- sures." *Tallahassee Democrat*, June 26, 2019. www.tallahassee.com/story

/news/2019/06/26/fsu-hazing-andrews-law-gov-desantis-florida-tougher-hazing
-measures/1566778001/.

Dockterman, Eliana. "Imagine if Half of All Tech Inventions and Start-Ups Came from
Women." *Time*, May 29, 2014. https://time.com/136598/snapchat-misogyny/.

Dorpat, Paul. "Delta Gamma Helped Pave the Way for UW's 'Greek Row.'" *Pacific North-
west Magazine (The Seattle Times)*, September 8, 2016. www.seattletimes.com
/pacific-nw-magazine/delta-gamma-helped-pave-the-way-for-uws-greek-row/.

Doyle, Sady. *Trainwreck: The Women We Love to Hate, Mock, and Fear . . . and Why*. New
York: Melville House, 2016.

Drake, Kalli. "Dawgy Style: UGA Ranked No. 1 Kinkiest School in the Country." *Red &
Black*, September 16, 2015. www.redandblack.com/variety/dawgy-style-uga-ranked
-no-kinkiest-school-in-the-country/article_b57e0d60-5c02-11e5-a194-6f196c47689d
.html/.

Dries, Kate. "Backlash Comes over UGA's Ban on Hoop Skirts at Greek Functions."
Jezebel, March 25, 2015. https://jezebel.com/backlash-comes-over-ugas-ban-on
-hoop-skirts-at-greek-fu-1693539661/.

Drouin, Michelle, Manda Coupe, and Jeff R. Temple. "Is Sexting Good for Your Relationship? It Depends." *Computers in Human Behavior* 75, no. 1 (October 2017):
749–56.

Dubner, Stephen J. "266: Trust Me." Produced by Greg Rosalsky. *Freakonomics Radio*,
29:49, November 10, 2018. http://freakonomics.com/podcast/trust-me/.

Dukcevich, Davide. "The Best Fraternities for Future CEOs." *Forbes*, January 31, 2003.
www.forbes.com/2003/01/31/cx_dd_0131frat.html?sh=911820499cfe/.

Duke University. "Duke Facts." Accessed January 7, 2021. https://facts.duke.edu/.

Dunbar, Robin. "Coevolution of Neocortical Size, Group Size, and Language in
Humans." *Behavioral and Brain Sciences* 16, no. 4 (1993): 681–735.

———. *How Many Friends Does One Person Need? Dunbar's Number and Other Evolutionary Quirks*. Cambridge, Mass.: Harvard University Press, 2010.

———. *Human Evolution: Our Brains and Behavior*. Oxford: Oxford University Press,
2016.

———. "Neocortex Size as a Constraint on Group Size in Primates." *Journal of Human
Evolution* 22, no. 6 (June 1992): 469–93.

Dunker, Chris. "UNL Frat Investigated after Members Steal Black Lives Matter Signs
from Neighborhood." *Lincoln Journal Star*, September 11, 2020. https://journalstar
.com/news/local/education/unl-frat-investigated-after-members-steal-black-lives
-matter-signs-from-neighborhood/article_2d55eb91-fe1f-5518-9465-9d9d91df7e40
.html/.

Dunn, Clouse. "SMU Student Sues Kappa Kappa Gamma Sorority over Secretly
Recorded Racy Video." PR Newswire, March 23, 2016. www.prnewswire.com
/news-releases/smu-student-sues-kappa-kappa-gamma-sorority-over-secretly
-recorded-racy-video-300240548.html/.

Dvorak, Robert D., Nicholas J. Kuvaas, Tess M. Kilwein, Tyler B. Wray, Brittany L.
Stevenson, and Emily M. Sargent. "Are Drinking Motives Associated with Sexual
'Hookups' among College Student Drinkers?" *Journal of American College Health* 64,
no. 2 (February 2016): 133–38.

"ECU Fraternity Shut Down after Drug-Related Investigation." WNCT CBS/CW News, April 11, 2018. www.wnct.com/local-news/ecu-fraternity-shut-down-after-drug-related-investigation/.

Edwards, R. H., J. M. Hartman, and G. M. Fisher. *Undergraduates: A Study of Morale in Twenty-three American Colleges and Universities.* New York: Doubleday, 1928.

Eldridge, Elizabeth. *Co-EDiquette: Poise and Popularity for Every Girl.* New York: E. P. Dutton, 1936.

Eligon, John. "The 'Some of My Best Friends Are Black' Defense." *New York Times,* February 16, 2019. www.nytimes.com/2019/02/16/sunday-review/ralph-northam-blackface-friends.html/.

Emelianchik-Key, Kelly, Rebekah Byrd, and Carmen S. Gill. "Dating Violence and the Impact of Technology: Examining the Lived Experiences of Sorority Members." *Violence Against Women* (2021): 1–20.

Emery, Lea Rose. "Is My Best Friend Toxic? 9 Signs to Look Out For, According to the Experts." Bustle, August 16, 2017. www.bustle.com/p/is-my-best-friend-toxic-9-signs-to-look-out-for-according-to-experts-75959/.

Engelmayer, Caroline S. "'Cultural' Fraternities and Sororities Offer Harvard Students Chance at Sanctions-Free Greek Life." *Harvard Crimson,* September 25, 2018. www.thecrimson.com/article/2018/9/25/cultural-frats-sanctions-unaffected/.

Engelmayer, Caroline, and Michael E. Xie. "Pro-Greek Life PAC Fights against Sanctions, Adds Porcellian Grad to Board of Directors." *Harvard Crimson,* April 17, 2018. www.thecrimson.com/article/2018/4/17/fspac/.

England, Paula. Online College Life Social Survey. "How Much Alcohol Did You Drink before or during the {Date/Hookup/Occasion}?" 2011. https://pages.nyu.edu/ocsls/2010/codebook/mixed.drinks.html/.

England, Paula, Emily Shafer, and Alison Fogarty. "Hooking Up and Forming Relationships on Today's College Campuses." In *The Gendered Society Reader,* edited by Michael Kimmel and Amy Aronson, 531–47. New York: Oxford University Press, 2007.

Ethridge, Maggie, and Jessica Milton. "An Eagle Becomes a Lion." *Adelphean* (Fall–Winter 2020): 10–11. https://editiondigital.net/publication/?m=17352&i=685431&p=10/.

Etters, Karl. "911 Tape from Andrew Coffey Death Released." *USA Today,* January 30, 2018. https://amp.usatoday.com/amp/1080372001/.

Evon, Dan. "Was a Noose Hung across from the U.S. Capitol?" Snopes, January 6, 2021. www.snopes.com/fact-check/noose-hung-outside-capitol/.

Fadel, Leila. "Cultural Appropriation, a Perennial Issue on Halloween." NPR, October 29, 2019. www.npr.org/2019/10/29/773615928/cultural-appropriation-a-perennial-issue-on-halloween/.

Fairbairn, Catharine E., Michael A. Sayette, Odd O. Aalen, and Arnoldo Frigessi. "Alcohol and Emotional Contagion: An Examination of the Spreading of Smiles in Male and Female Drinking Groups." *Clinical Psychological Science* 3, no. 1 (September 26, 2016): 686–701.

Fairlie, Anne M., William DeJong, John F. Stevenson, Andrea M. Lavigne, and Mark D. Wood. "Fraternity and Sorority Leaders: A Comparison of Alcohol Use, Attitudes, and Policy Awareness." *American Journal of Drug and Alcohol Abuse* 36, no. 4 (July 2010): 187–93.

Fardouly, Jasmine, Brydie K. Willburger, and Lenny R. Vartanian. "Instagram Use and Young Women's Body Image Concerns and Self-Objectification: Testing Mediational Pathways." *New Media & Society* 20 (2017): 1380–95.

Fass, Paula. *The Damned and the Beautiful: American Youth in the 1920s.* New York: Oxford University Press, 1977.

Fausset, Richard, and Campbell Robertson. "Beyond College Campuses and Public Scandals, a Racist Tradition Lingers." *New York Times*, February 8, 2019. www .nytimes.com/2019/02/08/us/northam-blackface-virginia.html/.

Feher, Sam. "The 50 Most Stunning Sorority Houses in America." *Cosmopolitan*, April 10, 2018. www.cosmopolitan.com/lifestyle/g19725690/the-22-most-stunning -sorority-houses-in-america/.

Feiler, Bruce. "Should Your Spouse Be Your Best Friend?" *New York Times*, October 12, 2017. www.nytimes.com/2017/10/12/style/should-your-spouse-be-your-best-friend .html/.

Feltman, Chandra, and Dawn M. Szymanski. "Instagram Use and Self-Objectification: The Roles of Internalization, Comparison, Appearance Commentary, and Femi- nism." *Sex Roles: A Journal of Research* 78, no. 5–6 (2018): 311–24.

Fern, Ashley. "11 Things Every Girl Does before Responding to a Text, as Told by 'Alice in Wonderland.'" Elite Daily, July 7, 2014. www.elitedaily.com/humor/everything -girl-responding-text/648090/.

————. "48 Signs She's Not Your Best Friend, She's Actually Your Soulmate." Elite Daily, April 23, 2015. www.elitedaily.com/women/your-bff-your-soulmate /1008949/.

Fernández, Stefanie. "Leaked Chat Shows FIU Frat Joking about Rape, Sharing Nude Female Pics." *Miami New Times*, October 25, 2017. www.miaminewtimes.com/news /florida-international-university-frat-caught-joking-about-rape-sending -nudes-9776775/.

Ferner, Matt, and Jessica Schulberg. "Here's What Yale Was Like for Women When Brett Kavanaugh Was There." Huffington Post, September 27, 2018. www.huffpost.com /entry/brett-kavanaugh-yale-women_n_5bac5776e4b082030e78204d/.

Fialka, Karolína. "It's Time to Stop Calling Women 'Crazy.'" Medium, May 2, 2020. https://medium.com/an-injustice/its-time-to-stop-calling-women-crazy -87f9aacb72d/.

Field, Andy Tsubasa. "Fraternities and Sororities Sue Harvard over Its Policy against Single-Sex Groups." *Chronicle of Higher Education*, December 3, 2018. www.chronicle .com/article/fraternities-and-sororities-sue-harvard-over-its-policy-against-single -sex-groups/.

Fielder, Robyn L., and Michael P. Carey. "Predictors and Consequences of Sexual 'Hook- ups' among College Students: A Short-Term Prospective Study." *Archives of Sexual Behavior* 39, no. 5 (October 2010): 1105–19.

————. "Prevalence and Characteristics of Sexual Hookups among First-Semester Female College Students." *Journal of Sex & Marital Therapy* 36, no. 4 (July 2010): 346–59.

Finney, Lauren, and Maggie Maloney. "The 22 Most Over-the-Top Sorority Houses in the Country." *Town & Country*, February 13, 2018. www.townandcountrymag.com /society/tradition/g2977/best-sorority-houses/.

First, Amanda. "What I Learned Living in a Sorority House." HerCampus, April 4, 2012. www.hercampus.com/life/campus-life/what-i-learned-living-sorority-house/.

"1st of 2 UC Berkeley Students Testifies Against Ex-Fraternity Member Accused in Violent Rapes." CBSN, September 12, 2019. https://sanfrancisco.cbslocal.com /2019/09/12/uc-berkeley-ex-fraternity-member-accused-violent-rapes/.

Fishbein, Rebecca. "Cornell Fraternity Kicked Off Campus for 'Sexually Humiliating' Hazing." Gothamist, January 12, 2013. https://gothamist.com/news/cornell -fraternity-kicked-off-campus-for-sexually-humiliating-hazing/.

Fisher, Helen E. *The Anatomy of Love: The Natural History of Monogamy, Adultery, and Divorce.* New York: W. W. Norton, 1992.

Fisher, Julia Freeland. "How to Get a Job Often Comes Down to One Elite Personal Asset, and Many People Still Don't Realize It." CNBC, December 27, 2019. www.cnbc.com /2019/12/27/how-to-get-a-job-often-comes-down-to-one-elite-personal-asset.html/.

Fischetti, Matthew. "Fraternity Suspended after Racist Messages Leaked amid Nationwide Anti-Racist Protests." *Washington Square News*, May 30, 2020. https://nyunews .com/news/2020/05/30/fraternity-suspended-after-racist-messages-leaked-amid -nationwide-anti-racist-protests/.

Flaherty, Colleen. "Consent Matters for Photos, Too." Inside Higher Ed, April 22, 2019. www.insidehighered.com/news/2019/04/22/photography-professor-accused -violating-rules-consent-new-book-greek-life/.

Flanagan, Ben. "Alabama Sorority Row 2016: The Houses, New and Old." AL.com. Accessed July 22, 2019. www.al.com/entertainment/2016/06/alabama_sorority _row_2016_the.html/.

Flanagan, Caitlin. "The Dark Power of Fraternities." *Atlantic*, March 2014, updated September 9, 2019. www.theatlantic.com/magazine/archive/2014/03/the-dark -power-of-fraternities/357580/.

———. "Death at a Penn State Fraternity." *Atlantic*, November 2017. www.theatlantic .com/magazine/archive/2017/11/a-death-at-penn-state/540657/.

Fleming, Crystal M. *How to Be Less Stupid about Race.* Boston: Beacon, 2018.

Florida, Richard. "Where There Are More Single Men Than Women." City Lab, February 11, 2015. www.citylab.com/equity/2015/02/where-in-the-us-are -there-more-single-men-than-women/385369/.

Forinash, Carter. "Duke to Create 'Residential Community' System on West Campus, New Task Force to Reshape Housing Experience." *Chronicle*, November 19, 2020. www.dukechronicle.com/article/2020/11/duke-university-residential-community -west-campus-next-generation-living-learning-housing-rush/.

Fox, Rob. "Some Pretty Bad Hazing Photos from Hofstra Sigma Pi Leaked and Are Gonna Blow Up, So Here They Are." Total Frat Move, December 7, 2016. https://totalfratmove.com/hofstra-sigma-pi-hazing-photos-pictures/.

fratcock_12. "When You Wait to Call an Ambulance, Your Friends Die." Comment on "Jared Borislow." Total Frat Move, February 7, 2017. https://totalfratmove.com /when-you-wait-to-call-an-ambulance-your-friends-die/.

"Frat Dudes Make Pledges Rub Hot Sauce on Their Crotches, Clutch Poop during 'Hell Night.'" Daily Caller, January 13, 2014. https://news.yahoo.com/frat-dudes-pledges -rub-hot-sauce-crotches-clutch-204750449.html;_ylt=A2KLfSJ7uTNd_ XAAyhhXNyoA;_ylu=X3oDMTEyZnBzbDVmBGNvbG8DYmYxBHBvcwMxBHZoa WQDQjY4MzNfMQRzZWMDc3I-/.

Fraternity and Sorority Political Action Committee. "It Shouldn't Take the Supreme Court to Get a School to Understand a Student's Freedom of Association Rights Don't Stop When They Set Foot on Campus." June 29, 2020. www.facebook.com /fspac/posts/3731311076885919/.

Freeman, Margaret L. *Women of Discriminating Taste: White Sororities and the Making of American Ladyhood.* Athens: University of Georgia Press, 2020.

Freid, Jared. "69: The Future of Greek Life." Produced by Micah S. Wiener. *Inside TFM Podcast,* June 8, 2017, 100:25. https://soundcloud.com/mindofmicah/episode -69-the-future-of-greek-life/.

Friedersdorf, Conor. "How Does Hookup Culture Affect Sexual Assault on Campus?" *Atlantic,* June 28, 2016. www.theatlantic.com/politics/archive/2016/06 /how-does-hookup-culture-affect-sexual-assault-on-campus/489098/.

Friedman, Ann. "The Importance of Friendship Diversity." The Cut, September 26, 2014. www.thecut.com/2014/09/importance-of-friendship-diversity.html/.

Frietas, Donna. *Consent on Campus: A Manifesto.* Oxford: Oxford University Press, 2018.

Frost, Natasha. "Mormon Women Are Caught between Economic Pressures and the Word of God." Quartz, December 31, 2019. https://qz.com/1778333/the-brigham -young-university-wage-gap-tells-the-story-of-mormon-feminism/?utm_source =YPL&yptr=yahoo/.

Fry, Richard. "U.S. Women Near Milestone in the College-Educated Labor Force." Pew Research Center, June 20, 2019. www.pewresearch.org/fact-tank/2019/06/20/u-s -women-near-milestone-in-the-college-educated-labor-force/.

Fuentes, Jairo N., and Alexander Hoffman. "Alcohol Consumption and Abuse among College Students: Alarming Rates among the Best and the Brightest." *College Student Journal* 50, no. 2 (Summer 2016): 236–40.

Gajilan, Chris A. "Greek Life More Popular Than Ever, Despite Recent Controversy and Deaths." CNN, December 8, 2018. https://edition.cnn.com/2018/08/22/us /fraternity-hazing-tim-piazza-death/index.html/.

Gallaga, Omar L. "Debauched, Yet Self-Aware, Total Frat Move Takes Off on the Web and in Print." *Statesman,* August 28, 2013, updated September 27, 2018. www .statesman.com/article/20130828/NEWS/308289603/.

Gallagher, Billy. "How Reggie Brown Invented Snapchat." TechCrunch, February 10, 2018. https://techcrunch.com/2018/02/10/the-birth-of-snapchat/.

Gallo, Andrea. "Why Matthew Naquin's Felony Conviction Makes LSU Case Stand Out from Other Hazing Trials." *Advocate,* July 19, 2019. www.theadvocate.com/baton _rouge/news/courts/article_3f9c09ca-aa5b-11e9-a0e4-eb79ecca89f7.html/.

Gamma Phi Beta. "BEDI Summit." Accessed March 27, 2021. www.gammaphibeta.org /gpb/39af2e76-0f23-4e5e-ba5d-cd9319fed1e8/BEDI-Summit/.

Garber, Megan. "The Summer of the #Squad." *Atlantic,* July 23, 2015. www.theatlantic .com/entertainment/archive/2015/07/the-summer-of-the-squad/399308/.

Garcia, Justin R., Amanda N. Gesselman, Shadia A. Siliman, Brea L. Perry, Kathryn Coe, and Helen E. Fisher. "Sexting among Singles in the USA: Prevalence of Sending, Receiving, and Sharing Sexual Messages and Images." *Sexual Health* 13, no. 5 (2016): 428–35.

Garcia, Sandra E. "'Pick My Cotton': Video of Mock Whipping Prompts Fraternity to Expel 4 Students." *New York Times*, March 24, 2019. www.nytimes.com/2019/03/24/us/uga-fraternity-racist-video.html/.

Gass-Poore, Jordan. "'They're Going to Get me F***ed Up': Final Text of Frat Pledge Who Died after Falling Down the Stairs at His Initiation Ceremony—and Help Wasn't Called for 12 Hours." *Daily Mail*, April 9, 2017. www.dailymail.co.uk/news/article-4394424/Chilling-final-text-frat-pledge-dead-event.html/.

Georgetown University. "Bulldog Tavern." Accessed December 14, 2019. https://auxiliary.georgetown.edu/bulldog-tavern/.

Germain, Lauren J. *Campus Sexual Assault: College Women Respond*. Baltimore, Md.: Johns Hopkins University Press, 2016.

Gesensway, Deborah. "The Sad Tale of Mortimer Leggett." *Cornell Daily Sun* 97, no. 108 (March 20, 1981): 6. https://cdsun.library.cornell.edu/?a=d&d=CDS19810320.2.18&e/.

Gladwell, Malcolm. *The Tipping Point: How Little Things Can Make a Big Difference*. Boston: Little, Brown, 2000.

Gold, Hannah. "6 Disturbingly Racist and Sexist Frat Party Themes—from Just This Past Year!" Salon, March 4, 2014. www.salon.com/2014/03/04/6_disturbingly_racist_and_sexist_frat_party_themes_%E2%80%94_from_just_this_past_year_partner/.

Gonçalves, Bruno, Nicola Perra, and Alessandro Vespignani. "Modeling Users' Activity on Twitter Networks: Validation of Dunbar's Number." *PLOS ONE* 6, no. 8 (August 3, 2011): 1–5.

Gordon, Jaime. "'Total Frat Move'—or Total Misogyny?" *USA Today*, May 30, 2016. www.usatoday.com/story/college/2016/05/30/total-frat-move-or-total-misogyny/37417863/.

Gordon, Michael. "Was Waller Ever Right? The Rating and Dating Complex Reconsidered." *Journal of Marriage and Family* 43, no. 1 (February 1981): 67–76.

Grand Forks Historical Preservation Commission. "University of North Dakota Historic District." Accessed September 18, 2018. www.gfpreservation.com/university-of-north-dakota-historic-district/.

Grawe, Nathan D. *Demographics and the Demand for Higher Education*. Baltimore, Md.: Johns Hopkins University Press, 2018.

Gray, Burke. "Fraternalism in America, 1860–1920." Phoenixmasonery Masonic Museum and Library. Accessed June 17, 2018. www.phoenixmasonry.org/masonicmuseum/fraternalism/fraternalism_in_america.html/.

"Greek Life Statistics." The Fraternity Advisor. Accessed March 7, 2021. https://thefraternityadvisor.com/greek-life-statistics/.

Griffis, Sean. "Have You Been Frexting Without Even Knowing It?" Brit+CO, May 10, 2015. www.brit.co/frexting/.

Grigoriadis, Vanessa. *Blurred Lines: Rethinking Sex, Power, and Consent on Campus*. Boston: Houghton Mifflin Harcourt, 2017.

Grimm, Beca. "'Frexts' Is a Thing Now and You Should Be Doing It." Bustle, May 4, 2015. www.bustle.com/articles/80793–8-reasons-why-frexting-is-the-thing-you-and -your-friends-should-already-be-doing/.

Grinberg, Emanuella, and Catherine E. Shoichet. "Brock Turner Released from Jail after Serving 3 Months for Sexual Assault." CNN, September 2, 2016. www.cnn.com /2016/09/02/us/brock-turner-release-jail/index.html/.

Gross, Doug, and Brandon Griggs. "Snapchat CEO 'Mortified' by Leaked E-Mails." CNN, May 29, 2014. www.cnn.com/2014/05/29/tech/mobile/spiegel-snapchat-leaked-e -mails/index.html/.

Gupta, Sujata. "The COVID-19 Pandemic Made U.S. College Students' Mental Health Even Worse." Science News, January 22, 2021. www.sciencenews.org/article /covid-19-coronavirus-pandemic-us-college-students-mental-health/.

Guttentag, Marcia, and Paul F. Secord. *Too Many Women? The Gender Ratio Question.* Beverly Hills, Calif.: Sage, 1983.

Gyan, Joe. "Days before Max Gruver Died, Ex-LSU Frat Member Says Matthew Naquin Warned but 'Blew Me Off.'" *Advocate*, July 15, 2019. www.theadvocate.com/baton _rouge/news/courts/article_24d9335c-a57d-11e9–8cbc-6f3e76cfda83.html/.

Gyee, Gregory Yee. "Five College of Charleston Fraternities Shut Down within a Year; Pi Kappa Phi Shutters Doors after Misconduct Investigation." *Post and Courier*, August 3, 2017. www.postandcourier.com/news/five-college-of-charleston-fraternities-shut -down-within-a-year/article_96e131f4–77c4–11e7-b4ff-6b74c68f5a30.html/.

Haas, Nathaniel. "The Price of Sex at USC." Medium, November 2, 2015. https:// medium.com/neon-tommy/the-price-of-sex-at-usc-ae347fd26814/.

Hacker, Holly. "Topless Dancing at SMU Sorority Leads to Lawsuit over Secret Video." Dallas News, March 24, 2016. www.dallasnews.com/news/news/2016/03/23 /partially-naked-dancing-at-smu-sorority-leads-to-lawsuit-over-secret-video/.

Hagan, Shelly. "IPO Could Value Tinder Rival Bumble at $1.1 Billion." *Bloomberg*, November 5, 2018. www.bloomberg.com/news/articles/2018–11–05 /tinder-rival-bumble-might-have-to-compromise-on-valuation-in-ipo/.

Hagerty, Barbara Bradley. "The Campus Rapist Hiding in Plain Sight." *Atlantic*, July 15, 2018. www.theatlantic.com/education/archive/2019/07/why-dont-more-college-rape -victims-come-forward/593875/.

Hakala, Kate. "This Is Why Men Outnumber Women Two-to-One on Tinder." Mic, February 18, 2015. www.mic.com/articles/110774/two-thirds-of-tinder-users-are -men-here-s-why/.

Hamilton, Hannah R., and Tracy DeHart. "Drinking to Belong: The Effect of a Friend- ship Threat and Self-Esteem on College Student Drinking." *Self & Identity* 16, no. 1 (January 2017): 1–15.

Hamilton, Laura. "Trading on Heterosexuality: College Women's Gender Strategies and Homophobia." *Gender and Society* 21, no. 2 (April 2007): 145–72.

Han, Crystal, Ozan Jaquette, and Karina Salazar. "Recruiting the Out-of-State Univer- sity: Off-Campus Recruiting by Public Research Universities." Joyce Foundation, March 2019. https://emraresearch.org/sites/default/files/2019-03/joyce_report.pdf.

Handler, Lisa. "In the Fraternal Sisterhood: Sororities as Gender Strategy." *Gender and Society* 9, no. 2 (1995): 236–55.

Harman, Justine. "What It Costs to Make a Sorority Recruitment Video This Outrageous." *Elle*, January 8, 2016. www.elle.com/culture/news/a33128/delta-gamma -recruitment-video/.

Harmon, Amy, Frances Robles, Alan Blinder, and Thomas Fuller. "'Frats Are Being Frats': Greek Life Is Stoking the Virus on Some Campuses." *New York Times*, August 18, 2020. www.nytimes.com/2020/08/18/us/coronavirus-fraternities-sororities .html/.

Harnish, Amelia. "The Horror of Being a Woman (in the Movies)." *Wall Street Journal*, December 11, 2019. www.wsj.com/articles/the-horror-of-being-a-woman-in-the -movies-11576082964/.

Harris, Cheryl. "Whiteness Is Property." *Harvard Law Review* 106, no. 8 (1993): 1709–91.

Harris, Frank, III, and Shaun R. Harper. "Beyond Bad Behaving Brothers: Productive Performances of Masculinities among College Fraternity Men." *International Journal of Qualitative Studies in Education* 27, no. 6 (2014): 703–23.

Harvard University. "Policy on Unrecognized Single-Gender Social Organizations." June 29, 2020. www.harvard.edu/president/news/2020/policy-on-unrecognized -single-gender-social-organizations/.

Hasinoff, Amy Adele. *Sexting Panic: Rethinking Criminalization, Privacy, and Consent*. Urbana: University of Illinois Press, 2015.

Hatch, Jenavieve. "Read the Sexist Email That Got This Univ. of Richmond Frat Suspended." Huffington Post, September 14, 2016. www.huffpost.com/entry/read -the-sexist-email-that-got-this-univ-of-richmond-frat-suspended_n_57d9745de4 b0fbd4b7bcb36b/.

Hathaway, Jay. "Sorority Girl Celebrates 21st Birthday with Racist Three-Layer Cake." Gawker, December 12, 2014. https://gawker.com/sorority-girl-celebrates-21st -birthday-with-racist-thre-1670470468/.

Hartmans, Avery. "Bumble, a Dating App That Forces Women to Make the First Move, Reportedly Turned Down at $350 Million Acquisition Offer." Business Insider, August 23, 2017. www.businessinsider.com/bumble-dating-app -match-iac-tinder-buyout-2017-8/.

Harwood, William S. "Secret Societies in America." *North American Review* 164, no. 486 (1897): 617.

Hauser, Christine. "Virginia Fraternity Is Suspended after Death of Student." *New York Times*, March 1, 2021. www.nytimes.com/2021/03/01/us/adam-oakes-vcu-delta-chi .html/.

"Hazing Defined." StopHazing.org. Accessed June 12, 2019. www.stophazing.org/jpeg/.

Hechinger, John. *True Gentlemen: The Broken Pledge of America's Fraternities*. New York: Public Affairs, 2017.

Hechinger Report Contributor. "Colleges Set to Fight for Fewer Students." *U.S. News and World Report*, September 10, 2018. www.usnews.com/news/education-news /articles/2018-09-10/colleges-set-to-fight-for-fewer-students/.

"'He Died in a Room Full of People': Read the Grand Jury Report into Andrew Coffey's Death." *Tallahassee Democrat*, December 19, 2017, updated December 20, 2017. www .news-press.com/story/news/2017/12/19/he-died-room-full-people-read-grand-jury -report-into-andrew-coffeys-death/967639001/.

Hernandez, Sean. "Sexual Economics: An Econometric Study of a University Greek System." Master's thesis, University of Southern California, 2014. http://digitallibrary.usc.edu/cdm/ref/collection/p15799coll3/id/445745/.

Hershey, George L. "Godey's Choice." *Journal of the Society of Architectural Historians* 18, no. 3 (October 1959): 104–11.

Hesp, Grahaeme A., and Jeffrey S. Brooks. "Heterosexism and Homophobia on Fraternity Row: A Case Study of a College Fraternity Community." *Journal of LGBT Youth* 6, no. 4 (2009): 395–415.

Hess, Amanda. "How Drunk Is Too Drunk to Have Sex?" *Slate*, February 11, 2015. https://slate.com/human-interest/2015/02/drunk-sex-on-campus-universities-are-struggling-to-determine-when-intoxicated-sex-becomes-sexual-assault.html/.

———. "Two Lawsuits Allege Rape at the 'Rapebait' Frat House." *Slate*, October 31, 2014. https://slate.com/human-interest/2014/10/rapebait-fraternity-two-lawsuits-allege-rape-at-the-georgia-tech-phi-kappa-tau-house.html/.

Higgins, Lauryn. "Experts on Hazing Say Incidents Have Reached Epidemic Levels." HerCampus, September 19, 2017. www.hercampus.com/news/experts-hazing-say-incidents-have-reached-epidemic-levels/.

Hirsch, Jennifer S., and Shamus Khan. *Sexual Citizens: A Landmark Study of Sex, Power, and Assault on Campus*. New York: W. W. Norton, 2020.

Holcombe, Madeline. "3 Fraternity Brothers Sentenced to Jail in Penn State Hazing Death." CNN, April 3, 2019. www.cnn.com/2019/04/03/us/tim-piazza-fraternity-member-hazing-sentences/.

Hollis, Hillary. "Greek Members Expect Renovations to Sororities and Fraternities." *Arkansas Traveler*, September 13, 2016. www.uatrav.com/news/article_c388f4d8-7939-11e6-9589-b707eb79737d.html/.

Hogg, Charlotte. "Sorority Rhetoric as Everyday Epideictic." *College English* 80, no. 5 (May 2018): 439–40.

"'Hooking Up'—What Does It Really Mean?" Huffington Post, October 12, 2011. www.huffingtonpost.com/2011/10/12/hooking-up_n_1007364.html/.

Horn, Leslie. "MTV Spring Break Used to Rule." Deadspin, March 15, 2015. https://theconcourse.deadspin.com/mtv-spring-break-used-to-rule-1690911924/.

Horn, Tina. "7 Tips to Elevate Your Nude Selfie Game." *Allure*, December 8, 2017. www.allure.com/story/how-to-take-nude-photos/.

Horowitz, Helen Lefkowitz. *Campus Life: Undergraduate Culture from the End of the Eighteenth Century to the Present*. New York: Knopf, 1987.

"Hottest Sorority Recruiting Videos 2018." *Slickster Magazine*. Accessed February 12, 2019. www.slickstermagazine.com/hottest-sorority-recruiting-videos-2018–2/.

Howell, Ryan T. "Why Are Emotions Contagious?" *Psychology Today*, April 17, 2012. www.psychologytoday.com/us/blog/cant-buy-happiness/201204/why-are-emotions-contagious/.

H.R.3128–Collegiate Freedom of Association Act, 116th Congress (2019–2020). Accessed December 1, 2021. www.congress.gov/bill/116th-congress/house-bill/3128?q=%7B%22search%22%3A%5B%22Freedom+of+collegiate+association+act%22%5D%7D&s=1&r=2/.

H.R.4508–Propser Act, 115th Congress (2017–2018). Accessed December 1, 2021. www.congress.gov/bill/115th-congress/house-bill/4508/.

Humphries, Monica. "A College Freshman Paid $1000 to Join a Sorority during the Pandemic—and All They Do Is Zoom." Insider, November 11, 2020. www.insider.com/sorority-college-greek-life-pandemic-cost-worth-it-2020-10/.

Husser, Bill. "The Condition of Education 2020." National Center for Education Statistics, May 2020. Accessed December 1, 2021. https://nces.ed.gov/pubs2020/2020144.pdf.

Irrera, Anna. "Exclusive: How Elite U.S. College Students Brought COVID-19 Home from Campus." Reuters, April 2, 2020. www.reuters.com/article/us-health-coronavirus-usa-vanderbilt-exc/exclusive-how-elite-u-s-college-students-brought-covid-19-home-from-campus-idUSKBN21K2CJ/.

IPSOS. "The IPSOS MORI Almanac." 2017. www.ipsos.com/sites/default/files/ct/publication/documents/2017-11/ipsos-mori-almanac-2017.pdf.

Isenberg, Nancy. White Trash: The 400-Year Untold History of Class in America. New York: Viking, 2016.

Iwamoto, Derek Kenji, William Corbin, Carl Lejuez, and Laura MacPherson. "College Men and Alcohol Use: Positive Alcohol Expectancies as a Mediator between Distinct Masculine Norms and Alcohol Use." Psychology of Men and Masculinities 15, no. 1 (January 2014): 29–39.

Jackson, Lily. "Campuses Are Short on Mental-Health Counselors. But They've Got Plenty of Antidepressants." Chronicle of Higher Education, June 28, 2019. www.chronicle.com/article/Campuses-Are-Short-on/246532/.

Janis, Irving. "Groupthink." In The Hazing Reader, edited by Hank Nuwer, 19–26. Bloomington: Indiana University Press, 2004.

Jenkins, Wesley. "After a Freshman's Death, Cornell U. Fraternities Ban Some of Their Own Events. But Is the Move Merely Symbolic?" Chronicle of Higher Education, November 12, 2019. www.chronicle.com/article/after-a-freshmans-death-cornell-u-fraternities-ban-some-of-their-own-events-but-is-the-move-merely-symbolic/.

Jennings, Rebecca. "Bama Rush TikTok, Explained and Explained and Explained." Vox, August 17, 2021www.vox.com/the-goods/22627638/bama-rush-tiktok-alabama-makayla-old-row-ootd/.

Jerkovich, Kate. "Chrissy Teigen Posts Completely Nude Photo for Friend's Birthday [PHOTOS]." Daily Caller, October 17, 2016. https://dailycaller.com/2016/10/17/chrissy-teigen-posts-completely-nude-photo-for-friends-birthdayphotos/.

Johnny_Fratkins. Comment on the post "Any Gay Frat Guys?" Reddit, April 20, 2018, 6:03 P.M. GMT. www.reddit.com/r/Frat/comments/8drajh/any_gay_frat_guys_what_has_your_experience_been/.

Johnson, Patrick Spencer. Fraternity Row. Los Angeles: Brewster, 1963.

Johnston, Norman. "Row Show." University of Washington, September 2001. Accessed December 1, 2021. www.washington.edu/alumni/columns/sept01/greekrow1.html/.

Jones, Allie. "#BamaRush, Explained." New York Times, August 17, 2021, updated August 24, 2021. www.nytimes.com/2021/08/17/style/bama-rush-explained.html/.

———. "A Child's Treasury of This Year's Most Offensive Halloween Costumes." Gawker, October 31, 2014. https://gawker.com/a-childs-treasury-of-this-years-most-offensive-hallowee-1652874318/.

Jones, Grace Latimer. "The Evil of Girls' Secret Societies." Ladies' Home Journal 24, no. 11 (October 1907). Women's Magazine Archive.

Jones, Leigh Ann. *From Boys to Men: Rhetorics of Emergent American Masculinity.* Urbana, Ill.: National Council for Teachers of English, 2016.

Joyce, S. Brian. "Perceptions of Race and Fit in the Recruitment Process of Traditionally, Predominantly White Fraternities." *Oracle: The Research Journal of the Association of Fraternity/Sorority Advisors* 13, no. 2 (Fall 2018): 29–45.

Junger, Sebastian. *Tribe: On Homecoming and Belonging.* New York: Twelve, 2016.

Juzwiak, Rich. "That's Not How Dicks Work: On Not Gay and 'Straight' Men Who Have Gay Sex." Gawker, August 12, 2015. http://review.gawker.com/page_1/.

Kappa Alpha Theta. "Alpha Xi Oregon." Accessed February 4, 2021. www.kappaalphatheta .org/find-a-chapter/college-chapters/alpha-xi/.

———. "Notable Thetas." Accessed November 26, 2018. www.kappaalphatheta.org /heritage/notable-thetas/.

Kappa Kappa Delta. "Meet Some Notable Kappa Deltas." Accessed November 26, 2018. www.kappadelta.org/about-us/notable-kds/.

Kappa Kappa Gamma. "Build a Home Where Kappa Standards May Be Shared by Those Who Seek Them When the Years Have Left Them Lonely." *Key* 55, no. 4 (December 1938): 367–68. https://wiki.kkg.org/images/d/d2/THE_KEY_VOL_55_NO_4 _DEC_1938.pdf.

———. University of Idaho. "Our House." Accessed February 4, 2021. http://uidaho .kappa.org/our-house/.

———. University of Michigan. "Fraternity and Sorority Life." Accessed February 4, 2021. https://fsl.umich.edu/resource/106/.

———. University of Montana. "Our House." Accessed February 4, 2021. http://umt .kappa.org/our-house/.

———. University of New Mexico. "Our House." Accessed January 18, 2018. http://unm.kappa.org/our-house/.

———. University of Oregon. "Our House." Accessed February 4, 2021. http://uoregon .kappa.org/our-house/.

———. University of Southern California. "Our House." Accessed February 4, 2021. http://usc.kappa.org/our-house/.

Karma, Allen. "5 Plead Guilty in Florida State University Student's Hazing Death." ABC News, April 17, 2018. https://abcnews.go.com/US/plead-guilty-florida-state -university-students-hazing-death/story?id=54520580/.

Kathryn Novak v. Brandon Simpson, Delta Sigma Phi, Jacob Pelkey, Andres Perales, Jonathan Landrum, and Matt Farley. U.S. District Court Middle District of Florida. Case 6:18-cv-00922-RBD-TBS. June 13, 2018. www.dropbox.com/s /exf6ldu57ig87d4/NComplaint.pdf?dl=0/.

Katz, Jackson. *The Macho Paradox: Why Some Men Hurt Women and How All Men Can Help.* Naperville, Ill.: Sourcebooks, 2006.

Katz, Jonathan Ned. *The Invention of Heterosexuality.* Chicago: University of Chicago Press, 2014.

Keating, Caroline F., Jason Pomerantz, Stacy D. Pommer, Samantha J. H. Ritt, Lauren M. Miller, and Julie McCormick. "Going to College and Unpacking Hazing: A Functional Approach to Decrypting Initiation Practices among Undergraduates." *Group Dynamics: Theory, Research, and Practice* 9, no. 2 (2005): 104–26.

Kelley, Sonaiya. "How 'Black Christmas' Became a 'Fiercely Feminist' Slasher Movie for the #MeToo Era." *Los Angeles Times,* December 11, 2019. www.latimes.com /entertainment-arts/movies/story/2019–12–11/black-christmas-feminist -horror-sophia-takal/.

Kellogg, H. L. *College Secret Societies: Their Customs, Character, and the Efforts for Their Suppression.* Chicago: Ezra A. Cook, 1874.

Kelly, Jason and Jack DeMarco. "UCF Suspends Fraternity." WFTV, September 10, 2020. www.wftv.com/news/local/orange-county/ucf-suspends-fraternity -sorority-not-following-schools-covid-19-policies/FKIDR4C3ZJHIHGC WUCMJZ3IUCU/.

Kendall, Diana. *The Power of Good Deeds: Privileged Women and the Social Reproduction of the Upper Class.* New York: Rowman & Littlefield, 2002.

Kenney, Erin. "Parties Don't Stop: Multiple UGA Sororities, Fraternities Criticized for Party Culture during COVID-19." *Red & Black,* August 22, 2020. www.redandblack .com/uganews/the-parties-don-t-stop-multiple-uga-sororities-fraternities-criticized -for-party-culture-during-covid/article_80140668-e427-11ea-807b-43d50a8f37ea .html/.

Kern, Lauren, and Noreen Malone. "Heirs to the Sexual Revolution." The Cut, October 15, 2015. www.thecut.com/2015/10/sex-lives-of-college-students.html/.

Khyati, Y. Joshi. *White Christian Privilege: The Illusion of Religious Equality in America.* New York: New York University Press, 2020.

Kiersz, Andy. "Here's When You're Probably Getting Married." Business Insider, February 6, 2019. www.businessinsider.com/average-marriage-age-united -states-2019–2?r=US&IR=T/.

Kilanski, Kristine M., and David McClendon. "Dating Across and Hooking 'Up': Status and Relationship Formation at an Elite Liberal Arts University." *Demographic Research* 37, no. 60 (December 14, 2017): 1917–32.

Kimmel, Michael. *Guyland: The Perilous World Where Boys Become Men.* New York: Harper, 2008.

———. *Manhood in America: A Cultural History.* Oxford: Oxford University Press, 2011.

Kingkade, Tyler. "'Butt Chugging' Allegations at University of Tennessee Fraternity Lead to Reforms." Huffington Post, July 23, 2013. www.huffpost.com/entry/butt -chugging-fraternity-tennessee_n_3635660/.

Kipnis, Laura. *Unwanted Advances: Sexual Paranoia Comes to Campus.* New York: HarperCollins, 2017.

Klinenberg, Eric. *Going Solo: The Extraordinary Rise and Surprising Appeal of Living Alone.* New York: Penguin, 2012.

Knapton, Sarah. "Facebook Users Have 155 Friends—But Would Trust Just Four in a Crisis." *Telegraph,* January 20, 2016. www.telegraph.co.uk/news/science/science -news/12108412/Facebook-users-have-155-friends-but-would-trust-just-four-in-a -crisis.html/.

Koman, Tess. "Why Getting Hazed by My Sorority Was Weirdly Worth It." *Cosmopolitan,* September 19, 2013. www.cosmopolitan.com/health-fitness/advice/a4802/why -getting-hazed-by-my-sorority-was-weirdly-worth-it/.

Konneker, Liz. "University 'Looking Into' Racist Snapchat Post Depicting Sorority Members." *GW Hatchet*, February 1, 2018. www.gwhatchet.com/2018/02/01/university-looking-into-racist-snapchat-post-depicting-sorority-members/.

Konnikova, Maria. "The Limits of Friendship." *New Yorker*, October 7, 2014. www.newyorker.com/science/maria-konnikova/social-media-affect-math-dunbar-number-friendships/.

Koplowitz, Howard. "UA Is 'Extreme Case' of State Schools Recruiting Out-of-State Residents, Report Finds." AL.com, March 26, 2019. www.al.com/news/2019/03/ua-is-extreme-case-of-state-schools-recruiting-out-of-state-residents-report-finds.html/.

Kosoff, Maya. "'People Are Going to Make Mistakes': Evan Spiegel Defends Snap against Charges of Sexism." *Vanity Fair*, May 30, 2018. www.vanityfair.com/news/2018/05/people-are-going-to-make-mistakes-evan-spiegel-defends-snap-against-charges-of-sexism/.

Koulogeoge, Nik. "Video Games: 4 Ways They Can Aid in Recruitment—Virtual or Not." Fraternity Man, August 17, 2020. https://fraternityman.com/video-games-recruitment/.

Knieriem, Declan, and Ema R. Schumer. "Harvard Drops Social Group Sanctions Following Supreme Court Sex Discrimination Decision." *Harvard Crimson*, June 30, 2020. www.thecrimson.com/article/2020/6/30/harvard-ends-social-group-sanctions/.

Kravitz, Jamie. "Your Best Friend Is Better Than a Boyfriend or Girlfriend & Here's Why." Elite Daily, June 5, 2018. www.elitedaily.com/p/your-best-friend-is-better-than-a-boyfriend-girlfriend-heres-why-9047913/.

Kulbaga, Theresa A., and Leland G. Spencer. *Campuses of Consent: Sexual and Social Justice in Higher Education*. Boston: University of Massachusetts Press, 2019.

Kurzban, Robert, and Jason Weeden. "HurryDate: Mate Preferences in Action." *Evolution and Human Behavior* 26, no. 1 (2005): 227–44.

Lakoff, George, and Mark Johnson. *Metaphors We Live By*. Chicago: University of Chicago Press, 1980.

Lake, Sydney. "Southern Sorority Recruitment Is Like the College Admissions Process, Rush Coach Says." *Fortune*, August 24, 2021. https://fortune.com/education/business/articles/2021/08/24/southern-sorority-recruitment-is-like-the-college-admissions-process-rush-coach-says/.

Land, Brad. *Goat*. New York: Random House, 2004.

Lang, Cady. "RushTok Is a Mesmerizing Viral Trend. It Also Amplifies Sororities' Problems with Racism." *Time*, August 19, 2021. https://time.com/6091217/bamarush-rushtok-tiktok-racism/.

Lautrup, Joey. "Abolish Greek Life? See How a Campus Debate Reflects the Nationwide Racial Justice Reckoning." *Time*, December 16, 2020. https://time.com/5921947/abolish-greek-life-debate/.

Lavender, Sebastian. "I Took My First Nudes . . . and Then Shared Them with Everyone I Knew." Femsplain, December 21, 2015. https://femsplain.com/i-took-my-first-nudes-and-then-shared-them-with-everyone-i-knew-3cb01ca65c38/.

Law, Tara. "Women Are Now the Majority of the U.S. Workforce. But Working Women Still Face Serious Challenges." *Time*, January 16, 2020. https://time.com/5766787 /women-workforce/.

Lee, Alfred McClung. *Fraternities Without Brotherhood*. Boston: Beacon, 1955.

Lee, Harrison. "TFM's 10 Best Universities for Greek Life in the United States of America." Total Frat Move, April 28, 2016. https://totalfratmove.com /tfms-10-best-universities-for-greek-life-in-the-united-states-of-america/.

———. "Video Surfaces of Alleged Nebraska Phi Kappa Psi Fraternity Members Branding a Pledge's Ass." Total Frat Move, January 13, 2016. https://totalfratmove .com/video-surfaces-of-university-nebraska-phi-kappa-psi-fraternity-members -allegedly-branding-a-pledges-ass/.

Leemon, Thomas A. *The Rites of Passage in a Student Culture: A Study of the Dynamics of Transition*. New York: Teachers College Press, 1972.

Lefkowitz, Melanie. "Anti-Hazing Efforts to Honor Antonio Tsialas '23." *Cornell Chronicle*, December 2, 2020. https://news.cornell.edu/stories/2020/12 /anti-hazing-efforts-honor-antonio-tsialas-23/.

Lehman, Alexandra. "A Brief History of Fraternity/Sorority Paddles and Recommendations." Fraternal Law Newsletter, July 2014. Accessed December 6, 2021. https:// fraternallaw.com/newsletter2/a-brief-history-of-fraternity-sorority-paddles-and -recommendations/ .

Levenson, Eric. "FSU Fraternity Pledge Died 'Alone in a Room Full of People' at Party." CNN, December 22, 2017. https://edition.cnn.com/2017/12/20/us/fsu-fraternity -pledge-death-grand-jury/index.html/.

Levinson, Alana Hope. "Girl, Send Me a Frext." Medium, April 30, 2015. https:// medium.com/matter/girl-send-me-a-frext-4ae41b9c832b/.

The Levo League. "Networking, Sorority Style: How Floating in College Helps You Network Now." Huffington Post, July 11, 2012. www.huffpost.com/entry /networking-tips-advice_b_1507559/.

Lewis, Casey. "This Ridiculous Sorority Recruitment Video Probably Cost More Than Your College Tuition." *Teen Vogue*, January 10, 2016. www.teenvogue.com/story /university-of-miami-sorority-recruitment-video/.

Lewis, Megan, Ruth Sanchez, Sarah Auerbach, Dolly Nam, Brennan Lanier, Jeffrey Taylor, Cynthia Jaso, Kate Nolan, Elizabeth A. Jacobs, Parker Hudson, and Darlene Bhavnani. "COVID-19 Outbreak among College Students after a Spring Break Trip to Mexico—Austin Texas, March 26–April 5, 2020." *Morbidity and Mortality Weekly Report*, July 3, 2020. www.cdc.gov/mmwr/volumes/69/wr/mm6926e1 .htm/.

Lewis, Melissa A., David C. Atkins, Jessica A. Blayney, David V. Dent, and Debra L. Kaysen. "What Is Hooking Up? Examining Definitions of Hooking Up in Relation to Behavior and Normative Perceptions." *Journal of Sex Research* 50, no. 8 (November–December 2013): 757–66.

Liang, Sherry. "UGA Fraternity Self-Suspends after Racist, Offensive Messages Released." *Red & Black*, September 20, 2020. www.redandblack.com/uganews /uga-fraternity-self-suspends-after-racist-offensive-messages-released/article _7c7faf6e-fb7b-11ea-9fb9-ef3e1f4bf3bc.html/.

Lieb, Ethan. *Friend v. Friend: The Transformation of Friendship—and What the Law Has to Do with It.* Oxford: Oxford University Press, 2011.

Lieberman, Jesse. "Fraternities Host Massive Pool Parties as COVID Cases Surge at UM." *Miami Hurricane*, February 5, 2021. www.themiamihurricane.com /2021/02/05/fraternities-host-massive-pool-parties-as-covid-cases-surge-at-um/.

Lindig, Sarah. "This Video Shows What History Would Look Like Without Men." *Elle*, October 11, 2015. www.elle.com/culture/career-politics/a31098/men -photoshopped-out-of-history-video/.

"Lodge Initiates Man; Kills Him." *Chicago Defender* 23, no. 50 (April 14, 1928): 20–21.

Lohse, Andrew. *Confessions of an Ivy League Frat Boy.* New York: Thomas Dunne, 2014.

Lopez, Mark Hugo, and Ana Gonzalez-Barrera. "Women's College Enrollment Gains Leave Men Behind." Pew Research Institute, March 6, 2014. www.pewresearch .org/fact-tank/2014/03/06/womens-college-enrollment-gains-leave-men-behind/.

Louisiana State University Greek Life. "Annual Report 2016–2017." Accessed June 23, 2019. www.lsu.edu/greek-life-taskforce/files/annual-report-2016-2017.pdf.

Maas, Megan K., Kyla Cary, Elizabeth Clancy, Bianna Klettke, Heather McCauley, and Jeff Temple. "Slutpage Use Among U.S. College Students: The Secret and Social Platforms of Image-Based Sexual Abuse." *Archives of Sexual Behavior* 50 (2021): 2203–14.

MacCarron, Pádraig, Kimmo Kaski, and Robin Dunbar. "Calling Dunbar's Numbers." *Social Networks* 47, no. 1 (2016): 151–55.

MacKinnon, Sean, Christian H. Jordan, and Anne E. Wilson. "Birds of a Feather Sit Together: Physical Similarity Predicts Seating Choice." *Personality and Psychology Bulletin* 37, no. 7 (April 2011): 879–92.

MacLean, Sarah. "Alcohol and the Constitution of Friendships for Young Adults." *Sociology* 50, no. 1 (2016): 93–108.

Macmillan, Amanda. "Why Friends May Be More Important Than Family." *Time*, June 7, 2017. http://time.com/4809325/friends-friendship-health-family/.

Mahtani, Nikhita. "The 15 Most Outrageous University of Alabama Sorority Houses." *House Beautiful*, August 24, 2021. www.housebeautiful.com/design-inspiration /a37376919/university-of-alabama-bama-sorority-houses/.

Maloney, Maggie. "Jack Rogers Now Creates Sorority-Specific Sandals." *Town & Country*, September 6, 2019. www.townandcountrymag.com/style/fashion-trends /g28938633/jack-rogers-sorority-sandals-shop/.

Manne, Kate. *Down Girl: The Logic of Misogyny.* Oxford: Oxford University Press, 2019.

———. *Entitled: How Male Privilege Hurts Women.* New York: Crown, 2020.

Marcantonio, Tiffany L., and Kristen N. Jozkowski. "Do College Students Feel Confident to Consent to Sex after Consuming Alcohol?" *Journal of American College Health* (2021): 1–9.

Marcus, Ezra. "The War on Frats." *New York Times*, August 1, 2020. www.nytimes .com/2020/08/01/style/abolish-greek-life-college-frat-racism.html/.

Marcus, Jon. "The Degrees of Separation between the Genders in College Keep Growing." *Washington Post*, October 27, 2019. www.washingtonpost.com/local /education/the-degrees-of-separation-between-the-genders-in-college-keeps -growing/2019/10/25/8b2e5094-f2ab-11e9-89eb-ec56cd414732_story.html/.

———. "Why Men Are the New College Minority." *Atlantic,* August 8, 2017. www.theatlantic.com/education/archive/2017/08/why-men-are-the-new-college-minority/536103/.

Marinova, Polina. "How Tinder Used Greek Life for More Than Just Hookups." *Fortune,* August 9, 2016. http://fortune.com/2016/08/09/entrepreneurs-greek-life-tinder/mar_lifebelike/.

Marquina, Sierra. "Chelsea Handler Posts Nude Mirror Selfie in Honor of Reese Witherspoon's Birthday—See the Funny NSFW Pic." *US Weekly,* March 22, 2016. www.usmagazine.com/celebrity-body/news/chelsea-handler-poses-nude-in-honor-of-reese-witherspoons-birthday-w199889/.

Marshall, Terry. *From High on the Hilltop: A Brief History of SMU.* Dallas: Southern Methodist University, 1993. https://sites.smu.edu/cdm/cul/vas/Hilltop_Chapter1.pdf.

Martin, Annie. "UCF Suspends Sorority after Accusation of Hazing, Drinking, Drug Use." *Orlando Sentinel,* November 27, 2019. www.orlandosentinel.com/news/education/os-ne-pi-phi-suspension-20191127-shdfhsrcxnhqpiiv6y6yw7g3vq-story.html/.

Martin, Patricia Yancy. "The Rape Prone Culture of Academic Contexts: Fraternities and Athletics." *Gender and Society* 30, no. 1 (February 2016): 30–43.

Martin, Sarah Ida Shaw. *The Sorority Handbook.* 11th ed. Boston: n.p., 1931.

Mathews, Jana. "The Oldest Sister." *Rollins Magazine,* Fall 2014. www.rollins.edu/magazine/fall-2013/the-oldest-sister.html/.

Mau, Dhani. "Selling the South: How Fashion Brands are Cashing in on Southern Charm." Fashionista, July 12, 2017. https://fashionista.com/2017/07/american-southern-fashion-brands-marketing-trends/.

McCann, Adam. "States with the Fewest Coronavirus Restrictions." WalletHub, January 26, 2021. https://wallethub.com/edu/states-coronavirus-restrictions/73818/.

McCreary, Gentry. "How Big Is Too Big?" Doctor Gentry's Blog, January 13, 2015. https://doctorgentry.blogspot.com/2015/01/how-big-is-too-big.html/.

McCreary, Gentry, and Joshua Schutts. "Toward a Broader Understanding of Fraternity—Developing and Validating a Measure of Brotherhood." *Oracle: The Research Journal of the Association of Fraternity/Sorority Advisors* 10, no. 1 (Summer 2015): 31–50.

McCreary, Gentry, N. Bray, and S. Thoma. "Bad Apples or Bad Barrels? Moral Disengagement, Social Influence, and the Perpetuation of Hazing in the College Fraternity." *Oracle: The Research Journal of the Association of Fraternity/Sorority Advisors* 11, no. 1 (2017): 1–15.

McEvoy, Jemima. "Outbreaks Hit Fraternities, Sororities and Dorms as College Parties Resume." *Forbes,* August 17, 2020. www.forbes.com/sites/jemimamcevoy/2020/08/17/outbreaks-hit-fraternities-sororities-and-dorms-as-college-parties-resume/?sh=d9f820a2050a/.

McGee, Jon. *Breakpoint: The Changing Marketplace for Higher Education.* Baltimore, Md.: Johns Hopkins University Press, 2015.

McGirr, Lisa. *The War on Alcohol: Prohibition and the Rise of the American State.* New York: W. W. Norton, 2016.

McIntosh, Peggy. "White Privilege: Unpacking the Invisible Knapsack." *Peace and Freedom Magazine*, July–August 1989, 10–12.

McKenzie, Bryan. "Watch Now: UVA Says COVID Surge Created by Student Noncompliance." *Daily Progress*, February 19, 2021. https://dailyprogress.com/news/local/watch-now-uva-says-covid-surge-created-by-student-noncompliance/article_502308fa-7310–11eb-85a6-bb84d2fbebe8.html/.

McMahon, Julie. "Syracuse Theta Tau Brothers Explain Crude Skits: 'We Thought It Was OK' (police video)." Syracuse.com, November 16, 2018, updated January 29, 2019. www.syracuse.com/su-news/2018/11/theta_tau_syracuse_university_students_interviews_dps.html/.

McMurtie, Beth. "The Fraternity Problem." *Chronicle of Higher Education* 61, no. 42 (August 7, 2015): A16–A21.

McQuade, Dan. "Cops Called after 20 Dudes Streak through Princeton Econ Class." *Philadelphia Magazine*, December 12, 2014. www.phillymag.com/city/2014/12/12/cops-called-20-dudes-streak-princeton-econ-class/.

Merriam-Webster. s.v. "playdate." Accessed October 1, 2019. www.merriam-webster.com/dictionary/playdate/.

Meyer, Dick. "Rush: MPs Just 'Blowing Off Steam.'" CBS News, May 6, 2004. www.cbsnews.com/news/rush-mps-just-blowing-off-steam/.

Meyerhofer, Kelly, and Emily Hamer. "UW-Madison Orders More Sorority and Fraternity Houses with COVID-19 Cases to Quarantine." *Wisconsin State Journal*, September 12, 2020. https://madison.com/wsj/news/local/education/university/uw-madison-orders-more-sorority-and-fraternity-houses-with-covid-19-cases-to-quarantine/article_dae3647c-ea87–5bf1-be69–53225e422891.html/.

Miller, Chanel. *Know My Name*. New York: Viking, 2019.

Miller, Joshua Rhett. "Sorority Sister Speaks Out on Racist Video That Got Her Booted from College." *New York Post*, January 17, 2018. https://nypost.com/2018/01/17/sorority-sister-booted-for-posting-profanity-laced-racist-videos/.

Miller, Michael E. "All-American Swimmer Found Guilty of Sexually Assaulting Unconscious Woman on Stanford Campus." *Washington Post*, March 31, 2016. www.washingtonpost.com/news/morning-mix/wp/2016/03/31/all-american-swimmer-found-guilty-of-sexually-assaulting-unconscious-woman-on-stanford-campus/.

Mills, Charles W. *The Racial Contract*. Ithaca, N.Y.: Cornell University Press, 1997.

Minow, Jacqueline Chevalier, and Christopher J. Einolf. "Sorority Participation and Sexual Assault Risk." *Violence Against Women* 15 (2009): 835–51.

Mississippi State Panhellenic Council. "Mississippi State University Panhellenic Council Chapter Score Card 2019." Accessed June 23, 2019. www.union.msstate.edu/sites/www.union.msstate.edu/files/Panhellenic_0.pdf.

Mitchell, Josh. *The Debt Trap: How Student Loans Became a National Catastrophe*. New York: Simon & Schuster, 2021.

Moisey, Andrew. "American Fraternity." Indiegogo. Accessed February 15, 2021. www.indiegogo.com/projects/american-fraternity#/.

———. *The American Fraternity: An Illustrated Ritual Manual*. Chapel Hill, N.C.: Daylight Books, 2018.

Mongell, Susan, and Alvin E. Roth. "Sorority Rush as a Two-Sided Matching Mechanism." *American Economic Review* 81, no. 3 (June 1991): 441–64.

Monroe, Amanda. "Sorority House Tour!!/Alpha Phi at the University of Arizona!!" YouTube video, 11:18, July 9, 2020. www.youtube.com/watch?v=dAPCk9G0DR4/.

Montemayor, Cristina. "Top 25 Best Universities for Greek Life." Total Sorority Move, June 17, 2016. https://totalsororitymove.com/top-25-best-universities-for-greek-life/.

Monto, Martin, and Anna Carey. "A New Standard of Sexual Behavior? Are Claims Associated with the 'Hookup Culture' Supported by General Social Survey Data?" *Journal of Sex Research* 51, no. 1 (2014): 605–15.

"More Than Cheese Fries: OSU's Partnership with Eskimo Joe's Proves Successful for Both." *State*, August 29, 2019. https://news.okstate.edu/magazines/state-magazine /articles/2019/fall/more_than_cheese_fries.html/.

Morgan, Demetri L., Hilary B. Zimmerman, Tanner N. Terrell, and Beth A. Marcotte. "'Stick With Yourselves; It's What's Normal': The Intergroup Racial Attitudes of Senior, White, Fraternity Men." *Journal of College and Character* 16, no. 2 (2015): 103–19.

Murdoch, Tim. "Xanax: An Unforeseen Danger in College." *Pitt News*, May 30, 2017. https://pittnews.com/article/120026/opinions/xanax-unforseen-danger-in-college/.

Muskal, Michael. "Racist Chant Taught on Fraternity Leadership Cruise, University of Oklahoma Says." *Los Angeles Times*, March 27, 2015. www.latimes.com/nation/la -na-sae-chant-20150327-story.html/.

Nadworny, Elissa. "I Need a Degree in Order to Move Forward: Why Some Adults Choose College." NPR, March 12, 2019. www.npr.org/2019/03/12/700326142 /over-24-and-thinking-about-college-youre-not-alone#:~:text=In%202018%2C%20 nearly%207.6%20million,last%20high%20school%20math%20class/.

Narins, Elizabeth. "30 Fitness Stars Everyone Is Following on Instagram." *Cosmopolitan*, December 14, 2018. www.cosmopolitan.com/health-fitness/a42715/everyone -is-following-these-instagram-fitness-stars/.

Nashrulla, Tasneem. "This Fraternity Held a 'Mexican-Themed' Party Where Some Dressed as Construction Workers." BuzzFeed News, May 1, 2017. www.buzzfeednews .com/article/tasneemnashrulla/kappa-sigma-baylor-racist-mexican-party/.

National Center for Education Statistics. "Digest of Education Statistics." Accessed January 14, 2021. https://nces.ed.gov/programs/digest/d19/tables/dt19_303.40.asp/.

——. "Fast Facts: Degrees Conferred by Race and Sex. Accessed January 24, 2022. https://nces.ed.gov/fastfacts/display.asp?id=72.

——. "Fast Facts: Enrollment." Accessed June 1, 2019. https://nces.ed.gov/fastfacts /display.asp?id=98.

National Panhellenic Conference. "2016–2017 Annual Survey Highlights: Fast Facts." Accessed May 23, 2019. www.npcwomen.org/wp-content/uploads/sites/2037 /2017/10/2017-Annual-Survey-Fast-Facts.pdf.

——. "Extension Information for College Panhellenics." Accessed January 14, 2021. www.npcwomen.org/wp-content/uploads/sites/2037/2020/07/Extension -Information-for-College-Panhellenics.pdf.

——. "National Panhellenic Conference to Call for Critical Change in Greek Life." January 11, 2018. www.NPCwomen.org/2018/01/11/national-panhellenic -conference-to-call-for-critical-change-in-greek-life/.

——. "NPC Community College Task Force Survey." n.d. https://www.surveymonkey .com/r/CJXCJQR/.

————. "NPC Fact Sheet." Accessed May 25, 2019. www.npcwomen.org/wp-content
/uploads/sites/2037/2019/04/2018-Annual-Meeting-Fast-Facts-FINAL.pdf.

————. "RFM Update 2018." Accessed May 25, 2019. www.NPCwomen.org/wp
-content/uploads/sites/2037/2018/05/RFM-Update-2018.pdf .

————. "Our Story." Accessed January 18, 2021. www.npcwomen.org/about/our-story/.

Nehamas, Alexander. *On Friendship.* New York: Basic Books, 2016.

Nelson, Shasta. *Frientimacy: How to Deepen Friendships for Lifelong Health and Happiness.*
New York: Seal, 2016.

Netter, Sarah. "Texas Fraternity Brother Branded, Family Furious over Ritual." ABC
News, January 29, 2010. https://abcnews.go.com/WN/texas-fraternity-brother
-branded-family-furious-ritual/story?id=9688654/.

Neumann, Daniel C., Mark A. Kretovics, and Elisabeth C. Roccoforte. "Attitudes and
Beliefs of Heterosexual Sorority Women toward Lesbian and Bisexual Chapter
Members." *Oracle: The Research Journal of the Association of Fraternity/Sorority
Advisors* 8, no. 1 (2013): 1–15.

New, Jake. "A Common Sign." Inside Higher Ed, August 28, 2015. www.insidehighered
.com/news/2015/08/28/sexist-banners-old-dominion-point-practice-many
-campuses/.

Newcomer, Mabel. *A Century of Higher Education for American Women.* New York:
Harper, 1959.

Newman, Deena Williams. "40 Years Ago, Ted Bundy Terrified City with Chi Omega
Murders." *Tallahassee Democrat,* January 13, 2018. www.tallahassee.com/story
/life/2018/01/13/lest-we-forget-remembering-margaret-and-lisa/1026999001/.

————. "Rutgers Has a Rope Rush: It Is Substituted for the Cane Rush, Which Was
Abolished as Brutal." Special to the *New York Times* (1857–1922), September 22,
1901, 20. ProQuest Historical Newspapers.

————. "What We Know about the Death of George Floyd in Minneapolis." *New York
Times,* April 3, 2021. www.nytimes.com/article/george-floyd.html/.

"No One Can Dim the Light Within." TikTok, August 15, 2021. www.tiktok.com/@mar
_lifebelike/video/6996692519903907077?referer_url=https%3A%2F%2Fembeds
.time.com%2F&referer_video_id=6996692519903907077&refer=embed&is
_copy_url=0&is_from_webapp=v1&sender_device=pc&sender_web_id=689172
3010732295685/.

Norberg, Melissa M., Alice R. Norton, Jake Olivier, and Michael J. Zvolensky. "Social
Anxiety, Reasons for Drinking, and College Students." *Behavior Therapy* 41, no. 4
(December 2010): 555–66.

North American Interfraternity Conference. "About Interfraternity Council (IFC)."
Accessed December 23, 2020. https://nicfraternity.org/about-interfraternity
-council-ifc/.

————. "Constitution of the North American Interfraternity Conference." Accessed
December 17, 2020. https://nicfraternity.org/wp-content/uploads/2019/12/NIC
-Constitution-and-Bylaws-L.R.-12.03.19.pdf.

————. "Member Fraternities." Accessed June 17, 2019. https://nicfraternity.org
/member-fraternities/.

————. "Policy Prohibiting Alcohol above 15% ABV." August 27, 2018. https://
nicfraternity.org/policy-prohibiting-alcohol-above-15-abv/#:~:text=27%2C%20

2018)%3A%20Each%20NIC,a%20licensed%20third%2Dparty%20vendor.&
text=1%2C%202019%2C%20will%20be%20granted,one%2Dyear%20
extension%20in%20adoption/.

Nuwer, Hank. *Broken Pledges: The Deadly Rite of Hazing.* Atlanta, Ga.: Longstreet, 1990.

———. "Hazing Deaths: 1737–2019." Hank Nuwer.com. Accessed July 14, 2019. www
.hanknuwer.com/hazing-deaths/.

———. "Hazing Deaths: A Note to the Reader." HankNuwer.com. Accessed March 1,
2021. www.hanknuwer.com/hazing-deaths-a-note-to-the-reader/.

———. *Wrongs of Passage: Fraternities, Sororities, Hazing, and Binge Drinking.* Bloomington: Indiana University Press, 2001.

O'Connor, Florence. "The Truth about Bama Rush Is Hiding in Plain Sight." The Cut,
August 19, 2021. www.thecut.com/2021/08/what-the-bama-rush-tiktok-trend-is
-hiding.html/.

Ofosu, Diana. "Brett Kavanaugh Was Socialized in a Culture of Unchecked Misogyny
at Yale." Think Progress, October 2, 2018. https://archive.thinkprogress.org
/brett-kavanaugh-socialized-in-misogyny-2bd826d84ccf/.

Ogozalek, Sam. "Second Theta Tau Video Shows Mimed Sexual Assault of Person with
Disabilities." *Daily Orange,* April 21, 2018. http://dailyorange.com/2018/04/second
-theta-tau-video-shows-mimed-sexual-assault-person-disabilities/.

Oluo, Ijeoma. *So You Want to Talk about Race.* New York: Seal, 2018.

O'Kane, Caitlin. "Georgia College Students Throw Massive Party Ahead of School
Starting, Ignoring COVID-19 Guidelines." CBS News, August 17, 2020. www
.cbsnews.com/news/university-of-north-georgia-college-students-party
-coronavirus-pandemic/.

"*Old School* (7/9) Movie Clip—The Cinder Block Test (2003) HD." YouTube video, 2:36,
October 11, 2011. www.youtube.com/watch?v=jJMXxv-hYP0/.

"1 In, 1 Out: Oxford Study Shows How People Put a Limit on Their Social Networks."
EurekAlert!, January 6, 2014. www.eurekalert.org/pub_releases/2014-01/u00
-oi0010214.php/.

Orendi, Josh. "New #1, Alabama Takes Over as Nation's Largest Greek Community."
Phired Up, June 27, 2012. http://blog.phiredup.com/new-1-alabama-takes
-over-as-nations-largest-greek-community/.

Orenstein, Peggy. *Girls and Sex: Navigating the Complicated New Landscape.* New York:
Harper, 2017.

Ortiz, Michael. "Alleged Sigma Pi Hazing Involved Induced Vomiting, a Cage, and Anti-
Semitic Imagery." *Hofstra Chronicle,* December 6, 2016. www.thehofstrachronicle
.com/archive-2016/alleged-sigma-pi-hazing-involved-induced-vomiting-cage-anti
-semitic-imagery?rq=hazing/.

Ortiz, Rebecca R., and Bailey Thompson. "Risky Recruitment: How Rape Myth Accep
tance among Potential New Sorority Members Is Related to Their Self-Efficacy to
Prevent Sexual Assault and Perceptions of University Sexual Assault Reporting."
Oracle: The Research Journal of the Association of Fraternity/Sorority Advisors 12, no. 2
(Winter 2017): 59–67.

Nguyen, Terry. "Why It's So Difficult to Abolish Sororities and Fraternities." Vox,
September 29, 2020. www.vox.com/the-goods/21492167/abolish-greek-life
-campus-covid/.

Packer, George. "Hillary Clinton and the Populist Revolt." *New Yorker*, October 24, 2016. www.newyorker.com/magazine/2016/10/31/hillary-clinton-and-the-populist-revolt/.

"PAC Profile: Fraternity & Sorority PAC." OpenSecrets.org. Accessed January 17, 2021. www.opensecrets.org/political-action-committees-pacs/fraternity-sorority-pac /C00410068/summary/2020/.

Paiella, Gabriella. "These Are the Winners of the Sorority-Recruitment Video Olympics." The Cut, August 19, 2016. www.thecut.com/2016/08/sorority-recruitment -videos-olympics.html/.

Parry, Mark. "Behind the Statistics on Campus Rape." *Chronicle of Higher Education*, January 16, 2015. www.chronicle.com/article/behind-the-statistics-on-campus-rape/.

Park, Julie J. "Clubs and the Campus Racial Climate: Student Organizations and Interracial Friendship in College." *Journal of College Student Development* 55, no. 7 (2014): 641–60.

Parks, Casey. "With White Students Becoming a Minority, Public Universities Push Harder to Diversify." *Birmingham Times*, April 14, 2019. www.birminghamtimes .com/2019/04/with-white-students-becoming-a-minority-public-universities -push-harder-to-diversify/.

Parks, Gregory S., and Matthew W. Hughey. *A Pledge with Purpose: Black Sororities and Fraternities and the Fight for Equality.* New York: New York University Press, 2020.

Parsons, Edward S. "The Social Life of the Coeducational College." *School Review* 13, no. 5 (May 1905): 382–89.

Paxton, Pamela, and James Moody. "Structure and Sentiment: Explaining Emotional Attachment to Group." *Social Psychology Quarterly* 66, no. 1 (March 2003): 34–47.

Pedersen, Olaf. *The First Universities: Studium Generale and the Origins of University Education in Europe.* Cambridge: Cambridge University Press, 2009.

Pequeño, Sara. "Report: Fraternities Cut Ties with Duke after University Creates New Restrictions." *INDY Week*, February 17, 2021. https://indyweek.com/news/durham /fraternities-cut-ties-duke-university/.

Perricone, Sophia. "BGSU Sophomore Dies after Alleged Hazing Incident." NBC 24 News, March 7, 2021. https://nbc24.com/news/local/bgsu-sophomore-dies -after-alleged-hazing-incident/.

Perrin, Andrew. "5 Facts about Americans and Video Games." Pew Research Center, September 17, 2018. www.pewresearch.org/fact-tank/2018/09/17/5-facts-about -americans-and-video-games/.

Petersen, Anne Helen. "The Genius of Taylor Swift's Girlfriend Collection." Huffington Post, January 8, 2015. www.huffpost.com/entry/the-genius-of-taylor-swif_n _6436068/.

Peterson, Sara. "Battle of the Big Three." *D Magazine*, September 1997. Accessed December 7, 2021. www.dmagazine.com/publications/d-magazine/1997/september /society-battle-of-the-big-three/.

Petit, Stephanie. "Why Everyone Needs to Back Off Alpha Phi at the University of Alabama." College Candy, August 17, 2015. http://collegecandy.com/2015/08/17 /university-of-alabama-alpha-phi-recruitment-video-controversy-back-off/.

Peyser, Eve. "10 Signs Your Best Friend Is Your Soul Mate." *Cosmopolitan*, July 7, 2016. www.cosmopolitan.com/sex-love/a60974/signs-your-best-friend-is-your-soulmate/.

Phi Delta Theta. "Phi Delt 2020." Accessed January 14, 2021. www.phideltatheta.org
/resources/phidelt2020.pdf.

Phi Mu. "Jobs." https://phimu.org/about-us/jobs/. Accessed January 14, 2021.

Phi Psi. "Redacted_Phi_Psi_1. pdf." In "Cult of Misogyny: Leaked Internal Documents
Reveal Silence Around Harmful Culture at Phi Psi," by Bayliss Wagner, Naomi Park,
Trina Paul, Ganesh Setty, Keton Kakkar, and Laura Wagner. *Phoenix*, April 18, 2019.
https://swarthmorephoenix.com/2019/04/18/47956/.

Phired Up, TechniPhi, and AFLV. "Fraternity & Sorority Will Endure: Immediate
Growth Recommendations for the Entire Fraternity/Sorority Industry to Weather the
Storm of COVID-19 Implications." Phired Up. Accessed March 1, 2021. http://blog
.phiredup.com/wp-content/uploads/2020/04/Endure.pdf.

Pi Beta Phi. "Stay Connected with Pi Beta Phi." Accessed January 14, 2021. www
.pibetaphi.org/connect/.

Pierson, Emma. "Is Sexist Rhetoric a Total Frat Move?" *New York Times*, May 9, 2016.
https://kristof.blogs.nytimes.com/2016/05/09/is-sexist-rhetoric-a-total-frat-move/.

Pietsch, Bryan. "Fraternity at University of Georgia Is Suspended after Racist Messages
Are Exposed." *New York Times*, September 22, 2020, updated September 24, 2020.
www.nytimes.com/2020/09/22/us/fraternity-university-of-georgia-suspended
-racist.html/.

Pi Kappa Phi. "Alumni Engagement." In *Uncommon Leadership Strategic Plan 2023*.
Accessed January 14, 2021. https://pikapp.org/wp-content/uploads/2019/08/2023
_Uncommon_Leadership_Strategic_Plan_2023_Final.pdf.

Piña, Christy. "Top 10 Colleges for Hookups." College Magazine, March 28, 2017. www
.collegemagazine.com/top-10-colleges-hookups/.

PingPongx. Comment on the Post "Any Gay Frat Guys?" Reddit, April 20, 2018 7:37 P.M.
GMT. www.reddit.com/r/Frat/comments/8drajh/any_gay_frat_guys_what_has
_your_experience_been/.

Pizarro, Citlali, Tiffany Wang, and Olivia Robbins. "'Phi Psi Historical Archives' Leaked
amidst Campus Tensions around Fraternities." Voices, April 18, 2019. https://
swarthmorevoices.com/content-1/2019/4/17/phi-psi-historical-archives-leaked
-amidst-campus-tensions-around-fraternities-86plg/.

"*Playboy* Releases Its List of the Top 10 Party Schools in America." PRNewswire, April
16, 2010. www.prnewswire.com/news-releases/playboy-releases-its-list-of-the-top
-10-party-schools-in-america-91023664.html/.

Poindexter, Katie. "Members of Greek Life Reflect on Virtual Recruitment." Talisman,
September 3, 2020. https://wkutalisman.com/members-of-greek-life-reflect-on
-virtual-recruitment/.

Pope, Melissa. "Greek Life: I Wish I Could Still Live in My Sorority House." Unigo,
May 29, 2015. www.unigo.com/in-college/college-experience/greek-life-i-wish
-i-could-still-live-in-my-sorority-house/.

Porta, Carolyn M., Sean Elmquist, Lauren Martin, Kira Sampson, Kasey Stack, Annie
Hill, Angeline Lee, and Molly C. Driessen. "'It Could Bring Down Greek Life as a
Whole': Greek Life Members' Perspectives on Party Culture, Safety, Responsibilities,
and Consequences." *Journal of American College Health*, July 9, 2021, 1–11. https://doi
.org/10.1080/07448481.2021.1942004.

Powell, Farran. "10 Universities with the Most Students in Sororities." *U.S. News*, June 28, 2016. www.usnews.com/education/best-colleges/the-short-list-college /articles/2016–06–28/10-universities-with-the-most-students-in-sororities/.

Purdue University Undergraduate Admissions. "Student Enrollment, Fall 2018." Accessed January 7, 2021. www.admissions.purdue.edu/academics/enrollment.php/.

Putnam, Robert. *Bowling Alone: The Collapse and Revival of American Community*. New York: Touchstone, 2000.

Raguso, Emilie. "UC Berkeley Student Charged with Rape at Cal Fraternity, Other Sex Crimes." Berkeleyside, May 16, 2019. www.berkeleyside.com/2019/05/16 /uc-berkeley-student-charged-thursday-with-multiple-rapes-other-sex-crimes.

———. "UC Berkeley Student Charged with Sexual Assaults Ordered to Stand Trial." Berkeleyside, September 17, 2019. www.berkeleyside.com/2019/09/17/uc -berkeley-student-charged-with-sexual-assaults-ordered-to-trial/.

Rankin, Susan R., Grahaeme A. Hesp, and Genevieve Weber. "Experiences and Perceptions of Gay and Bisexual Fraternity Members from 1960 to 2007: A Cohort Analysis." *Journal of College Student Development* 55, no. 6 (2013): 570–90.

Rao, Mythili, and T. J. Raphael. "Singles Now Outnumber Married People in America— and That's a Good Thing." PRI, September 14, 2014. www.pri.org/stories/2014 –09–14/singles-now-outnumber-married-people-america-and-thats-good-thing/.

Reade, Josie. "Keeping It Raw on the 'Gram: Authenticity, Relatability, and Digital Intimacy in Fitness Cultures on Instagram." *New Media & Society* 22, no. 3 (2021): 535–53.

Reddit. "Any Gay Frat Guys? What Has Your Experience Been Like?" April 20, 2018, 5:46 P.M. GMT. www.reddit.com/r/Frat/comments/8drajh/any_gay _frat_guys_what_has_your_experience_been/.

———. Comment on the Post "Any Gay Frat Guys?" April 21, 2018, 1:38 A.M. GMT. www.reddit.com/r/Frat/comments/8drajh/any_gay_frat_guys_what_has_your _experience_been/.

Reddy, Emily. "Students React to Fraternity Suspension over Nude Photos." WPSU Radio, March 18, 2015. https://radio.wpsu.org/post/students-react-fraternity -suspension-over-nude-photos/.

Reed-Tsochas, Felix. "Science May Explain Why Your Friendships Fall Apart." Huffington Post, December 6, 2017. www.huffpost.com/author/felix-reedtsochas/.

Reeves, Richard V. *Dream Hoarders: How the American Upper Middle Class Is Leaving Everyone Else in the Dust, Why That Is a Problem, and What to Do About It*. Washington, D.C.: Brookings Institute, 2017.

Reid, Rebecca. "Why Are Women Sending Nudes to Their Platonic Female Friends?" Grazia, April 11, 2019. https://graziadaily.co.uk/life/real-life/naked-pics-nudes -friends/.

Reilly, Katie. "Record Numbers of College Students Are Seeking Treatment for Depression and Anxiety—but Schools Can't Keep Up." *Time*, March 19, 2018. https://time .com/5190291/anxiety-depression-college-university-students/.

Rein, Kristen. "U of Alabama Sorority Criticized for Recruitment Video." *USA Today*, August 28, 2015. www.usatoday.com/story/news/nation-now/2015/08/18 /university-alabama-criticized-racially-homogeneous-recruitment-video/31900097/.

Relentless with Kate Snow. Season 1, episode 6, "Abby Honold: College Tailgate Turns into a Brutal Assault." Aired November 1, 2019, on Oxygen. YouTube video, 13:42, November 4, 2019. www.youtube.com/watch?v=TlC6tl-zrks/.

"Revealed: Threesomes, Snog an Uber Driver, and Drink a Bong: The Shocking Sexual and Drugs Tasks That Sorority Girls Were Forced to Do on 'Scavenger Hunt' That Got It Banned from Campus." *Daily Mail*, March 15, 2018. www.dailymail.co.uk /news/article-5503403/Sexual-tasks-sorority-girls-forced-scavenger-hunt.html/.

Rich, Adrienne. "Compulsory Heterosexuality and Lesbian Existence." In "Women: Sex and Sexuality," special issue, *Signs*, 5, no. 4 (Summer 1980): 631–60.

Riggio, Ronald E. "How Are Men's Friendships Different from Women's?" *Psychology Today*, October 9, 2014. www.psychologytoday.com/us/blog/cutting-edge -leadership/201410/how-are-men-s-friendships-different-women-s/.

Robbins, Alexandra. *Fraternity: An Inside Look at a Year of College Boys Becoming Men.* New York: Dutton, 2019.

Robbins, Alexandra. *Pledged: The Secret Life of Sororities.* New York: Hyperion, 2004.

———. "Sorority Secrets: The Dark Side of Sisterhood That No One's Willing to Talk About." *Marie Claire*, July 20, 2015. www.marieclaire.com/culture/news/a15160 /sorority-campus-sexual-assault/.

Robbins, Alexandra, and Georgianna L. Martin. "Should Colleges Get Rid of Fraternities?" *Wall Street Journal*, September 16, 2015. www.wsj.com/articles/should-colleges -get-rid-of-fraternities-1442368892/.

Roberts, Diane. "Black, White & Greek." *Atlanta Journal Constitution*, October 28, 1998. www.welcometothemachine.info/media.php?ID=59/.

Roberts, Sam G. B., and Robin I. M. Dunbar. "Communication in Social Networks: Effects of Kinship, Network Size, and Emotional Closeness." *Personal Relationships* 18 (2011): 439–52.

Robinson, David. "Private Investigators Focused on Frat Party in Cornell University Freshman's Death." *USA Today*, November 28, 2019. www.usatoday.com/story /news/education/2019/11/28/antonio-tsialas-death-investigation-focused -cornell-frat-party/4324482002/.

Roche, Jake. "Pike Might Be Able to Blacklist Me from Their Frats." TikTok, February 12, 2021. www.tiktok.com/@purrpooo/video/6928377092396584198?sender _device=pc&sender_web_id=6933655316912424454&is_from_webapp=v2&is _copy_url=0/.

Rocheleau, Matt. "BU Suspends Fraternity amid Hazing Investigation." *Boston Globe*, October 30, 2012. www.bostonglobe.com/metro/2012/10/29/boston-university -suspends-fraternity-amid-hazing-investigation/iuV5xIIsj9yLxdvTpSNQ5N/story .html/.

Rochester Institute of Technology. "Overview of RIT." Accessed February 1, 2021. www .rit.edu/about-rit/.

Rodger, Elliot. "My Twisted World: The Story of Elliot Rodger." *New York Times*, May 25, 2014. www.nytimes.com/interactive/2014/05/25/us/shooting-document.html/.

Rodick, Madison. "Most Beautiful Sorority Houses across the Country." *Teen Vogue*, August 25, 2017. www.teenvogue.com/story/most-beautiful-sorority-houses? verso=true/.

Roebuck, Jeremy. "Security Footage Details Penn State Fraternity Pledge's Final Hours in Fatal Hazing Ritual." *Philadelphia Inquirer,* May 7, 2017. www.inquirer.com/philly /education/Piazza-Penn-State-hazing-Beta-Theta-Pi-fraternity-charged-Centre -County.html/.

Rogers, Tim. "First Person: Sorority Girls Gone Wild." *D Magazine,* January 2003. Accessed December 13, 2021. www.dmagazine.com/publications/d-magazine /2003/january/first-person-sorority-girls-gone-wild/.

Rollins College. "Dave's Boathouse." Accessed December 14, 2019. https://rollinscollege .sodexomyway.com/dining-near-me/daves-boathouse/.

Romero, Dennis, and Stephanie Giambruno. "Lawsuit Accuses Frat Brothers of Sharing Nude Imagery without Woman's Consent." NBC News, June 14, 2018. www .nbcnews.com/news/crime-courts/lawsuit-accuses-frat-brothers-sharing -nude-imagery-without-woman-s-n883346/.

Roosevelt, Rodney W. "Deconflating Buffoonery and Hazing: A Two-Factor Model of Understanding Maladaptive New Member Activities." *Oracle: The Research Journal of the Association of Fraternity/Sorority Advisors* 13, no. 1 (2018): 16–31.

Rose, Suzanna M. "Same- and Cross-Sex Friendships and the Psychology of Homosociality." *Sex Roles* 12, no. 1–2 (1985): 63–74.

Rosenberg, Eli, and Kristine Phillips. "Accused of Rape, Former Baylor Fraternity President Gets No Jail Time after Plea Deal." *Washington Post,* December 11, 2018. www.washingtonpost.com/education/2018/12/11/accused-rape-former-frat -president-gets-no-jail-time-after-plea-deal-da/.

Rosenblatt, Kalhan. "University of Alabama Sorority Rush Has Taken Over TikTok. Users Can't Look Away." CNBC, August 13, 2021. www.cnbc.com/2021/08/13 /university-of-alabama-sorority-rush-has-taken-over-tiktok.html/.

Rosin, Hanna. *The End of Men: And the Rise of Women.* New York: Riverhead, 2013.

Ross, Lawrence. *The Divine Nine: The History of African American Fraternities and Sororities.* New York: Dafina, 2000.

Rotundo, Antony L. *American Manhood: Transformations in Masculinity from the Revolution to the Modern Era.* New York: Basic Books, 1993.

Ruland, Sam. "Messages from the Night of Bid Acceptance to the Days Following Piazza's Death." *Daily Collegian,* May 9, 2017. www.collegian.psu.edu/news/crime _courts/article_1c1e6914-350c-11e7-b3b1-436b96fe269f.html/.

"Rutgers Fraternity Accused of Spiking Punch with Xanax." CBS News, December 16, 2017. www.cbsnews.com/news/rutgers-fraternity-accused-of-spiking-punch-with -xanax/#:~:text=NEW%20BRUNSWICK%2C%20N.J.%20%2D%2D%20 A,punch%2C%20CBS%20New%20York%20reports.&text=Sorority%20mem- bers%20accused%20the%20fraternity,Xanax%20can%20produce%20those%20 symptoms.

"Rutgers Has a Rope Rush: It Is Substituted for the Cane Rush, Which Was Abolished as Brutal." Special to *New York Times* (1857–1922). September 22, 1901. ProQuest Historical Newspapers. *The New York Times,* 20.

Rutgers University. "Rutgers through the Years." Accessed December 13, 2021. https:// timeline.rutgers.edu/#event-first-classes-held-at-local-tavern/.

Safranek, Conrad. "Stanford Students Now Spend Four-Fifths of the Waking Day Staring at a Screen: Is This the New College Normal?" *Stanford Daily,* July 8, 2020.

www.stanforddaily.com/2020/07/08/stanford-students-now-spend-four-fifths-of-the
-waking-day-staring-at-a-screen-is-this-the-new-college-normal/.

Sales, Nancy Jo. *American Girls: Social Media and the Secret Lives of Teenagers*. New York:
Vintage, 2017.

———. "Tinder and the Dawn of the 'Dating Apocalypse.'" *Vanity Fair*, September 8, 2015. www.vanityfair.com/culture/2015/08/tinder-hook-up-culture
-end-of-dating/.

Salinger, Tobias. "Texas Sorority Members' Topless Dancing Ritual Prompts $1M Law-
suit over Secretly Recorded Video at Kappa Kappa Gamma." *New York Daily News*,
March 24, 2016. www.nydailynews.com/news/crime/sorority-members-topless
-dancing-ritual-prompts-1m-lawsuit-article-1.2576982/.

Salo, Jackie. "Frat Accused of Forcing Pledges to Do the 'Elephant Walk.'" *New York
Post*, February 7, 2019. https://nypost.com/2019/02/07/frat-accused-of-forcing
-pledges-to-do-the-elephant-walk/.

Samson, Frank L. "Fraternity Membership and Negative Racial Attitudes among U.S.
College Students." *Sociological Inquiry* 20, no. 10 (2021): 1–30.

Sanchez, Gabriel H. "15 Dark and Disturbing Pictures from Inside an American Frat
House." Buzzfeed, September 24, 2018. www.buzzfeednews.com/article
/gabrielsanchez/american-fraternity-greek-college-culture-photography-book/.

Sanday, Peggy Reeves. *Fraternity Gang Rape: Sex, Brotherhood, and Privilege on Campus*. New York: New York University Press, 1990.

Sanders, Chris. "UA Sophomore Says She's the First Black Sorority Member." *Tuscaloosa
News*, September 7, 2001. www.tuscaloosanews.com/article/DA/20010907/News
/606125062/TL/.

Sanua, Marianne R. *Going Greek: Jewish College Fraternities in the United States, 1895–
1945*. Detroit, Mich.: Wayne State University Press, 2003.

Saramäki, Jari, E. A. Leicht, Eduardo López, Sam G. B. Roberts, Felix Reed-Tsochas,
and Robin Dunbar. "Persistence of Social Signatures in Human Communication." *PNAS* 11, no. 3 (January 21, 2014): 942–47.

Saul, Stephanie. "Public Colleges Chase Out-of-State Students, and Tuition." *New York
Times*, July 7, 2016. www.nytimes.com/2016/07/08/us/public-colleges-chase-out
-of-state-students-and-tuition.html/.

Schallhorn, Kaitlyn. "Virginia College Students in Hot Water for 'Border Control'
Themed Party." *Washington Examiner*, November 24, 2013. www.washingtonexaminer
.com/red-alert-politics/randolph-macon-students-in-trouble-after-border-control
-themed-party/.

Schlenker, Barry R. "Liking for a Group Following an Initiation: Impression Management or Dissonance Reduction?" *Sociometry* 38, no. 1 (March 1975): 99–118.

Schrader, Alexis. "Art Book *The American Fraternity* Didn't Intend to Make a Statement
on Consent—but the Women in the Photographs Have Other Thoughts." *Bust*. Accessed February 15, 2021. https://bust.com/feminism/195653-american-fraternity
.html/.

Schmid, Eric. "The 2020 Census Is Underway, but Nonbinary and Gender-
Nonconforming Respondents Feel Counted Out." St. Louis Public Radio, March 17,
2020. https://news.stlpublicradio.org/politics-issues/2020-03-17/the-2020-census-is
-underway-but-nonbinary-and-gender-nonconforming-respondents-feel-counted-out/.

Schuster, Dana. "Inside the Harvard Clubs That Groom the 1%." *New York Post*, July 22, 2017. https://nypost.com/2017/07/22/harvard-wants-to-ban-elite-social-clubs-to-be-more-inclusive/.

Scott, John Finley. "The American College Sorority: Its Role in Class and Ethnic Endogamy." *American Sociological Review* 30, no. 4 (August 1965): 514–27.

Seabrook, Rita C., Sarah McMahon, and Julia O'Connor. "A Longitudinal Study of Interest and Membership in a Fraternity, Rape Myth Acceptance, and Proclivity to Perpetrate Sexual Assault." *Journal of American College Health* 66, no. 6 (August–September 2018): 510–18.

Sedgwick, Eve Kosofsky. *Between Men: English Literature and Male Homosocial Desire*. New York: Columbia University Press, 1985.

———. *Tendencies*. New York: Routledge, 1994.

Serna, Joseph. "Elliot Rodger Meticulously Planned Isla Vista Rampage, Report Says." *Los Angeles Times*, February 9, 2015. www.latimes.com/local/lanow/la-me-ln-santa-barbara-isla-vista-rampage-investigation-20150219-story.html/.

"Setting the Record Straight on '1 in 5.'" *Time*, December 15, 2014. https://time.com/3633903/campus-rape-1-in-5-sexual-assault-setting-record-straight/.

Setty, Emily. "'Frexting': Exploring Homosociality among Girls Who Share Intimate Images." *Journal of Youth Studies* (2021): 1–16.

———. *Risk and Harm in Youth Sexting: Young People's Perspectives*. New York: Routledge, 2020.

"7 Largest Sorority Houses in the Nation." The Daily Dropout, December 21, 2018. https://daily-dropout.squarespace.com/articles/2018/12/21/7-largest-sorority-houses-in-the-nation/.

Shah, Maham. "Is Snapchat Sexist?" Voice of Journalists, August 11, 2017. www.voj.news/is-snapchat-sexist/.

Shaw, David Odin, and Saman Ayesha Kidwai. "The Global Impact of the Black Lives Matter (BLM) Movement." Geopolitics, August 21, 2020. https://thegeopolitics.com/the-global-impact-of-the-black-lives-matter-movement/.

Shelton, Victoria. "Nunsploitation and the Figure of the Naughty Nun." The Mask, November 2014. www.maskmagazine.com/the-heretic-issue/sex/the-naughty-nun/ (no longer available).

Shinkman, Paul D. "Prosecutors: Capitol Rioters Intended to 'Capture and Assassinate' Elected Officials." *U.S. News*, January 15, 2021. www.usnews.com/news/national-news/articles/2021–01–15/prosecutors-capitol-rioters-intended-to-capture-and-assassinate-elected-officials/.

Sheridan, Jake. "Coronavirus Outbreak at USC's Fraternity Row Leaves at Least 40 People Infected." *Los Angeles Times*, July 30, 2020. www.latimes.com/california/story/2020-07-30/coronavirus-usc-greek-row-covid-19-colleges-prep/.

Shontell, Alyson. "Founder of $3 Billion Tinder Reveals the Clever Marketing Tricks He Used to Make the App Go Viral." Business Insider, February 15, 2017. www.businessinsider.com/how-tinder-went-viral-sean-rad-reveals-app-marketing-tricks-in-podcast-2017-2/.

———. "Meet the Genius Frat Dudes Who Turned Bro Humor into a Multimillion-Dollar Media Empire." Business Insider, March 21, 2014. www.businessinsider.com/how-total-frat-move-and-grandex-were-founded-2014-3/.

Sicurella, Savannah. "UGA Tri Delta Chapter Placed on Probation for 'Hazing' by National Organization." *Red & Black*, October 2, 2019. www.redandblack.com /uganews/uga-tri-delta-chapter-placed-on-probation-for-hazing-by-national -organization/article_3d6e3fdc-e53f-11e9-bebb-73070d6d3407.html/.

Sieczkowski, Cavan. "Lilly Pulitzer Sorority Prints: Which Five Sororities Won Their Own Lilly Print?" *International Business Times*, January 24, 2012. www.ibtimes .com/lilly-pulitzer-sorority-prints-which-five-sororities-won-their-own-lilly-print -400034/.

Sigma Chi. "Diversity & Inclusion." Accessed March 14, 2021. https://sigmachi.org /home/news/diversity-inclusion/.

Sigma Pi. "Our Chapter." Accessed January 2, 2021. www.sigmapivu.org/about-us .html/.

Silva, Tony J., and Rachel Bridges Whaley. "Bud-sex, Dude-sex, and Heteroflexible Men: The Relationship between Straight Identification and Social Attitudes in a Nationally Representative Sample of Men with Same-Sex Attractions and Sexual Practices." *Sociological Perspectives* 61, no. 3 (2018): 426–43.

Simmons, Todd. "Virtual Brotherhood Building Ideas." Phi Delta Theta, March 26, 2020. www.phideltatheta.org/2020/03/virtual-brotherhood-building-ideas/.

Simpson, Connor. "What Hazing Is Like at the Deadliest Frat." *Atlantic*, December 30, 2013. www.theatlantic.com/entertainment/archive/2013/12/what-hazing -deadliest-frat/356574/.

Skene, Lea. "At LSU, How a 'Bright Future' Ended amid Rise in Prescription Drug Abuse: 'Like Night and Day.'" *Advocate*, June 23, 2019. www.theadvocate.com/baton _rouge/news/crime_police/article_b66accfe-9385-11e9-baca-3f3c08c8f5a9.html/.

SKYN. "2019 SKYN Condoms Sex & Intimacy Survey." Accessed November 22, 2019. www.skyn.com/en-us/2019-intimacy-survey/.

Smith, Aaron. "What People Like and Dislike about Facebook." Pew Research Center, February 3, 2014. www.pewresearch.org/fact-tank/2014/02/03/what-people-like -dislike-about-facebook/.

Smith, Aaron, and Monica Anderson. "5 Facts about Online Dating." Pew Research Center, February 29, 2016. www.pewresearch.org/fact-tank/2016/02/29/5-facts -about-online-dating/.

Smith, Adam. "Snapchat Investigating Itself after Ex-Employees Speak Out against 'Racist' Work Culture, Reports Claim." *Independent*, July 22, 2020. www .independent.co.uk/life-style/gadgets-and-tech/news/snapchat-racist-sexist -black-dance-investigation-a9632046.html/.

Smith, Kylie Towers. "'We Should Live Together When We're Old!' Kappa's Boyd Hearthstone." Fraternity History and More, December 10, 2012. www.franbecque .com/we-should-live-together-when-were-old-kappas-boyd-hearthstone/.

Smith, Ray A. "Looking for a Friend without Benefits? Try Match, Bumble, and Tinder." *Wall Street Journal*, July 7, 2021. www.wsj.com/articles/looking-for -a-friend-without-benefits-try-match-bumble-and-tinder-11625675336/.

Smith-Rosenberg, Carroll. *Disorderly Conduct: Visions of Gender in Victorian America.* New York: Knopf, 1985.

———. "The Female World of Love and Ritual: Relations between Women in Nineteenth-Century America." *Signs* 1, no. 1 (1975): 1–29.

Smothers, Hannah. "A UT Fraternity Threw Another Racist Party." *Texas Monthly*, February 15, 2015. www.texasmonthly.com/the-daily-post/a-ut-fraternity-threw -another-racist-party/.

"SMU Allegedly Provided Sex for Recruits." *Los Angeles Times*, March 24, 1987. www .latimes.com/archives/la-xpm-1987-03-24-sp-91-story.html/.

Son, Changwon, Sudeep Hegde, Alec Smith, Xiaomei Wang, and Farzan Sasangohar. "Effects of COVID-19 on College Students' Mental Health in the United States: Interview Survey Study." *Journal of Medical Internet Research* 22, no. 9 (2020): e21279.

Soule, Eric K, Matthew E. Rossheim, Tammy C. Cavazos, Kendall Bode, and Abigail C. Desrosiers. "Cigarette, Waterpipe, and Electronic Cigarette Use among College Fraternity and Sorority Members and Athletes in the United States." *Journal of American College Health* 69, no. 5 (2021): 463–69.

Southern Methodist University Student Affairs. "Fraternity and Sorority Life." Accessed December 14, 2019. www.smu.edu/StudentAffairs/StudentActivities/FSL/.

———. "Frequently Asked Questions—Panhellenic Sorority Recruitment." Accessed June 18, 2019. www.smu.edu/StudentAffairs/StudentActivities/FSL/PAN/FAQ -SororityRecruitment/.

Sperber, Murray. *Beer and Circus: How Big-Time College Sports Is Crippling Undergraduate Education*. New York: Owl, 2000.

Stafford, Zach. "College Students Say They Were Kicked Out of Frat Party for Being Gay." *Advocate*, October 29, 2019. www.advocate.com/news/2019/10/29/college -students-say-they-were-kicked-out-frat-party-being-gay/.

Stancill, Jane. "ECU Sorority Suspended after Hazing Investigation. It's the Latest Greek Sanction at School." *News and Observer*, August 10, 2018. www.newsobserver .com/news/local/article216439545.html#:~:text=A%20sorority%20at%20East%20 Carolina,news%20release%20from%20the%20university/.

"States with Anti-Hazing Laws." StopHazing. Accessed July 20, 2019. www.stophazing .org/states-with-anti-hazing-laws/.

Statista. "Average U.S. Teen Instagram Follower Count 2015." April 9, 2015. www .statista.com/statistics/419326/us-teen-instagram-followers-number/.

Statt, Nick. "Former Snap Employee Says Company Has a 'Toxic' and 'Sexist' Culture." The Verge, May 29, 2018. www.theverge.com/2018/5/29/17406524 /snapchat-sexist-toxic-workplace-culture-diversity-numbers-report/.

Steecker, Matt. "Cornell Bans Phi Kappa Psi Fraternity One Year after Antonio Tsialas' Death." *Ithaca Journal*, October 1, 2020. www.ithacajournal.com /story/news/local/2020/.10/01/cornell-university-bans-fraternity-one-year -after-death-tsialas/5882767002/.

Stein, Joel. "Millennials: The Me Me Me Generation." *Time*, May 20, 2013. https://time .com/247/millennials-the-me-me-me-generation/.

Stepp, Laura Sessions. *Unhooked: How Young Women Pursue Sex, Delay Love, and Lose at Both*. New York: Riverhead, 2007.

"Stone-Cold Sober Schools." Princeton Review. Accessed February 14, 2021. www .princetonreview.com/college-rankings?rankings=stone-cold-sober-schools.

Stout, Hilary. "A Best Friend? You Must Be Kidding." *New York Times*, June 16, 2010. www.nytimes.com/2010/06/17/fashion/17BFF.html/.

Stover, Lauren. "The Selfie That Dares to Go There." *New York Times*, July 7, 2018. www
.nytimes.com/2018/07/07/style/vagina-selfies.html/.

Stroud, Katie. "Social Learning and Dunbar's Number." Association for Talent Development, October 13, 2016. www.td.org/insights/social-learning-and-dunbars-number/.

"Students at Georgia Institute of Technology." Niche. Accessed June 1, 2019. www.niche
.com/colleges/georgia-institute-of-technology/students/.

"Students at University of Georgia." Niche. Accessed June 1, 2019. www.niche.com
/colleges/university-of-georgia/students/.

Sutcliff, Alistair, Robin Dunbar, Jens Binder, and Holly Arrow. "Relationships and the
Social Brain: Integrating Psychological and Evolutionary Perspectives." *British Journal of Psychology* 10, no. 3 (2012): 149–68.

Sutter, John D. "Are Frats 'a Form of American Apartheid'?" CNN, March 10, 2015. www
.cnn.com/2015/03/10/opinions/sutter-oklahoma-fraternity-racist/index.html/.

Sweet, Stephen. "Understanding Fraternity Hazing." In *The Hazing Reader*, edited by
Hank Nuwer, 1–13. Bloomington: Indiana University Press, 2004.

Sykes, Stefan. "No Charges in Death of Cornell Freshman Hazed at Frat
Party." MSNBC, December 1, 2020. www.nbcnews.com/news/us-news
/no-charges-death-cornell-freshman-hazed-frat-party-n1249598/.

Synott, Marcia. "A Friendly Rivalry: Yale and Princeton Universities Pursue Parallel
Paths to Coeducation." In *Going Coed: Women's Experiences in Formerly Men's Colleges
and Universities*, edited by Leslie Miller-Bernal and Susan L. Poulson, 111–50. Nashville: Vanderbilt University Press, 2004.

Syrett, Nicholas. *The Company He Keeps: A History of White College Fraternities.* Chapel
Hill: University of North Carolina Press, 2009.

Talmadge, Stephanie. "The Sisterhood of the Exact Same Pants." Racked, August 30,
2017. www.racked.com/2017/8/30/16218066/sorority-dress-code-rush-t-shirts/.

Tanzi, Alexandre. "Women Are Outpacing Men in Higher Education: Demographic
Trends." *Bloomberg*, August 6, 2018. www.bloomberg.com/news/articles/2018
-08-06/u-s-women-outpacing-men-in-higher-education-demographic-trends/.

Tau Kappa Epsilon. "Goal Two: Programs." Accessed January 14, 2021. www.tke
.org/2025/.

Taylor and Jeff. "Coming Out in the South | Taylor Phillips." YouTube video, 19:50,
February 1, 2019. www.youtube.com/watch?v=uYZToSlxZi4&t=399s/.

Taylor, Lucy. "2: Meet the Greeks." *Snapped*, 23:00, May 25, 2020. https://podcasts
.apple.com/us/podcast/snapped/id1513433742/.

———. "3: Crash." *Snapped*, 16:00, June 10, 2020. https://podcasts.apple.com/us
/podcast/snapped/id1513433742.

Taylor, Z. W., Jennifer Zamora, Arianne McArdle, and Mario Villa. "A Positive Spin on a
Negative Narrative: How the Media Portrays Fraternities and What Fraternities Can
Do About it" *ORACLE: The Research Journal of the Association of Fraternity
/Sorority Advisors* 13, no. 1 (2018): 51–68.

Techno FAQ. "How Porn Drove Innovation in Tech." Accessed December 13, 2021. https://
technofaq.org/posts/2015/02/infographic-how-porn-drove-innovation-in-tech/.

"10 People Indicted in Death of 18-Year-Old Ohio University Fraternity Pledge." CNN
Wire, November 20, 2019. https://wreg.com/2019/11/20/10-people-indicted-in
-death-of-18-year-old-ohio-university-fraternity-pledge/.

"These 12 Everyday Words Used to Have Completely Different Meanings." Huffington Post, February 26, 2014. www.huffpost.com/entry/words-that-have-changed-meaning_n_4847343/.

"This University of Florida Sorority Video Is the Hottest Thing You'll See All Day." Maxim, September 21, 2017. www.maxim.com/women/sorority-recruitment-videos-2016-6/.

Thompson, Bailey A., and Rebecca R. Ortiz. "Frat Daddies and Sorostitutes: How TotalFratMove.com and Greek Identity Influence Greek Students' Rape Myth Acceptance." *Sexualization, Media & Society* 2, no. 4 (October–December 2016): 1–9.

Thompson, Derek. "America's Weird, Enduring Love Affair with Cars and Houses." *Atlantic*, February 25, 2014. www.theatlantic.com/business/archive/2014/02/americas-weird-enduring-love-affair-with-cars-and-houses/284049/.

Thompson, Kelsey. "A Moral Crisis Is Plaguing Fraternities." Business Insider, June 24, 2017. www.businessinsider.com/a-moral-crisis-is-plaguing-fraternities-2017-6/.

Tian, Emily. "Yale's Fraternities Enter National Spotlight." *Yale News*, May 13, 2020. https://yaledailynews.com/commencement2020/2020/05/13/yales-fraternities-in-the-national-spotlight/.

Tiger, Lionel. "Males Courting Males." In *The Hazing Reader*, edited by Hank Nuwer, 14–18. Bloomington: Indiana University Press, 2004.

———. *Men in Groups*. New York: Random House, 1969.

Tingley, Keith, Loni Crumb, Shelly Hoover-Plonk, Wes Hill, and Crystal R. Chambers. "Sorority and Fraternity Attitudes towards Initiation and Hazing." *Oracle: The Research Journal of the Association of Fraternity/Sorority Advisors* 13, no. 2 (2018): 46–60.

Tmaddog. "Penn State Has Indefinitely Banned Alcohol at All Fraternity Parties Following Student's Death." Comment on "Jared Borislow," Total Frat Move, February 10, 2017. https://totalfratmove.com/penn-state-fraternity-alcohol-ban/.

"Top Greek Schools According to the Princeton Review." GreekRank, February 2, 2018. www.greekrank.com/Top-Schools-For-Greek-Life-According-to-the-Princeton-Review/.

Torbenson, Craig L. "From the Beginning: A History of College Fraternities and Sororities." In *Brothers and Sisters: Diversity in College Fraternities and Sororities*, edited by Craig L. Torbenson and Gregory S. Parks, 15–43. Madison, N.J.: Fairleigh Dickinson University Press, 2009.

Total Frat Move. "ΦKT Member from Georgia Tech Sends Rapiest Email Ever—'Let Them Grind Against Your Dick.'" Accessed May 19, 2019. https://totalfratmove.com/%CE%A6kt-member-from-georgia-tech-sends-rapiest-email-ever/.

Total Sorority Move. "6 Steps to Being the Ultimate Wingwoman." Accessed November 5, 2016. https://totalsororitymove.com/6-key-steps-to-being-the-ultimate-wingwoman/.

Totenberg, Nina. "Supreme Court Delivers Major Victory to LGBTQ Employees." NPR, June 15, 2020. www.npr.org/2020/06/15/863498848/supreme-court-delivers-major-victory-to-lgbtq-employees/.

Traister, Rebecca. *All the Single Ladies: Unmarried Women and the Rise of an Independent Nation*. New York: Simon & Schuster, 2016.

"Trending Houses–Aphi: University of Arizona." *Trending Houses*, YouTube video, 3:52, May 19, 2016. www.youtube.com/watch?v=e4V4TKnnyAU/.

Tri Delta. "Preparing Our Members for Life after College." August 12, 2019. www
.tridelta.org/the-trident/life-after-college/.

Trump, Jack, and James A. Wallace. "Gay Males in Fraternities." *Oracle: The Research
Journal of the Association of Fraternity Advisors* 2, no. 1 (2006): 8–27.

Turk, Diana. *Bound by a Mighty Vow: Sisterhood and Women's Fraternities, 1870–
1920*. New York: New York University Press, 2004.

"21 SUNY Students Charged with Hazing Pledges Using Urine, Vomit, Alcohol."
NBC New York, October 31, 2017. www.nbcnewyork.com/news/local/suny
-hazing-fraternity-alcohol-plattsburgh/327559/.

"2019 Best Greek Life Colleges in America." Niche. Accessed December 2, 2019. www
.niche.com/colleges/search/best-greek-life-colleges/.

Uecker, Jeremy E., and Mark D. Regnerus. "Bare Market: Campus Gender Ratios, Romantic Relationships, and Sexual Behavior." *Sociological Quarterly* 51, no. 3 (Summer
2010): 409.

Unigo. "What Are the Most Popular Student Activities/Groups?" Accessed June 3,
2019. www.unigo.com/colleges/georgia-institute-of-technology-main-campus
/q-and-a/what-are-the-most-popular-student-activities-groups-17/1/.

University of Alabama. "Define Your Experience: Sororities and Fraternities at the
University of Alabama." Accessed July 3, 2019. https://ofsl.sa.ua.edu/wp-content
/uploads/sites/9/2017/08/2017-Definine-Your-Experience-Brochure.pdf.

———. "Fraternity and Sorority Life." Accessed June 22, 2019. https://ofsl.sa.ua.edu/.

———. "Greek Housing." Accessed June 22, 2019. https://ofsl.sa.ua.edu/housing/.

———. "The University of Alabama Interfraternity Council." Accessed June 23, 2019.
http://alabamaNIC.com/main.html/.

———. "The University of Alabama Panhellenic Association." Accessed June 23,
2019. www.uapanhellenic.com/.

University of Arkansas. "Fall 2016 11th Day Enrollment Report." Accessed September 2,
2019. https://oir.uark.edu/students/enrollment-reports/fall2016enrlrptsummary.pdf.

———. "New Arkansan Non-Resident Tuition Award Scholarship." Accessed July 29,
2019. https://scholarships.uark.edu/nrta/.

———. "U of A Ranked as Seventh-Fastest-Growing Public Research University."
August 21, 2014. https://news.uark.edu/articles/24891/u-of-a-ranked-as-seventh
-fastest-growing-public-research-university/.

———. "University Enrollment Hitting Record Highs at Start of Fall Semester." August
25, 2021. https://news.uark.edu/articles/57436/university-enrollment-hitting
-record-highs-at-start-of-fall-semester/.

———. "University of Arkansas Enrollment Grows by 5.8 Percent, Sets New Record."
September 20, 2012. https://news.uark.edu/articles/19202/university
-of-arkansas-enrollment-grows-by-5-8-percent-sets-new-record/.

———. "University of Arkansas Enrollment Reaches Record High for Second Consecu-
tive Year." September 13, 2002. https://news.uark.edu/articles/12580/university
-of-arkansas-enrollment-reaches-record-high-for-second-consecutive-year/.

———. "Welcome to Greek Life!" Accessed June 22, 2019. https://uagreeks.uark.edu/.

University of Georgia. "Greek Life." Accessed May 25, 2019. https://greeklife.uga.edu
/uploads/docs/GLO_Info_Handout_2019.pdf.

University of Missouri. "Greek Statistics." Accessed June 23, 2019. https://fsl.missouri
.edu/about/greek-statistics/.

University of North Georgia. "Quick Facts." Accessed January 27, 2021. https://ung.edu
/institutional-effectiveness/institutional-research/quick-facts.php.

University of Oklahoma Office of Student Life. "The University of Oklahoma Panhellenic Association Recruitment Look Book 2019." Accessed June 23, 2019. https://
issuu.com/oufsps/docs/pan_look_book_2019/.

University of Southern California. "Traditions." Accessed February 17, 2017. www
.usctraditions.com/.

University of Texas at Austin Panhellenic Council. "Discover Sorority Life." Accessed
June 23, 2019. https://issuu.com/texaspanhellenic/docs/university_of_texas_at
_austin_panhe/.

"USC Alpha Phi 2016." College Weekly, YouTube video, 3:08, August 1, 2016. www
.youtube.com/watch?v=6tCQ-kBnSjY/.

U.S. White House–Office of the Press Secretary. "Fact Sheet—Not Alone: Protecting
Our Students from Sexual Assault." April 29, 2014. https://obamawhitehouse
.archives.gov/the-press-office/2014/04/29/fact-sheet-not-alone-protecting
-students-sexual-assault/.

U.S. Bureau of Labor Statistics. "Table 11A. Time Spent in Leisure and Sports Activities for the Civilian Population by Selected Characteristics, Averages Per Day, 2018
Annual Averages." Accessed June 23, 2019. www.bls.gov/news.release/atus.t11A
.htm/.

"UVA Confirms COVID-19 Violations Are Being Brought against Five Fraternities."
Cavalier Daily, February 20, 2021. www.cavalierdaily.com/article/2021/02/u-va
-confirms-covid-19-violations-are-being-brought-against-five-fraternities/.

Vance, J. D. Hillbilly Elegy. New York: Harper, 2016.

Van Beusekom, Mary. "In-Person Classes, Greek Life Tied to College COVID Outbreaks." Center for Infectious Disease Research and Policy, January 7, 2021.
www.cidrap.umn.edu/news-perspective/2021/01/person-classes-greek-life
-tied-college-covid-outbreaks/.

Vander Ven, Thomas. Getting Wasted: Why College Students Drink Too Much and Party So
Hard. New York: New York University Press, 2011.

Véliz-Calderón, Daniela, and Elizabeth J. Allan. "Defining Hazing: Gender Differences." Oracle: The Research Journal of the Association of Fraternity/Sorority Advisors 12, no. 2 (2017): 12–25.

Velzer, Ryan Van. "FSU Student Who Died, Andrew Coffey, to Be Honored." South
Florida Sun Sentinel, November 17, 2017. www.sun-sentinel.com/news/florida
/fl-reg-andrew-coffey-service-20171117-story.html/.

Victor, Daniel. "Florida Fraternity Sued over Intimate Videos Shared on Facebook."
New York Times, June 14, 2018. www.nytimes.com/2018/06/14/us/delta-sigma
-phi-revenge-porn.html /.

Vrangalova, Zhana. "In Hookups, Alcohol Is College Students' Best Friend." Psychology
Today, January 30, 2014. www.psychologytoday.com/us/blog/strictly-casual/201401
/in-hookups-alcohol-is-college-students-best-friend/.

Wade, Lisa. American Hookup: The New Culture of Sex on Campus. New York: W. W.
Norton, 2017.

———. "Why Colleges Should Get Rid of Fraternities for Good." *Time*, May 19, 2017. https://time.com/4784875/fraternities-timothy-piazza/.

The Wall. "Our Menu." Accessed January 3, 2020. https://thewallbyu.com/menu/.

Wagner, Bayliss, Naomi Park, Trina Paul, Ganesh Setty, Keton Kakkar, and Laura Wagner. "Cult of Misogyny: Leaked Internal Documents Reveal Silence around Harmful Culture at Phi Psi." *Phoenix*, April 18, 2019. https://swarthmorephoenix .com/2019/04/18/47956/.

Walch, Tad. "Stone-Cold Sober XXIII: BYU Repeats (and Repeats) atop Princeton Review List." *Deseret News*, August 18, 2020. www.deseret.com/faith/2020 /8/18/21372855/stone-cold-sober-xxiii-byu-repeats-and-repeats-atop-princeton -review-list/.

Walker, Emma E. "Pretty Girl Papers IV: 'Crushes' Among Girls." *Ladies' Home Journal* 21, no. 2 (January 1904), 21.

Walker, Kristen M., and Pamela A. Havice. "Student Affairs Practitioners' Perceptions of the Career Development of Sorority Members." *Oracle: The Research Journal of the Association of Fraternity/Sorority Advisors* 11, no. 1 (Fall 2016): 16–30.

Wallace, Emily. "17 Things You Should Never Do at a Frat Party." Spoon University. Accessed December 14, 2019. https://spoonuniversity.com/lifestyle/17-things -you-should-never-do-at-a-frat-party/.

Waller, Willard. "The Rating and Dating Complex." *American Sociological Review* 2, no. 5 (October 1937): 729–30.

Walsh, Jennifer L., Kate B. Carey, and Michael P. Carey. "Do Alcohol and Marijuana Use Decrease the Probability of Condom Use for College Women?" *Journal of Sex Research* 51, no. 2 (2014): 145–58.

Wang, Connie. "10 Women Share Their Sexy Selfie Tips." Refinery 29, June 28, 2018. www.refinery29.com/en-us/2017/02/140123/sexy-selfies-picture-tips/.

Ward, Jane. *Not Gay: Sex between Straight White Men, Sexual Cultures*. New York: New York University Press, 2015.

———. *The Tragedy of Heterosexuality*. New York: New York University Press, 2020.

Ward, Robbie. "Fraternity Grounded after 'Cripmas' Party Backlash." *USA Today*, December 8, 2014. www.usatoday.com/story/news/nation/2014/12/08/clemson -fraternity-cripmas-party-increases-racial-tension/20083415/.

Washington, Michael, and Cheryl L. Nuñez. "Education, Racial Uplift, and the Rise of the Greek-Letter Tradition." In *African American Fraternities and Sororities: The Legacy and the Vision*, edited by Tamara L. Brown, Gregory S. Parks, and Clarenda M. Phillips, 141–82. Lexington: University Press of Kentucky, 2012.

Wasserman, Sydney. "The Most Beautiful Sorority Houses in America." *Architectural Digest*, September 8, 2017. www.architecturaldigest.com/story/the-13-most-beautiful -sorority-houses-in-america/.

Wechsler, Henry, and Bernice Wuethrich. *Dying to Drink: Confronting Binge Drinking on College Campuses*. New York: Rodale, 2002.

Wechsler, Henry, George Kuh, and Andrea E. Davenport. "Fraternities, Sororities, and Binge Drinking: Results from a National Study of American Colleges." *NASPA Journal* 46, no. 3 (2009): 395–416.

Wellemeyer, James. "Students at Vanderbilt Leave Fraternities and Sororities, Alleging Racism and Insensitivity." NBC, August 1, 2020, updated August 3, 2020.

www.nbcnews.com/news/us-news/students-vanderbilt-leave-fraternities-sororities
-alleging-racism-insensitivity-n1235375/.

Weigel, Moira. *Labor of Love: The Invention of Dating*. New York: Farrar, Straus & Giroux, 2016.

Wenerd, Brandon. "Arizona State's Alpha Phi Sorority Recruitment Video Is Packed with Babes in Yoga Pants." BroBible, 2016. Accessed December 13, 2021. https://brobible.com/college/article/asu-alpha-phi-sorority-recruitment-video-2016/.

WER Architects/Planners. "Chi Omega House." Accessed June 23, 2019. https://werarch.com/projects/chi-omega-house/.

West, Lois A. "Negotiating Masculinities in American Drinking Subcultures." *Journal of Men's Studies* 9, no. 3 (Spring 2001): 371–92.

Westerman, Ashley, Ryan Benk, and David Greene. "In 2020, Protests Spread across the Globe with a Similar Message: Black Lives Matter." NPR, December 30, 2020. www.npr.org/2020/12/30/950053607/in-2020-protests-spread-across-the-globe -with-a-similar-message-black-lives-matt/.

Whaley, Deborah. *Disciplining Women: Alpha Kappa Alpha, Black Counterpublics, and the Cultural Politics of Black Sororities*. Albany: State University of New York Press, 2010.

"When Did the Word 'Playdate' Come About?" *Mothering*, May 18, 2007. www .mothering.com/forum/35-parenting/677047-when-did-word-playdate-come -about.html/.

White, Kaila. "ASU Sorority: Our Recruitment Video Didn't Cost $200,000." AZ Central for the *Arizona Republic*, August 16, 2016. www.azcentral.com/story /news/local/tempe/.2016/08/16/asu-sorority-alpha-phi-recruitment-video-cost /88797200/.

White, Sarah. "How to Use Your Sorority Network after College." Miss Millennial Magazine, February 26, 2016. https://missmillmag.com/millennial-mindset /how-to-use-your-sorority-network-after-college/.

Whitford, David. *A Payroll to Meet: A Story of Greed, Corruption, and Football at SMU*. New York: Macmillan, 1989.

Wiest, Brianna. "15 Moments That Turn Your Best Friend into Your Soulmate." Bustle, October 15, 2015. www.bustle.com/articles/82351–15-moments-that-turn-your -best-friend-into-your-soulmate/.

Wilcox, Holly C., Amelia M. Arria, Kimberly M. Caldeira, Kathryn B. Vincent, Gillian M. Pinchevsky, and Kevin E. O'Grady. "Prevalence and Predictors of Persistent Suicide Ideation, Plans, and Attempts during College." *Journal of Affective Disorders* 127, no. 1 (2010): 287–94.

Wilkie, Laurie A. *The Lost Boys of Zeta Psi: A Historical Archaeology of Masculinity at a University Fraternity*. Berkeley: University of California Press, 2010.

"Will Supreme Court Ruling Mean More Transgender Sorority Members?" Higher-EducationLaw, August 10, 2020. www.highereducationlaw.org/url/2020/8/10 /will-recent-supreme-court-ruling-mean-more-transgender-soror. html#:~:text= On%20June%2015/.

Winton, Richard, Rosanna Xia, and Rong-Gong Lin II. "Isla Vista Shooting: Read Elliot Rodger's Graphic, Elaborate Attack Plan." *Los Angeles Times*, May 24, 2014. www .latimes.com/local/lanow/la-me-ln-isla-vista-document-20140524-story.html/.

Witters, Dan. "Hawaii Tops U.S. in Wellbeing for Record 7th Time." Gallup, February 27, 2019. https://news.gallup.com/poll/247034/hawaii-tops-wellbeing-record-7th-time.aspx/.

Wong, Alia. "Where Are All the High-School Grads Going?" *Atlantic*, January 11, 2016. www.theatlantic.com/education/archive/2016/01/where-are-all-the-high-school-grads-going/423285/.

"Woo Horns Sooiree: In 2022, More Texans Than Arkansans to Attend University of Arkansas." Best of Arkansas Sports. Accessed July 5, 2019. www.bestofarkansassports.com/woo-horns-sooiee-ua-its-veritable-texas-salad-bowl-of-out-of-state-students/.

Wray, Matthew. *Not Quite White*. Durham, N.C.: Duke University Press, 2006.

Wright, Gwendolyn. *Building the Dream: A Social History of Housing in America*. New York: Pantheon, 1981.

Wright, Jennifer. "Women Aren't Crazy." *Harper's Bazaar*, December 28, 2017. www.harpersbazaar.com/culture/politics/a14504503/women-arent-crazy/.

Vang, Kristyn E., Elisabeth R. Krow-Lucal, Allison E. James, Michael J. Cima, Atul Kothari, Namvar Zohoori, Austin Porter, and Ellsworth M. Campbell. "Participation in Fraternity and Sorority Activities and the Spread of COVID-19 among Residential University Communities—Arkansas, August 21–September 5, 2020." *Morbidity and Mortality Weekly Report*, January 8, 2021. www.cdc.gov/mmwr/volumes/70/wr/mm7001a5.htm/.

Yagoda, Maria. "The Satisfying Joy of Sending Platonic Nudes to Your Friends." VICE, November 2, 2017. www.vice.com/en_us/article/j5jj78/the-satisfying-joy-of-sending-platonic-nudes-to-your-friends/.

Yen, Mallun. "How Friendship Holds Women Back in Their Careers—and What They Can Do About It." *Fortune*, August 1, 2018. https://fortune.com/2018/08/01/women-friendships-careers-leadership/.

Yenisey, Zeynep. "5 Sorority Recruitment Videos You Have to See to Believe." *Maxim*, August 4, 2016. www.maxim.com/women/best-sorority-recruitment-videos-2016-8/.

Young, Sean. "The Social Psychology of the Naked Selfie." Tech Crunch, November 30, 2014. https://techcrunch.com/2014/11/29/the-psychology-of-the-naked-selfie/.

"You've Never Seen Sorority Houses Like These Before." *Southern Living*. Accessed April 17, 2019. www.southernliving.com/home/decor/southern-sorority-houses-video/.

Zaydenberg, Izabella. "7 Things to Know Before Taking the Perfect Vagina Picture." Elite Daily, January 22, 2016. www.elitedaily.com/women/how-to-take-vagina-pictures-sext/1355435/.

Zhu, Christine. "Virtual Sorority Recruitment Brought Unexpected Advantages for New Members and Recruiters." *Diamondback*, February 14, 2021. https://dbknews.com/2021/02/15/umd-sorority-recuitment-zoom-covid-19/.

Zimmerman, Hillary B., Demetri L. Morgan, and Tanner N. Terrell. "'Are We Really Not Going to Talk about the Black Girl?' The Intergroup Racial Attitudes of Senior, White, Sorority Women." *NASPA Journal about Women in Higher Education* 11, no. 2 (2018): 191–210.

Zucchino, David. "Duke Protests Frat Party That Mocked Asians." *Los Angeles Times*, February 6, 2013. www.latimes.com/nation/la-xpm-2013-feb-06-la-na-nn-asian-slurs-duke-20130206-story.html/.

INDEX

Abbie, 114–15
Abelson, Max, 208
Abolish Greek Life movement, 201–2,
    203, 237, 244
abolishing sororities and fraternities, 16,
    191–94, 201–2, 203, 237, 244
absent homosexuality, 2
Abu Ghraib, 159–60
accountability, 139, 160
Adderall, 80
Addison, 213–14
Adelphean, 202
admissions models, 30
African American sororities and
    fraternities, 194–97, 266n52
Aidan, 57–58, 60
A.J., 73
alcohol consumption: binge drinking, 21,
    77–78, 165, 166–69, 241; death and,
    35, 167–72, 175, 241–42; drugs and,
    80; at fraternity and sorority houses,
    24, 34–35, 82–83, 86–87; hazing
    and, 151, 165–67, 241–42; history of,
    81–87; hookups and, 78–79, 89–90;
    on-campus bars and, 83, 84–86; and
    rescuers and rescuees, 166–67
Ali, 41–42
All-American Rathskeller, 84
Allan, Elizabeth, 152
alligators, 32
Allmendinger, David, 157
all-women residential communities, 117
Alpha Chi Omega, 131, 134, 146

Alpha Delta Pi, 202, 228, 267n76
Alpha Gamma Delta, 268n37
Alpha Kappa Alpha, 196–97, 266n52
Alpha Phi, 14, 73, 110, 111–12, 121
Alpha Phi Alpha, 266n52
Alpha Xi, 122
alumnae initiate programs, 227
alumni of fraternities and sororities:
    affluence and prominence of, 21–22,
    176, 217; clubhouses of, 125; missing
    Greek life of, 124–25; networking and,
    219–20, 221, 223; professions of, 176,
    208–9, 217; recruitment and, 102; as
    school donors, 131, 192, 239; silence
    of, 217–18
Alumni Weekend, 223
Amanda, 33–34
American Fraternity (Moisey), 59, 75–76
American Girls (Sales), 44
American Hookup (Wade), 27, 99, 191–92
American Time Use Survey, 142
Anderson, Jacob Walter, 98
Andrew, 233–34, 235, 236
Animal House (film), 86, 163
anti-hazing, 152–53, 171, 262n10
anxiety, 79–81
apologies for buddy system breakdowns,
    97, 98
Arizona Republic, 111
Arizona State University, 110
Arkansas, 129, 259n4
Armstrong, Elizabeth A., 28–29
Aronson, Elliot, 153–54

317

Ashley, 223, 224
assistance while drinking, 166–67
associate degree students, 226–29
Association of American Universities
    survey, 92
Atlantic, xi, 8, 78, 103, 119, 207
Austin, J. L., 91
Ava, 203, 220

Bach, Henning, 2
Bacow, Lawrence S., 194
bad apple argument, 170
Badeen, Jonathan, 36
Bailey, 51–52, 53
*Baird's Manual of American Colleges and
    Fraternities*, 11
Baker-Jordan, Skylar, 56, 57
banana photo, 242
ban of alcohol consumption at sorority
    houses, 34
Barber, Harley, 182
bars, on-campus, 83, 84–86
Barstool Sports, 14, 72
Bauerlein, Mark, 142, 143
bed-sharing, 58, 117
beer, 77–78, 83, 84, 86
Beer and Circus (Sperber), 77
Bella, 113
Bennett, Amanda, 75
Bennett, Drake, 138
benzodiazepines, 80–81
Berbary, Lisbeth, 148
Bernholdt, Chris, 5
best friends, 6–7, 50, 55, 140–41
Beta Omega, 228
Beta Theta Pi, 164, 168–69
Bid Day, 126–28, 145, 233–35, 236
Big Brother Night, 167–68
Big/Little relationships, 61, 142, 146,
    167–68, 170, 223
binge drinking, 21, 77–78, 165, 166–69,
    241. *See also* alcohol consumption
Birger, Jon, 26
birthrate, national, 259n1
Blackballed (Ross), 185
Black Christmas (film), 221

Black Greek letter organizations, 194–97,
    266n52
Black Lives Matter (BLM) movement, 201,
    202–3, 237
blame: for hazing deaths/injuries, 169–
    70; for sexual assault, 96–97, 98
Bloomberg, 138, 208, 210
bonding, 95, 115, 135, 141–42, 155, 166
Boston University, 27, 151
Bound by a Mighty Vow (Turk), x, 125, 191,
    216–17
Bowling Alone (Putnam), 207
Bowling Green State University, 242
Brady, 41–42
Brain, Robert, 7
brains and relationships, 135–36
brands, preppy, 13, 14, 243
Brigham Young University (BYU), vii,
    85–86
BroBible, 72, 169
brocabulary, 72–75
bro humor sites, 72
brotherhood, 21, 54, 91, 160–62, 167
Brunsma, David, 86
buddy system, 19, 94–100
Buenneke, Katie, 103
Bumble, 6, 37, 39, 40
Bumble BFF, 6
Bumble Honeys, 39
bump groups, 108–9
Bundy, Ted, 218
Business Insider, 13, 36
Bust, 5–6, 75
Bustle, 65

California Polytechnic University, 181
Campbell, Lily Bess, 123
campus bars, 83, 84–86
Carly, 134
Carmel, Ind., 122
Carnes, Mark C., 177, 208
Carroll, Rebecca, 190
Carsyn, 187
Cassidy, 96–97, 98, 144–45, 146–48
Center for Responsive Politics, 193
Chapman, Nathaniel, 86

Chappelle, Dave, 183, 184
chapter size, 19, 30–31, 134, 139. *See also* superchapters
chapter tiers, 15. *See also* top-tier chapters
Charlie, 186–87
Charlotte, 65–66
Chase, 48, 49–50, 52–53, 56
Cheever, Susan, 83, 165
children and alcohol consumption, 83
Chi Omega, 112, 131, 134, 218
Chopik, William, 5
Christakis, Nicholas, 190
Chronicle of Higher Education, 129, 172
cinderblocks, 162–64, 165
Civil War–themed events, 157, 181
Claire, 179–80, 242–43
Clark, Clifford E., 120
Clark, Phillip, 170
class, social, 16–17, 120, 206–7, 208, 211
class warfare, college, 157–58
Clemson University, 151, 180–81
Clinton, Hillary, 183, 184
closing chapters, 244, 268n46
Clover app, 26
Coates, Ta-Nehisi, 207
coeducation, 25–26, 177, 216
Coffey, Andrew, 153, 155, 168, 169, 170, 172, 262n10
cognitive dissonance experiment, 153–55
Cohen, Rhaina, 8
Cohen, Sarah, 139
Cole, 79–81
Colgate University, 147, 209, 211
college attendance, decline in, 129, 259n1
College of Charleston, 49
College of William and Mary, 83, 155–56
College of Wooster, 84
College Weekly (YouTube channel), 117
comedy, amateur, 13, 183–84
common purpose, 139
community colleges, 226–29
Company He Keeps, The (Syrett), x, 12, 58–59, 157
CONNECTDDD, 221
consent: to sex, 79, 90, 91; to take photos or videos, 68, 69, 75, 76

conversations, face-to-face, 42–43, 82, 137
Cooper, Brittney, 6
Cooper, Katherine, 74
Corbin, 32–33
Cornell University, 25, 59, 157, 171–72, 173
Cosmopolitan, 5–7, 121, 146
Courtney, 130
courtship culture, traditional, 5
COVID-19 pandemic, 6, 22, 230, 234–37, 239–42, 243, 244, 268–69n1
"Cowboy Casanova" incident, 118–19, 128
craft beer, 86
crazy, calling women, 149–50
Cribs, 117
cross-dressing, 115–16, 151, 212–13
Culpepper, Makayla, 187
Cut, The, 110

Daisy, 202–3
Dallas, 105
Damian, 73
Dan, 60
Daniel, 197–98
Dara, 198–99
"darty," 32–33
Dartmouth College, 58–59, 156
date rape drugs, 95
"dates," 2, 5, 27, 28, 54–55, 89, 109
dating apps, 6, 26, 36–40. *See also specific dating apps*
dating websites, 6
Davis, 51
death causes of college students, 170–71
Debt Trap (Mitchell), 133
deferred recruitment, 50, 102, 144, 238
degradation of women, 71–73
Delta Gamma, 110, 112, 114, 117, 122, 131, 194
Delta Kappa Epsilon (DKE), 176, 178, 242
Delta Tau Delta, 159
Delta Zeta, 117, 124, 221
demographics of college students, 31, 226
depression, 79–81, 240

DeSantis, Alan, 217
DiAngelo, Robin, 190
diversity, 180, 185–86, 190–94, 198–99,
    201–2, 265n15
Divine Nine, 194–97, 266n52
Dockterman, Eliana, 74
Doe, Donna, 98
Dog Pound (Facebook page), 69
domestiques, 45, 47
Down Girl (Manne), 74
Doyle, Sady, 149–50
Dream Hoarders (Reeves), 211
dressing up, 181, 206, 208, 212–13
Drill-Mellum, Daniel, 87, 88
drinking age, legal, 83–84
drug dealing, 80–81
drugs, 79–81
drunk support, 166–67
Dubner, Stephen, 207
Duke University, 34, 181, 201, 202–3, 238
Dunbar, Robin, 20, 135–36, 137–38,
    141–42, 261n34, 261n36
Dylan, 160–62, 163, 169

Eastern Carolina University (ECU),
    80–81, 145
Eighteenth Amendment, 83
Elaine, 230
elephant walks, 60
Elite Daily, 6–7, 43
Elizabeth, 33, 65–66
Elle, 110, 264n2
Eloquent Rage (Cooper), 6
emails, 69–72, 75, 76
Emeline, 77
Emma, 118
emojis, 43
England, Paula, 78
enrollment caps and quotas, 30
epistemology of ignorance, 182–83, 200
Epsilon Kappa Phi, 58
Eskimo Joe's, 84
Everyone Sexts, 64–65
"Evils of Girls' Secret Societies, The"
    (Jones), 116
exceptionalism, 21, 124, 169, 174, 191

Facebook, 67, 69, 136–38, 220, 261n36
fake-out hazing, 162–65
Family Bottle, the, 168
family metaphor, 91–92, 99, 120
Family Weekend, 209
Faux, Zeke, 208
faux lesbianism, 118
Fern, Ashley, 43
Fernandez, Sean, 34, 35
fictive families, 91–92, 99, 120
finance industry, 208, 209, 219
Finstagram, 66
First, Amanda, 125
first-year students, 144–45
Fish, Kathy, 153
Fisher, Helen, 113
Flanagan, Caitlin, xi, 35, 78, 168
Fleming, Crystal M., 17, 199
Florida, Richard, 38–39
Florida International University, 67
Florida State University (FSU), 117, 153,
    167–68, 169, 218
Floyd, George, 200–201
Foltz, Stone, 242
Forbes, 211
formals, 89–90
Fortune, 102
Fortune 500 companies, 21–22, 176
founding members, of fraternities and
    sororities, 11–12
Fowler, James, 190
Fraternal Information and Programming
    Group, 86
fraternal orders, secret, 156–57,
    177–78, 208
fraternities: Black members of, 198–200;
    high-risk appeal of, 171–73; history
    of, 155–57, 177; interaction with other
    Greek letter organizations by, 30–31,
    92; LGBTQ+ community and, 49;
    LGBTQ+ networking and, 210, 211,
    215, 222; pipeline of, 21–22, 177,
    208–10; professional development
    and, 222; and religion, 17–18, 116; sex
    ratio manipulation by, 29–36, 38; U.S.

presidents as members of, 176. *See also houses, fraternity; LGBTQ+ fraternity and sorority members; North American Interfraternity Conference; and specific aspects of fraternity and sorority life*

fraternity and sorority life (FSL) professionals, 8–9

Fraternity and Sorority Political Action Committee (FratPAC), 193–94

Fraternity Row, 164

fratire, 13

FratPAC (Fraternity and Sorority Political Action Committee), 193–94

Frazier, Aubrey, 225–27, 229

Freedom of Collegiate Association Act, 193

Freeman, Margaret L., x, 11, 12, 122, 123

frexting, 62–67

friend groups, 44–45, 48, 92, 93, 126, 140–41

friendifying the lover, 6

friends: being related to, 190; having too many, 136–37; making, 5, 6, 20

friendship: importance of, 93; mutuality of, 46; romanticizing, 115–19

frientimacy, 66

fuck boys, 28

Gabe, 60–61, 62

Gainesville State College, 226

Gallagher, Billy, 69

gaming, 158–59

Gauntlet, the, 168

gay best friends, 50, 55

gay community. *See* LGBTQ+ community

gay Greek members. *See* LGBTQ+ fraternity and sorority members

gender expression, 51, 53

gender ratio imbalance. *See* sex ratio imbalance

Generation Z, 43, 49, 63

George, 51

Georgetown University, 84

George Washington University (GW), 198–99, 242–43

Georgia Institute of Technology (Georgia Tech), 26–27, 37–38, 39–40

gifs, 43, 65

Girls Gone Wild, 117

girl squads, 140–41

"God Damn Independents" (GDI), 105

Godey's Lady's Book (magazine), 120

Greek Preview Day, 133

Grimm, Beca, 65

group chats, 34, 43, 65, 67–72, 75, 76

GroupMe, 67, 203

Gruver, Max, 170, 172

Guttentag-Secord theory, 25–26

Halperin, David, 207

Hamilton, Laura T., 28–29, 118

Handler, Chelsea, 64

Handler, Lisa, 45–46

harassment for reporting sexual assault, 92–93

hard-liquor bans, 35

Harris, Cheryl, 17

Harvard School of Public Health's alcohol survey, 165

Harvard University, 156, 192–94, 266n52

hazing: alcohol and, 151, 165–67, 241–42; anti-, 152–53, 171, 262n10; appeal of, 171–74, 175; background and overview of, 21, 151–53; class warfare and, 157–58; consequences for, 172–73; COVID pandemic impact on, 239–40; deaths from, 167–72, 174, 241–42; fake-out, 162–65; history of, 157–58; pain and, 153–55; playing war and, 155–62; and rescuers and rescuees, 162; sexual, 59–60, 61; sorority, 119, 145–47

Hazing Prevention Week, 152–53, 172

headquarters, fraternity and sorority, 8, 13, 119, 122–23, 158, 221, 239

Hearthstone, Boyd, 125

Hechinger, John, 95, 181

Hernandez, Sean, 34, 35–36

heterosexuality, xii, 2, 60

Hinge, 37

Hirsch, Jennifer S., 88, 98

"historically white," 17, 21, 199–200

Hofstra University, 160
Hogg, Charlotte, 12
homes, 119–20. *See also* houses, fraternity;
    houses, sorority
homoerotic behavior, 2, 55, 60, 114–19
homophobia, 49, 52, 55, 118
Honold, Abby, 87, 88–89, 92–93
hookups: alcohol and, 78–79; fraternity
    parties and, 89–90; meaning of, 2–3,
    6; sex and, 99; sex ratio and, 18–19,
    24, 26–28, 31, 36, 251n11; sexual
    assault and, 90; women and, 28–29
horizontal relationships, 20–21,
    141, 142
Horowitz, Helen Lefkowitz, 115–16
House Beautiful, 124
houses, fraternity: alcohol consumption
    at, 24, 34–35, 82–83, 86–87;
    construction and renovation of, 130,
    134; the Manor, 23–24; sexual assault
    at, 87–88; sexual behavior at, 59–60;
    tours of, 117
houses, sorority: about, 12–13, 20; alcohol
    consumption ban at, 34; construction
    and renovation of, 131, 134; design
    and beauty of, 121–22, 123–24; early,
    120–21; love of living in, 124–25; men
    and, 123; playing house at, 123; tours
    of, 117–18, 124
house tours, virtual, 117–18
Houston, Christina, 185
Houzz, 124
How to Be Less Stupid about Race
    (Fleming), 17, 199
"How to Use Your Sorority Network after
    College," 220
Hughey, Matthew, 180, 194–95

ignorance, epistemology of, 182–83, 200
immigration, 83
Indiana University, 117
Indiana University–Purdue University
    Fort Wayne research, 62
Indiegogo, 75
INDY Week, 238
in-group status, 179, 184

initiation rituals, 18, 59, 153–54, 157, 164–
    65, 173–74, 178, 196–97
Inside TFM Podcast, 192
Instagram, 14, 44, 64, 66, 67, 137,
    140, 201
Institutional Review Board (IRB), 15–16
insurance, 34–35
interaction between Greek letter
    organizations, 30–31
Interfraternity Council (IFC), 31, 134, 170,
    192, 238, 241
internships and jobs, 210, 211, 213–16,
    218–20, 221–24, 268n37
interpersonal communication, 42–43,
    82, 137
interracial love, 199
interviews for this book, about, 9–11, 16
intimacy *vs.* sex, 3, 4

Jack, 68
Jack Rogers, 13
Jake, 56–57
Jane Doe 1, 89, 90, 92
Jane Doe 2, 90–91, 92
Jenkins, Wesley, 172
Jo, 107
jobs and internships, 210, 211, 213–16,
    218–20, 221–24, 268n37
John, 215
Johnson, Mark, 91
Jones, Grace Latimer, 116
Jones, Leigh Ann, 12, 91
Joyce, Brian, 191
J. P. Morgan, 208
Junger, Sebastian, 155, 162

Kahangi, Linda, 111
Kansas State, 182
Kappa Alpha (KA), 87, 171–72, 178, 181,
    186
Kappa Alpha Theta, 113–14, 122–23, 125,
    128, 191, 219–20, 267n27
Kappa Kappa Gamma, 108, 112, 118–19,
    121–22, 125, 128, 131, 201
Katherine, 218–19, 220
Katz, Jackson, 94

Kavanaugh, Brett, 176, 178

Kayla, 37

Kelsey, 107, 108

Kendall, Diana, 11

Khan, Shamus, 88, 98

Khyati, Y. Joshi, 18

Kimmel, Michael, 6, 178

Klonopin, 79–80

Knapton, Sarah, 138

Koman, Tess, 146

Konnikova, Maria, 137

Koulogeoge, Nick, 158–59

Krissy, 213

Krista, 132

Kylie, 43, 44, 62, 64, 67

Lacy, 125

Ladies Home Journal, 115, 116

Lake Jessup darty, 32–33

Lakoff, George, 91

Lambda Chi Alpha, 204

Lambda Phi Epsilon, 203

Lavender, Sebastian, 65

leaking nude photos and videos, 67–71

"leave no man behind," 162, 169, 175

Lee, Marissa, 187

Leggett, Mortimer, 171–72

legislation, anti-hazing, 152–53, 262n10

Lehigh University, 146

Leifer, Jane, 25

"lesbian tourism," 118

Lewin, Michelle, 66

LGBTQ+ community: acceptance of, 48–49; discrimination against, 193; faux lesbianism and, 118; same-sex, non-gay affections and, 57–59; same-sex sexual encounters and, 60–61

LGBTQ+ fraternity and sorority members: acceptance of, 49–52, 53, 55–57, 253n15; background and overview of, 17, 19, 48–49; second-class status of, 54–55; as third-party romance assistants, 52–55, 57, 62

Lieb, Ethan, 136, 137

Lila Grace, 138

Lilly Pulitzer, 13

Limbaugh, Rush, 159–60

Louisiana State University (LSU), 135, 159, 170, 172–73

lower-tier chapters, 15

loyalty, 55–56

Lucas, 209, 211

Lucy, 214–15

Lucy Ewing, 105

Mackenna, 51, 55

Madden, Mary, 152

Madison, 28

Madyson, 107

Make America Great Again (MAGA) caps, 205, 207

Mallory, 132, 142

Manne, Kate, 74

Manor, the, 23–24

Marie Claire, 106

Marissa, 215–16

marriage, 125, 126

marriage metaphors, 20, 113–15, 205–6

Martin Prosperity Institute, 38

masculinity, 6, 49, 50–51, 56, 60, 86, 155, 162

Mashable, 162

Massachusetts Institute of Technology, 46, 109

matchmaking, 19, 46–48, 78

Mateen, Justin, 36, 39

Maxim, 110

Mbunwe, Arianna, 203–4

McCreary, Gentry, 139–40, 160

McGirr, Lisa, 83

McIntosh, Peggy, 17

media on Greek letter organizations, 110, 121, 171, 173–74

membership and quotas, 30

membership models, 30

members of fraternities and sororities: counts of, viii, xii, 104–5; older, 230–32; stereotyping of, 217–18. *See also* LGBTQ+ fraternity and sorority members

methodology of this study, 8–10, 15–16

Miami Dade Community College, 228
Miami University (Ohio), 159
mid-tier chapters, 15
Milktoberfest, 86
millennials, 43, 63, 143
Miller, Chanel, 87
Mills, Charles W., 180, 182–83
Mills, Judson, 153–54
Misha, 230–32
misogyny, 74–75, 178–79; and imagining murder of women, 73
Mitchell, Josh, 133
mixers, 30–31
models, membership, 30
Mohammed, 189–90
Moisey, Andrew, 59, 75–76
Molly, 27
Monica, 43, 62, 64, 67–69
Moorjani, Dinesh, 36
Morgan, 57
MTV, 117
Munoz, Joe, 36
Murray, Charles, 206
mutual assistance, 21, 160–62, 167, 175, 198, 207, 210, 216
My Story (Snapchat), 69, 71

Naquin, Matthew, 170, 172
narrative timelines, 69–71
Natalie, 37–38, 39–40
National Center for Education Statistics, 179
National College Health Assessment Survey, 79
National Hazing Prevention Week, 152–53, 172
National Longitudinal Study of Freshman, 17
National Panhellenic Conference (NPC): admission model of, 30; alcohol consumption and, 35; background and overview of, vii, 8–9, 17, 249n1; community colleges and, 226–27, 228; hazing and, 61; membership rules of, 226–27; mixers and, 31; race and,

199–200; reaction to Pledged by, 106; recruitment and, 109, 144, 240; sex ratio and, 29–30
Nelson, Shasta, 66
nepotism, fraternal, 208–10
networking, 210, 211, 213–16, 219–20, 221–24, 225, 268n37
new member education process, 11, 197
New York Daily News, 119
New Yorker, 137, 206
New York Times, 140, 201
New York University, 27, 203
NIC (North American Interfraternity Conference). See North American Interfraternity Conference (NIC)
nicknames, 189
Nicole, 33
Nikki, 37–38
Nora, 218, 220
normalization, 60, 63, 68, 72, 79
North American Interfraternity Conference (NIC): admissions and, 30; alcohol consumption and, 35; background and overview of, ix, 8–9, 17, 249n5; community colleges and, 228, 268n46; discrimination and, 180; hazing and, 61, 173; PNM bidding and, 233; race and, 199–200; sex ratios and, 19, 29–30, 251n19
North Carolina State University (NC State), 195–97
North Georgia College and State University, 226
Novak, Kathryn, 69
NPC (National Panhellenic Conference). See National Panhellenic Conference (NPC)
NPR, 212
nude photos, 63–69, 71, 75–76
Nuwer, Hank, 160, 170

Oakes, Adam, 242
Ohio University, 151
Oklahoma State University, 84
Old Dominion University, 178

Old School (film), 162–63, 165
Oluo, Ijeoma, 180
150 rule, 135–36, 137–38, 139, 141, 142, 261n34
Onward Christian Soldiers, 157
OOTD (outfits of the day), 243
OpenSecrets.org, 193
opportunity hoarding, 211
Order of the Oddfellows, 157
"others," 178–79
Owen, Kent Christopher, 176
ownership of pledges, 174–75

paddles, wooden, 59, 61–62, 151, 159, 164
Padma, 44
parental help, 209–10
Park, Julie, 17
Parker, 28
Parks, Gregory S., 194–95
Parsons, Edward S., 120–21
parties: COVID pandemic and, 230, 241–42; LGBTQ+ community and, 49; racism at, 180–81, 182, 183, 205–6; sex ratios at, 27, 32–33; sexual assault at, 38, 89–90; venues for, 24, 34–35. *See also* alcohol consumption
Paying for the Party (Armstrong and Hamilton), 28–29
Pennsylvania State University (Penn State), 25, 31, 67, 84, 164, 168–69, 251n6
Pequeño, Sara, 238
Petersen, Anne Helen, 140
Petit, Stephanie, 111
petting, 31
Pew Research reports, 43, 136, 158
Peyton, 138
Phi Beta Kappa, 83, 155–56
Phi Delta Theta, 158, 159, 170
Phi Kappa Psi, 172–73
Phi Kappa Tau, 38, 80–81, 252n37
Phillips, Taylor, 54
Phi Mu, 131, 134, 187, 268n37
Phi Psi, 67, 89, 183–84
PhiredUp, 133

photos, 43–44, 63–69, 71, 75–76
photo shoots, 64
Piazza, Jo, 39
Piazza, Timothy, 168–69, 172
Pi Beta Phi (Pi Phi), 70, 112, 114–15, 131, 145–46, 185, 268n37
Pig Run, 127
Pi Kappa Alpha, 130, 151, 242
Pi Kappa Phi, 49, 167–68
pipeline, fraternity, 21–22, 177, 208–10
play dates, 5
playing house, 123
pledge classes, 99, 141–42
Pledged (Robbins), 20, 105–6
Pledge with Purpose, A (Parks and Hughey), 194–95
pledging, 146, 150, 174–75. *See also* recruitment, fraternity and sorority; *and specific aspects of*
Ponytail Gate, 105
Pope, Melissa, 124
pornography, 67–69
Porteus, Richard, Jr., 193
potential new members (PNMs): Bid Day and, 233–34; female degradation and, 73; preference day and, 113–15, 244–45; racism and, 188; recruitment of LGBTQ+, 51; sorority recruitment and, 14, 101–4, 107, 111–12, 144, 233
preference day, 113–15, 244–45
Preston, 52–53, 54–55, 57–58, 60
Princeton University, 25, 59
privilege: gender and, 26, 48, 88, 184, 212; of Harvard University, 192; minorities and, 224–25; white, 16–17, 18, 21, 179, 183, 184, 203, 207
probates, 196–97
probationary periods, 152
professional development, 221–23, 224
professions of fraternity and sorority alumni, 176–77, 217, 264n2
Prohibition, 82–83
PROSPER Act, 193
prostitution, 105

Public Religion Research Institute study, 190
punctuation, in texting, 43
punishment for sexual assault, 98
Purdue University, 33, 197
Putnam, Robert, 207

queer Greek members. *See* LGBTQ+ fraternity and sorority members

race, 16–17, 21, 198–200, 206. *See also* diversity; racism
Rachel, 97
Racial Contract, The (Mills), 180, 182–83
racial uplift, 195
racism, 180–85, 186–90, 198–200, 203–4
Rad, Sean, 36–37
Raguso, Emilie, 89, 90, 92
rape. *See* sexual assault
"rape bait" email, 38
Ravelo, Connor, 168, 170
Rebecca, 219–20
recruitment, college, 129–30, 133–34, 260n22
recruitment, fraternity and sorority: background and overview of, 101–4; Bid Day and, 126–28; buddy system and, 98–99; computer algorithm and, 233; deferred, 50, 102, 143–44; LGBTQ+ individuals and, 51, 52; online, 240; preference day and, 113–15; probation and, 152; racism and, 186–89; skits for, 109, 112–13; at SMU, 101, 102–3, 104–9, 257n8; at University of Alabama, 133–34; video gaming and, 158–59; videos for, 14, 20, 102, 109, 110–13, 117
recruitment coaches, professional, 102
recruitment counselors, 107
Reddit posts, 53–54
Reed-Tsochas, Felix, 138
Reeves, Richard, 211
Regnerus, Mark, 28
résumés, 211, 217–18, 221
Rich, Adrienne, 2

Rick, 210
ridesharing apps, 99
Riggio, Ronald, 214
rituals, 18, 20, 59, 116, 157. *See also* hazing; initiation rituals
Rizzo, Greg, 164
Robbins, Alexandra, 20, 105–6, 127
Rochester Institute of Technology (RIT), 33–34
Rodger, Elliot, 73–74, 75, 218
Rollins College: alcohol consumption at, 84; background and overview of, vii–viii; COVID pandemic at, 234–35, 236; deferred recruitment at, 50; Family Weekend at, 209; fraternity revoking at, 238–39; hazing at, 146; LGBTQ+ community at, 49, 51, 52, 54–55; racism at, 181, 182, 188–90
romantic assistance, 41–47
romantic capital, 144–45
romantic friendship, 115–19
Rose, 34, 230
Ross, Lawrence, 185, 194
Rotundo, E. Anthony, 156
Rutgers University, 83, 157
Ryan, 27–28
Ryan, Jim, 235

Sacramento State University, 59–60
Sage, 229–30
Sales, Nancy Jo, 44
Salisbury University, 151
Salon, 56
same-sex, non-gay affections, 57–59
same-sex eroticism, 115–19
same-sex friendship, 4–7; in the nineteenth and early twentieth century, 115–17
Samson, Frank, 225
Sanchez, 35–36
Sara, 132
scavenger hunts, 146, 161–62
Schrader, Alexis, 75
Schutts, Josh, 139
Scott, John Finlay, 8–9

Sedgwick, Eve Kosofsky, 2
selfies, nude, 63–67
"send nudes" party, 65
settlement houses, 125
sexist speech, 72–75
sex ratio imbalance: background and
    overview of, 4, 18–19, 24; gay fraternity
    members and, 50; hookup culture and,
    25–26, 27–29; manipulation of, 29–36,
    38; privilege and, 224
sex ratio theory, 26, 27, 29, 31
sexting, 6, 62–67, 254n57
sexual assault: buddy system breakdowns
    and, 95–100; fictive families and,
    87–94; insurance claims and, 35; Phi
    Kappa Tau and, 38, 252n37; prevention
    of, 19, 94–95; punishment for, 98;
    reporting of, 92, 97; scope of, 95,
    256n57
sexual hazing, 59–60, 61
Sexual Health (journal), 62
sex vs. intimacy, 3, 4
Shakur, Tupac, 183, 184
Shantelle, 195–96
Shaw, Sarah Ida, 121
Shelton, Todd, 30, 228
Shontell, Alyson, 36
Shutts, Joshua, 160
Sigma Alpha Epsilon (SAE), 181,
    194, 208
Sigma Chi, 194, 211
Sigma Nu, 178
Sigma Phi Epsilon, 87
Sigma Pi, 160, 268n46
Sign of the Red Lion, 83
Silva, Tony J., 60
Simpson, Brandon, 69
Simpson College, 123
single-sex communities, 125–26
single womanhood, 125–26
sisterhood, 11, 99, 139, 167
sizes of chapters. *See* chapter sizes
skits, recruitment, 109, 112–13
SKYN Condoms Sex and Intimacy
    Survey, 63

slut-shaming, 106, 147–50
Smith College, 115–16
Smith-Rosenberg, Carroll, 115
Snapchat, 14, 57–58, 69, 71–72, 136
Snapped (podcast), 148
snowball sampling, 10
sober socials, 224
social capital, 35, 144, 207, 208
social media, 13, 42–44, 102, 136–38, 148.
    See also specific apps
social networks, 135, 136, 137
solidarity, 21, 160, 162, 167
Sonya, 188–89
Sophie, 42
sororal pacts, 45–48
sororities: dropping out of, 202–3;
    friendships and, 45–48; history
    of, 216–17; LGBTQ+ networking
    and, 213–16, 219–20, 221–24, 225,
    268n37; professional development
    and, 221–23; relationships between
    chapters of, 230; and religion, 17–18,
    116; and repression, 200. *See also*
    houses, sorority; LGBTQ+ fraternity
    and sorority members; National
    Panhellenic Conference
Sorority Handbook (Shaw), 121
"Sorority Recruitment Video
    Olympics," 110
southern aesthetic, 11, 12–14
Southern Living, 12, 124
Southern Methodist University (SMU):
    "Cowboy Casanova" incident at, 118–
    19, 128; diversity at, 185; fraternity and
    sorority recruitment at, 20, 101, 102–3,
    104–9, 112–15, 126–28, 257n8; same-
    sex friendship at, 118
Southern Tide, 13
So You Want to Talk about Race
    (Oluo), 180
speech, sexist, 72–75
speed dating, 108
Sperber, Murray, 77
Spiegel, Evan, 69–72, 75
spring break, 117

Springer, Paul, 162
Stacy, 62, 64, 66, 67
Stanford University, 42, 87
Start Up (podcast), 212
State University of New York at
    Plattsburgh, 59
Stein, Joel, 142–43
Stella, 43, 62, 64
Stepp, Laura Sessions, 2–3
StopHazing.org, 152
Stout, Hilary, 140
Stroud, Katie, 137
study halls, 223–24
suicide, 171
superchapters: about, 20, 30, 134–35;
    friendship and, 136, 138–40,
    141, 142
Supreme Court justices, 176
Suzanne, 51, 54
Swarthmore College, 67, 183–84
Sweet, Stephen, 150
Swift, Taylor, 140–41
Syracuse University, 184–85
Syrett, Nicholas, x, 12, 58–59, 157

Tatum, 24, 32
Tau Kappa Epsilon (TKE), 181
tax-exempt status, 222
Taylor, Lucy, 148–49
technology, 42, 62, 69, 76, 99, 137. *See
    also* social media
Teen Vogue, 13, 110, 121
Teigen, Chrissy, 64
Telegraph, 138
texting, 6, 41, 42–43, 62–67, 254n57
TFM (Bolen), 13–14
TFM (Total Frat Move), 13–14, 72, 130, 159,
    160, 169, 192
Theta Connect, 219–20
Theta Tau, 184–85
third-party assistance, 41–47
Thomas, Keith, 207
Thompson, Derek, 119
Thompson, Taylor, 201
Tiger, Lionel, 165, 209

Tik-Tok, 14
Till, Emmett, 181
Time, 5, 74, 142–43, 191, 256n57
Tinder, 36–37, 38–40
"Tinder and the Dawn of the Dating
    Apocalypse" (Piazza), 39
Title IX, 98, 193
tokenization, 52, 198
Tom, 27
top-tier chapters, 15, 35, 51, 144, 229–30
Total Frat Move (TFM), 13–14, 72, 130, 159,
    160, 169, 192
Total Sorority Move (TSM), 13–14, 47,
    260n17
Town & Country, 13, 124
*Tragedy of Heterosexuality,
    The* (Ward), 74
Trainwreck (Doyle), 150
Trending Houses (YouTube series),
    117, 124
Tribe (Junger), 155, 162
Tri Delta, 74, 145, 218, 221
Trump, Donald, 207
trust walks, 163–64
Tsialas, Antonio, 172, 173
TSM (Total Sorority Move), 13–14, 47,
    260n17
Tulane University, 151
Turk, Diana, x, 125, 191, 216–17
Turner, Brock, 87, 88, 98
Twitter, 13, 136, 137, 203
two-year students, 226–29

Uecker, Jeremy, 28
underage drinking, 24, 84, 87, 197
unfair advantages, 212
Unigo, 124
University of Alabama, 14, 111–12, 124,
    133–34, 182, 243
University of Arizona, 111, 121, 133
University of Arkansas at Fayetteville
    (UA): college recruitment at, 129–30,
    260n9; fraternities and sororities at,
    130–33, 141, 142, 260nn11–12, 260n17;
    philanthropy event at, 131–32

University of California, Berkeley, 59, 84, 89

University of California at Santa Barbara (UCSB), 73–74

University of Central Florida (UCF), 145–46, 236

University of Delaware, 49

University of Florida (UF), 222–24

University of Georgia (UGA): hazing at, 145; hookup culture at, 26–27, 251n11; racism at, 181, 203–4; sex ratio imbalance at, 31; sorority comparison to University of North Georgia, 229–30

University of Idaho, 59, 122

University of Maryland, 182

University of Memphis, 49

University of Miami, 110, 235

University of Michigan, 25, 121

University of Minnesota (UM), 87, 88–89, 93

University of Mississippi (Ole Miss), 51, 54, 181, 236

University of Montana, 122

University of Nebraska–Lincoln, 203

University of New Mexico, 121–22

University of North Dakota, 121

University of North Georgia (UNG), 225, 226–27, 229–31, 240–41

University of Oklahoma, 135, 181

University of Oregon, 122

University of Richmond, 178

University of South Carolina, 186

University of South Dakota, 122

University of Southern California (USC), 34–36, 84, 122

University of Tennessee, 151

University of Tennessee at Knoxville, 124

University of Texas at Austin, 135, 181, 236

University of Virginia, 25, 235

University of Washington, 121

U.S. Capital attack, 242–43

U.S. News survey, 104–5

U.S. Supreme Court, 176, 193

utility, 207–8

Vanderbilt University, 201, 235–36

Vander Ven, Thomas, 166

Vanity Fair, 39

Vassar College, 116

vertical relationships, 141, 143–50

Victoria, 95–97, 98

video gaming, 158–59

videos: racist, 181–82, 184–85; recruitment, 14, 20, 102, 109, 110–13, 243; sexual, 59, 67, 68–69, 117, 119

violence, 62, 156, 159, 164–65, 174. *See also* sexual assault

Virginia Commonwealth University (VCU), 242

Virginia Tech, 187

Volstead Act, 82, 83

Wade, Lisa, 27, 99, 191–92, 236

Wake Forest University, 51–52

Wall, The, 85–86

Waller, Willard, 25, 31, 251n6

Wall Street Journal, 106

Ward, Jane, 2, 59, 60, 74

Washington Post, 75

Washington State University Pullman, 31

wealth, 185–86

Weatherford, Dani, 222, 228

websites, 6, 13–14, 124, 217, 222. *See also specific websites*

Weigel, Moira, 90

Weiss, Veronika, 74

West, Lois, 166, 263n58

White Fragility (DiAngelo), 190

white privilege, 16–17, 18, 21, 179, 183, 184, 203, 207

white supremacy, 191

white trash wedding, 205–6

Wickham, Madison, 13

Wilkie, Laurie A., 82

wingmen, gay, 52–55, 57, 62

wingwomen, 46–47, 53, 62

Wolfe, Whitney, 36, 39, 40

Wolff, Finn, 89, 90–91
womanhood, national ideal of, 11
women, collegiate history of, 125,
   216–17
Women of Discriminating Taste (Freeman),
   x, 11, 12, 122, 123
women's colleges, 115–16, 125
Wortham, Jenna, 64–65
Wright, Gwendolyn, 120

Xanax, 80–81

Yale University, 25, 157, 176, 178
Yen, Mallun, 214
Yik Yak, 93
Young, Noraleen, 122
Young, Ryan, 13
Young, Sean, 63
YouTube, 14, 54, 102, 117, 124, 182

www.ingramcontent.com/pod-product-compliance
Lightning Source LLC
Chambersburg PA
CBHW032343280326
41935CB00008B/426